THE WAGNER CLAN

For more than three decades Jonathan Carr served as a foreign correspondent, initially in Geneva, Paris and Brussels, later as bureau chief of the *Financial Times* and *The Economist* in Germany. A regular visitor to the Bayreuth festival since 1970, his interest grew steadily in the saga of the Wagner family – above all as a mirror of German (and in part European) history.

His other books include biographies of the former German chancellor Helmut Schmidt (1985) and of Gustav Mahler (1997), as well as *Goodbye Germany* (1993), a far from solemn obituary of the pre-unity Federal Republic. The winner of several press awards for his reporting from Germany, he received the CBE in 2000 for services to British–German relations.

Born in 1942, Jonathan Carr lived with his wife in a village overlooking the Rhine, near Bonn, until his death in 2008.

Praise for *The Wagner Clan*:

'Gripping.' Michael Church, *Independent*

'Compendious and enthralling.' *The Economist*

'A saga Carr tells with great pace and assurance.' Bill Jamieson, *Scotsman*

'This level-headed book . . . tells you the story at rattling speed. Jonathan Carr is also especially good at placing each episode in the family story within the context of what was happening in Germany at the time.' A. N. Wilson, *TLS*

'Carr's grasp of the complex events and personalities involved – particularly the family's long and unsavoury involvement with Hitler and the Third Reich – impresses at every point, the more so for his refusal to praise or demonize individuals. The genre is genuine information-packed documentary, not polemic. What a family. But (let's face it) never dull.' Malcolm Hayes, *Classic FM Magazine*

'An engaging group biography . . . Carr's levelheaded and meticulous approach is best displayed in his treatment of the Master's anti-Semitism and the family's links to Hitler, a regular houseguest and devoted fan affectionately referred to as "Uncle Wolf".' *New Yorker*

'Well written, entertaining and well informed.' Simon Heffer, *Literary Review*

# The Wagner Clan

JONATHAN CARR

First published in 2007
by Faber and Faber Limited
3 Queen Square London WC1N 3AU
This paperback edition first published in 2008

Typeset in Sabon by Faber and Faber Ltd
Printed in England by CPI Bookmarque, Croydon, CR0 4TD



A CIP record for this book
is available from the British Library

ISBN 978-0571-20790-9

2 4 6 8 10 9 7 5 3 1

To David,
my brother,
in proud memory

# Contents

# Plates

# Preface

It is often said that more books have been written about Richard Wagner, probably the most adored and detested creative artist in history, than about anyone else bar Jesus Christ and Napoleon. That claim is hard to prove; but it is true that the literature by and about the so-called 'Master of Bayreuth' – composer and dramatist, essayist and architect, racist and revolutionary – is bewilderingly vast and breathtakingly contradictory. Less, but still much, has been written about Cosima, Liszt's illegitimate daughter by a French countess, who left her pianist-conductor husband Hans von Bülow for Wagner, bore him three children and outlived him by forty-seven years. Yet what of the clan that Richard and Cosima founded? For well over a century – two world wars, Nazi dictatorship and foreign occupation notwithstanding – the Wagners have run the Bayreuth festival, played host to many of the greatest and ghastliest figures in the arts and politics and battled one another like the warriors in the music dramas they stage. For better or worse, they are Germany's most famous family. Yet next to no serious attempts have been made to tell their story.

Even for those with little interest in history and still less in marathon music drama, the Wagner saga is absorbing in its own right. The greed and jealousy, plotting and scrapping in and around the ill-named family seat Wahnfried – which roughly translates as 'Peace from Delusion' – more than match the most lurid episodes of *Dallas* or *Dynasty*. Nike Wagner, Richard's sharp-tongued great-granddaughter, who strongly resembles Cosima (in looks if hardly in character), refers to a 'diffusely expanding family hydra, a selfish, pretentious mass with prominent noses and thrusting chins . . . in which fathers castrate sons and mothers smother them with love . . . in which men are feminine and women masculine and in which a great-grandchild nibbles on the liver of another great-grandchild'.[1] To be strictly accurate, she should have added that at least some Wagners have been blessed with a sense of justice and an ironic humour uncharacteristic of the rest of the tribe. Beyond that human drama, though, the Wagner tale is a matchless mirror of Germany's convulsive rise, fearful fall and resurrection over nearly two hundred years.

Richard Wagner himself belonged to what now seem very distant times; born in Leipzig in 1813 when Napoleon Bonaparte's troops were at the gates, and dying in Venice in 1883 – twelve years after Germany achieved the unity he had yearned and fought for. His son Siegfried, on the other hand, forms a link to an era almost too close for comfort. Although he died in 1930, three years before the Nazis founded their so-called 'Third Reich', he lived long enough to see his family, especially his wife Winifred, become deeply involved with Adolf Hitler. Of Siegfried's four children one daughter, Friedelind, despised the Nazis and fled to America, while the other, Verena, stayed at home and married a senior SS officer. After the war the two sons, Wieland and Wolfgang, were able largely to shrug off the family's long liaison with 'Uncle Wolf' (i.e. Hitler), and in 1951 they restarted the Wagner festival in Bayreuth, the little town where their grandfather had started the whole show nearly eight decades before. Verena and Wolfgang have survived into the new millennium and the latter, at the time of writing (2006), continues to direct the festival despite sporadic bids to dislodge him.

Every summer, the celebratory start of the new Bayreuth season is one of Germany's top social occasions – less dazzling than Ascot, more earnest than Glyndebourne, but with elements about it of both. At the Festspielhaus (festival theatre) set on a hilltop on the outskirts of town, Wolfgang, together with his wife and daughter, receive the visiting notables, like royals in residence, as crowds gape and cameras flash. Back in the 1930s Winifred stood on the selfsame spot amid a hysterically cheering throng to greet Hitler and his pack. When the very first festival was held, in 1876, it was the Master himself who received guests ranging from the Kaiser and the King of Bavaria to Nietzsche, Liszt and Bruckner – not to mention a swarm of monied grandees from whom Wagner hoped, largely in vain, to extract more funds for his deeply indebted enterprise. Audiences and artists come and go; a Kaiser gives way to a Führer who is followed by a string of (democratically elected) federal presidents; but the programme stays relentlessly the same – Wagner's works (albeit not all of them), performed in the theatre that Wagner built and that is still run, although no longer owned, by a Wagner. Anyone looking for evidence of long-term continuity in Germany, no easy search, will surely find it in this unassuming corner of northern Bavaria.

In view of their role and history, it seems obvious to call the Wagners 'German through and through', or simply *typisch Deutsch*. What, though, do those words that trip so easily off the tongue really imply? Something specially good, or specially bad, or specially baffling – or all together, perhaps? Thanks to Goethe and Schiller, Kant and Schopenhauer – the list can be extended almost indefinitely – Germany has long been thought of as a land of particularly profound *Dichter und Denker* (poets and thinkers). Thanks to composers such as Bach, Beethoven, Brahms and – of course – Wagner, music in all its expressive power and indefinable substance has been called 'the most German of the arts'. How odd, therefore, that these 'rulers in the airy kingdom of dreams', as Heine defined his countrymen, only half ironically, should have been at the same time so industrious, well organised, worthy, even – yes – plodding. And on the face of it, how unfathomable that this same people, lusting for self-assertion and *Lebensraum* (living space), should have unleashed so much slaughter and misery on its neighbours – and on itself.

No one was more baffled by his compatriots than Wagner himself. In an essay called 'What is German?' he set out to get to the bottom of the matter; he might, one feels, have simply answered his own question by writing 'Me – in all my explosive genius and self-contradiction'. But after a long discourse on art and politics, laced with some of his sadly familiar swipes at Jews, the Master instead concluded that he was stumped. Others, he opined, should look further into the question. Many indeed have done so, but more than a century on the answer remains uncommonly elusive. With respect to the Wagners, it needs noting at the outset that the fiercest German nationalists among them – Houston Stewart Chamberlain (husband of the Master's daughter, Eva), as well as Cosima and Winifred – all married into the family and were not German-born. They were or became, as the trite phrase goes, 'more German than the Germans'. As for other members of the clan it is striking how many of them, including Richard himself, often felt most comfortable and even safest outside the borders of their strenuous *Vaterland*. No doubt there was something *typisch Deutsch* about that. Those looking for evidence of German national character in the Wagner saga will surely find it in abundance, but they are also in for some surprises.

# Family Tree

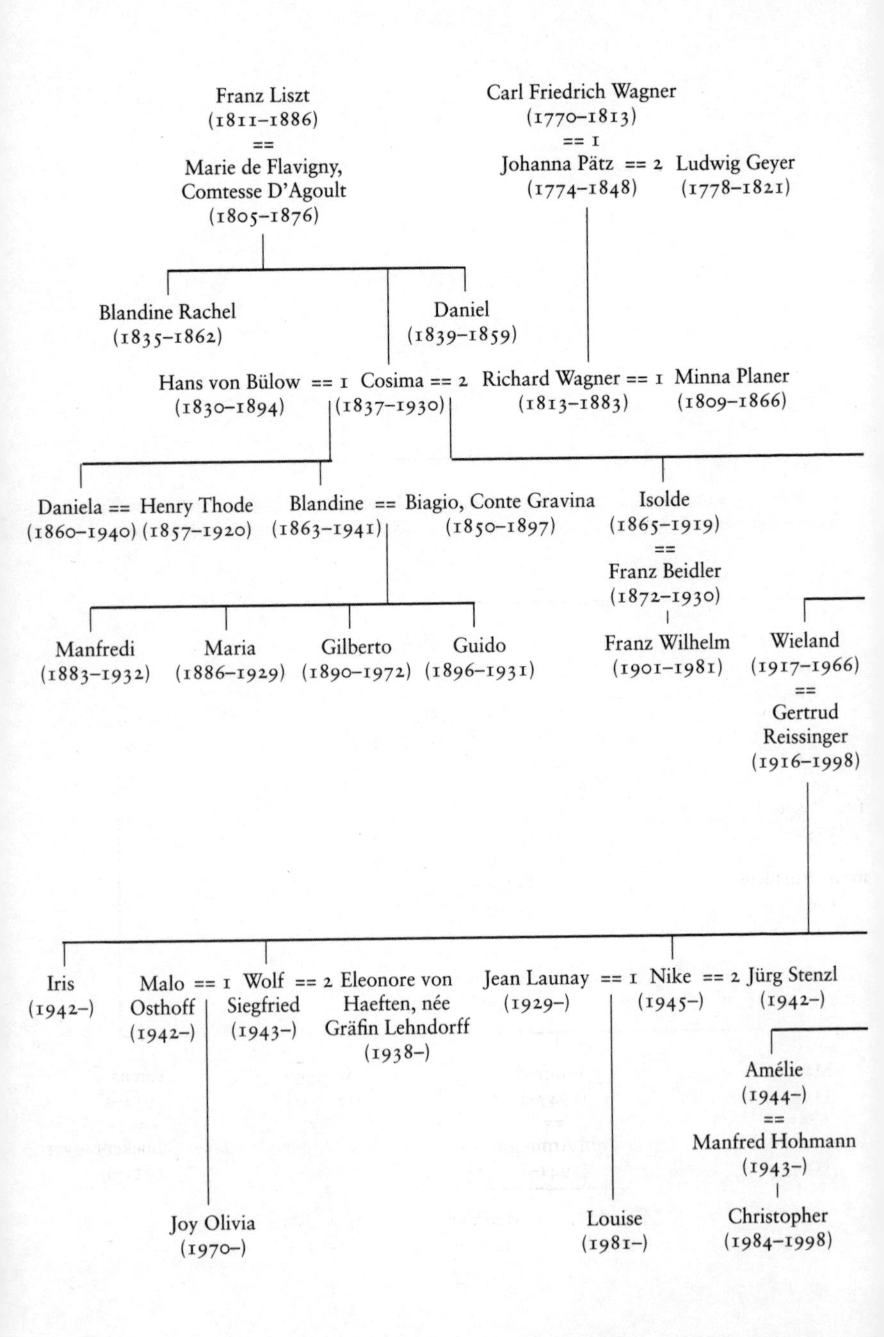
Franz Liszt
(1811–1886)
==
Marie de Flavigny,
Comtesse D'Agoult
(1805–1876)
Carl Friedrich Wagner
(1770–1813)
== 1
Johanna Pätz == 2 Ludwig Geyer
(1774–1848) (1778–1821)
Blandine Rachel
(1835–1862)
Daniel
(1839–1859)
Hans von Bülow == 1 Cosima == 2 Richard Wagner == 1 Minna Planer
(1830–1894) (1837–1930) (1813–1883) (1809–1866)
Daniela == Henry Thode
(1860–1940) (1857–1920)
Blandine == Biagio, Conte Gravina
(1863–1941) (1850–1897)
Isolde
(1865–1919)
==
Franz Beidler
(1872–1930)
Manfredi
(1883–1932)
Maria
(1886–1929)
Gilberto
(1890–1972)
Guido
(1896–1931)
Franz Wilhelm
(1901–1981)
Wieland
(1917–1966)
==
Gertrud
Reissinger
(1916–1998)
Iris
(1942–)
Malo == 1 Wolf == 2 Eleonore von
Osthoff Siegfried Haeften, née
(1942–) (1943–) Gräfin Lehndorff
(1938–)
Jean Launay == 1 Nike == 2 Jürg Stenzl
(1929–) (1945–) (1942–)
Amélie
(1944–)
==
Manfred Hohmann
(1943–)
Joy Olivia
(1970–)
Louise
(1981–)
Christopher
(1984–1998)

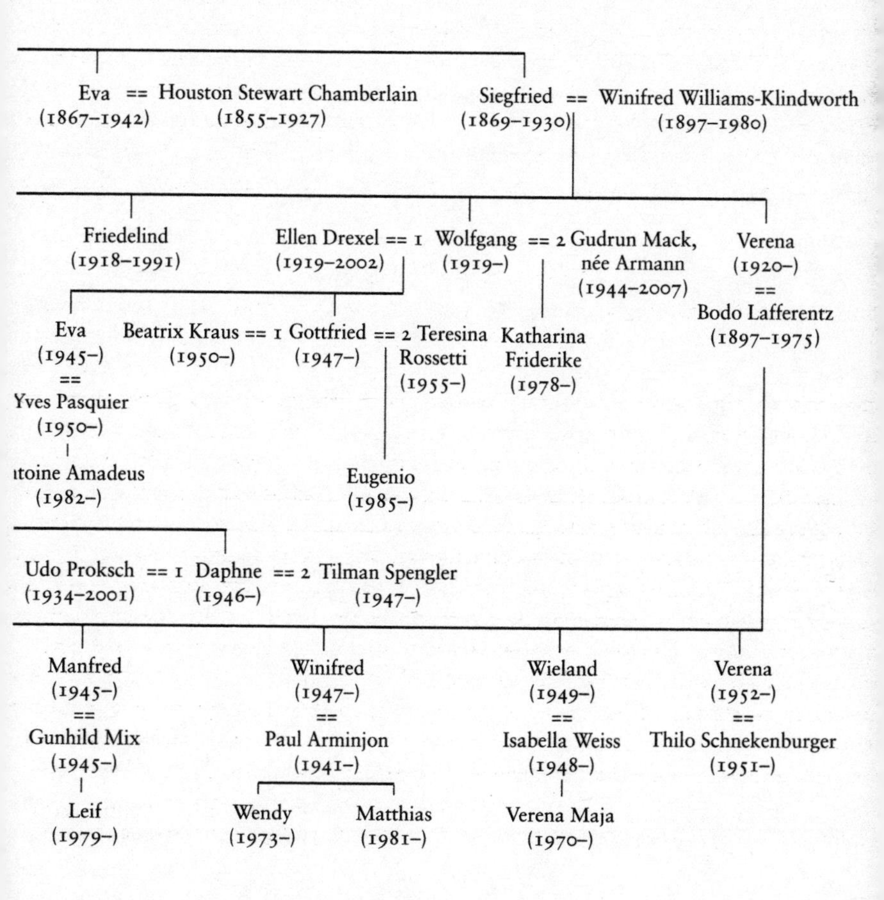
Eva == Houston Stewart Chamberlain
(1867–1942) (1855–1927)
Siegfried == Winifred Williams-Klindworth
(1869–1930) (1897–1980)
Friedelind
(1918–1991)
Ellen Drexel == 1 Wolfgang == 2 Gudrun Mack,
(1919–2002) (1919–)
née Armann
(1944–2007)
Verena
(1920–)
==
Bodo Lafferentz
(1897–1975)
Eva
(1945–)
==
Yves Pasquier
(1950–)
itoine Amadeus
(1982–)
Beatrix Kraus == 1 Gottfried == 2 Teresina
(1950–) (1947–)
Rossetti
(1955–)
Eugenio
(1985–)
Katharina
Friderike
(1978–)
Udo Proksch == 1 Daphne == 2 Tilman Spengler
(1934–2001) (1946–) (1947–)
Manfred
(1945–)
==
Gunhild Mix
(1945–)
Leif
(1979–)
Winifred
(1947–)
==
Paul Arminjon
(1941–)
Wendy
(1973–)
Matthias
(1981–)
Wieland
(1949–)
==
Isabella Weiss
(1948–)
Verena Maja
(1970–)
Verena
(1952–)
==
Thilo Schnekenburger
(1951–)

# I

# A Sublime but Glaucous Sea

Of all the buildings in which Richard Wagner lived during his peripatetic career, Tribschen near Lucerne in Switzerland was easily the loveliest. The three-storey villa with its rows of green-shuttered windows stood, and still stands, high on a wooded peninsula with dazzling views across the Vierwaldstätter Lake to distant Alpine peaks. It was more elegant than Wahnfried, the mausoleum-like residence Wagner later planned and built in Bayreuth, more light and airy than the Palazzo Vendramin on the Grand Canal in Venice, where he died. Summer was much the best time. The rooms filled with the sweet scent of flowers and cut grass, the family would often picnic on the meadow and, when his work had gone well or (more often) when he just wanted to show off, Wagner did headstands and climbed trees. The elder children played 'brigands' for hours in the shrubbery or cooed over the latest addition to the family, Siegfried Helferich Richard Wagner, affectionately known as Fidi.

Trippers were the main pest, sailing across the lake armed with telescopes in the hope of spying Tribschen's notorious inhabitants. For Wagner was a former left-wing revolutionary who now seemed to be changing the face of music with the backing of unlikely allies, notably King Ludwig II of Bavaria, who was widely regarded as mad. His mistress, Francesca Gaetana Cosima von Bülow, was an illegitimate daughter of Marie d'Agoult, a French countess, and Franz Liszt, whose devilish virtuosity as pianist and lover had long been the talk of Europe. To general astonishment, Liszt had meanwhile become an Abbé after curbing his wilder ways and taking minor Catholic orders, while the countess, despite (or because of) her pedigree, had turned into a writer with strong republican sympathies. Siegfried, born in the early morning of 6 June 1869, was Richard's and Cosima's third child, but they had yet to marry. Politics, art, nobility, sex – no wonder voyeurs by the boatload set daily course for Tribschen, or as close to it as they could get.

At least in the circumstances of his birth, Siegfried lived up to his extraordinary parents. Just as he uttered his first cry, according to an entry in Cosima's voluminous diary, early rays of dawn sunlight flickered out from behind the mountains and bathed the villa's rooms in orange fire. Caught in this blaze and reflecting it, Cosima's portrait set in a gold-framed jewel case was 'transfigured in celestial splendour'.[1] Oddly enough it was Richard himself, not Cosima, who wrote that particular entry and the scene described might well have been taken from one of his own music dramas. It might also have appeared in one of the more poetic works of the philosopher Friedrich Nietzsche, say his *Also Sprach Zarathustra* (Thus Spake Zarathustra); and by an extraordinary chance Nietzsche, who had enjoyed a 'wondrous' first meeting with Wagner in Leipzig a year earlier, was a house guest at Tribschen that night. Disappointingly, it seems that he slept through the whole thing, but the mere fact of his presence in that very place at that very time is enough to set the imagination racing. Wasn't the Siegfried of Wagner's massive *Ring* cycle the prototype blonde, fearless, Teutonic hero, prone to slay dragons and plunge unharmed through fire? And didn't Nietzsche with his concepts of the 'superman' and the 'will to power' help blaze a trail for the Nazis? How easy, therefore, to see all this not so much as a striking coincidence as an omen.

Easy but wrong. It is hard to imagine anyone less like a hero of the *Ring* or a Nietzschean superman than the gentle, affable, bisexual Siegfried who was born at Tribschen that night. Because Wagner junior lacked his father's genius, as well as his ruthless egocentricity, he remains far less well known than his life and talent justify. Although busy enough as boss of the Bayreuth festival, he also ran a parallel career as producer and conductor, besides composing nearly a score of operas – works sneered at with depressing regularity, especially by people who have never heard them. Not that the ignorant can be much blamed. The Wagner family itself, who stood guard over Siegfried's scores after his early death, for the most part did precious little to propagate them in the wake of the Second World War. Even leaving aside the compositions, much remains to be uncovered about

Siegfried's personal and professional life. A couple of biographies of him have appeared in German, but his own memoirs are thin, his letters in part still not disclosed, his true feelings often masked by irony and bonhomie.

The problem with getting a clear view of Siegfried's parents is rather the opposite. The near-limitless sea of material by and about the couple is one in which even expert navigators can lose their bearings for good. Cosima's diary alone, belatedly published in full in 1976, runs to nearly a million words. She was also a compulsive correspondent, albeit no match for Richard, who fired off so many letters, more than ten thousand at the last count, that experts are still toiling to collect and classify them all. Overall, Wagner's writings on just about everything under the sun (and including the texts of his music dramas) fill sixteen fat tomes. Nor is it just a matter of sheer quantity. Cosima's diary reveals much to fascinate and infuriate, but it is wrong to take it, as many tend to do, as a verbatim record. Wagner's near-thousand-page autobiography *Mein Leben* (My Life) is in part a compulsive read, but it is about as frank and reliable as you would expect, given that the text was written for a rich patron, King Ludwig, and dictated to Cosima. His essays, tracts and stories can be thought-provoking like *Die Kunst und die Revolution* (Art and Revolution), practical like *Über das Dirigieren* (On Conducting) – even funny like *Eine Pilgerfahrt zu Beethoven* (A Pilgrimage to Beethoven). They are usually trenchant, sometimes violent. But often it seems that Wagner takes up his pen not because he knows at the outset what he wants to say but because he wants to find out what he really thinks. To put it mildly, he does not always succeed. In any case he changed some of his key views over the years, in part radically. There is nothing odd about that of course, but he rarely acknowledged the fact publicly and probably did not always admit it to himself.

None of that would matter if Wagner had been a mediocre composer. It is doubtful whether much of his prose would be read nowadays for intrinsic merit. But because Wagner's music is, at its best, of rarely matched power and beauty, his writings have become by association an irresistible lucky dip into which just about anyone – be it sage or crank, pacifist or warmonger, vegetarian or meat-eater, semite or anti-semite – has been able to plunge a fist and pull out a prize. Zealots can find plenty of goodies there alone to back up their view of 'The Master' as a near-deity whose intellectual abilities matched his musical genius. Those who hold this opinion enjoy flanking support, thanks to the strenuous efforts of Cosima and her devoted circle to doctor the record after Wagner's death and declare his life unimpeachable. Similar obfuscation, albeit less blatant, has gone on intermittently ever since. On the other hand Wagner's many foes can easily assemble more than enough 'evidence' from his literary meanderings and chequered career to demonise him, even to make him seem personally responsible for Hitler. Innumerable books and articles have been launched from both implacable camps. Behind many of them you can hardly miss the sound of axes being ground.

The six years Wagner spent at Tribschen (1866–72), when so many strands of his life came together, offer plenty of ammunition to fans and foes alike. It was, on the face of it, a period of almost unmatched joy and productivity. During it Wagner completed *Die Meistersinger von Nürnberg* (The Mastersingers of Nuremberg) and recommenced work on the *Ring* after a twelve-year break. Cosima joined him for good in 1868 and, after her divorce from von Bülow, who seemed almost relieved to lose her to someone he too felt was the 'better man', the pair finally married in Lucerne in 1870. 'What a lucky old donkey I am,' Wagner burst out one evening at Tribschen – and up to a point, that is just what he was. Literally worshipped by a woman twenty-four years younger, surrounded by his adored children and favourite animals – including two dogs and two peacocks called Wotan and Fricka – he seemed to have come as close as he ever did to finding a real home. He did later own Wahnfried, whereas Tribschen was merely rented; but since the bill for the latter was footed by the sorely tried but still not wholly estranged King Ludwig, that particular distinction did not matter much to Wagner. And there were peaks of domestic bliss at Tribschen that seem never quite to have been scaled later.

One of these was the famous birth of the *Siegfried Idyll*, which combines so many of those qualities such as charm, lightness and intimacy that the rest of Wagner's music is widely but wrongly said to lack. Even those who can resist the *Idyll* itself can hardly deny the romance of its origin; how Wagner secretly composed the piece in 1870 as a birthday present for Cosima; how she failed to guess what was in the offing despite surreptitious rehearsals in and around the villa; how she awoke on Christmas morning (she was born on 24 December but celebrated on the twenty-fifth) to the strains of the premiere given by fifteen musicians crammed onto the staircase leading to her bedroom.

Cosima wept. She often did that anyway, especially when listening to Wagner, but then whose eyes would have stayed dry on such a day? 'Now let me die,' she sighed to him after the work had been repeated twice more, albeit in less cramped conditions. 'It would be easier to die for me than to live for me,'[2] Wagner replied – an observation very likely true.

Wagner was partly out to match (or rather surpass, since he despised mere equality) the birthday treat Cosima had secretly concocted for *him* seven months earlier. Overnight she had decorated Tribschen's stairwell with hundreds of roses and in the early morning a forty-five-piece military band filed into the garden at her behest to play the *Huldigungsmarsch* (March of Homage), a far from idyllic piece Wagner had composed six years before for King Ludwig. But of course there was more behind the *Idyll* than a ritual move in an elevated game of tit-for-tat. Joy at the birth of his son, love for Cosima, a sense of peace in so ideal a place – all flowed into the piece and were reflected in the title Wagner gave it: 'Tribschen Idyll with Fidi-Birdsong and Orange Sunrise presented as a symphonic birthday greeting to his Cosima by her Richard, 1870.'

It was not only the Wagners who found the Tribschen experience magical. Judith Gautier, a visiting French beauty whom Wagner seduced (or at least tried to) years later, told Cosima that 'Now, at last, I comprehend that happiness of paradise so extolled by believers, the seeing of God face to face.' The mistress of the house, Judith somewhat superfluously noted, 'thought quite as I did'.[3] Likewise Elisabeth Nietzsche, Friedrich's sister who later devoted much of her life to falsifying his writings, recalls an enchanted walk by the lake under the full moon. Wagner wearing his famous velvet biretta and black cloak, Cosima in a pink cashmere gown, eloquently held forth with Nietzsche on the greatness of the Greeks, the promise of the Germans and the tragedy of human life until – bit by bit – they fell into a wistful silence. For the youthful philosopher, thirty-one years Wagner's junior, Tribschen initially brought *the* revelation of joy (his unrequited love for Cosima notwithstanding) in a tortured, lonely life. Decades later and close to madness, he recalled his twenty-three visits – let's say pilgrimages – to the spot, and confided that 'at no price would I have my life deprived of those days at Tribschen – days of confidence, of sublime flashes of insight and of profound moments. I know not what Wagner may have been for others; but no cloud ever obscured our sky.'[4]

The first part of that statement is no doubt true, the last is nonsense. Even during that much-prized Tribschen era, Nietzsche's slowly growing differences with Wagner brought down on him Cosima's censure: as she put it in her diary, he was mistakenly 'trying to resist the overwhelming effect' of the Master's personality.[5] Later, feeling used, betrayed and humiliated, Nietzsche launched attacks on Wagner that for bitterness and ferocity, not to mention stylistic skill, remain unsurpassed to this day despite huge and ever-growing competition. Yet he could refer to a cloudless sky in the above passage from *Ecce Homo*, written in 1888 but only published twenty years later. One explanation might be that his madness had set in rather earlier than generally thought. More likely, at this particular moment he simply blended out painful memories to ensure that happy ones stayed untainted. Selective recollection is certainly, to quote Nietzsche again, *Menschlich, Allzumenschliches* (Human, All-Too-Human). But whether such distortion is unconscious, as it may well have been in Nietzsche's case, or deliberate, it bedevils the Wagner saga often, all-too-often. And, of course, it works both ways.

Just how idyllic really was the Tribschen era? It was certainly a period when Richard and Cosima took their deception of King Ludwig, long blissfully unaware of their adultery, to new depths, with a barrage of lies and obsequiousness breathtaking even by Wagner's abject standards. It was also just at this time that Wagner chose to reissue *Das Judentum in der Musik* (Jewishness in Music), an antisemitic tract he had published under a pseudonym two decades before. Now he worded it still more viciously (Cosima recorded her 'great delight in its terseness and pithiness'[6]) and issued it under his own name. Similarly repulsive was *Eine Kapitulation* (A Capitulation), a jingoistic farce seemingly glorying in French humiliation in the war against Prussia, which he gleefully produced in late 1870, more or less simultaneously with the *Siegfried Idyll*. Wagner later argued that the piece was really meant to show that artistically the Germans were even more puerile than the French, and indeed his contempt for his own countrymen, Wagner fans excluded, at times seemed boundless. But whatever Wagner's real intentions with *Eine Kapitulation*, there is no mistaking the joy with which he and particularly Cosima followed the progress of the Prussian onslaught. 'Nine battles within a month, and all victorious,' she exulted in her diary in September 1870. 'What a christening present for Fidi.'[7] In this and most other things, Cosima, with her

French mother and Hungarian father, felt more intensely and chauvinistically German than most Germans. Hers was an example that other non-German members of the Wagner clan were disastrously to follow.

Wagner's conduct can be, and often is, cast in a more favourable light. It is at least arguable that King Ludwig mainly had his own naivety to blame for trusting his 'heavenly friend' for so long, and for continuing to back him (much to posterity's benefit) even when it was clear the trust was misplaced. Besides, it is widely claimed that geniuses have a higher calling that justifies any amount of subterfuge – or at least makes those who draw attention to it seem petty if not contemptible. Above all great love is said to set its own rules or, as Cosima more eloquently wrote, it 'works on us like a Plutonian eruption, it bursts through everything, throws all strata into confusion, raises mountains, and there it is – utmost transformation and utmost law'.[8] Even those who consider themselves less than 'perfect Wagnerites' usually praise Cosima for striking courage and self-sacrifice, risking everything the world of convention had to offer to go to the man she adored. By so doing, she gave him vital stability, a family and fostered his creativity. 'Richard is working,' she joyfully noted time after time in her diary. Wasn't this relationship at least pretty close to a love that, as Wagner put it, emerges 'only once in five thousand years'?[9]

Yes and no. By mid-1864, when Wagner and Cosima are first known to have slept together ('consummated their union' as it is often more delicately put), and four years before they finally settled in at Tribschen, he had already composed the bulk of his work, including more than half the *Ring*, part of *Die Meistersinger* and the whole of *Tristan und Isolde*. It is tempting to speculate that the tension produced by Wagner's long and unhappy first marriage to Minna Planer, and by his relatively brief infatuation for Mathilde Wesendonck, the wife of a rich German businessman in Zurich, may have spurred him to creativity at least as much as life with Cosima ever did. Tempting – but hardly fruitful. At least Cosima's omnipresence did not stop him completing his unfinished works and composing the whole of *Parsifal*, often claimed to be his finest piece. Besides, the love that happens 'only once in five thousand years' was itself far from tension-free.

Take that flowery account of Siegfried's birth in Cosima's diary. Isn't it strange that Wagner should have written it there? He did have a lovely diary of his own in brown leather decorated with malachite stones, given him by Cosima years before. One explanation could be that Wagner felt so totally at one with her on that splendid June morning that her thoughts and feelings – and hence her diary – became his own, as it were. No doubt he also wanted to spare her the effort of writing so soon after giving birth. That seems plausible, except that Wagner had written another long entry in Cosima's diary a few days before, without at first telling her what he was up to, and it was anything but considerate. Instead he bitterly complained because Cosima, still married to von Bülow and apparently embarrassed with her elder children in the house, refused to move into an apartment on the ground floor with a bedroom next to his. Such treatment, Wagner charged as he returned the volume to his pregnant mistress, tormented him 'like the fear of death.'[10] Cosima was not just remorseful. As the very next entry (in her own hand) makes clear, she felt that barely seven months after moving in with Wagner she had been given the '*coup de grâce*'.[11]

This was no isolated storm. Like a spoiled brat, Wagner could never bear to be away from the centre of attention, sometimes emitting a piercing scream simply to shut up guests who had the effrontery to chat among themselves. But when Cosima was distracted for an hour or two, say minding the children or doing embroidery, his tantrums could become especially vindictive. Even before the Tribschen era, he particularly resented Cosima's continuing contacts with her father – that same Franz Liszt who had proved such a staunch friend to Wagner when he was down and nearly out, as he so often was. And later in Bayreuth a 'distracting' letter from Liszt sparked such a bitter outburst from Wagner that Cosima in distress abandoned her beloved diary for twelve days. How could she put up with such treatment? The truth is she enjoyed it. 'I am glad of my suffering,' she wrote, 'and fold my hands in grateful prayer.'[12]

The Tribschen idyll with its peaks of physical joy and its 'sublime flashes of insight' was no sham. That birthday music for Cosima unforgettably sums up the best of it. But as so often with Wagner, it was also a time shot through with peculiarly intense envy, prejudice and cruelty. Both extremes belong to the true picture of a life that, to cite Charles de Gaulle's forbidding words between the two world wars about Germany, was like 'a sublime but glaucous sea where the fisherman's net hauls up monsters and treasures'.[13] No wonder Wagner's descendants staggered under the weight of so glorious but poisoned a legacy.

# 2

# Revolution and Reverse

At the start of 1848, revolution sparked by poverty, famine and unrealised democratic ideals began to sweep through Europe – unstoppably, it seemed at first. In February Karl Marx and Friedrich Engels issued their *Communist Manifesto*, not an immediate cause of the uprisings, it is true, but very much a sign of the times. The same month King Louis-Philippe of France, threatened by street battles in Paris and fearing for his head, hastily abdicated after eighteen years of rule and fled to England. A republic was promptly declared – the second in France since the bloody revolution begun in 1789, bringing about a reign of terror, the execution of Louis XVI and the end of the monarchy for more than two decades.

With the 1848 insurrection victorious in Paris, demonstrations erupted in March in Vienna, capital of the Habsburg (Austrian) empire, forcing the flight of Clemens von Metternich, the power behind the throne for nearly forty years, and later the abdication of Emperor Ferdinand himself. For a time the far-flung but loosely integrated empire itself seemed about to fall apart. Meanwhile regimes in the patchwork of states that made up Italy and Germany lost their nerve with startling speed, promising all sorts of democratic reforms to keep the mobs at bay. More or less at the geographical centre of this turmoil, though not at first directly involved in the violence swirling around it, was Dresden, capital of Saxony. And at the core of Dresden's musical life was the energetic but chronically impecunious Richard Wagner, since 1843 Hofkapellmeister (court conductor) to King Friedrich August II, a post that brought more than local prestige.

Surely such an establishment figure, with his regular duties, smart livery and ex-actress wife who adored being called 'Frau Hofkapellmeisterin', would be firmly committed to the status quo. Not so. Bursting with frustration and increasingly anarchic visions, Wagner backed the drive for sweeping reform at home and greeted the outbreak of street fighting in Vienna with a signed poem published in the Austrian press. None of that lost him his job. His monumental opera *Rienzi, der letzte der Tribunen* (Rienzi, the Last of the Tribunes), set in ancient Rome and packed with insurrection, death and destruction, was indeed removed by the management from the programme of the Royal Court Opera – hardly a drastic rebuke in the circumstances. But in September Wagner was still very much active in His Majesty's service, conducting a concert including excerpts from his latest work *Lohengrin* to mark the three-hundredth birthday of the Court Orchestra (forerunner of the superb Dresden Staatskapelle, still going strong today despite everything war and dictatorship has flung at its home city). Wagner's friends marvelled at his ability to bounce back; his foes seethed at his knack, as it seemed to them, of getting away with murder. Whatever you called it, the truth was that this phenomenal court employee had already packed far more scandal and sheer adventure into his thirty-five years than most men do into a lifetime.

Twelve years before, Wagner had made his public debut as an opera composer with *Das Liebesverbot* (The Ban on Love), an over-long but witty piece based on Shakespeare's *Measure for Measure*, which lampoons sham morality in general and puritanism in particular. It still deserves a staging but rarely gets one anywhere; it is never produced at the Bayreuth festival, where its lightish relief would be a boon. It was not Wagner's first completed opera – that was the easily forgettable *Die Feen* (The Fairies) – but it was the first to get a hearing, albeit a brief one. The premiere in Magdeburg where Wagner regularly conducted was a fiasco, and a second performance was scrapped after onstage fist fights broke out before the curtain rose. The company then went bankrupt. It was during his involvement with the Magdeburg troupe that Wagner wooed and won – perhaps one should rather say wore down – Christine Wilhelmine 'Minna' Planer, a fetching, blue-eyed actress four years older than himself with an illegitimate daughter named Natalie whom she passed off as her sister. They were wed in 1836 in Königsberg, a marriage that was rocky from the first but somehow survived poverty, sickness and a stream of affairs, not to mention a basic difference of outlook, until Minna's death thirty years later.

Not quite all the extra-marital adventures were Wagner's. Six months after the wedding Minna, battered and bewildered by her husband's lightning switches of mood from towering rage to tearful remorse, ran off with a merchant. She finally rejoined Wagner in the Baltic town of Riga (then in the Russian empire) where he had become music director. But when his contract was not renewed and his passport impounded because he failed to pay his debts, Wagner decided in 1839 to flee west with Minna and a huge hound called Robber to seek his fortune in Paris, at that time the capital of the opera world. According to Natalie, Minna was so injured in a cart accident during the perilous trip that she was unable to have another child. That may or may not be accurate. Natalie was not present in Riga and only rejoined the household in Paris, so her report made decades later is second-hand. But both Wagner and Natalie in their separate accounts do agree that there was an accident – and it is a fact that Minna henceforth stayed childless.

After dodging Cossack guards on the border with East Prussia, hiding in the hold of a small merchant ship and surviving a storm-wracked, zigzag voyage, the dazed couple arrived in London barely able to stand upright. Wagner aimed to make some useful contacts there and also to track down the score of his grandiose overture *Rule Britannia*, which had vanished into thin air after he had posted it two years before to the Philharmonic Society. Having failed in London on both counts (though the score, worth an occasional outing at the Last Night of the Proms, did eventually reappear), Wagner pressed on with wife and hound to Paris. His hopes of a breakthrough there were still high, but not for much longer. Even allowing for Wagner's often deliberate distortions in *Mein Leben*, from which he tends to emerge as a victim of idiot critics and envious rivals, there is little doubt that his two and a half years in the French capital were among the most frustrating and degrading he ever suffered. He spent much of the time begging for cash, writing articles (some still gripping, many hack-work) and knocking on doors of the music establishment, which usually stayed shut.

One door that opened more than a crack, however, was that of Giacomo Meyerbeer, born Jakob Liebmann Beer into a wealthy Jewish family near Berlin, who had lived in Paris for years and whose grand operas were the toast of much of Europe. In one sickeningly sycophantic letter, a genre of which he proved a lifelong master, Wagner offered to become Meyerbeer's 'slave, body and soul, in order to find food and strength for my work, which will one day tell you of my gratitude'.[1] Meyerbeer's genuine efforts on Wagner's behalf brought little direct result in the French capital; but they did help get *Rienzi* and *Der fliegende Holländer* (The Flying Dutchman), both completed in Paris, to the stage in Germany. Wagner was later to repay this backing not with the promised gratitude but with some of the most vindictive attacks even he could muster. Deeply envious of Meyerbeer's success, he was also filled with self-hatred; not just because he had felt forced to beg (he was often doing that), but because in *Rienzi* he came close to producing the kind of superficial spectacle he despised in contemporary opera in general – and in his benefactor's work in particular. Did Wagner come to hate Meyerbeer so much because he was Jewish, or did he come to hate Jews because of Meyerbeer? Of that grubby question, alas, more later.

With such a long march of misery behind him, Wagner could hardly believe it when his luck began to turn and Dresden agreed to stage *Rienzi*. After agonies of apprehension before the premiere on 20 October 1842, he stopped the clock in the Court Theatre during the six-hour marathon for fear an impatient public might bolt before the end. He need not have worried. Nearly everyone stayed until after midnight to cheer. It was one of the biggest first-night successes Wagner ever had, paving the way for his appointment as Hofkapellmeister. Three months later Dresden premiered *Holländer* (to less acclaim) and in 1845 *Tannhäuser*, the latter even drawing a reluctant salute from Robert Schumann, influential both as critic and composer, who claimed to have little against Wagner except that he 'never stops talking'.[2] Wagner's income still far from matched his spending, but that apart he seemed to have real cause to celebrate. Minna was clearly overjoyed and, after the vagabond existence since Magdeburg, who could blame her? From her point of view, only a fool would deliberately endanger a 'good life' so hard won; but then her point of view was emphatically not her husband's. If that had not been wholly plain in the years of shared privation, it became so in the relative security of Dresden. For Minna, the world at large could more or less drift on as it was. For Wagner it had to change.

And changing it was, despite all the efforts of the old order to maintain the status quo. Germany still existed merely as a Confederation of grotesquely unequal parts – including five kingdoms, six grand duchies, eleven duchies, ten principalities, one landgraviate and four free cities – created by the Congress of Vienna in 1815 after Napoleon's final defeat. The continued division of a potentially serious rival suited the big powers like Russia, Britain and Austria (the latter formally part of, and dominant within, the Confederation). It did not suit Germans fired by the ideals of the 1789 French Revolution, who reckoned liberal reforms could only make headway if the petty potentates in the regions lost their clout in a truly united nation. Nor did it remotely suit German business, envious of Britain's economic success but trapped in a web of customs tariffs between and sometimes even within the member states. There was no common currency and no uniform system of weights and measures.

The creation under Prussian pressure in 1834 of the Zollverein, a customs union that included much of the Confederation but not Austria, went some way to meet German business demands. Arguably it gave a more decisive prod to the cause of German unity than any of the philosophies, speeches and demonstrations then current (a point not lost just over a century later on those who set up the Common Market while seeking a united Europe). But economics and pragmatism alone could not satisfy those Germans genuinely seeking liberal reform, let alone those impatient for a powerful base, democratic or not, from which to repay the French for past humiliation. It was around this time that Wagner became involved with *Junges Deutschland* (Young Germany), a loose literary grouping at odds in detail on many things but broadly united in a yearning for the overthrow of the existing order – political, artistic and moral. In Germany pressure for change built up slowly like distant thunder, noted Heinrich Heine, the Jewish-born poet who was the group's most distinguished adherent; but one day a drama would be enacted there 'compared with which the French Revolution will seem like a harmless idyll'.[3]

Wagner's political stance was not at first as radical as that, although part of *Junges Deutschland*'s 'free love' philosophy quickly flowed into *Das Liebesverbot* and some of Heine's work later served as a source for *Holländer* and *Tannhäuser*. But his views hardened under the humiliating blows he suffered in hated Paris and, more surprisingly at first glance, they continued to do so even in Dresden. Why? For one thing Wagner failed to win reform even in the limited field in which he fondly imagined that, as Hofkapellmeister, he had direct influence. In 1846 he produced a report proposing ways to rationalise the hiring of orchestral players and boost their salaries while offering more concerts. It is one of a handful of constructive, practical documents that show that Wagner did not always have his head in the clouds or the slime of the Rhine. But it did not persuade local bureaucrats who carefully mulled over the scheme for a year, then carefully shelved it. Nothing loath, Wagner came up with another even more far-reaching plan two years later. Under it the Court Theatre was to be renamed the National Theatre and given a form of collective self-management that would remove it from direct political or royal infuence, though Wagner cannily built in a clause that would have enhanced his own position. No doubt a servant (even a superior one) who thinks he can afford to bite his master's hand so blithely must be judged more than a bit naive. At any rate nothing came of this scheme either.

Those setbacks alone would hardly have taken Wagner to the barricades, but there was much else simmering in his head and heart. Perhaps already in Paris, but at the latest in Dresden, he was fired by the ideas of the contemporary French anarchist Pierre-Joseph Proudhon, now most widely remembered and falsely judged for his unsubtle remark that 'property is theft'. What Proudhon really opposed was not property earned by personal effort, but the kind used to exploit the labour of another. No wonder that struck a chord with Wagner, who had so often felt forced to sell his compositions for a pittance, pawn his pathetic belongings and beg for help in cash and kind, not least from Jews. But he was even more decisively influenced by the philosophy of Ludwig Feuerbach, one of whose key works, *Das Wesen des Christentums* (The Essence of Christianity), was published in 1841 just before Wagner and Minna packed their bags in Paris and retreated to the Fatherland. Claiming that man created God in his own image, Feuerbach urged people to stop projecting their own highest qualities, and shuffling off responsibility, onto a non-existent deity. In a nutshell, he issued a clarion call to human beings to grow up and take their lives into their own hands.

For Wagner Feuerbach was simply, as he put it in *Mein Leben*, 'the ideal exponent of the radical release of the individual from the thraldom of accepted notions'.[4] Many budding revolutionaries of the time felt the same. One was Marx, a keen Feuerbach admirer at least for a while. Another was August Röckel, deputy conductor in Dresden, a man of minor musical talent but such explosive eloquence on his favourite topic of insurrection that even Wagner sometimes found it hard to get a word in edgeways. It was thanks to Röckel that in 1849 Wagner fell in with Mikhail Bakunin, the very model of a Russian anarchist (and naturally a Proudhon fan), who was always looking for trouble and found plenty of it in Dresden that year.

By that time Wagner was more than ready to back an uprising with action as well as words. Back in 1846 he had told a fellow radical, Alfred von Meissner, that there had already been a revolution in people's heads and that 'the new Germany was ready and waiting like a bronze cast that needed only a hammer blow on its clay shell in order for it to emerge.'[5] Two years later, with Europe increasingly in turmoil, Wagner went public with his view of what this 'bronze cast' should look like. In a speech in June 1848 to more than a thousand backers of the fiercely republican *Vaterlandsverein* (Fatherland Union), he called among other things for national unity, universal suffrage, abolition of censorship and removal of the aristocratic 'lackeys and flunkies' at court (though not of the king himself). He also came close to demanding the abolition of money, a step that presumably would have seen off his ineluctably rising debts, which already far exceeded his annual salary. Out of all that, Wagner claimed, a new and free Germany would emerge, which would establish colonies and thus carry civilisation across the globe. 'The sun of German freedom and German gentleness', as he put it, 'should alike warm and elevate Cossack, Frenchman, Bushman and Chinese . . . '[6]

With the sad benefit of hindsight, it is hard not to sneer at Wagner's vision of Germanic global warming. As for his other points, the woolly ranting against money was much in tune with the times and the call for greater unity and democracy surely justified. But bit by bit that year the conservatives in much of Europe steadied themselves and began to take back concessions they had promised in the initial panic. A national assembly began meeting in Frankfurt to try to unite Germany and produce a constitution, but to the frustration of many – including Wagner – it proved unrepresentative and ultimately powerless. Finally, in May 1849, violence came to the streets of Dresden at last and the court composer, along with his pals Röckel and Bakunin, was in the thick of it. Exactly what part Wagner played is not clear and presumably never will be. But he certainly issued leaflets to Saxon soldiers urging them not to make common cause with Prussian forces called in by the King to help put down the uprising. He also reported on troop movements from the steeple of a Dresden church with bullets pinging about him, and he may have helped order hand grenades for the rebels.

Anyway, the rebellion flopped and a warrant was issued for Wagner's arrest. He narrowly escaped capture and thanks to help from Franz Liszt, then music director in Weimar, he managed to make it with false papers over the border to Switzerland. There poor Minna, her worst fears confirmed, later joined him. Wagner stayed in exile for eleven years, sometimes with Minna, often without her. Röckel was not so lucky. Caught and tried, he was condemned to death, a sentence later commuted to life imprisonment. Bakunin was jailed for seven years, then exiled to Siberia. He escaped in 1861 and popped up in Europe again to spread more unrest, still trumpeting that 'the passion for destruction is also a creative passion'.[7]

The tale so far might seem to suggest that Wagner was dropping composing to become a professional revolutionary. Almost the opposite is true, although he did spend his first period in exile turning out one theoretical tract after another but no music. He had come to believe that only through revolution would a society emerge in which true art, notably his own, was able to flourish. It was therefore wholly in his interest to spend some time giving revolution a helping hand. What good were all those pathetically provincial and near-bankrupt little theatres, Wagner fumed, or those grand opera houses crawling with bureaucrats and subject to the patronage of musically illiterate grandees? He had seen more than enough of both from the inside. Not for him the superficial gestures and empty pomp of works by Meyerbeer and his ilk – mere sops tossed into a gilded trough for frivolous audiences that tended to come late, leave early and chatter in between. What a difference, he reflected, to the role of art in ancient Greece, where works fusing instrumental music, singing, poetry and drama had touched the deepest human thoughts and feelings. Moreover, the performances had been given in theatres of a practical design where all present could see and hear well, not in ornate buildings with tiered boxes that emphasised wealth and social status. The Greeks who imbibed all-encompassing art under ideal conditions came away feeling uplifted and united, with a better understanding of the world and of themselves. That at least is how Wagner saw it, so fired during his last years in Dresden by reading Greek texts, especially the *Oresteia* of Aeschylus, that he later claimed, 'I have never since been really able to reconcile myself with modern literature.'[8]

Despite his rose-tinted view of antiquity, Wagner did admit that economically Greek society had been flawed because it was based on slavery. But so too, he argued, was the modern world, in which all had become slaves to capital in one way or another. What's more, over the centuries 'the great synthesis of the arts' that had plumbed and reflected the public consciousness of the Greeks had split apart. What remained were mere fragments such as opera, plays and ballet – superficial and commercialised like the alienated, class-ridden society they intermittently titillated. The answer? Overthrow capitalism, stop treating culture as a commodity and reunite the sadly splintered arts as co-equal partners. And who, despite two years of largely abortive revolution in Europe, might be bold or crazy enough to try his hand at forging a *Gesamtkunstwerk* (total work of art) modelled on that long-shattered Greek ideal? Why, the all-but jobless, henpecked exile Richard Wagner. In Dresden he had already sketched part of the plot for a suitable opus; a parable of human kind eventually called *Der Ring des Nibelungen* (The Ring of the Nibelung), beginning in primeval slime, ending in fire and showing how greed for power and wealth destroys love. He also had some original ideas about how this colossus should be displayed; over four evenings before an audience that did not have to pay, and in a wooden building designed along the lines of a Greek theatre, which would be burned down after the last night. All that remained to be settled were the practical details like composing the music and raising the money. And in the latter skill, as in the former, Wagner was a much-practised virtuoso.

He needed to be. Zurich is a city where traditionally much money can indeed be raised (and hidden from prying eyes), but not by just anyone. And here among its solid citizens was a perfect example of the sort of person seemingly bound not to get a *sou*; a rather undersized (not quite five feet seven inches) Saxon musician with an oversized head, a thick accent, dreadful manners and an often venomous glare, who wrote and babbled incessantly about chimeras like *Das Kunstwerk der Zukunft* (The Artwork of The Future). His marriage was clearly shaky and he had no fixed address. Yes, he had had some success and status in Dresden and he had made something of a mark since arriving in Zurich, both as a conductor and as actor/narrator of his near-interminable Nibelung tale – recited to a dogged little throng over four nights in the luxury Hotel Baur au Lac. But surely one would sooner invest in an enterprise to make silver from moonbeams than inject cash into this Saxon windbag?

And yet Wagner – the master-pumper from Leipzig – extracted a steady stream of loans and largesse, even managing repeatedly to tap a canny silk merchant, Otto Wesendonck, while dallying with Otto's young and lovely wife Mathilde. Much of Wesendonck's backing was, in fact, pledged only in exchange for future income from performances of Wagner's works. But since most of the latter had so far proved anything but box-office hits, and the projected *Gesamtkunstwerk* was of unparalleled length and complexity, to be staged in a theatre that did not yet exist, Wesendonck's 'security' looked shaky indeed. How did Wagner manage to turn so many usually steady heads? Some well-wishers, of course, quickly grasped that his was music for the ages; most people were anyway susceptible to his silver tongue, his air of life-or-death conviction and his sheer effrontery: 'I must have beauty, radiance, light. The world owes me a living.'[9] Like all the greatest actors he did not so much charm and bully his audiences (onstage and off) as spellbind them. Of all the roles he created, from the ever-wandering Dutchman through the passionate outsider Tannhäuser to the lovesick knight Tristan, perhaps the one that matches Wagner best is Klingsor – the wizard in *Parsifal*, making magic from a dark tower above his dangerously seductive magic garden.

Although still smarting under the Dresden setback, living from hand to mouth and close to the age of forty, Wagner remained committed – fiercely for a time – to leftist revolution. It is true that he condemned communism (but capitalism too!) and that when he invoked the *Volk*, a dangerously vague word easily misused, he was thinking not of the working masses but of a kind of German spiritual brotherhood. Moreover, he claimed to favour a continued role for monarchs (not to mention a special place for outstanding artists – like himself) in the post-revolutionary world he dimly foresaw. All that might seem to show that Wagner was more of a bourgeois-liberal reformer than a socialist rebel, that like many of his countrymen he favoured a soft 'revolution from above' over a violent French-style one from below. It is often claimed that this national trait – in principle endearing but in practice calamitous – helps explain why Germany never had a thoroughgoing revolution and stayed all too vulnerable to authoritarian and dictatorial regimes. Be that as it may, Wagner surely does not fall under Lenin's caustic definition of Germans as people so law-abiding that they will first buy platform tickets before storming a railway station. He really had been penniless and hungry and he had seen at close quarters the stifling power of entrenched privilege. He could easily have chosen to throw in his lot with the establishment for good, but instead he risked jail and even his life to try to overturn it. He was certainly not averse to violence, except against animals.

Physically safe and halfway solvent in his Zurich oasis, Wagner struggled to create a work revolutionary in aim and form from a bewildering array of sources. The Greek example clearly played a big role in the forging of the *Ring* – surprisingly big, no doubt, for those who tend to think of the cycle as Teutonic through and through. It shows up in the bid to give music and words equal status, as well as in parts of the plot that echo the work of Aeschylus. It may even help account for the cycle's four-part format, which recalls the tetralogies of Athenian drama. Nordic myth and Germanic saga went into Wagner's crucible too. But what caused him to want to weld all this disparate material into shape in the first place? That is a dangerous question to ask about any creative artist. But it is surely plausible to conclude that without a deep sense of injustice and the yearning for a new order, bred by bitter personal experience and fostered by the philosophy of revolution, Wagner would not have begun the *Ring* as and when he did, perhaps not at all. His blueprint showing how disaster inevitably springs from greed for riches and lust for power would surely have drawn a nod of assent from Proudhon. Likewise Feuerbach would in principle have enthused over the fearless, taboo-breaking optimism of the *Ring*'s young Siegfried, though he might well have had doubts about the uses to which Siegfried put these qualities.

In view of all that it seems sad, even tragic, that the leaders of the German Left did not try harder to adopt Wagner either during his lifetime or later. Didn't the social and political views he held for much (perhaps most) of his life strongly resemble their own? Wasn't this stance made manifest in the great parable of the *Ring*, at least in much of it? And surely the scheme for a 'classless theatre' making performances available even to the impecunious should have warmed the hearts of all leftist culture-vultures. In his incisive *The Perfect Wagnerite* (1898), the Irish socialist George Bernard Shaw brilliantly explored the *Ring* as an allegory of capitalism. No doubt he stressed that aspect too much at the expense of others. The tetralogy is a muddling (and muddled) beast that can be defined in many weird and wonderful ways. But the point is that no German figure of the left with remotely similar clout produced a thesis comparable to Shaw's. Nor was it until 1976 that a *Ring* production taking the socialist approach, with all its insights and flaws, finally reached the Bayreuth stage – and then it came from a Frenchman, Patrice Chéreau. Instead Wagner disastrously became the hero of the conservative bourgeoisie and increasingly of the far right. That is partly because his widow Cosima and her Bayreuth disciples strenuously remoulded the Master's image into one they approved of and wanted the world to believe in. But it is also because Wagner did what most people, including revolutionary firebrands, tend to do in the fullness of time. He changed.

One reason why Wagner changed was that the world in the 1850s stayed much the same, or at least was not transformed in the way he yearned for. It was a good time for reactionaries, not revolutionaries. After a coup d'état in Paris in 1851, France's short lived Second Republic gave way to a Second Empire with Napoleon III (Bonaparte's nephew) at its head. Germany remained the patchwork Confederation that had emerged after 1815, with much the same sort of old guard in control. National unity and democratic reform seemed as far distant as ever. In fact the apparent lull in 1850s Germany was deceptive. Prussia became increasingly dominant, building up its industry and starting to modernise the army that would shortly humble first the Austrians (in 1866) and then the French (in 1870–1). Meanwhile, thanks not least to the 'deregulation' boost of the Zollverein, most of the Confederation enjoyed an economic boom. New factories were built, railways laid, banks founded to finance it all. In 1871 national unity emerged at last, driven by economics and sealed by Prussian military might. 'Iron and blood' proved more effective than 'speeches and majority verdicts' (not to mention revolutionary idealism), just as Otto von Bismarck, Prussia's chancellor and master of *Realpolitik*, had predicted. Not surprisingly Wagner did not foresee all that in the early 1850s as he plugged away at his *Ring* in Zurich. He continued to pay lip service to the cause and kept in sporadic contact with old leftist pals. But his revolutionary ardour was fading.

Then he came across the philosophy of Arthur Schopenhauer. That discovery has been seen by one scholar after another, not to mention the composer himself, as a 'road to Damascus' revelation after which Wagner was never the same again. Up to a point that seems true. In late 1854 a friend gave him a copy of Schopenhauer's massive *Die*

*Welt als Wille und Vorstellung* (The World as Will and Representation), which Wagner promptly devoured although he was in the throes of composing. Suddenly, it seemed to him, the clouds rolled away and the largely unpalatable truth about the world and himself became clear. He read the work four times within a year, went on reading it for the rest of his life and tried with typical fervour to ram what he took to be its message down as many throats as possible. His keenness was not misplaced. Whatever its flaws, *Die Welt als Wille und Vorstellung* is almost uniquely wide-ranging and, unlike most of Wagner's own pseudo-philosophical writings, a pleasure to read. Schopenhauer's relentless logic brought perceptions like those of Buddhism but by the unexpected route of western thought. His insights into the power of the subconscious presaged those of Sigmund Freud. His analysis of matter and energy, fantastic though it seemed at the time, fits uncannily well into the world of quantum physics. All in all, a startling achievement for an odd little man with a near-insatiable appetite, at least for food and intellectual activity, who preferred his cat to people and who was widely ignored for much of his life.

In a nutshell, Schopenhauer argued that the world we poor humans perceive with our limited faculties and different standpoints is our own representation of reality, but not reality itself. Behind this empirical world, the one our senses and intellect register, lies what Schopenhauer (and in part Immanuel Kant before him) calls the 'thing in itself'. This 'real reality' is not strictly knowable but it distressingly manifests itself through what Schopenhauer confusingly calls 'Will', best thought of as energy or force, not conscious intent. This force is all-encompassing. People can dimly see it at work within themselves in the urge to live, to reproduce, to 'get on'. But for Schopenhauer it drives everything animate and inanimate; the whole universe is engaged in a blind and ceaseless chase to satisfy desires that, if met at all, are at once replaced by new ones. Result – misery. Is there no escape? Schopenhauer sees two possible ways. One is that people can by a process of self-denial withdraw from the eternal rat race into something much like the Buddhist state of Nirvana. This rather optimistically implies that, like Schopenhauer, they realise the awful truth and that, rather unlike him, they fully apply the appropriate remedy. The other way to win an at least short-term respite is, as it were, to lose oneself in art. Schopenhauer greatly valued the arts and judged much the greatest to be music – a direct manifestation, he believed, of inner consciousness.

For Wagner, Schopenhauer was the right philosopher at the right time. The aging revolutionary was starting to despair and here was Schopenhauer telling him, in a sense, not to worry because the whole struggle was useless anyway. Overturn one system and the next one will be no better, nor the one after that and so on ad infinitum. Moreover, Wagner had spent immense time and energy telling himself and other people that music and words were equal partners in the *Gesamtkunstwerk*, and here was Schopenhauer saying instead that music was best by far. On the face of it that looks inconvenient. But hadn't Wagner in his heart of hearts believed it anyway, whatever his intellect had tried to tell him? He was first and foremost a musician. And if he had fancied himself as a writer too, every one of Schopenhauer's clear and elegant sentences put him firmly in his lowly place.

Wagner readily agreed that Schopenhauer had a key impact on his work, but he did not, perhaps could not, fully and frankly state what that impact was. When he came across *Die Welt* he had just completed the music for *Das Rheingold* (The Rhine Gold), the first part (or so-called *Vorabend* – 'preliminary evening') of the *Ring,* and was hard at work on the next part, *Die Walküre* (The Valkyrie). In *Mein Leben*, he admits that after reading *Die Welt* he at first felt embarrassed because much of the theory behind his Nibelung project did not match what he felt Schopenhauer was telling him. However, when he took a further look at his own 'poetical conception' he concluded there was no contradiction after all. In other words, at a deeper level than that of conscious theory he had really been a Schopenhauerian all along.

Stretching a point, you can indeed fit much of Wagner's earlier work into the gospel according to Schopenhauer, especially the struggle between flesh and spirit in *Tannhäuser.* As for the *Ring*, Wagner found it terribly hard to cobble together a libretto consistent with his revolutionary ideals, and rewrote the ending of the whole cycle several times even before he read *Die Welt*. The truth is that Schopenhauer jerked the rug from under a concept for the *Ring* that had already been made shaky by Wagner's growing pessimism about his own future, and the world's. Why did he largely drop the project (tinkering apart) in 1857 for twelve whole years, when he was already well into *Siegfried*, the next-to-last part of the cycle? One all-too-familiar reason was that he needed cash, and clearly the *Ring* would not be complete and available as a money-spinner for ages, if at all. Besides, *Tristan und Isolde* and *Die Meistersinger* were welling up in him, both works that with crass misjudgement he reckoned almost any opera house would be able to stage with ease. Although it demands some intellectual effort (and self-deception?) to find a place for the often buoyant *Meistersinger* in Schopenhauer's bleak universe, the desolate *Tristan* – fusing love and death in music of agonising intensity – seems to slot into it rather well. And in the late 1850s after his doomed affair with Mathilde Wesendonck, Wagner was in a near-suicidal mood – arguably ideal for *Tristan*.

Above all, though, Wagner simply became bored with the Nibelungs. He admitted as much almost in passing in a letter in 1856, and when he finally got the cycle under way again his style as well as his world-view had changed. His music dramas, he blithely claimed in 1872 – in flat contradiction to his *Gesamtkunstwerk* theories of two decades before – were 'deeds of music made visible'. He never did wholly solve the knotty problem of the *Ring*'s ending (optimistic or pessimistic, Feuerbachian or Schopenhauerian?) to his own satisfaction. When asked what it meant, he rather testily replied that the meaning was in the music. A very sensible remark. Theories about Wagner come and go, some edifying, many absurd. 'Explaining' his work is a serious industry offering employment to legions of scribes who might otherwise go hungry. But what really counts is the music. Sir Thomas Beecham, that master of barbed wit and backhanded compliment, once said of the British that they knew nothing about music but loved 'the noise it makes'. By no means everyone loves the noise Wagner makes, but as a rule simply listening to it is more rewarding than imbibing any of the theories that circulate around it, including Wagner's own.

The amazing thing is that Wagner managed to produce so much 'noise' at all, especially in the post-Dresden era when he was a wanted man. The last music he managed to compose before scuttling off to Zurich with the police at his heels was *Lohengrin*, finished in 1848. The faithful Liszt premiered the work in Weimar in 1850, but Wagner did not attend for fear of arrest. Even in Venice, part of the Austrian empire, he was harassed by police (admittedly rather cultured and understanding police) while working on *Tristan* in 1858–9. He was safe enough in London, where in 1855 he conducted a few concerts panned by the press and even got to meet Queen Victoria ('not at all pretty with, I am sorry to say, a rather red nose'[10]). The longish arm of Saxon law could not catch up with him in Paris either, but he grew to hate the city more than ever, especially after the performances of

*Tannhäuser* in 1861 were drowned in an uproar organised by political foes and nitwit aristocrats. A year before that debacle, Wagner had at last been granted a partial amnesty, allowing him to visit most of Germany again, but the full pardon that included his home state of Saxony came through only in 1862.

Apart from being on the run for so long, there was much else to keep Wagner from his work. His health was dreadful for most of his life; typhoid fever in France, dysentery in Italy, boils, colds, stomach troubles, haemorrhoids – it would be rather easier to list what he did *not* suffer from. Persistent rashes, probably of psychosomatic origin, at least gave him a fine excuse to do something he loved anyway – wear silk and satin against his skin. In later years he suffered growing chest pains, foreshadowing the heart attack that killed him. All this discomfort helps explain his frequent bouts of foul temper, but it did not stop him plunging into one affair after another. How many of his 'conquests' he actually slept with is unclear and hardly important, except to those who claim that much of his work, especially *Tristan*, is a product of sublimated physical passion. Would the pieces have been very different, or even failed to emerge at all, if the passion had not been sublimated? Leaving aside that fruitless question, Cosima quotes Wagner in her diary as saying that a tall story he had once told about composing part of *Parsifal* was 'as far-fetched as my love affairs'.[11] Admittedly, he may well have told Cosima what he thought she wanted to hear, or she may have reported what she chose to remember.

One thing seems sure. Wagner invested at least as much time and effort in his lady friends as he did in pondering Schopenhauer's counsel about self-denial. He did, in fact, once write a letter to Schopenhauer arguing that since the sexual act induced a sense of other-worldly peace, it should be seen as a road to salvation from the near-irresistible pressures of Will. But he never posted this ingenious document, perhaps fearing the great man might judge the argument a mite self-serving. Be that as it may, although the names of all Wagner's amours will never be known, the spectrum even of the identifiable ones is wide indeed. There was Mathilde Wesendonck with her delicate beauty and literary pretensions; and there was Marie Völkl with more tangible assets, including 'pink drawers' that Wagner begged her by letter to make ready for his impending arrival. There was Jessie Laussot, a Bordeaux wine merchant's English-born wife with whom

Wagner briefly planned to elope to some distant spot in Asia Minor; and there was the 'obliging' teenager Seraphine Mauro, much beloved by the composer Peter Cornelius, one of the many friends Wagner betrayed but who trotted back for more. There was the temperamental actress Friederike Meyer from Frankfurt, not to be confused with the sweet-natured Mathilde Maier from Mainz who was rather deaf (no liability, cynics may feel, for anyone spinning in Wagner's immediate orbit). The list is easily expandable.

Wagner's insecure childhood offers a happy hunting ground for all those seeking to explain (away?) his later instability in general and partner-swapping in particular. His mother was, without a shadow of doubt, Johanna Rosine Wagner (née Pätz), a baker's daughter from Wessenfels near Leipzig. But was his real father the Leipzig police actuary Carl Friedrich Wagner, who died six months after Richard's birth on 22 May 1813? Or was it the actor, writer and painter Ludwig Geyer, a close family friend (sometimes claimed contrary to the evidence to have been Jewish), who married Johanna when Richard was a year old? Nobody knows for sure and, barring exhumation and DNA tests, presumably no one ever will. Wagner was not sure either. In *Mein Leben* he claims he was baptised two days after birth but in fact the ceremony took place only three months later, after Johanna had made an unexplained trip through war-torn territory to visit Geyer, who was on tour with his theatre troupe. For much of his childhood, the boy was called Richard Geyer rather than Richard Wagner. Uncertain of his identity, brought up by a 'stepfather' who was a rival for his mother's attention; no wonder, the theory goes, that Wagner spent his life seeking the love he lacked in childhood, and that redemption thanks to self-sacrificing women is such a big theme in his operas.

There may be something in that. But it is not clear that Wagner really was starved of affection by his mother, busy woman with a big family (Richard was her ninth child) though she was. And throughout his life he referred to his 'rival' Geyer with respect and gratitude, not sentiments he often mustered for anyone else. Perhaps being 'flighty' simply ran in the family. Johanna had been a mistress of a local prince in earlier years and Carl Friedrich dilly-dallied with local actresses, often returning home after supper-time with the less than original excuse that he had been kept late at the office. As for the handsome, articulate, multi-talented Geyer, he could and did charm the ladies with a snap of his elegant fingers.

Besides, for all his roving eye and hands Wagner did stay true to Minna in his own erratic fashion, and she evidently stayed true to him, that one affair in the first year of marriage apart. Every one of their 'kiss and make-up' bids over the decades ended in hellish scenes but they never divorced. He continued to support her financially and when his foes claimed otherwise shortly before her death in Dresden in 1866, she issued a furious public rebuttal. From the first, he played along with the fiction that Natalie was Minna's sister, not her illegitimate daughter, and he continued to support her even after Minna died. Natalie seems to have learned the truth about her birth only late in life. In any case she rarely had anything bad to say of 'kind Richard'. To her he was a generous protector, hard used by the world and at the mercy of his volatile temperament. In a way so he was, just as he was also a lying, spiteful philanderer. One moment he would drown anyone who dared to contradict him under torrents of words so emotional that they emerged as gulps and barks; the next he would act like a mischievous schoolboy who thinks the girls are watching, sliding about the floor and shinning up drainpipes. And always he adored the sensuous; the sweetest of perfumes, the thickest of rugs, the softest of – just everything.

No wonder that, above and beyond offering insights into Schopenhauer and readings from the *Ring*, Wagner managed to dazzle the ladies at least as comprehensively as he did his financiers. Sometimes these were one and the same. Julie Ritter, a friend of Jessie Laussot, paid him an annual allowance for eight years. Countess Marie Muchanoff, a rich Polish admirer, gave him ten thousand francs to help him out of the red in Paris. Other *grandes dames* rewarded him for a piano trifle or a poetry reading with a thousand thalers here, a thousand roubles there. Wagner's female fans rarely offered him loans rather than gifts, evidently judging the prospects of repayment more realistically than his male creditors did. Julie Schwabe, wealthy widow of a Manchester industrialist, did lend him money and tracked him down relentlessly for years until she got it back. But she was the exception.

Finally, in 1864, Wagner's luck seemed to run out. After he had spent most of his earnings from a Russian tour on lavish presents, and on having the walls of his latest 'nest' near Vienna lined in silk, his creditors got close to him at last, wings flapping, beaks snapping. He fled to a dismal hole in Stuttgart and, not for the first time, considered suicide. If Wagner had been the unhappiest of heroes in the corniest of pantomimes, this would have been the moment for a fairy godmother to waft onstage, wand fluttering, and grant his every wish. Such a miracle does not happen in real life, of course, except that in this case it preposterously did. Wagner was summoned to Munich in May by King Ludwig II, who had just ascended to the Bavarian throne at the age of eighteen and who had swooned over *Lohengrin*, above all, for years. Wagner's debts were wiped out in a trice and he was urged to get on with composing – money, apparently, no object.

Hard on the heels of the miracle, Cosima von Bülow-Liszt descended on Haus Pellet, a splendid villa by Lake Starnberg, south of Munich, which the king had put at Wagner's disposal. Only cynics, surely, would see any unworthy connection between Cosima's sudden appearance and her host's dramatically improved circumstances, but it is clear that her arrival took Wagner aback. He had, indeed, invited his friend and colleague von Bülow to visit and bring his wife with him, but he had also written shortly before to Mathilde Maier begging her to come and be his 'housekeeper'. When Cosima turned up on 29 June, a week ahead of her husband, Wagner had to write hastily to Mathilde (who had wisely treated the 'housekeeper' scheme coolly in any case) telling her not to come after all. It is virtually certain that during that week before von Bülow himself arrived, Richard and Cosima's first child was conceived – a daughter appropriately named Isolde. When Liszt had talked about the future of his choosy but impecunious daughters, Cosima and Blandine, he had been inclined to shake his head sadly and complain that each sought a husband who combined the genius of Beethoven or Raphael with the wealth of a nabob. In 1864 Cosima seemed on the right track: she was netting Wagner and he was backed by the resources of a king.

# 3

# Ugly Duckling and Swan King

'All our peace in this miserable life is found in humbly enduring suffering rather than in being free from it,' wrote the German mystic Thomas à Kempis in his *De Imitatio Christi* (Imitation of Christ). It was Cosima's favourite passage in a book she first read as a girl, continued to read as an adult and urged her children to read. It goes on: 'He who knows best how to suffer will enjoy the greater peace, because he is the conqueror of himself, the master of the world, a friend of Christ and an heir of heaven.'[1]

Cosima learned very well how to suffer long before her life with Wagner began, though he gave her exceptional scope for further practice. Born on 24 December 1837 in a lakeside hotel in Como, Italy (not on Christmas Day in the more exclusive resort of Bellagio, as some starry-eyed biographers maintain), she was the second of three illegitimate children spun off, as it were, from the tumultuous liaison between the countess Marie d'Agoult and Franz Liszt. Her elder, prettier sister, Blandine-Rachel, died aged twenty-six, soon after giving birth to a son. Her younger brother Daniel, blessed with Liszt's sea-green eyes and much of his irresistible charm, died at twenty of a lung ailment. Cosima, an 'ugly duckling' with a nose too long and a mouth too wide, dearly loved both of them – probably more than she loved anyone. 'I am always seeking in my heart for these two beings who were so young, so rare, so truly sacred, so utterly my own,' she wrote to a friend after Blandine's death. 'I feel nothing but emptiness.'[2]

The empty feeling had, in fact, begun long before. She lost her brother and sister as a young woman, but as a child, she hardly knew her exotic, volatile parents. Liszt and the countess had begun their affair in 1833 and eloped two years later – Parisian society was shocked (or at least affected to be) but romantics everywhere were exhilarated. It was not every day that a French aristocrat's wife, moreover one blessed with beauty and literary talent, deserted her husband and child to run off with a travelling pianist – albeit a bewitchingly good one – from some obscure spot in Hungary. But the ties between the two were already starting to loosen when Cosima was born. Her father pursued his international concert career, and other women, with still greater intensity, and her equally restless mother went back to Paris. There she worked as a political journalist and later wrote books, including a 'kiss and tell' novel based on life with Liszt and a three-volume history of the 1848 French revolution, whose liberal aims she applauded. The couple continued to see one another sporadically, but finally split amid angry scenes caused not least by Liszt's fleeting involvement with the Irish-born dancer known as Lola Montez – an affair the countess found simply degrading.

The children, meanwhile, were shuttled between nurses, boarding schools and long stays with Liszt's mother Anna in Paris. Liszt, who paid the bills, forbade them to see their own mother, and when the two daughters broke the ban in 1850 he decided to put them under firmer control. In this course he was egged on by his latest mistress, Princess Carolyne Sayn-Wittgenstein, whom he had met in Kiev three years before while on a concert tour and who had since settled down with him in Weimar. With her dumpy figure, blackish teeth and liking for foul-smelling cigars, this Polish-born wife of a hugely rich Russian was easily the least glamorous of all Liszt's known conquests. But she had quick intelligence and a sharp tongue of which even Wagner, who got to know her through Liszt, learned to beware. Irritated by her embarrassingly detailed questions about the exact meaning of the *Ring*, Wagner once told her that four weeks in her company would be the death of him. She laughed in his face.

It was Carolyne who persuaded Liszt to give up touring, settle in Weimar where he had been a (largely absentee) Kapellmeister since 1842, and devote far more time to composition. How right she was. Liszt began to produce work of the kind Marie d'Agoult had always tried but usually failed to extract from him, and thanks to his influence Weimar became a key centre for new music, rather like Darmstadt after the Second World War, but less doctrinaire. Not that Carolyne herself was a liberal – on the contrary. Fiercely Catholic and a foe of revolution, she disapproved of Marie for her republican sympathies and was naturally jealous of her as Liszt's former mistress and the mother of his children. Just as naturally, the daughters hated Carolyne from afar, all the more so since she sent her fearsome ex-governess, Madame Patersi de Fossombroni, from St Petersburg to Paris in 1850 to take them in hand for five interminable years. A fanatic for discipline and correct deportment, who is said to have crossed most of Europe in a railway carriage at the age of seventy-two without once leaning back in her seat, Madame Patersi and her similarly aged sister sought to create young ladies of whom Carolyne, Liszt and suitable suitors (in that order) would approve. That meant instilling into both girls reverence for the Catholic Church and, equally important, for that aristocratic, imperial France – given a new lease of life from 1852 under Napoleon III – that their mother had come to despise. It also meant ensuring that both of them learned just enough about most things, barring science, to be able to keep up an appropriate patter in the social circles into which they were carefully propelled. Their mail was vetted by Madame Patersi and they had next to no friends their own age. Once in a while Blandine threw a scene to protest against this treatment. Cosima never did. She was too proud to show her elders what she really felt, and learned to dissemble skilfully in her letters, an art that stood her in good stead later. Besides – didn't her beloved Thomas à Kempis advise that by conquering oneself, one mastered the world?

Such was the domestic scene at the neat but claustrophobic apartment in the rue Casimir Périer, literally in the shadow of the church of St Eustache, when Liszt turned up on 10 October 1853 to visit the children he had last seen eight years before. He was accompanied by two composers whose work he was trying hard to promote: Hector Berlioz, who seems to have stayed quiet for much of the time, and Richard Wagner, who as usual did not. After supper Wagner treated the others to a reading of the last act of *Götterdämmerung* (then called *Siegfrieds Tod* – 'Siegfried's Death'), drawing tears of ecstasy from Cosima even though she could hardly follow the German words. Wagner hardly noticed her, simply reporting that both Liszt's daughters seemed very shy. Marie Hohenlohe, the attractive teenaged daughter of Carolyne who had already caught Wagner's fancy, was more observant. Years later in her memoirs Marie recalled 'poor Cosima's' adolescent awkwardness – how tall and angular she had seemed and how the tears had run down her nose that evening. But that was not all.

'Dark passion and boundless vanity pulsated through her veins,' Marie recorded, 'and now and then the Parisienne's inborn mockery played wantonly on her thin lips.'[3] Perhaps part of that picture was embellished with hindsight. But suppressed passion, vanity and mockery were always important parts of Cosima's make-up, and of her icy attraction.

After nearly four years the paths of Cosima and Wagner crossed again, but the second meeting proved hardly more propitious than the first. Cosima, now aged nineteen, had just married Hans von Bülow, an ex-pupil of her father and eight years her elder, and he could think of no better way to spend a memorable honeymoon than in the company of Wagner, whom he venerated as much as he did Liszt. So the newly-weds travelled in September 1857 to Zurich to find the lovesick composer trapped between his anguished wife Minna and the adored but already 'taken' Mathilde Wesendonck. Cosima thought little of either woman, and hardly any more of Wagner, however affecting his music. The uncouth ways and Saxon accent of the ageing ex-revolutionary outraged her Patersi-induced sense of etiquette, and she reacted with a coldness still manifest when the von Bülows visited Zurich again a year later. Indeed, so upset was Hans by his wife's standoffish attitude during this trip that he wrote to Wagner afterwards to make excuses for her. The honoured Master should get to know Cosima better, von Bülow advised, and then he would realise how lovable she really was.

If anyone urgently needed to know Cosima better it was von Bülow himself. He must have been surprised, and no doubt gratified, when Cosima abandoned her reserve for a few brief moments at the end of the stay, threw herself weeping at Wagner's feet and kissed his hands. Wagner himself seems to have been nonplussed (he omitted details of the scene from *Mein Leben*) but then he had much else on his mind at the time. The atmosphere in and around the Wagner household during that summer of 1858 was even more doom-laden than usual. Minna made one jealous scene after another. Mathilde saw Wagner often but stayed tied to her husband. Wagner had the passion and desolation of *Tristan und Isolde* welling up in him and felt cornered. He was about to make another bolt for 'freedom' and everyone knew it, including Cosima. But even that did not seem fully to explain her uncharacteristic outburst.

By this time Wagner had certainly noticed how intensely Cosima responded to his work. After her first Zurich visit he had even sent her a letter, to which she seems not to have replied, apologising with awkward humour for his bad manners. But that gesture was probably meant to ensure that he did not indirectly estrange von Bülow, a fine musician and willing tool whom Wagner (rightly) felt could prove useful to him. Cosima simply does not seem to have struck him as particularly desirable: too prim and proper, too uptight. However much he adored having women at his feet, he seems to have been frankly surprised and a mite embarrassed to find Cosima there.

Wagner's eyes were unexpectedly opened soon afterwards when he fled from Zurich to Venice accompanied only by his disciple Karl Ritter, son of his benefactress Julie Ritter. The young man had an extraordinary tale to tell – one, moreover, that seems to have percolated through to von Bülow only twelve years later. Ritter claimed that during a recent trip, he and Cosima had poured out their hearts to one another and she had asked him to help her drown in Lake Geneva. She only dropped the idea when Ritter said he would kill himself too. The story naturally enthralled Wagner, hard at work on *Tristan* and yearning hopelessly for Mathilde. Even so, when he recorded it in his Venice diary he still seemed to be keeping his emotional distance from Cosima, simply expressing surprise at her conduct and intense curiosity about her 'further development'. Did the incident in fact take place as Ritter claimed and/or as Wagner recorded it? It hardly seems to fit the picture of the haughty stoic who would sooner die than lose her self-possession. Or does it? Perhaps it was precisely because her feelings were so firmly suppressed for most of the time that their rare eruptions proved so fierce. Anyway, in a letter to a confidante in 1864 (only published in full more than a century later), Wagner not only referred to this abortive suicide attempt but claimed there were more. Cosima, he wrote, had later made repeated, and conscious, attempts to contract various fatal illnesses.[4] And he had no doubt about the cause of her desperation. It was her marriage to von Bülow.

Wagner might fairly have pinned some of the blame on Cosima's largely loveless childhood too, but it is true that her husband was about the last man likely to help her find emotional fulfilment. Born in 1830 into a noble but impoverished family and rocked in his youth by his parents' divorce, von Bülow concealed a deep-seated emotional insecurity behind irascibility and sarcasm. Already in a letter to Liszt in 1856 asking for Cosima's hand, he seems to have had more than an inkling that he was embarking on a doomed enterprise. 'I swear to you', he wrote, 'that however much I feel bound to her by my love, I should never hesitate to sacrifice myself to her happiness and release her, were she to realise that she had made a mistake in regard to me.'[5] Cosima soon realised it all too well but – as usual – she gave few outward signs. Fearful that Hans would react cuttingly on learning she was pregnant with their first child, she could only pluck up enough courage to whisper the news in his ear when he was asleep. The child, Daniela Senta – known as Lulu – was born in 1860. Three years later a second daughter arrived, Blandine Elisabeth. According to Cosima, Hans greeted the birth with sullen silence.

So why did they marry? In von Bülow's case the answer seems clear. In taking the daughter he felt he was nearing the father, his mentor. 'For me Cosima Liszt transcends all other women,' he confided to his future father-in-law, 'not only because she bears your name, but also because she so resembles you, because she is in so many ways the exact mirror of your personality.'[6] Cosima's motives were less straightforward. She was surely tired of being shunted around, and marriage offered a way out. The most recent indignity was that Princess Carolyne, concluding in 1855 that Cosima and Blandine were still too close to their mother in Paris, had seen to it that the girls were whisked off willy-nilly to Berlin, to live with Franziska von Bülow and her son Hans, who would give them piano lessons. Barely six weeks after her arrival, Cosima waited up late for Hans after a concert at which he had been hissed. She showed every sympathy and Hans, unused to such treatment from anyone, let alone from a Liszt daughter, was deeply grateful. They became secretly engaged.

Marriage was more than a bolt-hole for Cosima, all the same. In his twenties, Hans was already a remarkable musician and Cosima aimed to make him a great one. As a pianist of uncommon stamina and virtuosity, he had no rival in Berlin and few in Europe. All that stood in the way of still greater success was his insistence on spicing his programmes with modern works his audiences found indigestible. He had, for instance, given the first public performance of Liszt's B minor sonata, a work that in its tonal ambiguity and structural daring was as innovative as anything by Wagner – and much more concise. As a conductor he was only gradually making his mark but he promised to become truly outstanding, as Liszt and especially Wagner well realised. But all that was not enough for Cosima, just as Liszt's keyboard wizardry alone had not been enough either for Marie d'Agoult or Carolyne. She, like them, wanted to be the muse to a creative genius, and Hans yearned to fill the bill. He mulled over composing an opera based on the Merlin legend, and Cosima helped ensure he got a libretto. Then he was commissioned to produce the piano reduction of an entirely different opera, and as he pored over the astounding manuscript he felt all his own creativity draining away. The work was *Tristan und Isolde*.

So it was that Wagner unintentionally began to destroy von Bülow's urge to compose – some years before he seduced his wife, or was seduced by her. It is hard to say whether 'poor Hans' would have produced anything to win a firm place in the repertory even without Wagner's despotic influence. The few piano and orchestral pieces he did complete do not suggest that he would. In any case the blow delivered by *Tristan* in 1859 was followed by a still more crippling one in the summer of 1862. While visiting Wagner at Biebrich on the Rhine with Cosima, von Bülow perused the as yet unfinished score of *Die Meistersinger* and lost heart altogether. Compared with that masterpiece, he reflected, his own work was '*Lappaliendreck*' – trifling filth. For a while he felt suicidal – just like his wife, for whom 1862 was another dreadful year. Her sick and wasted brother Daniel had expired in Berlin in her arms three years earlier, and now her sister Blandine, weakened by a difficult birth, succumbed in France. By September, when Blandine died, Cosima was pregnant with her second child, but the knowledge brought her no joy. Quite the opposite – she knew what Hans would think about it.

Amid the misery, there were nonetheless signs that Wagner and Cosima were becoming closer. At the end of a meeting with friends and family in 1861 she gave him a 'timid, quizzical glance' that stuck in his mind. A year later he remarkably offered to transport her across a square in a wheelbarrow – she, the strait-laced Cosima von Bülow. Even more remarkably she accepted, at which Wagner lost his nerve. Wagner relates both incidents in *Mein Leben*, perhaps giving them a significance they hardly had when they happened. But it is a fact that over the next year or so Wagner and Cosima saw one another four times, and that the last occasion was special; so special, in fact, that the key details of it were deleted for decades from all editions of *Mein Leben* available to the public. According to the full version, the two of them took a carriage ride in Berlin on 28 November 1863, while von

Bülow was rehearsing a concert, and 'in an urgent desire for truth between us [we] felt constrained to acknowledge our mutual unhappiness for which there was no need of words. With tears and sobs we sealed our vow to live for each other alone.'[7]

Wagner did not by any means live for Cosima alone in the ensuing seven months, and seemingly did not intend to. At first he continued to enjoy female company in his silk-lined home near Vienna; later, after his flight and rescue by King Ludwig, he issued that invitation to Mathilde Maier, hastily revoked on Cosima's arrival, to join him at his villa by Lake Starnberg. These facts used to lead some Wagnerians to conclude that the vow of eternal fidelity said to have been pledged in Berlin must in fact have been made later. But in an entry of her (long unpublished) diary dated 28 November 1869 Cosima, now separated from von Bülow for good and living with Wagner at Tribschen, makes the truth clear. 'Six years ago today R. came through Berlin, and then it happened that we fell in love; at that time I thought I should never see him again, we wanted to die together. – R remembers it, and we drink to this day.'[8]

So much happened to Wagner in Munich between his triumphant arrival and summary ejection that it almost comes as a shock to realise that he actually lived there for only nineteen months, though he made occasional visits later. That period from May 1864 to December 1865 includes the five months he spent at his villa by Lake Starnberg, often visiting King Ludwig at nearby Schloss Berg, before moving into the Bavarian capital itself. At first most things seemed to go nicely his way. Thanks to his urgent recommendation, Hans von Bülow was offered a job by the king and came to live with Cosima and the children in fashionable Luitpold Strasse in the town centre. Wagner held court in nearby Brienner Strasse in a rent-free residence equipped with all the things he loved, like silk and satin hangings and peacocks strutting in the garden. After supervising the daily chores at home, Cosima was easily able to slip round the corner and look after the Master's needs, secretarial and otherwise. Wearing the latest gowns from Paris and exuding an air of 'big city' superiority, she soon began to glide from one society salon to another, extolling the greatness of Wagner's work to those still sadly unconverted. In due course she also started on a long exchange of letters with the king, finding just the right blend of ecstasy and idolatry with which to make palatable her demands in what she took to be Wagner's interest.

Not that Cosima was the sole reason why Wagner wanted the von Bülows in Munich. 'Were I to die today Hans Bülow would be the only man to whom I could entrust my works,' he wrote to the king, one occasion on which he was surely telling Ludwig what he truly believed. 'Bülow has all the attributes of a very great artist, and in addition abilities of a kind I myself do not possess. He lacks only one thing: imaginative productivity.'[9] Hans was at first employed only as '*Vorspieler* [performer] *des Königs*', a suitably vague title for a task that mainly involved drawing the king, with the help of piano examples, into the deeper mysteries of Wagner's music. But it was not long before he was moved up several rungs to the post of 'court conductor for special services', just as Wagner had intended. Hence it was von Bülow who conducted the world premieres in Munich of both *Tristan* in 1865 and *Die Meistersinger* in 1868. These were probably the finest performances of any Wagner work given in the composer's lifetime, the Bayreuth *Ring* of 1876 and *Parsifal* of 1882 not excluded. Munich had the cash and technical resources, and in von Bülow, who never worked in Bayreuth, it had the outstanding Wagner conductor of the time.

Did Hans already realise that Cosima and Wagner were having an affair? Even allowing for his long-standing ignorance of his wife's feelings, it is hard to believe he did not sense something was in the wind. During the summer of 1864, he suffered ailments including temporary paralysis and bad migraines, perhaps signs of a mental and emotional conflict he found it impossible to resolve. At any rate Liszt knew what was going on, because Cosima soon told him. He was not amused, still less so since he happened to be entering a particularly pious phase. Three years before, Princess Carolyne had failed in her long battle to win the Pope's sanction for a divorce from her Russian husband. She and Liszt had therefore abandoned their plan to marry and now lived apart in Rome, where he was preparing to take the four minor Catholic orders and she was starting to write a survey of church problems that finally ran to twenty-four volumes. Liszt had never felt less in a mood to condone anything that might lead to the break-up of his daughter's marriage; but on reflection he concluded that the affair was a temporary infatuation, a condition on which he rightly regarded himself something of an expert. He even strongly urged von Bülow to go ahead and take the king's offer of a Munich job, advice he would hardly have given had he foreseen the consequences. When he did realise that more than a passing fling was involved he took tougher action to try to save the marriage, extracting Cosima from Wagner's immediate proximity for weeks at a time. The ruse did not work. Wagner wrote bitter letters to his distant mistress expressing contempt for her father's 'sanctimoniousness', and as soon as Cosima returned to Munich the affair was resumed, if anything more passionately. Probably Liszt would have had no better success if he had tried to put his foot down earlier. For Cosima, her father was not the most credible source of counsel on the inviolability of holy matrimony.

Most of that suited Wagner very well, but trouble was brewing and his relationship with the king was at the heart of it. In part this was due to jealousy at court and worry in the government because Ludwig seemed so much in thrall to a mere composer, and a non-Bavarian at that. But there were other reasons too, less obvious nowadays because the real Ludwig has tended to recede behind popular legend. Variously called the 'mad king,' the 'swan king' and the 'dream king' – though not (so far) the 'gay king', despite his homosexuality – Ludwig is widely thought to have been a political simpleton who nearly bankrupted Bavaria with his profligate backing of Wagner and his passion for building fairy-tale castles. Add in his doomed engagement to his cousin, the lovely Princess Sophie, and his mysterious death by drowning in Lake Starnberg, and it is easy to see why he has been deemed ideal material for films and a hit musical. Despite the sturdy efforts of scholars to set the record straight, the Ludwig caricature is in danger of replacing historical fact as firmly as Shakespeare's Richard III has done.

It is surely true, however, that Ludwig was not the ideal leader for the strained political situation into which he was unexpectedly catapulted by the early death of his father Maximilian II. When Prussia, propelled by the far-sighted and ruthless Bismarck, declared war on Austria in 1866, Bavaria backed the latter and was trounced along with it. In 1870, Bavaria reluctantly joined the war against France and saw Prussia emerge from it a year later as the strongest single German state by far, one able to compel the creation of a united nation. It even fell to Bavaria to invite King Wilhelm of Prussia, Ludwig's uncle, to accept the crown of the newborn German Reich. None of that was glorious. Ludwig hated militarism and quickly became bored by campaigns. But he realised very well early on that Bismarck was picking off Prussia's rivals one by one, and tried to stop him by supporting Austria. When that failed he did what he could to preserve Bavaria's independence in the Prussian-dominated German empire that was becoming inevitable, as he saw all too clearly. In that he was largely successful – admittedly helped by the realism of Bismarck, who found Ludwig intelligent and did not want a permanently humiliated Bavaria on Prussia's doorstep.

Ideally Ludwig would have liked to let politics simply go hang and to concentrate on 'art' in its broadest sense. He shared the fascination of his professorial father for mythology and the passion of his grandfather, Ludwig I, for building. What he did not share was his grandfather's particular weakness for women. Ludwig I had been forced to abdicate in 1848 after a stormy affair with Lola Montez, that very same adventuress who had helped bring the final split between Liszt and Marie d'Agoult a few years before. Instead of succumbing to a Lola, so the Munich wags had it, Ludwig II had fallen for a 'Lolus' – alias Richard Wagner. That was not necessarily meant to suggest that the two were lovers, though the longer the king failed to marry the more tongues wagged. But it certainly implied that Ludwig II, like Ludwig I, was letting a rank outsider have too much money and influence on affairs of state.

Despite appearances, though, Ludwig was by no means in Wagner's pocket. It is true that the two of them exchanged hundreds of letters couched in embarrassingly purple prose – 'O my glorious, my heavenly friend' is a fairly typical introductory flourish – but on ploughing through the full texts it is hard not to feel present at an elaborate charade. Each said what the other wanted to hear, and neither quite meant it. Ludwig was also amazingly naive for a long period about the real relationship between Wagner and Cosima, and by issuing a public letter at their outrageous instigation to 'defend the honour' of von Bülow he made himself look stupid. But in other respects he was more hard-headed than is usually claimed.

When Wagner started to talk about politics, Ludwig is said to have looked up to the ceiling and whistled, not just because he was bored but as a signal that his interlocutor was exceeding his brief. Wagner's demand that a politician he favoured be made prime minister was answered by Ludwig with several pages of flowery nothingness, followed by a sharp rebuff. Likewise Wagner's effort via an anonymous newspaper article to force the dismissal of ministers he hated ended in ignominy. The king told his 'beloved friend' to leave town. He acted sadly, under great pressure from his cabinet and family, and he had sporadic contact with Wagner for years to come – but act he did. Not least, Ludwig rejected Wagner's (and Cosima's) intense antisemitism, holding that he found 'nothing more objectionable, nothing more distasteful' than hatred of Jews, because 'we are all basically brothers'.[10] Wagner responded with an agitated letter claiming the king was only able to adopt such an attitude because 'these people never touch upon his royal sphere'. The truth was, he went on, that the Jewish race was 'the born enemy of pure humanity and all that is noble in man: it is certain that we Germans especially will be destroyed by them.'[11] Ludwig did not bother to reply.

In foreign affairs Wagner vainly advised Ludwig to keep Bavaria independent in the strife between Prussia and Austria. But once Prussia had won and began to look still more like the land of the future, Wagner changed his tune. He reckoned that Bismarck, whom he had initially detested, could be useful to him if Ludwig's support were to wane. In this he was mistaken. Bismarck had no intention of bending to any demands, especially not those of an interfering musician, that might fray the delicate ties with Bavaria. When the two finally met briefly in Berlin in 1871, Bismarck handled the talk so skilfully that the question of money for the planned but as yet unfinanced Bayreuth festival was not even raised. Wagner's irritation became greater as the years passed and Bismarck still proved no material use to him. Particularly galling was that Bismarck turned out to be no more antisemitic than Ludwig; indeed Gerson Bleichröder, a Jew, was his private banker and one of his closest counsellors.

As for Ludwig's alleged extravagance, his non-recoverable spending on Wagner was hefty but not astronomical and it all came from the civil list (the sums annually made available to the crown by law). Including all payments such as salary, rents and gifts, the total going to Wagner over nearly twenty years amounted to almost 563,000 marks. On top of that, interest-bearing loans of more than 300,000 marks were made at Ludwig's behest to save the Bayreuth festival. These credits were gradually repaid in full by the Wagner family from royalty income. All in all, the financial needs of the Master cut a biggish swathe through Ludwig's own funds, and it is easy to see why long-serving government officials and courtiers seethed at the good fortune of what they held to be a busybody interloper. But the sums involved did not even begin to break the back of the Bavarian exchequer. The more than thirty-one million marks Ludwig spent building his weird and wonderful castles at Herrenchiemsee, Linderhof and Neuschwanstein came closer to doing so; but since that sum has in the meantime been recovered many times over through tourist income, it is arguable that Ludwig in his 'madness' really did rather well for Bavaria's future.

Besides, the king's support for Wagner was far from selfless, whatever the unctious tone of his 'I am yours for ever' letters may seem to suggest. In return for services rendered, or at least promised, he received the copyright to the *Ring* (which, typically, Wagner had disposed of twice before), as well as a cluster of precious manuscripts including the autograph full scores of *Die Feen*, *Das Liebesverbot* and *Rienzi* along with autograph copies of *Das Rheingold* and *Die Walküre*. Unfortunately nearly all these treasures later came into the unsafe hands of Adolf Hitler and seem to have been destroyed along with him in the real-life *Götterdämmerung* of Berlin in 1945. But it was not simply possession of original manuscripts that interested Ludwig. He longed to be able to sigh and thrill to new works and, above all, he urgently wanted Wagner to complete the *Ring*. He arguably wanted that more than Wagner himself did.

Ludwig raised the question of ending the *Ring* at that very first meeting in 1864, when Wagner had arrived post-haste in Munich from his Stuttgart hideaway, dazed by the somersault in his fortunes. The king later repeatedly referred to 'our Nibelungs' and wrote that 'we want to make of this wonderful work a gift to the German nation and show both it and other nations what "German Art" is really capable of'.[12] In other words, Ludwig was far from unambitious although he despised the glory of the battlefield and the might of the new Reich. He aimed to become the undisputed King of German Art and Wagner was going to help him do it, firstly by finishing his 'greatest' work. In principle Wagner had similar ambitions, although in his revolutionary phase he had hardly reckoned that a king would make it possible for him to realise them. He too wanted to reveal what German Art could do and he had long viewed a completed *Ring* as the main showpiece. But he had dropped the project in mid-spate seven years before and in the meantime his style and view of life had changed, as *Tristan* well shows. Might it not have been better had he quietly let the thing slip altogether and moved on to other work –

unbound by a concept in which he no longer fully believed?

For many, perhaps most, Wagnerians the question is at best absurd, at worst heretical. What, no completed *Siegfried*, no *Götterdämmerung* – and perhaps no Bayreuth either, since the festival theatre there was built in the first place for the *Ring*? Unthinkable! On the other hand *Rheingold* and *Die Walküre* fit rather well together – the latter largely complementing with a heart-rendingly human tale the forbidding saga of the former with its gods, giants and dwarfs. Ending the 'cycle' with Wotan's farewell to his sleeping daughter Brünnhilde on her fire-encircled rock would have left questions unanswered, but what fun Wagnerians would have had arguing ever since over what probably happened next. Besides, it would have avoided the muddled ending of *Götterdämmerung* and the stylistic break that Wagner could not wholly conceal, despite his immense ingenuity, when he resumed composing *Siegfried*. It would also, admittedly, have deprived audiences of the most unintentionally hilarious scene in all opera: the one in which Siegfried pulls off the breastplate of the sleeping Brünnhilde (his aunt, according to the *Ring*'s tangled genealogy) and cries '*Das ist kein Mann*' (That is no man).

Speculation aside, it is plain that even with the backing and prodding of Ludwig from mid-1864, Wagner was not burning to get the *Ring* on the road again. 'I keep hesitating as to what I should start on first,' he wrote to a friend in September. 'In the end I expect I shall put everything aside and complete the Nibelungs: if I tell the King this I shall be even better off.'[13] He did tell the king exactly that a fortnight later, combining the glad news with a request for 'suitable accommodation' and more funds – which he promptly received. Wagner then took up again those parts of *Siegfried* on which he had already worked years before, making a fair copy of Act I and scoring Act II. But he did not actually get down to composing new material – Act III – until 1869, when he had long since left Munich and had settled in with Cosima for that 'Tribschen Idyll' described in the first chapter.

There were initially several good reasons for Wagner to delay. They included the accident-prone preparations for the premiere of *Tristan* on 10 June 1865 and the birth of his daughter Isolde on 10 April – the date of *Tristan*'s first orchestral rehearsal, conducted by the child's putative father, von Bülow. But hitherto Wagner had never allowed anything or anyone to distract him when he was in the throes of creation. Nor was he keen, as one might have expected, on Ludwig's scheme, foreshadowing Bayreuth, to build a festival theatre in Munich as a worthy home for the completed *Ring*. 'How I hate this planned theatre,' he wrote in September 1865, 'indeed how childish the King seems for insisting on this project so passionately.'[14] Wagner had indeed long felt a special theatre to be essential to the planned tetralogy but he wanted a simple one, probably of wood, not the imposing pile Ludwig had in mind. Irritatingly he now found himself being widely accused, wrongly for once, of making extravagant demands for which the king alone was responsible. Still worse, he felt he was being put under unwelcome pressure. What if the theatre were finished before the *Ring* itself was?

He need not have worried. The project flopped, though it proved a headache for years to Gottfried Semper, one of Wagner's old revolutionary friends from his Dresden days who was drafted in as designer. Another Munich scheme, for a new school whose prime aim was to teach the art of singing German music properly, was much closer to Wagner's heart, but it too came to nothing. Well after the Ludwig era Munich did in fact get round to building a theatre meant mainly for performing Wagner – despite fierce opposition from Cosima, who by that time (the turn of the century) had long since been running the Bayreuth festival and abhorred competition. Her concern was far from groundless. With its shell-shaped auditorium and steeply rising rows of seats allowing an unimpeded view of the stage, the Munich house (the Prinzregententheater that exists to this day) was plainly a clone of the Bayreuth one and might just have emerged as a real rival to it. In fact it never did so. Bayreuth's status for perfect Wagnerites as a place of pilgrimage, largely free of big city distractions, turned out to be unbeatable.

Ludwig got his *Ring* bit by bit almost despite Wagner. Tired of waiting until all four parts were available for performance together, as the composer intended, he insisted in 1869 that the world premiere of *Rheingold* be given at the Munich Court Theatre. Wagner collaborated with intense reluctance, drafting in the devoted young Hans Richter to conduct, replacing von Bülow, who had left town close to a nervous breakdown. When rehearsals went badly Wagner, pulling the strings from Tribschen, tried to stop the whole thing unless all his demands were met to the letter. He hastened to Munich but Ludwig refused to see him. 'The behaviour of Wagner and the theatre rabble is absolutely criminal and impudent,' wrote the king. 'It is an open revolt against my orders and this I will not stand.'[15] *Rheingold* was finally premiered on 22 September under Franz Wüllner, a local conductor, but without Wagner present. Wüllner also premiered *Walküre* in Munich nine months later, on 29 June 1870. Again Wagner stayed away, thus missing a performance hailed as a triumph by the public and much of the press. When Ludwig demanded a year later that *Siegfried* be staged too, Wagner told him the score was not yet complete – although in fact it was.

Ironically, when the premiere of the whole *Ring* cycle was finally given in August 1876 under Wagner's aegis in his 'own' Bayreuth festival theatre and with Richter conducting, it was Ludwig who was absent. He came to the general rehearsals and returned for the third and final performance of the cycle at the end of the month. But he was determined to avoid 'first night' fuss and in particular the company of Kaiser Wilhelm, who had done nothing to help bring the work to the stage but had agreed to drop by from Berlin for the premiere. Ludwig regarded the *Ring* as his creation as much as Wagner's. He believed in it, bought it and pushed it. He injected extra funds after Wagner had repeatedly lied to him and had decided, without adequate finance, to set up his theatre in provincial Bayreuth, not in Munich as Ludwig had offered. The king could well understand Wagner's point that the music dramas would make their full impact only before an audience not distracted by big city temptations, but he found the choice of Bayreuth hard to accept all the same. The town was in the far north of Bavaria, on the road to Berlin – a point that had certainly not escaped Wagner when, with an eye on possible Prussian largesse, he had chosen it in 1871 as his future headquarters. Indeed, it was the Margravine Wilhelmine, the favourite sister of Frederick the Great of Prussia, who had really put Bayreuth on the artistic map in the eighteenth century with, among other things, an opera house that was acoustically unsurpassed (though too small for Wagner's needs). Despite these irritating Prussian connections, Ludwig even put up the cash that enabled Wagner to build Wahnfried, his unlovely but roomy Bayreuth villa by the Hofgarten in the centre of town. Whatever else the king may have been (the diagnosis of 'madness' was made by doctors who never examined him), he was certainly not petty. In Wagner he backed a winner, however volatile and disreputable – and whatever the flaws of those first Bayreuth *Rings*.

In several ways, the 1876 festival was a compromise. That was certainly true of the performances, despite all that Wagner could do. Having composed the music, written the texts, helped design the theatre and raise the funds, he would surely have liked to play all the instruments, take every role and coordinate his manifold selves from the conductor's perch. He came quite close to doing just that during rehearsals. Now aged sixty-three, he leapt about the stage like a mountain goat, as one eyewitness put it, teaching giants how to lumber, Rhinemaidens how to swim and lovers how to embrace. When Sieglinde failed to clasp Siegmund to her bosom with adequate ardour, Wagner thrust her to one side and hurled himself with passion on the startled tenor, almost knocking him down. When the mist machine began to leak vapour into the sunken orchestra pit, Wagner had the hole plugged. But once the cycle began even Wagner could not exercise total control. In *Rheingold* a premature scene change revealed embarrassed workmen standing around in shirtsleeves. In *Siegfried* the mechanical dragon Fafner aroused more titters than terror. Made in Wandsworth in south London, it lacked a vital part of its anatomy, which had apparently been despatched by mistake to Beirut. The *Ring*'s ring itself went missing several times, bringing unscheduled treasure hunts in the wings. As for maestro Richter, Wagner complained, no doubt a trifle unfairly, that he had not been sure of a single tempo.

The 1876 public represented, if anything, a still bigger compromise. Wagner had originally aimed to attract post-revolutionary, non-paying pilgrims who would flock to the theatre to confront the underlying realities of life and death. But there had been no successful revolution and, since the festival project hovered on the brink of bankruptcy, most of those who attended had to pay for their seats. They could well afford it. Many of the audience were rich bourgeois, titillated by Wagner's scandalous reputation and looking for a novel 'event' to help bridge the summer doldrums. Droves of German aristocrats were initially there too, drawn mainly by the knowledge that their peers – and above all Kaiser Wilhelm – planned to be present. Their attendance did not signal a taste for marathon music drama, any more than did that of the prominent Nazis who some six decades later glumly accompanied their fanatically Wagnerian Führer on *his* Bayreuth trips. The Kaiser, in fact, stuck it out only for *Rheingold* and *Walküre*, then left for military manoeuvres. The ranks of the assembled grandees promptly thinned.

Naturally some visitors really did come for Art's sake. Fellow composers who sweated their way up to the suburban 'temple on the Green Hill' included Liszt (of course) as well as Anton Bruckner, Edvard Grieg, Camille Saint-Saëns and Pyotr Ilyich Tchaikovsky – the latter sighing even more than most over cramped lodgings and the daily battle for food in Bayreuth's gravely overstretched restaurants. There were painters, poets and, less to the Master's taste, around sixty reviewers – among them the redoubtable Eduard Hanslick from Vienna, whose critical but perceptive pieces are well worth rereading and belie his notoriety as an incorrigible Wagner-basher. Although this was not a point he would have cared to stress to Cosima, Wagner must also have been tickled by the presence of lady friends including Mathilde Wesendonck, Mathilde Maier, Jessie Laussot (now in love with a historian in Florence whom she later married) and – above all – Judith Gautier. But all in all the assembled throng was hardly a cross-section of that 'German nation being reborn through art' about which Wagner had enthused to Bismarck in an unanswered letter a year before.

One of those most shocked by the festival was Friedrich Nietzsche, that former devotee from the 'Tribschen Idyll' days who attended some rehearsals and the first *Rheingold* but gave away the tickets he had for other performances. He also avoided most of the receptions – 'papal audiences', he called them – that Wagner hosted almost daily at Wahnfried. Nietzsche was already suffering from those agonising headaches, possibly caused by syphilis, that presaged the onset of his madness more than a decade later, but his conduct in, and abrupt departure from Bayreuth cannot only be put down to disgust at what he saw and heard there. Even before his arrival Nietzsche had begun to have grave doubts about his former mentor, as his notebooks in particular show. Wasn't Wagner's art so much rhetoric, the work of an undeniably brilliant but tyrannical dilettante? Wasn't he becoming a banner-waver for just that kind of society he had aimed to overthrow? Where was that cosmopolitanism once meant to be at the core of the enterprise? After all Wagner had once claimed, and Nietzsche had endorsed, that whilst Greek art had 'expressed the spirit of a fair and noble nation, the artwork of the future must embrace the spirit of free people unshackled from all national boundaries'.[16] The festival, with its superficial German pomp and circumstance, did not mark the final break between the two men, but it was a key stage on the way to it. '*What had happened*?' Nietzsche later wrote, using italics for emphasis.

'Wagner had been translated into German! The Wagnerian had become master of Wagner! – *German* art! The *German* Master! *German* beer!'[17]

However just Nietzsche's critique of Wagner and Bayreuth may be in other respects, this particular charge misses the point. Five years after the surge of patriotism that accompanied victory over the French and the founding of the empire, Germany had by no means embraced Wagner despite all Wagner's admittedly intense efforts at courtship. Of course he had many German friends and disciples, among them real nationalist tub-thumpers; but Bismarck had shunned him and the Kaiser had largely ignored him. Nor did a patrons' scheme launched in 1871 to bring in funds for the great Bayreuth enterprise have anything like the success hoped for. Only about a third of the offered certificates, entitling their holders to festival seats, were actually sold. Hard cash stayed just as scarce after the premieres as before them, despite the well-heeled public, the endless receptions and the pats on the back. 'What was my reward for it all?' Wagner snapped later. 'Baa baa! I thought they would simply make up the deficit for me – oh yes, they came along, the women with their trains, the men with their moustaches, enjoyed themselves, and, since emperors and kings were also there, people ask: My God, what more does Wagner want?'[18]

The answer was simple. Wagner wanted to die, or so he told Cosima soon after the last visitors had gone home. He had had his grave dug in the garden behind Wahnfried a few years before and had clambered into it once or twice while the workmen were still shovelling. Now he felt like staying there. When all the sums were totted up, the festival turned out to be 148,000 marks in the red. Eight fund-raising concerts given in 1877 by Wagner and Richter in London's Royal Albert Hall netted just seven hundred pounds, less than a tenth of the sum essential to keep the Bayreuth show going. An anguished appeal to the patrons brought in exactly a hundred marks. Disgusted with Germany, Wagner considered emigrating. He even tried to negotiate a deal via his American dentist, under which the United States would gain his services 'for all time' and the right to the first performance of *Parsifal*, his latest (and last) work, for a price of one million dollars. America oddly failed to snap up the bargain. In 1878 more financial backing from Ludwig finally saved the day. But the theatre stayed closed until 1882 and the *Ring* was not staged there again until 1896, by which time Wagner had long since been lowered into his tried and trusted Wahnfried grave.

# 4

# The Fortress on the Hill

At the second Bayreuth festival in 1882 nearly everything went right that had gone wrong at the first one. Sixteen performances of a single work, *Parsifal*, were on offer, instead of the total of twelve performances of the four parts of the *Ring* given in 1876; the technical challenges were easier to master and the singers had more chance to dig deeper into their roles. As for the conductor Hermann Levi and the orchestra – supplied to Bayreuth, thanks to King Ludwig, by the Munich Court Theatre – both proved more expert than Richter and his players had been six years earlier. Not that this caused Wagner unalloyed joy. He hated having to entrust his *Bühnenweihfestspiel* (Stage-Consecrating Festival Play), as he grandly called *Parsifal*, to the Jewish Levi; but he feared with good reason that if he refused the conductor on non-musical grounds then the king would deny him the orchestra. That outcome would, in fact, have delighted many of the players, who abhorred having to trek off to a provincial outpost for extra work in the summer heat. As one cellist scrawled with relief on his score at the end of the ordeal: '*Ende! Gott sei Dank. Auf nach München*' (It's over! Thank God. Let's be off to Munich).

Something else Wagner found irritating was the applause, or rather the lack of it. Because of misunderstandings, for which his own garbled announcements were in part responsible, audiences sometimes stayed reverently silent when the cast and the composer would have loved them to cheer – *Bühnenweihfestspiel* or no. To the Master's particular chagrin he found himself hissed by several over-pious souls when, unrecognised in the gloom of the theatre, he bestowed an excited 'Bravo' on the flower maidens undulating sensuously around Parsifal in Act II.

Although the 'underlying meaning' of *Parsifal* (Christian, Buddhist, racist?), is at least as hotly disputed among aficionados as that of the *Ring*, even a single hearing should be enough to convince most people that the work has much to do with redemption through compassion and renouncing the 'sins of the flesh'. As such, the 'sacred drama' is probably Wagner's deepest bow before Schopenhauer – which is not to suggest that the aged but still lustful composer now found the stringent counsel of his favourite philosopher any easier to follow. Did Wagner really have an affair with Carrie Pringle, an enticing soprano from England who was one of the solo flower maidens? The claim has been made so often down the years that it seems a shame to cast doubt on it (as serious researchers now do[1]) – all the more so since it rescued Miss Pringle from the oblivion into which history would otherwise have cast her. Levi, for one, judged her to lack talent and her conduct at rehearsals to be unseemly. But if the evidence that Wagner adored Carrie Pringle looks flimsy, the proof that he fell in a big way for Judith Gautier is overwhelming.

Falling for Mademoiselle Gautier was in any case a sweet fate to which many men, before and after Wagner, blissfully succumbed. Besides her striking southern looks – jet-black hair, ivory teeth and golden skin – she was one of the most temperamental and talented young women of her generation. Nicknamed 'the hurricane' (who would sink many) by Charles Baudelaire and the inspiration for one of Victor Hugo's finest love poems, Judith inherited much of the literary skill of her father, Théophile Gautier, as well as the musical sensibility of her mother, the Italian opera singer Ernesta Grisi. Her links to Wagner's cause went right back to 1861 when, as a precocious teenager, she had heaped scorn on the numbskulls who barracked *Tannhäuser* in Paris. Eight years later when she first visited Tribschen with her husband, the writer Catulle Mendès, she had already produced several articles on Wagner – forerunners of her three-volume book about him more than a decade later. By the time she visited the first Bayreuth festival she had separated from Mendès and, now aged thirty, had begun an affair with Louis Benedictus, an amateur composer. That new liaison did not deter Wagner. On the contrary, the lovely lady of Tribschen days, for whom he had performed cartwheels and climbed trees to show off his still-youthful vigour, suddenly seemed to him more desirable than ever.

Judith later claimed that she was never Wagner's mistress, and that may be true. Dazzled though she had been by him at Tribschen, and devoted though she remained to his art (even translating *Parsifal* into French), there was more than a touch of farce about their relationship in the Bayreuth period. At one point during the *Ring*, Wagner eased himself into the seat he had arranged to be free between Judith and Benedictus, seized her hand and whispered that he yearned to hear all his works in her arms (a feat that, even assuming the swiftest of tempi, would have lasted well over fifty hours). One evening, it seems, he went to her rooms and fell prostrate at her feet, weeping. After she returned to Paris he plied her with letters in comical French, begging her to send him perfumes, oils and various exotic materials, including six metres of silk to cover a chaise longue that he dubbed 'Judith'. Remarkably, most of this at first escaped Cosima's eagle eye, mainly because Wagner and Judith conducted their correspondence via a Bayreuth barber and general factotum called Schnappauf. When Cosima did realise in early 1878 what was going on she firmly rapped the Master across his roving fingers. Judith may well have felt some relief that her more taxing duties as postmistress were now at an end and, with an eye on her planned Wagner book, she seems to have reached a wary 'business understanding' with Cosima. At any rate, she was back at Bayreuth in 1881 with Benedictus. In a diary entry dated 27 September and oozing unstated reproof, Cosima noted that 'When I come downstairs I discover R. at the piano and our friend Judith in rich, rather revealing finery: "I was taken by surprise," he tells me.'[2] Was the discomfited Master sent to bed without any supper, one wonders?

Since Wagner composed the music for *Parsifal* between 1877 and early 1882 – the 'late Gautier era', as it were – it is tempting to identify him with Amfortas, the tormented ruler of the Knights of the Grail, who longs to die, and Judith with Kundry, the eternal seductress. But such simple connections rarely convince, not even in the case of Mathilde Wesendonck and *Tristan und Isolde*, let alone here. There is, of course, something tragi-comic about Wagner composing his sternly Schopenhauerian epic while yearning for Judith and stuffing his trousers with her perfumed powder sachets. Perhaps it was exactly the hypertension between spiritual idealism and all-too-human desire that caused Wagner's long-dormant scheme for a work based on the Parsifal legend to erupt when it did. Perhaps that familiar dichotomy accounts for much artistic creativity, not just Wagner's. Who really knows, even after Freud? And if the information were available would it help us better appreciate the works themselves?

What we can be fairly sure of is that the only regularly practising disciple of Schopenhauer in the Wagner household was Cosima. How much of her self-denial and masochistic embrace of suffering was inborn is a matter of conjecture. She can hardly have inherited those traits direct from her father and mother. At any rate she surely learned from her revered Thomas à Kempis, long before she came across Schopenhauer, about the admirable rewards to be expected from 'conquering oneself'. To that inner conviction was added the emphasis on rigid control and correct deportment that she imbibed from her old governess Madame Patersi.

Wagner had much to thank Cosima for. She bore him three children, including his only son, and worshipped most of his work, egging him on even when he toiled gloomily over a chore like the *Centennial March*, a lucrative piece of hack-work commissioned to mark the hundredth anniversary of the American Declaration of Independence. She put up with his moods, managed to smile at his often coarse jokes and dealt cannily with bankers, lawyers and like threats to the Wagnerian way of life. Not least, she was the most gracious of hostesses although the company she encouraged at Wahnfried was not always to Wagner's taste. Already in Munich, Peter Cornelius had complained that it was barely possible for Richard's old friends, ex-revolutionaries and other 'disreputables', to get at him without going through Cosima first. That trend became still more marked in Bayreuth. The social 'upper crust' that assembled for the *Ring*, to Nietzsche's disgust and in part to Wagner's contempt, was a milieu in which Cosima felt completely at home.

The heart of the matter, though, was that while Wagner passionately over-embraced every aspect of life, despite his professed love of Schopenhauer and his occasional flirtations with suicide, Cosima did just the opposite. She saw that very well herself, noting in an early diary entry that Richard 'relishes existence and lovely things, whereas I almost prefer to do without rather than enjoy'.[3] Wagner poked fun at her, not always kindly. Less than a year after she had joined him for good, he observed that she wanted to bring her 'renunciation regime' to Tribschen too, and several times complained that she was 'wearing [her] Catholic face' again. But it was not just lovely things in general that Cosima felt to be dispensable. 'If only we could curb passion,' she wrote in May 1870, barely a year after Siegfried's birth, 'if only it could be banished from our lives! Its approach now grieves me, as though it were the death of love.'[4] No single woman or combination of women had managed to satisfy Wagner's sexual drive for long, and certainly Cosima was not cut out to be the first. Wagner felt frustrated. When Judith reappeared on the scene in 1876, she seemed to glow with the promise of all those things Cosima could not or would not adequately provide. A familiar drama, saved from banality only by the extraordinary cast.

A fortnight after the last 1876 *Ring* cycle, Wagner and Cosima took a three-month break in Italy that boosted them both, despite news of the festival deficit that reached them in Venice and a last, troubled, meeting with Nietzsche in Sorrento. They even found the time and inclination to pay a few calls in Rome on Princess Carolyne Sayn-Wittgenstein, whom neither had seen for years and who was still toiling over her twenty-four-volume *magnum opus* on church problems. The accompanying children hated the stuffy apartment that reeked of strong-smelling flowers and candle grease, but could not help giggling when forced to kneel before the princess for a farewell blessing. To their relief they were not invited back.

Henceforth Italy became Wagner's salvation, or something close to that. When grey clouds gathered, Siegfried recalled years later, his father would shake his fists at them, call them 'damned potato sacks' and dream of fleeing to 'the land where the lemons grow'. His early stays in Italy had been brief, apart from that spell in Venice in 1858–9 while he was working on *Tristan*. But the older he became, the worse his aches and pains and the greater the bother over Bayreuth, the more often he trekked south across the Alps and the longer he stayed away.

Moving the whole family around posed grave logistical problems, solved mainly by Cosima, helped on and off by a governess and several servants including the ubiquitous Schnappauf. If anything the difficulties grew in Wagner's very last years, from 1880 until his death in Venice on 13 February 1883, during which he spent more time in Italy than he did at home. Besides ensuring safe carriage for the Master with his books and scores, there were five children of varied age – and, indeed, paternity – to keep an eye on. The two eldest daughters, Daniela and Blandine, born to Cosima and von Bülow in 1860 and 1863 respectively, were in principle able to look after themselves. Not that this stopped Wagner from fretting when the girls were invited to dances by Italian hosts whose moral probity and financial resources might, he feared, be no better than his own. The third daughter Isolde, born in 1865 and attributed to von Bülow though tacitly assumed to have been sired by Wagner, was enterprising but headstrong and liable to land in scrapes. Eva and Siegfried, born in 1867 and 1869 respectively, were the 'babies' of the family, and Wagner was without any doubt their father. Whether despite or because of that, they gave precious little trouble to anyone – at least, not while young.

All the Wagner children loved Italy, but two of them were marked by it for life. One was Blandine, who was not only younger than Daniela but also prettier and more easy-going. Of the two girls Daniela, already aged eight when Cosima left von Bülow for good, may have suffered more from the ongoing tension and the final split in the family. Or perhaps she already had an inkling that fate was cutting out an unhappy future role for her, as a buffer and go-between for her divorced parents. Whatever the reason, she became so irritable and rebellious in Bayreuth that Cosima put her in a boarding school, a fate her more pliant sister suffered only briefly. And when it came to marrying, Blandine made an earlier and at first far happier match. During a family stay in Sicily in early 1882, she went to a ball where her looks and serenity attracted a local nobleman, count Biagio Gravina, who promptly asked for her hand. Blandine was eighteen and the count thirty-one but Wagner and Cosima could hardly complain that an age difference was an obstacle to marriage. So despite Wagner's initial grumbles that the suitor, distinguished though he seemed to be, had no firm occupation, the two soon became engaged and wed in Bayreuth in August. Blandine bore her husband four children but the marriage ended tragically: beset by money troubles and subject to bouts of deep depression, the count took his life at the age of forty-seven. Blandine lived on in Italy until 1941 – keeping a mental and usually a geographical distance from the storms in Germany, and Bayreuth in particular.

The other Italy fanatic was Siegfried, of whom there will later be much more to say. Enough to note here that as a child, the future 'Master of Bayreuth' showed little enthusiasm for composition; indeed in a notebook he kept at the age of thirteen he sketched several music exercises, drew an unsavoury black hole next to them and wrote a less than elegant proposal for combining the two. At that stage it was the visual arts above all that Siegfried adored and it was Italy that gave the decisive impetus. In his memoirs he recalls how, on his very first visit at the age of seven, he trotted from church to church and palace to palace, awkwardly trying to reproduce what he saw with paper and pencil. By the time of that trip to Sicily that netted Blandine her husband, Siegfried was twelve and could draw well. In Palermo he became almost as familiar a figure as his father, sketching for hours in the streets and squares and exchanging comments in quite fluent Italian with passers-by. Already his big ambition was to become an architect. That stayed a dream, but time after time he returned to Italy to view the landscapes, buildings and paintings he loved. Ideally, he would have liked to settle there for good.

Unlike his son, Wagner was not deeply struck by the art-works he saw – or if he was, he rarely mustered other than banal remarks about them. Even the Sistine Chapel seems to have drawn from him only the comment that 'This is as in my theatre, you realise it is no place for jokes.'[5] Nor is it clear that Italy directly influenced Wagner's work as much as he said it did. Although he stated in *Mein Leben* that seeing Titian's *Assunta* (Assumption of the Virgin) inspired him to start composing *Die Meistersinger*, a private letter shows that he was already planning to get down to work on the piece before he clapped eyes on the painting. Likewise his claim that a vision in La Spezia in 1853 gave him the start of *Rheingold* seems to owe more to his imagination than his memory. It is hardly Wagner's fault that posterity has so often overstated the significance of his 1880 trip to the Palazzo Rufolo in Ravello as an inspiration for *Parsifal*. He did indeed visit Rufolo's splendid grounds, perched high above the Amalfi coast, and wrote in the visitor's book that the (Act II) garden of the evil Klingsor had at last been found. But he had finished the text of *Parsifal* and had also completed the music in draft well before his Ravello trip. Even the claim that Rufolo's neatly laid-out gardens served as a model for *Parsifal*'s 1882 stage design, with its suffocatingly weird and wonderful vegetation, seems unconvincing. But at least there is little doubt that the temple of the Grail Knights in Acts I and III was modelled on Siena Cathedral – the likeness is too clear to miss.

What Italy did for Wagner above all, apart from regularly lifting his spirits and warming his creaking limbs, was give him an unmatched stage on which to perform the high drama of being himself. That goes especially for Venice. Wagner was far from the first to be seduced by the glorious unreality of *La Serenissima*, with its black, bobbing gondolas and slowly sinking palaces. But seduced he was, so much so that it is hard to avoid the thought that he may have selected the city as the ideal backdrop for his final exit. When he left Bayreuth for Venice in September 1882, he said farewell to his beloved dogs with special intensity, as though he would never see them again. Nor did he. Five months later his heart ruptured and he slumped dead across his desk in one of the eighteen rooms the family had hired in the Palazzo Vendramin, a superb pile overlooking the Canal Grande.

Then the legends began, as they usually do when illustrious people die. According to one famous story, based on remarks reported to have been made much later by Isolde, Wagner expired after a furious row with Cosima over an impending visit by that will o'the wisp flower maiden, Carrie Pringle. That claim can be neither proved nor disproved, but Cosima's diary shows that Wagner's temper and his heart pains had been getting worse for many months, even without Miss Pringle as an excuse. It is also often claimed that Cosima remained prostrate over the body for more than twenty-four hours, although the rather precise account given to Liszt a week later by Paul von Joukowsky, the Bayreuth stage designer who was present, suggests that is a mite exaggerated. Minor details, no doubt, but ones that help make up a false mosaic. As for King Ludwig, legend has it that when he heard of Wagner's death he let out a scream and stamped so heavily that he broke a floorboard. But the note made of Ludwig's reaction by the court secretary, Ludwig von Bürkel, gives a rather different impression. 'Oh! I'm sorry, but then again not really,' the king is reported to have said. 'There was something about the man I didn't really like.'[6] Is such a reaction credible? We know at least that Wagner was deeply hurt because Ludwig had failed to attend *Parsifal* in 1882, pleading ill health. Perhaps by the end the king had swum wholly free of the Master, and had his mind fixed more on his castles.

'A scoundrel and a charmer he must have been such as one rarely meets,' wrote Virgil Thomson, an American composer and one of the most rewarding of critics, about Wagner. 'Perfidious in friendship, ungrateful in love, irresponsible in politics, utterly without principle in his professional life. His wit was incisive and cruel; his polemical writing was aimed usually below the belt.' Quite so. At this point Thomson might have been expected to argue that, despite all those personal flaws, it is Wagner's art that really counts, that twentieth-century music is hardly imaginable without it, and so on. Instead, he pays tribute to the composer's 'sheer guts' and confesses that, fine though the music often is, he would most have liked 'to have known the superb and fantastic Wagner himself'.[7] That is a refreshing point of view. At least it takes account of the man's diabolical attraction, even to those who had most cause to shun him.

Because Cosima was later well-nigh worshipped at Bayreuth and lived on for nearly half a century, it is easy to forget how vulnerable she really was in those first years as a widow – and with her the family and the festival itself. Her first and biggest hurdle was that Wagner had made no will, perhaps because he had usually had only debts to bequeath, perhaps because despite all his talk of death he really thought himself immortal. Whatever the reason, Cosima was left out on a limb with a still partly dependent family and, for all her nimbus, a lot of critics. Amazingly, there is not a shred of evidence that Wagner thought she might take over the festival once he had gone. Sometimes he groaned that he could see no one able to step into his shoes, sometimes he mentioned his son as a possible successor. But Siegfried was only thirteen when his father died and besides, he was far keener on the visual arts than on music.

From an artistic standpoint, the argument that Cosima and/or her offspring should run the festival thus looked pretty thin. Nor did the family have a financial hold. The festival theatre had been built on land donated by the town of Bayreuth, Wagner fans had raised much of the cash for construction (albeit less than the Master had hoped for) and King Ludwig had stepped in with a loan when the enterprise faced catastrophe. With Wagner gone, many patrons and friends of Bayreuth who had put up funds felt entitled to a big say in the festival's future – if there was to be one. The most orthodox of them actually rejected Cosima on two main grounds: she was not thought pure enough to be Bayreuth's high priestess (although her adultery had been, as it were, 'in the Master's cause'); and she was not considered German enough – she who revered German culture *über alles*, who literally had nightmares about losing the German language and who had ticked off Nietzsche for a lack of true German style. As late as 1896, when Cosima produced a festival *Ring* that Siegfried conducted, such critics were still lamenting a dangerous 'internationalism' at Bayreuth allegedly promoted by Cosima's Gallic spirit. The 'older, better

Wagnerians', railed the singer and composer Martin Plüddemann, were moved to 'hostility and loathing by the lifestyle and goings-on at the thoroughly un-German court of Princess Cosima'.[8]

Despite these obstacles Cosima quickly won the upper hand, ran the festival for some twenty years and hovered in the background as a grey-black eminence for over twenty more – further evidence, if it is needed, of that often ruthless will she had shown from childhood. But she would never have seized power so soon after Wagner died, nor kept it so long, without the backing of one particularly devoted ally. He advised her on every vital step, legal and financial, built up the Wagners' fortune, protected them from scandal, pulled innumerable strings to help the festival run smoothly and, so it seems, never personally took so much as a *sou* for his trouble. This paragon, who deserves (but has never been given) a book to himself, was Adolf Wilhelm Benedikt von Gross. The name of his initial boss in Bayreuth, the banker Friedrich von Feustel, is better known, mainly because it was Feustel who early on helped arrange the offer to Wagner of a site for the proposed festival theatre. But it was von Gross who forged the closer personal links with Richard and especially Cosima the moment they arrived from Tribschen in 1872. At first the Wagners stayed at the Hotel Fantaisie, a cosy nest next to a splendid park outside Bayreuth, and every evening after work von Gross would ride out on horseback to visit them – partly on banking business but soon as a friend. Although Feustel indirectly benefited from these contacts, his relations with his brilliant and ambitious employee, then aged twenty-seven, were far from tension-free. In contrast to his boss, von Gross had a real love of music that quickly helped him gain favoured entry to the Wagner circle. Besides, he had long been courting Feustel's adored daughter Marie whom the father evidently hoped would make a more splendid match. The marriage went ahead all the same shortly after the Wagners came to town.

When Wagner died, von Gross and his wife sped at once to Venice and for weeks were the only people, apart from family, with whom Cosima would speak. In a way von Gross almost *was* family since Wagner, planning ahead that far at least, had appointed him the children's future guardian. He quickly extracted the go-ahead for the 1883 festival from Cosima and, crucially, had a document drawn up that amounted to a retroactive will naming Cosima and Siegfried as Wagner's heirs. As a means of bolstering Cosima's position and securing a clear line of succession for the Wagner dynasty, this prompt action was something of a masterstroke. It presented others keen to muscle in on the festival with a fait accompli and, at least for a few decades, headed off a family power struggle. It is not plain whether Cosima herself first proposed this solution at the expense of her daughters – Eva, after all, was certainly fathered by Wagner and Isolde was assumed to have been so – or whether her omnipresent adviser took the initiative. What evidence there is suggests the latter. In the immediate aftermath of Wagner's death Cosima did partly lose her bearings and later became briefly but seriously ill. It thus fell to von Gross to nudge her to the prompt action that kept foes and rivals at bay.

To that limited extent there is something to be said for the well-worn tale that Cosima became an inconsolable widow, far keener on preparing for the next world than on manoeuvring for power in this one. Her suffering was real enough but, as so often before, she won new strength from it. By autumn 1883 she was privately drawing up a detailed plan for the festival to the end of the decade, although she was not yet by any means in charge. *Parsifal* was to be given every year, *Tristan und Isolde* from 1885, *Holländer* from 1886, *Lohengrin* from 1887 and *Tannhäuser* from 1888. The bumper year 1889 would include *Meistersinger* and the first rerun of the *Ring* in Bayreuth since the festival theatre opened in 1876. Cosima sketched cast lists with comments on the singers and optimistically pencilled in her former husband Hans von Bülow to do much of the conducting. Much of this failed to happen on schedule, there was no festival at all either in 1885 or 1887 and von Bülow, not surprisingly, never fell in with Cosima's scheme despite his undimmed love of Wagner's music. But the scope of the plan shows that the emerging Mistress of Bayreuth was already thinking big.

In 1884 Cosima went a step further. Before the final rehearsals, she had a screen erected at the side of the stage in the festival theatre and, like Beckmesser in *Meistersinger*, sat hidden behind it marking down what she felt was going wrong. With all the authority of an oracle relaying wisdom from the Master's grave, she then handed on her 'advice' to the participants. Allegedly Cosima felt forced to step in because she was appalled by reports that, without the stamp of Wagner's authority, the work on *Parsifal* was going to the dogs. In fact a detailed account of the preparations, drawn up by the technical director Fritz

Brandt and sent to Cosima just before she intervened, reveal the sort of ups and downs common before any major opera staging. But the festival needed a firm hand in the long run and clearly Cosima decided she would be the one to supply it. When emissaries from the swelling ranks of the Wagner Societies tried to visit her to discuss Bayreuth's future she refused to receive them. When proposals were made for a Wagner Foundation that would dilute if not erase the family's role, she airily waved them aside – although the scheme resurfaced several times in modified form and was actually implemented nearly a century later.

During the festival-free year of 1885 Cosima announced almost in passing that she was taking over the helm, and in 1886 she made her debut as a producer with *Tristan und Isolde*. It was, on the whole, an artistic success. Cosima understandably stuck closely to the staging supervised by the Master himself for the 1865 Munich premiere; the singing was much praised and the thirty-year-old conductor Felix Mottl, making the first of many appearances in the Bayreuth pit, held the thing together well enough. The work played to half-empty houses all the same, evidence of the shaky ground on which the festival still stood. With Wagner dead, it was far from plain that Bayreuth under the new aegis had anything better to offer than rival opera houses that were easier to reach, at least as well equipped, and staged the Master's works ever more often. Even in the late 1890s seats were available at the last moment for many festival performances, unbelievable though that may seem nowadays to most pilgrims, who have to apply for about a decade on average before they are granted tickets.

Undeterred by the many empty seats at *Tristan*, Cosima pressed on. In 1889 she presented a well-received and better-attended *Meistersinger,* also based on the Munich premiere, and two years later she scored a real breakthrough, staging *Tannhäuser* despite fierce opposition from Bayreuth diehards who felt the work with its opening Venusberg bacchanalia was too profane for the festival theatre. These were the just the kind of self-appointed allies Wagner had once called more of a menace than his foes. Cosima faced them down and won plaudits for her production, the first for which she had no model approved by her husband to work from, and hence the first that was truly her own. But the battle over *Tannhäuser* revealed a touchy issue that raises hackles to this day, especially within the Wagner family. Just which works should be performed in Bayreuth?

Back in his days of exile in Switzerland, remember, Wagner had dreamed of a temporary structure built on the lines of a Greek theatre where his (so far non-existent) *Ring* would be given before a non-paying audience. He had to make compromises, but broadly speaking in Bayreuth he got the kind of building he was after and in 1876 the *Ring* was performed there. According to the original scheme that would have been that. But Wagner went on to compose *Parsifal*, the only work he conceived with a full knowledge of the festival theatre's acoustics, and without doubt the one that sounds best there. Since he prepared the Bayreuth premiere in 1882 and was looking forward to a repeat in 1883, there could hardly be any argument about continuing to present *Parsifal* in the festival theatre after his death. Indeed, it was argued then and later that the Master insisted that his 'Stage-Consecrating Festival Play' should be put on only in Bayreuth and nowhere else. That is not quite true. In this as in so many things Wagner contradicted himself. In 1881 he agreed that a company proposed by Angelo Neumann to go on tour with Wagner's works (and that did, in fact, later present the *Ring* throughout much of Europe and Russia) might eventually include *Parsifal* in its repertoire. He even repeated this view to Neumann a year later.[9] So Wagner not only agreed that a Jew (Levi) should conduct *Parsifal* at Bayreuth; he did not rule out the idea that a Jewish impresario might stage the work elsewhere.

The *Ring* and *Parsifal* manifestly belonged to a Bayreuth repertoire but what else did – if anything? Hardliners baulked at *Tannhäuser*; more open-minded Wagnerians felt the festival should include, as draft statutes for the still-born Foundation put it, the 'stylistically pure presentation' of musical works by other German masters – a proposal Cosima termed 'a joke'. In an 1880 letter, Wagner himself stated that once *Parsifal* had been staged, he aimed to present all his earlier works – one per year in chronological order – in 'exemplary performances' in Bayreuth. This, he stressed, would constitute his 'artistic legacy'.[10] Moreover, at one time, at least, the Master did not believe that a (mainly) Wagner festival should only look back; quite the contrary. In an introduction to the *Ring* text published in 1863, long before his Bayreuth era, Wagner proposed that such a festival be held every two or three years in the context of a prize-giving for a new 'musical-dramatic' work. The prize itself would be no more but no less than a well-prepared performance at the festival of the new piece. In this way, Wagner argued, his own works would gain from repetition under ideal circumstances and new ones also worthy of 'the German spirit' would steadily emerge.[11]

It is impossible to judge whether Wagner would really have done all that had he lived longer. But his proposals, even his self-contradictions, show he was far more open about the festival he founded than the many – above all his widow – who claimed to speak in his name once he was gone. It was Cosima who drew up the Bayreuth menu, basically unchanged to this day, offering huge dishes of Wagner and nothing but Wagner – later spiced with a few helpings of Beethoven's 'Choral' Symphony. It is easy to see why she acted as she did. So long as Bayreuth concentrated on the Wagner canon alone (excluding the earliest works – *Die Feen*, *Das Liebesverbot* and *Rienzi*) it stayed manifestly special. For devotees the Master's spirit there was never far away: his widow and children were constantly visible. Poky hotel rooms and unpalatable fare seemed sacrifices worth making to belong for a while to the big Bayreuth family. Indeed, the truest of the pilgrims like Friedrich Eckstein, a friend of Bruckner, spurned the relative comfort of train or carriage and plodded to Bayreuth with staff and knapsack. Throw in works by other composers, though, and the festival stood to lose the exclusiveness that was its main competitive advantage. Cosima knew that. As one of her descendants put it in private, she was 'an astute old bird' who saw the value of a well-defined brand and who was 'great at PR'.

That refreshingly disrepectful judgement is no doubt true as far as it goes, but it hardly gets to the heart of Cosima's achievement or of its limitations. She faced a dangerously tricky balancing act. On the one hand, she did not want to dissuade houses elsewhere from performing Wagner; indeed, the more they did so the more much-needed royalty income would flow to the debt-plagued family the Master had left behind. On the other, she needed to prevent the emergence of any real rival to Bayreuth. *Parsifal* was a special case. By using its 'sacred' character and 'the Master's wish' as arguments, the work was to be reserved for Bayreuth, thus forcing anyone who wanted to see it to go there. That alone ensured a steady stream of Wagnerians to the Green Hill, but it also attracted a lot of the unconverted who simply wanted to know what the fuss was about. As a result, *Parsifal* was better attended from the outset than other Bayreuth offerings.

By sheer force of character and a talent for self-dramatisation hardly less than the Master's, Cosima achieved much; imperiously nodding approval of a production or artist when this seemed in Bayreuth's interest, giving the thumbs down when she scented danger to its supremacy. But she did not always get her way. As already noted, she vainly tried to stop Munich building its Bayreuth imitation, the Prinzregententheater. More importantly, she petitioned the Reichstag in 1901 to extend copyright protection from thirty years to fifty, a step that would have ensured Wahnfried handsome royalty income beyond 1913, the thirtieth anniversary of Wagner's death (and the hundredth of his birth). For *Parsifal* she wanted even more: a permanent ban on performances outside Bayreuth. Cosima failed on both these counts too, providing her with a further cause for disgust with democracy in general and 'Berlin' in particular. Not that dictatorship proved more reliable. Adolf Hitler later solemnly promised at Wagner's graveside that *Parsifal* would be 'given back to Bayreuth' – but it never was. In any case *Parsifal* had been staged beyond the reach even of Cosima's long arm well before the thirty-year copyright expired, notably in New York from 1903 – an act denounced by the Wagner faithful as 'the rape of the Grail'. Cosima fumed and artists who took part in the New York 'treachery' were banned from the Green Hill. Otherwise she was powerless. The United States had not signed the Berne convention on international copyright protection, so no law had been broken – other than a 'moral' one drawn up in Bayreuth.

On the artistic side, Cosima generally secured outstanding singers, although she pettily drove some of the best away again – for example Lilli Lehmann, a soprano of Jewish descent who was, among many other things, a legendary Brünnhilde, and Anton van Rooy, one of the finest Wotans ever but outlawed from Bayreuth as one of the New York 'traitors'. She attracted some good conductors but not quite the best (although she kept on Levi who was unsurpassed in *Parsifal* ). Hans Richter was one of her favourites, despite the fact that his erratic handling of the *Ring* in 1876 had driven the Master to despair. Still, Richter was almost a family heirloom, having played the trumpet in that unforgettable premiere of the *Siegfried Idyll* on the staircase to Cosima's bedroom at Tribschen. The dynamic young Richard Strauss appeared for just one season, conducting *Tannhäuser* in 1894 a few weeks before he married Pauline de Ahna, a soprano with a sweet voice and a sharp tongue. The match displeased Cosima, who would have loved to have won Strauss for Bayreuth as a conducting son-in-law, although she thought little of him as a composer. For that and other reasons Strauss vanished from the Bayreuth scene for nearly forty years, finally popping up with abominable timing as a replacement for Arturo Toscanini, who dropped out when Hitler came to power in 1933.

From 1896 the able but initially reluctant Siegfried began regular service in the Bayreuth pit and from 1901 the punctilious Karl Muck took over *Parsifal*, becoming well-nigh as indispensable a 'guardian of the Grail' (particularly in his own opinion) as Levi had long been. Missing from the list were two of the greatest all-round conductors of the age: Hans von Bülow and Gustav Mahler. The former shunned the chance to appear at his ex-wife's court and died in Cairo in 1894; the latter was a Jew, and for Cosima Levi was already one Jew too many. She even plotted behind the scenes in a vain bid to stop Mahler winning the directorship in 1897 of the Vienna Court Opera, the most influential post in European music. After failing, she switched tack and sent him fawning letters extolling her son's operas, the first of which – *Der Bärenhäuter* (The Man in a Bear's Skin) – Mahler did indeed present in Vienna. But she never invited him to conduct in Bayreuth.

As for Cosima's stagings, the journalist Moritz Wirth snapped after seeing her *Ring* that if she had applied for a job as producer in any house but Bayreuth she would have been shown the door after fifteen minutes. That seems too tough by half. Cosima could think big and organise as well as anyone, as the massive spectacle of her *Tannhaüser* planned down to the tiniest detail well shows. But the stylised action and singing she endorsed, in presumed accord with Wagner's wishes, too often drained away the passion on which he of all people had insisted. Not surprisingly she had no time for the radical ideas of a new generation of stage designers, sticking instead to naturalistic sets and monotonous lighting.

'Frau Wagner was tireless as a producer,' wrote the conductor Felix Weingartner, who as a young protégé of Levi often saw Cosima at work. 'She combined a clear, flexible mind with a compelling way of arguing that made it hard to resist her.' But he added 'that Frau Wagner came to believe she had a kind of divine mission was less tragic than that no one had the courage to point out . . . that even a highly gifted person taking over a new and unusual task makes pardonable, understandable and natural mistakes.'[12] Weingartner did in fact contradict Cosima several times to her face and attacked Bayreuth's dogmatism in print, drawing charges from the faithful that he resented not being invited to conduct on the Green Hill. More likely Weingartner's version – that he loathed the servility around Cosima and was not prepared to make her Bayreuth the focal point of his career – is the right one. In his memoirs he recalls one particularly ghastly evening at Wahnfried when Levi was treated by the Wagner family with faint but constant contempt 'ill-concealed beneath the smiling mask of friendship'. Far from showing offence, the victim simply bowed and scraped. After leaving, Weingartner furiously asked his mentor how he could put up with such degrading treatment. Levi looked at him sadly and replied, 'It's easy enough for you in that house – Aryan that you are.'[13]

'Servile' would not correctly describe the least dispensable of the Wahnfried inner circle, namely von Gross. 'Devoted' fits better, although it was not always easy for outsiders to tell the difference. It was von Gross, for instance, who argued for festival-free years to help consolidate Bayreuth's finances, and for postponement until 1891 of the huge expense bound to be involved in a *Tannhäuser* production. Cosima objected on both counts but she finally backed down, well aware of her adviser's worth. In a letter, she once told the parable of the drowning man and the four bystanders. One of the four wondered what to do, another called for help, another went to fetch a boat but the fourth hurled himself into the water and pulled the victim to the shore. The festival had been the drowning man, Cosima said, and von Gross the rescuer.

It is misleading to see von Gross, as some have, as a philistine constantly putting business before culture. His many surviving letters to Bayreuth stalwarts like Richter and Levi, as well as to well-wishers like the composer Engelbert Humperdinck (Siegfried's music tutor) and the French conductor Charles Lamoureux, show how much he had the festival's artistic success at heart. It was he who drew the soprano Rosa Sucher to Bayreuth, initially at his own expense, where she became a much-feted Isolde. But it was as financial adviser and canny negotiator that von Gross showed his greatest worth; not least when King Ludwig died in 1886 and the Bavarian government sought to withdraw from Bayreuth the rights to the *Ring* and *Parsifal* that the monarch had ceded to it. In a confrontation with von Gross in Munich, the minister involved argued that as Ludwig had been declared mad his waiver of the rights was invalid. Gross retorted that in this case the minister's appointment by Ludwig must have been invalid too. The day was saved. Von Gross continued to guard the interests of family and festival so closely, and to invest royalty income so wisely, that the final tranche of Ludwig's loans to the Master could be paid back in 1906. By the time copyright protection ran out in 1913, royalty income earned on Wagner's works at home and abroad in the three decades since his death amounted to over six million marks and the wealth of the Wagner family itself totalled around seven million. That was above all von Gross's doing. If any charge can fairly be levelled at him, it is that he kept too many threads in his hands for too long and failed to prepare Siegfried adequately for his role as the next Master of Bayreuth.

The Cosima/von Gross tandem thus drew artistic and business success from near ruin but, for the faithful, Bayreuth was far more than music and money. It was, as Cosima put it, 'our mighty fortress on the hill' – the heart of a crusade aimed at achieving that 'regeneration' of mankind Wagner had dreamed of. Just what this brave new regenerated world would involve was no longer clear, if indeed it ever had been; but evidently German-ness, above all the work of the Master, was to be at the heart of it. One thing was certain. Jews would play a role only on sufferance, at best none at all.

# 5

# The Plastic Demon

Was it just coincidence? In 1869 Wagner issued a more sharply worded version of his antisemitic pamphlet *Das Judentum in der Musik*, and in the same year most German Jews were finally granted the emancipation for which they had long struggled. Historic event though it surely was, the act of emancipation slipped into being by stealth. Under a one-paragraph law that came into force in the North German Confederation, the Prussian-dominated alliance of states north of the River Main, the civil and political rights of all subjects were declared wholly 'independent of religious affiliation'.

Jews were not specifically mentioned, which helps explain why the move caused little public fuss at the time. Besides, in preceding decades German Jewry had moved step by painful step towards full civic equality, so that the new law simply removed the remaining restrictions, in the north at least. Two years later, after Prussia's victory over France, the northern states as well as the southern ones like Bavaria, Baden and Württemberg were absorbed into the newly proclaimed Reich and the 1869 law became valid throughout Germany. Thanks to the flourish of a pen combined with Bismarck's drive for national unity all 'Jews in Germany' thus became, on paper, fully fledged 'German citizens of Jewish faith.' Thousands of them had, in fact, already had the 'privilege' of serving in the war against France, just as, some four decades later, tens of thousands more would march off to fight for *Kaiser und Vaterland* in the First World War. German Jews and Gentiles, it seemed, could now die and live together on an equal footing. 'There is', declared the noted Jewish writer and lawyer Isidor Kaim in 1869 with misplaced optimism, 'no longer any Jewish question.'[1]

This is no place to attempt a thorough account of the age-old hostility to Jews, but without offering at least a background sketch the tale told here would lack perspective. Like a killer whale, antisemitism rears up and sinks from view in the Wagner family saga but it is rarely far away. Were the Wagners in general and Richard in particular specially responsible for the events that led to the Holocaust? Should one speak of 'Wagner's Hitler', the title of a fairly recent German book,[2] as though the Führer's drive to destroy the Jews was a largely inevitable product of the Master's antisemitism? Or can one fairly talk only of 'Hitler's Wagner', implying that because he loved Wagnerian music drama the Führer was instinctively drawn to the family and the Bayreuth festival, no less but no more? Although the Wagners' involvement with Hitler belongs to later chapters, it is high time to look more closely at the hostility Richard and Cosima felt for Jews long before the Führer was born. Where did it come from? What caused it? How 'special' was it?

Already in pre-Christian times Jews were pilloried by Greeks, among others, for believing in one God. With the rise of the church, they were branded all but indelibly with the stigma of Christ's crucifixion. The diaspora, in which Jews became dispersed far beyond Palestine, was interpreted as a sign of divine punishment, fulfilling the Biblical prophecy that 'the Lord will scatter you from one end of the earth to the other . . . and among those nations you shall find no rest.' In Europe even Jews sometimes found rest, but never for long. They were routinely massacred by crusaders travelling east to 'liberate' the Holy Land; like other 'heretics' they were tortured by the Inquisition; and they were expelled from (but later usually readmitted to) one country after another. Forbidden to own land or join craft guilds, they struggled to survive by begging, trading and especially by lending money at interest, an activity banned to Christians. Most had to live in ghettos, and as early as the thirteenth century many were forced to wear a yellow star, one of the vile traditions the Nazis revived.

That the Jews survived at all seems amazing. Some survived well – court Jews, for instance, whose skills in finance and organisation European rulers keen to raise armies or build palaces could ill afford to shun. These privileged Jews in turn often helped win better conditions for their less fortunate brethren. A long and faltering 'march out of the ghettos' began, not just physically but mentally, as Jews, egged on by intellectuals like Moses Mendelssohn in Germany, began to explore the broader culture on whose fringes they had subsisted for so long. All that was under way when the 1789 French Revolution with its 'liberty, equality, fraternity' ideals gave a mighty boost to the cause of Jewish emancipation, first in France and then further afield as Napoleon brought one part of Europe after another under his control. In Germany many ghetto walls were literally hammered down by French forces, but that alone did not bring German Jews equality, let alone fraternity with other Germans. Emancipation was only won bit by bit, and was often accompanied by a violent backlash.

The process of emancipation coincided with two other huge upheavals: the drive for a united Germany and the industrial revolution. The latter brought particular benefits to many Jews (though far from all). It is easy to see why. For generations they had had to be quick-witted, daring and adaptable to survive. The financial, trading and entrepreneurial skills they had honed were just the ones now most needed in a German economy growing and changing with bewildering speed. Traditionally excluded from the craft guilds, Jews were mainly insulated from sectors that now had the biggest problems to adapt. Concentrated in towns and cities because they had been banned from owning land, they were now at the heart of the action. They thus seemed peculiarly representative of all that was 'modern' – in the sense of rootless, flashy, 'on the make' – to Germans who had lost out from the new economy or who still lived from the soil. This perception was not changed by that formal step to full emancipation that emerged in 1869. If anything, resentment of Jewish success became more intense, and this in turn coincided with a surge of national pride over the birth of a united Germany. No matter that Jews, through business and on the battlefield, had helped bring the new Reich about. For many Germans they remained outsiders who had somehow managed to win a place on the inside track.

Suppose that after unity the economy had steadily done well and prosperity, flanked by the social security measures that Bismarck introduced, had spread to most Germans. Might the hostility to Jews have faded, or might future catastrophe at least have been avoided? In 1871 the number of Jews in the Reich totalled only 512,000, just 1.25 per cent of the population. Although the numerical figure steadily rose (to a peak of well over 600,000 before the First World War), the overall number of Germans grew faster still, so that the proportion of the population who were Jewish dropped to less than one per cent and stayed there. Reason suggests that the Jews were far from becoming an unmanageable minority, especially since they were now citizens with full rights and duties, but then reason plays little role in this tale. It was not statistical evidence that bothered those with fears and grudges back in 1871, let alone later. It was the prominence of Jews in influential fields, especially finance, trading and the press, against an age-old background of religious bigotry and superstition.

For two years after unification the economy boomed unhealthily, fuelled by 'the sky's the limit' euphoria and by five billion francs in war indemnity extracted from the French. Then in 1873 the stock market crashed and the country plunged into recession. A scapegoat was sought and easily found in the Jews – or rather, in international Jewry, which the Prussian historian Heinrich von Treitschke claimed had gained a stranglehold on Germany without having any real stake in the nation's future. Treitschke's nationalist, authoritarian theses, presented in undeniably elegant prose, had a special appeal to intellectuals who claimed to despise rabble-rousers. Wilhelm Marr, on the other hand, prided himself on touching the nerve of the masses. A journalist and troublemaker generally held to have coined the word 'antisemitism', Marr published his influential *Der Sieg des Judenthums über das Germanenthum* (The Victory of Jewishness over Germanism) in 1869 and simultaneously founded a movement called the *Antisemiten Liga* (League of Antisemites). A year earlier Adolf Stöcker, the eloquent Protestant chaplain at the Imperial Court, had formed a *Christlich-soziale Arbeiterpartei* (Christian-Social Workers' Party), intended mainly to woo support away from the growing ranks of the newly founded Social Democrats. Stöcker failed in that aim, but he gained broader backing when his speeches became overtly antisemitic. A petition organised in 1880 by one of his allies, Bernhard Foerster, urging that the influence of Jews in Germany be curtailed and Jewish immigration restricted, quickly won 225,000 signatures. One of those pressed to sign was Wagner. That he refused has since been widely counted in his favour, and even interpreted as a sign that in his last years the Master was becoming less intensely antisemitic. The matter is not as straightforward as that, as we shall see.

Treitschke, Marr and Stöcker were just three of the prominent Germans fanning hostility to Jews in the new empire. Scores of other writers and agitators joined in, often flaunting the pseudo-science of racial degeneration set out most thoroughly back in the 1850s by the French diplomat and ethnologist, Joseph-Arthur Comte de Gobineau, in his four-volume *Essai sur l'inégalité des races humaines* (Essay on the Inequality of Human Races). Gobineau himself did not despise Jews but, despite the impact of post-revolutionary emancipation, many of his countrymen did – including some of the most prominent ones. A historic strain of French intellectual antisemitism included such famous figures as Voltaire and Diderot, just as a German one covered Fichte and Kant. Similarly, antisemitism stayed rife throughout the Habsburg empire despite laws in the mid-nineteenth century giving Jews greater rights. In the Russian empire (which included much of Poland), repeated pogroms forced some million and a half Jews to flee for their lives between 1880 and 1914 alone, many to America. Compared to the ever-threatened *Ostjuden* (Jews in the east), most German Jews felt fairly secure. It is easy in retrospect to see how false that feeling was. But despite the hostile clamour, differences between and within the German antisemitic parties helped ensure that before the First World War no laws were passed to repeal Jewish emancipation. Many Jews thought that with time the sound and fury would blow itself out.

On the face of it that judgement was rational, but it was made in relation to a scourge that, whatever the modish scientific jargon being used to justify it, was irrational through and through. Jews who for centuries had mainly been viewed as inferior if not subhuman suddenly came to be regarded as creatures of infinite cunning, pulling all manner of international strings behind the scenes. If they stuck together they were held to be clannish, if they tried to assimilate they were accused of unhealthy infiltration. If they took insults quietly they were said to grovel, if they stood up for themselves they were 'getting too big for their boots'.

This inconsistency was served by an imprecise vocabulary. Marr came up with the word *Antisemitismus* because it had a scientific ring likely to be more widely acceptable than the old-fashioned but far more explicit *Judenhass* (hatred of Jews). Strictly speaking, his choice of word was inaccurate, since Arabs as well as Jews are Semites and Arabs were surely not the intended target. This imprecision did not stop the word catching on so far beyond its inventor's wildest dreams that it has become virtually impossible to avoid using it. Something of the same goes for *Arier* and *Arisch* (Aryan). Thanks to misappropriation by racists the words have become widely identified with Nordic supermen, rather than with their correct meaning of a prehistoric people (and group of languages) originating in Persia and northern India.

Even the word Jew is subject to manifold definition, ensuring that it is often unclear just who is meant. Karl Lueger, the antisemitic mayor of Vienna in the late nineteenth century, famously solved the problem to his own satisfaction. '*Wer Jude ist bestimme ich*' (I decide who is a Jew), he declared. That is clear, at least. The Nazis took much the same line, although in doing so they put up a thicker smokescreen of pseudo-science. Under their Nuremberg racial laws of 1935 (and subsequent 'clarifications') they claimed to have identified degrees of Jewishness mainly according to blood heritage. People with at least three 'fully Jewish' grandparents, for instance, were regarded as undilutedly Jewish and therefore a particular danger to the 'pure German race'; those with one Jewish grandparent as less harmful *Mischlinge* (hybrids) of the second degree. But how were 'fully Jewish' grandparents to be defined? Lamely, the Nazis here felt forced to abandon their sham precision on blood and race, identifying these forebears simply by their membership of the Jewish religious community.

So it was that when Wagner first went public (albeit under the pseudonym K. Freigedank) with his *Das Judentum in der Musik* in 1850,[3] he was working within an ancient and pernicious tradition. Even the specific application of antisemitism to music, rather than to religion or politics, was not unheard of. At the very start of his article in the *Neue Zeitschrift für Musik* (New Journal for Music), Wagner noted that there had recently been a set-to over a piece in the same periodical mentioning 'Hebraic artistic taste'. He now proposed to get to the root of the matter. There followed a stream of unproven statements, non sequiturs and insults. Wagner stated flatly that any contact with Jews brought 'instinctive repulsion', that Jewish speech sounded like a 'creaking, squeaking, buzzing snuffle' and that the only music Jews could offer, that of the synagogue, was characterised by 'gurgle, yodel and cackle'. Taking a backhanded swipe at Heine, whose work and ideas he had once seen as a model, Wagner grandly but vacuously claimed that the poet (long since a convert to Protestantism) was 'the conscience of Judaism, just as Judaism is the evil conscience of our civilisation'.

Buried among the vituperation, though, lurked one point of substance: that since Jews had so long lived only on the fringes of other cultures, they had been unable to produce music (or indeed any art) that tapped and reflected those cultures at the deepest level. It is of course true that no Beethoven or Goethe had emerged directly from the ghettos, but beyond that insight Wagner got onto shakier ground. Citing the case of Felix Mendelssohn Bartholdy (Moses Mendelssohn's grandson), he sought to show that even converted Jews of real talent and taste could at best produce only well-finished, diverting work, not great art. This amounts to a racist argument in embryo. although Wagner did not identify it as such.

One can argue about Mendelssohn's artistic stature, even about Heine's. But that aside, it evidently did not strike Wagner that the freeing of Jews from their age-old ghetto restrictions might, and indeed soon did, bring an upsurge in the arts and sciences (from Mahler to Freud, Schoenberg to Einstein) all but unmatched in history. He did get as far as charging that Jews, backed by their kind in finance and the press, were becoming increasingly dominant in music; but that, he explained, was because the art of music itself had been in a parlous state since Beethoven. Naturally Wagner exempted his own music from this charge; indeed, it was precisely his kind of *Gesamtkunstwerk* that he believed would reverse the decline. Meanwhile, though, Jews had won success by purporting to slake the thirst of bored audiences with 'sips of Art', and one famous opera 'tone-setter' had made this stultifying process the task of his life. Wagner disdainfully (or diplomatically?) gave no name, but his readers easily guessed who was meant – the Master's erstwhile mentor Meyerbeer.

After this doom-ridden onslaught, it comes as a shock when in a last brief paragraph Wagner suggests there is hope after all. Like a conjurer drawing a rabbit from a hat, he produces the writer Ludwig Börne (born Löb Baruch in Frankfurt in 1786), a converted Jew who played a key role in that revolutionary *Junges Deutschland* movement that had influenced the young Wagner. The final passage, often partly or even wrongly quoted, needs giving in full with Wagner's own italics:

From out of his isolation as a Jew, [Börne] came among us in search of redemption: he failed to find it and was forced to realise that he would only do so *when we ourselves were redeemed as true human beings*. But for the Jew to become human with us is tantamount to his ceasing to be a Jew. This Börne achieved. But Börne in particular teaches us that this redemption cannot be achieved in ease and cold, indifferent complacency but costs – as costs it must for us – sweat, want, anguish, and an abundance of suffering and pain. Join unreservedly in this self-destructive and bloody battle, and we shall all be united and indivisible. But remember that one thing alone can redeem you from the curse which weighs upon you: the redemption of Ahasverus – *going under!*

The word Wagner actually uses at the very end is *Untergang*, which is often rendered into English here as destruction. It *can* mean that at a pinch, but tends to imply a more gradual process, like the sinking of the sun or the decline of the West. If Wagner had wanted a still more drastic last word he had plenty of options. Even leaving that point aside those last two lines can bring a chill to the spine, especially after the Holocaust; but are they really as savage as they at first seem? Wagner himself had second thoughts about the penultimate one and in his reissued version of 1869 he dropped the reference to a bloody battle, one of the few places in the whole article where he softened the original text. The later passage reads 'Join unreservedly in this work of redemption that you may be reborn through the process of self-annihilation.' That is still a repulsive statement, but it does suggest that the '*going under*' Wagner refers to is of the kind he claims Börne went through by blotting out all in himself that was Jewish. Given the context it is hard to argue convincingly, although some scholars do try, that Wagner is here calling for the physical annihilation of the Jews.

It is not only the Jews who, according to Wagner, have hard work to do. He emphasises this with his italicised '*when we ourselves were redeemed as true human beings*' and his later reference to 'as costs it must for us'. What he seems to have in mind ('seems' is a word much needed in connection with Wagner's prose) is some kind of transformation of the whole of humankind, presumably within a new society in which his own art would play a major role. This transformation, he indicates, is hard enough for Gentiles to achieve but it is still tougher for Jews, who are coming, as it were, from further behind. But he evidently believes it is feasible all the same. It is worth stressing that *Judentum* was one of those works Wagner wrote just after he fled Germany into exile. Despite the failure of the Dresden uprising, he still firmly believed at that stage that revolution was possible in art, politics and society. Seen in that context, his *Judentum* tract might almost be construed as pointing the stony way to the brotherhood of man.

Almost but not quite. That last nebulous paragraph about redemption is too flimsy to counterbalance all the spite that has preceded it. After the salvos of animosity, the final lines have about them the air of an afterthought. Nor is it clear just what Wagner thinks Jews must do to ensure their Jewishness is wiped out, and the reference to Börne does not help. If Börne is considered by Wagner to be saved why not the now-slighted Heine? Apparently conversion alone is not enough. Besides, when Wagner republished the article as a pamphlet nearly two decades later, he included with it a text called *Aufklärungen über das Judentum in der Musik* (Some Explanations about Jewishness in Music) in the guise of an open letter. Here assimilation is only one conceivable solution he mentions to 'the Jewish problem'. He writes that 'Whether the downfall of our Culture can be arrested by a violent ejection of the destructive foreign element I am unable to decide, since that would require forces with whose existence I am unacquainted.'[4] He does not say he is against violent ejection, just that he does not know how it could be done. Would he prefer that solution to 'redemption through assimilation' if it were possible? He does not say.

Regrettably, the 1869 publication did not mark the last of Wagner's sallies into print on the Jewish question. Far from it. Particularly in the last five years of his life he returned to the topic in essays and pamphlets like *Modern* in 1878 and *Religion und Kunst* (Religion and Art) in 1880, as well as *Erkenne dich selbst* (Know Thyself) and *Heldentum und Christentum* (Heroism and Christianity), both in 1881. He also mentioned Jews frequently in letters and made many private comments about them, diligently recorded by Cosima who even in the worst of her many nightmares surely never dreamed that her diary, meant for her children, would one day be made public in full. One might think, or at least hope, that this mass of material would clarify Wagner's position. In fact the opposite is true because the Jewish issue becomes entangled with a host of others, including vegetarianism, vivisection, temperance, socialism and eastern religion – all heavily laced with doses of Schopenhauer and, at the very end, a dash of diluted Gobineau. Downing this heady brew can bring an occasional flash of insight but only at the serious risk of a bitter aftertaste and bad indigestion. These late works, sometimes called the 'regeneration writings', offer great scope for selective quotation both by those who seek to show that Wagner was a vicious antisemite and by those keen to prove the opposite – or at least to indicate that he was not such a bad chap after all.

Taking the defence case first, we find Wagner in July 1878 claiming that 'if the Catholics consider themselves to be of a higher rank than we the Protestants, then the Jews are of the highest rank, the oldest'.[5] The Master was here responding to Levi, who would conduct *Parsifal* four years later; with his sadly habitual self-abasement Levi had groaned that as a Jew – and a rabbi's son at that – he felt himself to be a 'wandering anachronism'. So it might be argued that Wagner was simply making a rare effort to be kind to a man he and Cosima later found plenty of occasions to torment. But only four months afterwards Wagner told Cosima that 'If ever I were to write again about the Jews, I should say I have nothing against them, it is just that they descended on us Germans too soon, we were not yet steady enough to absorb them.'[6] In other words, like Shakespeare's Cassius, Wagner reckons that the fault 'is not in our stars but in ourselves'. Three years later he takes up the point again in *Erkenne dich selbst*, referring to 'the Jew' as 'the most astonishing example of racial consistency that world history has ever offered'. Wagner acknowledged that Jews had become virtuosi in the vile art of handling money, but he charged that 'our Civilisation' had invented the system it now bungled. It was Germans, in the first place, who needed to go in for intense self-searching. Hence the title of his essay.[7]

It is hard not to notice a certain admiration in these remarks, albeit tinged with envy and even fear. Stretching a point, you might almost conclude that Wagner rather wished he were a Jew himself (and as we shall shortly see, some people claim he really was). He certainly had many Jewish friends; from Samuel Lehrs, a sympathetic philosopher from the dog days in Paris, to Joseph Rubinstein, 'house pianist' at Wahnfried; from Heinrich Porges, a young conductor who backed Wagner when he was at a particularly low ebb, to Angelo Neumann, that opera director and impresario who, with Wagner's blessing, took the *Ring* on tour across Europe. The list can easily be lengthened. Wagner did indeed partly turn against Heine and humiliated Levi, but he double-crossed and wounded countless non-Jews too. Friendship with Wagner meant total devotion verging on slavery. Many people readily made that sacrifice and among those Wagner most prized were Jews. Had he lived in the Nazi era, Wagner's personal contacts would surely have been regarded with the utmost suspicion, at least for as long as he found any Jews to befriend.

Despite all that, the prosecution evidence is at least as bulky. Probably its most shocking item is Wagner's retort that all Jews should be burned, during a performance of *Nathan der Weise* (Nathan the

Wise), a play espousing religious tolerance by Gotthold Ephraim Lessing, a (Gentile) friend of Moses Mendelssohn. All sorts of extenuating circumstances have been offered to try to account for this monstrosity. It emerged late in Wagner's life (on 18 December 1881) when he was in increasing pain and prone to still more splenetic outbursts. It was made in private and meant to be what the indefatigable Cosima calls 'a drastic joke' – a notable insight into Wagnerian humour. And it came in the context of a hobnob about a recent theatre fire in Vienna in which some nine hundred people died, nearly half of them Jews. If everyone's off-the cuff remarks were recorded for posterity, so the Master's defenders argue, who would escape censure?

Wagner was indeed never quite as drastic in public as he was in private. But in his final essays, alongside the kind of admiration quoted above, he railed against Jewish influence in the press, scorned state moves to bring about full Jewish emancipation and even called Jews 'the plastic demon of the decline of mankind'.[8] It is hard to be sure just what he meant by 'plastic demon', but it sounds pretty dreadful and that, no doubt, was the main thing. We also know that he had good things to say, albeit not consistently, about Marr and Stöcker as well as several other notable antisemites of the day. Cosima reports in 1879 that 'I read a very good speech by Pastor Stöcker on Judaism. R.[ichard] is for total expulsion. We laugh over the fact that really, it seems, his essay on the Jews marked the start of the struggle.'[9] So in private at least, according to his wife, Wagner backed the idea of expulsion that he had raised only as a very distant theoretical possibility in his reissued *Judentum* brochure a decade before.

Why then did Wagner not sign that petition repeatedly thrust under his nose in 1880 by Bernhard Foerster urging, among other things, that Jewish immigration be restricted? What could he possibly have against it, except perhaps a feeling that the wording was too weak? Cosima gave several explanations, among them that her husband had already done as much for the cause as he could, that a petition he had signed against vivisection had proved a failure and that the new appeal was addressed in servile language to Bismarck, whom by this time the Master loathed. Besides, even Wagner found the over-persistent petitioner lacked balance – a judgement too mild by far. A few years later Foerster and his wife Elisabeth, Nietzsche's bigoted and mendacious sister, founded a colony called Neu Germania aimed at raising a pure Teutonic race in Paraguay. When the project flopped Foerster committed suicide. Wagner died before this crazy scheme was launched, but he was rightly wary of the early planning for it. Explaining his failure to back the petition in a letter to Neumann, whom he addressed as 'Dear friend and benefactor', Wagner stressed that 'I have absolutely no connection with the present "anti-semitic" movement.' He added that a forthcoming article (*Erkenne dich selbst*) 'will prove this so conclusively that it will be impossible for anyone of *intelligence* to associate me with that movement'.[10]

That little word 'present' in the Neumann letter suggests Wagner was not against antisemitism as such, an implication the Master's apologists tend to overlook. Wagner surely did feel that his own approach to the Jewish question ('drastic' private outbursts apart) was on a higher level than that of mere petitioners and politicians, but he had a more pressing reason than that for shunning the Foerster initiative. Cosima's ex-husband von Bülow had signed the petition although, he grumbled, Jews would boycott his concerts as a result and cause him a sharp drop in income. He went ahead all the same because, he said, he wanted to show 'civic courage' and thought Wagner would sign too. When Wagner failed to join in, von Bülow was livid, but he should not have been surprised. Wagner had been preaching against what he regarded as excessive Jewish influence in music for decades and in 1880 he had a single, financially disastrous, Bayreuth festival behind him. He must have reckoned he could bear the consequences of too overt an act of so-called 'civic courage' still less than von Bülow.

So is the truth of the matter that Wagner aired his real antisemitic views in private but was cautious in public so as not to lose backing from Jews and their allies? Not altogether. Even in private Wagner found good things as well as bad to say about Jews, and while in public he fell short of endorsing expulsion (let alone burning) his comments were often manifestly offensive. A more credible explanation is that Wagner was muddled and inconsistent. That does not only apply to his attitude to Jews. In *Religion und Kunst*, for example, he draws an apocalyptic (and thoroughly modern-looking) picture of the arms race, warning that 'art, science, courage and honour, life and property could one day go up in the air through an incalculable oversight'.[11] Had he forgotten the glee with which he greeted the Franco-Prussian war a decade before; how he had voiced hope that Paris would be burned to the ground 'as a symbol of the world's liberation'; how he had composed a tub-thumping *Kaisermarsch*, probably the worst of his late works, to mark German victory?

Naturally Wagner had the right to change his mind, although even in his last years mention of Paris and the French (barring one or two favoured individuals like Judith Gautier) could draw from him a venom hardly compatible with his theoretical pacifism. Something of the same goes for his theoretical vegetarianism. In the Tribschen days we find Wagner scorning Nietzsche, who had refused meat on the grounds that it was 'ethically important not to eat animals'.[12] A few years later at Wahnfried, Wagner in principle adopted Nietzsche's stance – partly for the same moral reason, partly because by this time he had decided that eating the flesh of slaughtered beasts was mainly responsible for the degeneration of mankind. If man were to return to the right road he had to go over to a vegetable diet. Wagner even urged mass migration from northern climes to sunny spots where people would feel less impelled to tuck into juicy steaks. Most accounts nonetheless suggest that when it came to moving from theory to practice the Master honoured vegetarianism more in the breach than the observance. When two acolytes heeded his words in 1880 and really did give up meat, Wagner was contemptuous. 'R[ichard] sees his ideas reflected back at him as in a distorting mirror,' Cosima sighed, 'a great perception mistakenly converted into a petty practical act.'[13]

Not that Wagner thought vegetarianism alone would be enough to regenerate mankind. Great art, notably the *Gesamtkunstwerk*, had to make available again the sacred content that the church had lost when, Wagner claimed, it had perverted the teaching of Jesus Christ and become obsessed with empty dogma. At the same time man had to embrace a true religion founded on compassion and through which all races, even the lowest, could be purified by Christ's blood. Exactly how this is to be achieved Wagner does not say, but at least one argument for his antisemitism slips out here. He raises strong doubts over whether Jesus really was a Jew, and anyway deplores Judaism on the grounds that compassion is not at the heart of it. Here Wagner follows the involved, not to say contorted, reasoning of his hero Schopenhauer, who argued that Judaism wrongly held the world to be improvable, thus encouraging false optimism and fruitless activity. Only faiths such as Buddhism that advocated denying the self and the world were capable of generating acceptance of one's fate, and hence compassion for one's fellow men – stranded, as it were, in the same ghastly boat.

One reaction to all this is simply to ridicule it, as Bernard Shaw notably did in a despatch from Bayreuth six years after Wagner's death. Shaw reflected that being a Wagnerian had once meant commitment to nothing more than relishing the music: 'What it commits a man to now, Omniscience only knows.' He went on:

Vegetarianism, the higher Buddhism, Christianity divested of its allegorical trappings . . . belief in a Fall of Man brought about by some cataclysm which starved him into eating flesh, negation of the will-to-live and consequent Redemption through compassion excited by suffering (this is the Wagner–Schopenhauer article of faith); all these are but samples of what Wagnerism involves nowadays. The average enthusiast accepts them all unhesitatingly – bar vegetarianism. Buddhism he can stand; he is not particular as to what variety of Christianity he owns to; Schopenhauer is his favourite philosopher; but get through *Parsifal* without a beefsteak between the second and third acts he will not.[14]

Shaw (a practising vegetarian, incidentally, unlike Wagner) did not say whether being an 'average enthusiast' also meant implicitly accepting convoluted ideas about race and Jews. If this topic crossed his mind then he evidently felt that raising it in such an article would spoil the fun. But by underlining even jokingly how much Wagnerism had become a near-impenetrable jungle of faiths, fads and fancies, he puts his finger on the core of the matter.

Right up to the end Wagner the over-productive writer and incessant talker failed to make himself clear – not just on the admittedly woolly topic of regeneration in general, but on racism and the Jews in particular. When he maintains that even the 'lowest races' can be purified through Christ's blood, does that mean everyone can be – therefore also Jews, whom he actually refers to in another context as of 'the highest rank'? If it does, why does he rant about expulsion or (in passing) worse? Or is it only those Jews that fail to convert who will have to suffer serious consequences? Would conversion alone be enough? In *Judentum* he had implied it would not be, without specifying what else was needed. Questions upon questions which, if they simply referred to the nasty private hang-up of a fine composer, would hardly be worth putting. But Wagner the incorrigible self-publicist was bandying his undigested ideas about at a time of hitherto unparalleled Jewish emancipation and the backlash to it. By leaving the door wide open to interpretation he gave the most implacable of antisemites – then and later, in Bayreuth and beyond – scope to select what they wanted from his huge output and to use his prestige as an artist to bolster their cause. It is not enough to pass off Wagner's stance as irrelevant or even as something of a joke. It was deeply and dangerously ambivalent.

All of this can be discovered by anyone who really wants to do so thanks mainly to the evidence of Wagner's own writings and, latterly, of Cosima's diary. It is much harder to decide how far, if at all, Wagner's attitude to race and Jews penetrated his music dramas. Wildly diverging interpretations of *Parsifal* in particular show that best. Some believe Wagner's 'last card', as he called it, to be racist through and through, a paean to blood purity and exclusivity with Kundry the wandering temptress and Klingsor the castrated wizard as Jewish caricatures. Others see it as a masterpiece of compassion offering what Ernest Newman, the finest English-language biographer of Wagner, called one of the two or three most moving spiritual experiences of his life. After hearing *Parsifal* during his first visit to Bayreuth in 1883, the young Gustav Mahler – not yet converted from Judaism to Catholicism – evidently felt much the same. 'When I walked out of the Festspielhaus, incapable of uttering a word,' he wrote to a friend, 'I knew I had come to understand all that is greatest and most painful and that I would bear it within me, inviolate, for the rest of my life.'[15]

At least one widely touted myth can be disposed of rather easily, namely that Wagner created *Parsifal* under the baleful influence of Gobineau. This tale has gone on being told even after the publication of Cosima's diary in 1976 confirmed it as fiction. The diary shows that it was only in 1880 that Wagner first read a book by Gobineau (and then it was not the most famous one about racial inequality); before that he had met the count only fleetingly in Italy. On the other hand Wagner's letters show he was already pondering the *Parsifal* plot right back in the 1850s; he first drafted a libretto in 1865 and completed the final one in 1877. The music was composed between 1877 and January 1882. It is true that Gobineau stayed at Wahnfried for nearly a month in 1881, but Wagner did not rush back to his desk and revamp his work in the light of what his guest had to tell him about race. On the contrary, the two of them argued loud and long. Wagner found the count a fascinating companion but disagreed with his claim that the degeneration of the human race was unstoppable. As Cosima later recorded, 'He reproaches Gobineau for leaving out of account one thing that was given to mankind – a Saviour, who suffered for them and allowed himself to be crucified.'[16]

Naturally that chronology does not show Wagner never pondered matters of race at all before he met Gobineau. We know very well that he did, so it is not in principle impossible that race is at least part of what *Parsifal* may be 'about'. The questions really start when you try to pin down that 'about' in detail. Is Wagner warning of a Jewish threat to pure Aryan stock? Is he extolling Christian salvation, as so much of his talk in his last years about redemption and the blood of Christ would suggest? Is Buddhist and Schopenhauerian self-denial the key? Is *Parsifal* in some way all these things together: the essence of religion as Wagner saw it but of no specific faith? If so, what conclusion did he mean us to draw?

Part of the trouble is that while music can have the utmost power and depth it does not possess the precision available to words. Thanks to the sound of the cuckoo and the thunderclaps, we would know without being told that Beethoven's Sixth is a 'Pastoral' symphony. But would we connect his 'Eroica' with Bonaparte or even heroism if faced with the notes alone, without the title and some background history? Could there be such a thing as an antisemitic symphony? The questions here are not wholly fair because with Wagner we are dealing with music *and* words *and* stage action, a *Gesamtkunstwerk* no less. But that does not clarify things much, if at all. Not one of the characters in the music dramas is specifically identified as a Jew (with the partial exception of the Flying Dutchman) and no direct references to Jews are made. This seems odd since we are faced with dozens of hours of music drama of *almost* Shakespearian diversity. With Shylock, the grasping but proud moneylender in *The Merchant of Venice*, Shakespeare created one of the most famous and controversial of all stage Jews. Wagner did nothing comparable. The reason may simply be that he felt Jewish characters were not fit for inclusion in his music dramas, or indeed in any stage work of worth. He is on record as saying very much that, although he also claimed that Jews could not be really good actors and later changed his mind.

None of that proves there are no Jews in Wagner's work, only that *if* they are there they must be in disguise. But who might they be and what are we supposed to think of them? A popular suspect is Mime, the wheedling, double-crossing dwarf in the *Ring* who for his own nefarious aims brings up the young Siegfried. Mahler for one said he was sure Mime was meant to be a Jew but curiously added, 'I only know *one* Mime and that is *me*. You would be amazed what there is in that role . . .'[17] To which Wagner might have responded, 'You can't be Mime – because I am.' At least, Wagner began to describe Mime in detail in an early stage direction for *Siegfried* but gave it up because, according to the German writer and musician Theodor Adorno, he probably thought he was coming too close to portraying himself. That incident has naturally been used as ammunition by those who argue that Wagner feared he was indeed Jewish; but perhaps Adorno was over-interpreting and Wagner did not see a self-portrait, just a caricature of a Jew of precisely the sort that he wanted to keep out of his *Ring*. Then there is Beckmesser, the town clerk in *Die Meistersinger*, whose fussy manner and high-pitched voice are held by some scholars to be Jewish, just as his disagreeable ditties in Acts II and III are held to be like synagogue chant. But all these unpleasant elements can well be explained in other ways too.

It is easy to scorn the theory of disguised Jews in Wagner's work as the product of an over-fertile imagination; to claim that Mime is just a vile dwarf and Beckmesser an allegedly 'typical' town clerk. Since at least 1906, when a critic seriously claimed to find evidence in the music of *Götterdämmerung* that Brünnhilde was pregnant after her roll on the fire-encircled rock with Siegfried, Wagnerians have been reading things into the scores that common sense suggests are simply not there. Once in a while, though, it is worth at least suspending judgement, and that is the case here. Might not characters like Mime and Beckmesser be sending coded antisemitic signals that would have been more readily apparent to audiences in and around Wagner's time than in our own? One modern study in particular amasses enough evidence to suggest this could well be so.[18] But even if it were, that does not mean Wagner in his music dramas simply damns Jews and extols non-Jews. If Mime is a Jew so presumably is Alberich, who is invested by Wagner's music not only with nastiness but with tragic grandeur. Kundry is a character for whom one feels in sum more attraction and pity than abhorrence. And what of the supposed Aryans? Siegfried has one or two great moments, especially when he dies, but he is manifestly naive if not stupid. Wotan is a philanderer, liar and cheat. If Wagner intended to put over a clear racial message he did not do it very well. Perhaps when he got down to composing rather than theorising, the characters he created took on lives of their own. Or perhaps the music simply reflects Wagner's ambivalence on the whole question from the very start.

Where did it come from, Wagner's confusing intermingling of fierce hostility to Jews with respect and even friendship for them? There must have been more to this peculiarly personal mix than the impact of traditional, widespread antisemitism. So there was, but red herrings by the shoal complicate the search for it. Nietzsche produced one of the first and biggest of them when, consumed with the anti-Wagnerian fury of his late, post-Tribschen phase, he asked whether the composer was really German at all. Writing in a postscript to *Der Fall Wagner* (The Wagner Case) in 1888, Nietzsche claimed it was hard to discover any German characteristics in Wagner, mysteriously adding that '*Ein Geyer ist beinahe schon ein Adler*' (A vulture is almost an eagle). To those in the know this was a pun meant to shock. Ludwig Geyer was the name of Wagner's stepfather, whom Nietzsche reckoned was Wagner's real father. It is possible that Wagner thought so too, or at least did not rule it out, although when Cosima once faced him with the question he replied, apparently with no special display of emotion, 'I do not believe so.'[19] Anyway, to return to the pun, Adler was a common Jewish name. Ergo: Wagner, according to Nietzsche, was Jewish – or nearly.

Nietzsche produced no facts to back up his heavy hint and nor has anyone else since. On the contrary, records going back to the seventeenth century show the Geyers were Protestant church musicians. That has not stopped Nietzsche's pun gaining the force of an oracle, seemingly bolstered by bits and pieces of circumstantial 'evidence'. Take Wagner's birthplace, the Brühl area of Leipzig. This has often been described as 'the Jewish quarter' and it is true that it was a centre for Jewish merchants, especially when the regular Leipzig trade fairs were under way. But in 1813, when Wagner was born, fewer than a hundred Jews lived there, a minority of its population. Why did the Wagners set up their home in the Brühl? Probably because it was handy. Carl Friedrich Wagner, Richard's 'official' father, worked in an office nearby as a police actuary. Then there is Wagner's appearance; a smallish body with an oversized head and a prominent nose – attributes of 'Wagner the Jew baiter' satirical cartoonists during and after his day gleefully stressed. Add Wagner's hyperactivity, his love of learning, indeed his genius and you have plenty of familiar elements,

How a Leipzig Jew gradually became "Richard Wagner. This drawing published in the Viennese satirical magazine „Der Floh" (undated) was prompted by rumours that Wagner had a Jewish father. Although no firm evidence has ever emerged to back up these tales, they persist even to the present day.
(Taken from „Musik und Musiker in Karikatur und Satire" by Karl Storck, Oldenburg 1910)

positive and negative, of caricatures of Jews. That does not amount to proof that Wagner really was Jewish. Did Wagner nonetheless think he might be? If so, there is no record of it. Some argue that the very absence of evidence shows Wagner's shame was so deep that he never brought the matter up. With that puerile approach you can 'prove' anything.

A partial but more persuasive explanation for Wagner's anti-semitism is that, from early in his career, his profligacy put him in hock with moneylenders who were usually Jews. Already in Magdeburg where he courted Minna, he railed at having to deal with 'Jewish scum' because 'our people' offered no credit. In Paris he pawned his goods to Jews and did work he felt was menial for, among others, Maurice Schlesinger, a Jewish music publisher. Schlesinger's cash helped the Wagners ward off starvation but that made the struggling composer feel no better. Quite the opposite: he became ever more resentful and desperate. But none of that, surely, would have brought the eruption of *Judentum* without Meyerbeer, the opera king of Paris and Europe when Wagner was a mere serf.

Naturally Wagner envied Meyerbeer's phenomenal success with public and press alike. It would have been odd had he not done so. The first hundred performances of Meyerbeer's *Le Prophète* in Berlin alone netted the composer 750,000 marks, almost 200,000 marks more than the entire sum Wagner received over nearly two decades from King Ludwig. During 1850, when *Judentum* first appeared in Leipzig, the influential *Neue Berliner Musikzeitung* carried fulsome reports on Meyerbeer and his work in almost every issue: Wagner was mentioned in only six brief dispatches and *Lohengrin*, premiered by Liszt in Weimar in August, was variously spelled *Longrie* and *Lognin*. Even a composer with an ego far smaller and a skin much thicker than Wagner's might well have felt miffed. But there was more behind Wagner's fury than that. He had obsequiously begged Meyerbeer for help and he had gone down the Meyerbeerian opera road with *Rienzi* – even scored a local hit with it in Dresden. In short, his enmity was directed not least – perhaps mainly – at himself, not because he feared he was Jewish but because he felt he had debased himself before Jews. He even half admitted as much in a letter to Liszt. Describing Meyerbeer as 'infinitely repugnant' to him, Wagner remorsefully added that basically he had himself to blame for having 'wilfully allowed' himself to be taken in.[20]

For all its later notoriety as 'a classic antisemitic text of the nineteenth century', *Judentum* created only a short-lived stir among a limited public when it first appeared. The Leipzig *Neue Zeitschrift für Musik*, where Wagner placed the piece, was an insider publication with only some eight hundred subscribers and probably not more than two thousand readers. Although its editor, Franz Brendel, later claimed the article had caused a 'real storm' in the German press he was (unsurprisingly) exaggerating his own clout. There was indeed a set-to in Leipzig music circles and one or two shafts were hurled at 'Freigedank' from further afield. But the fuss soon died down – and once down it stayed dormant for years, not just because Wagner failed to launch another public onslaught but because the time was not ripe for one. Germany had entered that decade or more of deceptive lull that followed the failed uprisings of 1848–9. The political status quo seemed confirmed, the energy for new strife was either exhausted or channelled into revolutionising the economy, not the social order. Given this unreceptive national mood, the fierce piece of 1850 fluttered into a black hole.

Why then did Wagner suddenly publish a tougher version of *Judentum* as a pamphlet bearing his own name after a break of nineteen years? In a letter coinciding with the reissue to the young pianist Carl Tausig, yet another of his Jewish friends, Wagner explained that he had been incensed by the 'unheard of insolence of the Viennese press' after the *Meistersinger* premiere in Munich in June 1868.[21] By 'Viennese press' Wagner meant above all Hanslick, his former admirer turned stern critic. In fact Hanslick's report was not as vitriolic as Wagner's fierce reaction might suggest and as has often been claimed. It summed up *Meistersinger* as an 'interesting experiment' that, if taken as the rule, would spell the death of art; but it also called the piece a lot more stimulating than a dozen workaday operas by composers of far less talent. It is hard to read into this simply the personal vendetta Hanslick is widely said to have harboured because Wagner toyed for a while with calling the beastly Beckmesser in *Meistersinger* Hans-lick instead. What does emerge clearly from the report is Hanslick's conviction that Wagner was a genius who was taking music down the wrong road.

Furious though he was about the *Meistersinger* reaction in particular, Wagner's decision to republish was more deeply grounded. In that letter to Tausig he also mentioned a 'constant spinning of lies about me'. And in the introduction to the new *Judentum* text, he claimed that many baffled people had been asking him why all his 'artistic doings' were run down not only in Germany but abroad. The truth is that by this time Wagner had become convinced he was the victim of a far-flung Jewish conspiracy of which Hanslick (of Jewish descent on his mother's side) was only a part. This drive against him, he believed, had been sparked by the original *Judentum* article, had continued through the *Tannhäuser* scandal of 1861 in Meyerbeer-besotted Paris, and showed itself in widespread hostility or silence from the press towards his work. The fact that by 1869 his music was being more widely performed and that he had a growing band of allies, Jews among them, evidently did not impress him. Nor did the pretty muted public reaction to his 1850 text. For Wagner the very lack of a response from his foes, including Meyerbeer, revealed their cunning in deciding not to attack head-on but to undermine him bit by bit.

In his paranoia, Wagner even saw Jews as at least indirectly connected with his ejection from Munich in December 1865. A few months earlier he had sent King Ludwig a memorandum, harshly worded even by Wagner's standards, comparing the role of Jews to that of maggots attacking a dying body. Not that Jews alone were lambasted. In the document, which he published in modified form thirteen years later as the essay *Was ist deutsch?*, Wagner also hit out at various other 'J's' including Jesuits, Journalists, *Juristen* (lawyers) and *Junker* (Prussian landowners like Bismarck). But he plainly felt Jews presented the gravest danger, warning the king that action was needed to save the 'German spirit' from 'a shameful doom'. As usual Ludwig rejected his house composer's anti-semitism; indeed, the following year he visited a synagogue and pledged further backing for Jewish emancipation. In the meantime Wagner was forced to leave Munich and retreated to Switzerland. He had his own political interference as well as jealous courtiers to blame for that. But he surely linked his own fate to that broader danger to the 'German spirit' of which he had fruitlessly warned the king.

Seen in this context, the reissue of *Judentum* takes on an extra dimension. In 1850 Wagner was aiming largely at Meyerbeer while purporting to write a general piece about Jews and music; in 1869 he was mainly warning of the broader threat he felt Jews posed to Germany while claiming to defend himself against his critics. What had happened in the intervening period? Jews had continued to move bit by bit towards winning full civic rights, in addition to the private influence they already wielded, and in Wagner's view this spelled a danger of which not even Ludwig, let alone Bismarck, seemed aware. The Master finally decided it was up to him to sound the alarm. He must have felt still more justified when, months after his new text was published, Jews in the North German Confederation and later throughout Germany were formally granted full emancipation.To answer the question posed at the start of this chapter: it was a coincidence that Wagner's pamphlet and the act of emancipation emerged almost simultaneously. But the two developments were indeed linked and they had been brewing for years.

This time Wagner's tract did not drop into a void. In contrast to 1850 a storm really did blow up in the press, some performances of Wagner's works were hissed or postponed and attendance dropped off for a while. Jews were not the only ones incensed. But the setback was not permanent and in private Wagner was much praised for speaking out, especially by antisemites at the time too timid to do the same. That timidity evaporated over the next few years with the rise of national feeling that accompanied victory over France and the founding of the empire. Then came the 1873 stock market crash widely blamed, in the Habsburg empire as well as Germany, on the phantom of Jewish conspiracy. Whereas the anti-Meyerbeer Wagner of the 1850s had been largely ignored, the antisemitic Wagner of the 1870s and early 1880s found himself increasingly in the swim – although not quite in the mainstream. He still had all those Jewish friends, however much he terrorised many of them, and his increasingly baffling world outlook seemed to leave open a door to Jewish 'redemption'. Although the Master proved useful to the most rapacious antisemites, in part for his record and especially for his fame, he nonetheless brought furrows to their brows.

Antisemites had no need to worry about ambivalence on Cosima's part. Both her diary and many of her letters, written both before and long after Wagner's death, show her abhorrence of Jews to have been complete and obsessive. When there was anything to deplore, from supplies of rotten food for the army to a badly tuned instrument, as like as not Cosima found 'Israel' or 'Jewish revenge' behind it. She loathed Jewish faces and Jewish beards of which, to her particular irritation, she saw many among the public at performances of Wagner's works. At least she let the devoted Porges off relatively lightly, simply complaining in her diary that there was nothing obviously Jewish about the young conductor except that he 'can't listen quietly'. But for the most part, in contrast to the Master's bursts of impulse and self-contradiction, his wife's antisemitism was chillingly implacable.

On the face of it, Cosima's prejudice looks harder to explain than Wagner's. She was not forced to borrow from Jews when young, either through personal extravagance or early career struggles. Nor did she have grounds for the kind of envy Wagner felt for Meyerbeer. Might her antisemitism have been grounded in self-hatred because she feared she was of Jewish descent? This claim has often been made – even, by implication, in the documentation accompanying the exhibition *Wagner und die Juden* (Wagner and the Jews) organised by the Richard Wagner Museum at Wahnfried in 1985.[22] On examination this story turns out to be as ill-founded as the one about Wagner's alleged Jewish ancestry via Geyer. While it is true that Cosima's maternal grandmother was a daughter of the noted Bethmann banking family in Frankfurt, it is not correct to say, as many do, that this family was Jewish.[23] The mistake is easily made, partly because the name looks Jewish, partly because the rise of the Bethmanns as bankers coincided with that of the similarly influential Rothschilds, who were indeed

Jewish, in the same city. But there is no sign of Jewishness in the Bethmann genealogy, which can be traced right back to a certain Heinrich Bethmann living in Goslar near the Harz mountains in 1416. It is unclear where the Bethmanns came from and what they were doing before that, but even the most assiduous seeker after possible Jewish ancestry has to call a halt somewhere and the fifteenth century seems a fair place to stop.[24] Perhaps Cosima feared she might be Jewish all the same, despite the Bethmanns' provable lineage, but if so she seems never to have mentioned it. As with Wagner, the self-hatred case can thus be built only on the flimsy grounds of an absence of evidence supposedly caused by shame.

The root of Cosima's hatred of Jews most probably lay not in fears about her ancestry but in her intensely Catholic, authoritarian upbringing, followed by her marriage to the antisemitic von Bülow. The evidence is mixed on how far Cosima's usually absent father, Liszt, felt similar hostility. But there is no doubt that his mistress, Princess Carolyne, despised Jews and it was she who dispatched her old governess to Paris to look after Liszt's children for years in the illiberal spirit of the *ancien régime*. It may seem odd that Cosima imbibed her antisemitism in that very city where more than half a century earlier, revolution had, among other things, pioneered Jewish emancipation in Europe. But then time and again in nineteenth-century France the forces of liberalism were driven back by those – naturally including monarchists and the church – who despised the revolution and all its works, not least the boost it had given to the Jewish cause. Not every aristocrat was illiberal, as the example of Cosima's mother Marie d'Agoult well shows, nor was by any means every leftist a fan of the Jews. But broadly speaking conservative reaction fed antisemitism, and in her teens in particular, Cosima was in the thick of its influence. Her years under Madame Patersi's thumb in Paris coincided with the breakdown of the Second Republic and its replacement by the Second Empire under Napoleon III – initially at least, an era in which civil liberties and parliamentary power were sharply curtailed.

French soil still proved fertile for antisemitism, arguably more so, even after the birth of the insecure Third Republic in 1871. Monarchists sought for years to claw back their lost power, national humiliation over the defeat by Prussia ran deep, the economy was shaky and Jews as usual served as handy scapegoats, although there were even fewer of them than in Germany – about eighty thousand, or less than

0.2 per cent of the population. When finance scandals erupted in the 1880s and 1890s, notably over the collapse of a Catholic bank and of the Panama Canal Company, phantom Jewish conspirators were blamed – much as they had been in Germany for the 1873 stock-market crash. When it emerged in 1894 that military secrets had been betrayed to Germany it was an officer of Jewish descent, captain Alfred Dreyfus, who was arrested, convicted on trumped-up evidence and sentenced to life imprisonment on Devil's Island.

Although Dreyfus was finally cleared, '*L'affaire*' (so notorious that no more precise designation was needed) reverberated for decades in France and beyond. It helped persuade Theodor Herzl, who went to Paris to report on the Dreyfus trial, to found Zionism, on the grounds that antisemitism left Jews no course but to seek a homeland of their own. And it caused French nationalists like Charles Maurras, appalled by Dreyfus's 'treason' and still more by his pardon, to found *L'action française,* a proto-fascist movement that later backed the Vichy government during the Nazi occupation of France. All in all, an unbiased observer at the turn of the century might well have concluded that the future of the Jews looked less secure in France than in Germany. That the opposite proved true was due to two main factors. Although often under threat, republicanism *did* survive in France and antisemitism, though present, rarely enjoyed even implicit governmental approval. Moreover, when it next came to a major war in Europe, Germany lost it and the Weimar Republic that emerged from the debris turned out to be all but stillborn. Conditions were ideal for extremists, notably Hitler, and Jews as usual were handy scapegoats.

That is jumping on a lot, although Cosima lived to see much of it. Enough to stress here that her antisemitism was born in France, confirmed by her first marriage and intensified by her second. She shared all Wagner's paranoia about Jewish conspiracy and almost none of his fondness for individual Jews. After his death she even turned that paranoia to advantage, emphasising the specialness of Bayreuth as a temple of pure art and true German-ness under unrelenting siege. As high priestess, Cosima preserved the Wagnerian faith as she saw it, greeted pilgrims, blessed true believers and excommunicated all those who fell short. Her acolytes were many, but her most effective evangelist by far came from a wholly unexpected source, and she came to love him as her son – perhaps even more.

# 6

# The Spin Doctor

The man was a voracious reader. His now unused library in a sturdy villa at Number 1 Wahnfriedstrasse, one of Bayreuth's best addresses, is packed from floor to ceiling with more than twelve thousand volumes, many well thumbed. But from the evidence of the books alone you would find it hard to judge the owner's nationality, let alone his occupation. Here are complete editions of Goethe and Luther, there the collected works of Shakespeare and Sir Walter Scott along with shelf after shelf of Voltaire and Balzac, Hugo and Mérimée, Gautier and Maupassant – all in the original languages. A history of Sumerian art seems to have been consulted at least as often as the Tibetan Book of the Dead and a three-volume (German) survey of the Jews at the time of Christ.

Who was he, this man of many letters? Theologian, historian, literary critic? Something of all those things and much besides: philologist, botanist, photographer – even, as a hobby, an astronomer. When his work was done for the day he would often climb to a domed observatory on the roof and sit for hours behind his telescope. Retreating to survey the heavens and, with luck, forget the earth was a habit he adopted as a child after constant bullying at school. In those days, he pathetically confessed, stars were his only friends – apart from Jesus Christ. A lonely, timid intellectual, then? In a way, yes. He hated crowds and admitted he would often pass several times before the door of a cafe trying to raise the courage to enter, then retreat hungry. Yet he was a keen mountain hiker, made a hazardous trip with his first wife through the Balkans on horseback and somehow found time for a string of mistresses.

Above all, he became much the most influential propagandist for the racist, ultra-nationalist clique centred on Wahnfried after Wagner's death. The Kaiser and Hitler were among those who revered him. After his second marriage, this time to the Master's youngest daughter Eva in 1908, he held sway for years over the whole Wagner clan, to a greater degree than the domineering but aged and ailing Cosima, let alone the even-tempered Siegfried. Time was when a Bayreuth road proudly bore his name and that erstwhile residence of his sported a stone memorial plaque. But the road has been re-christened and the plaque removed. The ground floor of the villa now houses a museum devoted to Jean Paul, a once hugely popular novelist who lived in Bayreuth in the early nineteenth century. The upper floors, including the library and the now empty observatory, are in principle off limits. Curious visitors who nonetheless win entry may spot that dismantled plaque, evidently thought too shameful to show but too precious to pulverise, propped up in a corner. It is doubtful whether the name on it will ring a bell with them, or if it does it may be the wrong one, bringing a vague association with an ill-starred former British prime minister. For how many people nowadays know much, if anything, about Bayreuth's once-adopted son – the erudite but wildly misguided Houston Stewart Chamberlain?[1]

He was the youngest of a British admiral's three sons, born on 9 September 1855 in Southsea, a genteel adjunct to the naval dockyard city of Portsmouth on the south coast of England. With four of his uncles also in the armed forces, it seemed quite likely that young Houston would one day take the same road. One of his brothers, Harry, at first did so, following his father into the navy; the other, Basil, eventually became a professor of Japanese and philology at Tokyo University but seemed to stay fond of Britain from afar. Houston, by contrast, came to despise almost everything about the land of his birth; its military might, its empire, its commercialism and what he saw as its crass superficiality. The best thing that could happen to the British, Houston believed in later life, would be defeat by the Germans with their deeper and truer culture. When the opposite happened in 1918 his world fell apart.

One might put Houston's bitterness down to an unhappy, uprooted childhood; but his brothers, only a few years older, suffered much the same early strains and yet emerged, if not exactly smiling, at least more balanced. When the boys' mother died months after giving birth to Houston, the often-absent admiral put his offspring in the care of his own wealthy, widowed mother, Anne Chamberlain, who, supposedly for reasons of her health, lived in Versailles. This formidable old lady brought the boys up to believe that 'British is best' (climate excepted), but all three of them initially attended the local *lycée* and spoke French more fluently than English. Harry and Basil took to this schizophrenia better than Houston, who tended to be sickly and hated games. Worried that his youngest son in particular was losing contact with 'the old country', the admiral had Houston hauled back across the Channel at the age of eleven for further education. He meant well but the result was disastrous. At his first English school the child suffered physical and mental torment he never forgot; at his second he was simply lonely and homesick, although strictly speaking he had no real home to yearn for. When his health worsened, probably for psychological reasons, doctors diagnosed a breathing ailment and proposed treatment at a foreign spa. Accordingly, the youth was withdrawn from school and went abroad in 1870 accompanied by his devoted aunt Harriet, a near-substitute for his long-dead mother. He never returned to England again for long.

For much of the next decade or so Chamberlain drifted through agreeably clement continental spots like Montreux, Cannes and Florence, mainly at the expense of relatives worried that serious work might break his delicate health for good – a concern he seems to have done his best to foster. Torn between passion for the arts and an unexpected brilliance in natural science, Chamberlain finally enrolled at Geneva University, easily won a bachelor's degree in 1881 and began work for a doctorate in plant chemistry. His course finally seemed more or less clear – but not for long. He abruptly shelved further study and to the amazement of his friends joined a brokerage partnership in Paris. With France still reeling after post-war reparation payments to Germany and stock markets shaky throughout Europe, Chamberlain could hardly have chosen a worse time to go into business. The partnership foundered and it was thanks only to an injection of funds by the long-suffering aunt Harriet that Chamberlain was narrowly saved from ruin. Back in Switzerland he had a nervous breakdown. Unable to read for more than a few minutes at a time without getting a splitting headache, his future looked bleak indeed.

In fact, Chamberlain was at last on the way to finding his real métier. Throughout his years roaming Europe one emotion above all had proved strong and growing – a love of all things German. It had seized him on that very first trip with aunt Harriet that took them to the German spa of Bad Ems in the summer of 1870, just at the outbreak of the Franco-Prussian war. In principle he abhorred the armed services, no doubt fearing his father might yet force him into a military career. But in Bad Ems he was stirred by the bands and uniforms and spent hours watching soldiers leave for the front. That same year, when it was clear he would not soon be returning to England, Chamberlain was put in the hands of a Prussian tutor who fired his interest in Germany's language and culture. By 1874, when he went to winter on the French Riviera and there met Anna Horst, a Prussian woman ten years his senior, he had become a fervent Germanophile. Indeed it may have been Anna's nationality as much as anything more personal that first attracted him. His family opposed the liaison but Chamberlain persisted and in 1878 the two were married.

Anna has had a 'bad press' – on the rare occasions, that is, when she has been noticed at all. The daughter of a public prosecutor in Breslau, she was shy, rather plain and was often sniffed at by her husband's friends as 'second-rate' or 'the governess type'. Chamberlain managed to concoct his four-hundred-page memoirs, written a decade after he divorced Anna to marry Eva Wagner, without once mentioning her by name, although they had lived together for the best part of thirty years. Yet she shared many of his interests, especially botany, cleared up his affairs in Paris after his abortive sally into finance there, repeatedly nursed him through his mysterious illnesses and set up the several homes where he found the relative tranquillity to write his most (in)famous works. Her own little-known memoirs are neither sweeping in scope nor a model of style, but they wholly lack rancour – even over the divorce, in which Chamberlain (as other documents show) displayed a mean spirit and a tight fist.

What Anna did not share was her husband's passion for Wagner; or rather, while she was stirred by the music she shunned the quasi-religious dogma laid down from Wahnfried. So did Chamberlain at first. In later years he came to see his gradual transformation from mere Wagnerian to 'Bayreuthian' (a word he coined to identify one of the true faithful) as a Parsifal-like pilgrimage from simpleton to saviour. The very beginning of the odyssey seemed to him in retrospect to have been ordained by a higher power. Shortly after that stay in Bad Ems at the start of his continental travels, he had moved on with aunt Harriet to Switzerland and taken a boat trip on the Vierwaldstätter Lake.

Those around him pointed to the elegant villa Tribschen on a headland and chattered about the wild composer and his mistress who lived there 'in sin'. Chamberlain could not recall ever having heard of Wagner before, but the name stuck in his mind along with the splendid view and the intriguing gossip. The date was August 1870, just before his fifteenth birthday, and the very month in which Richard and Cosima finally married in nearby Lucerne.

Step by step Chamberlain began to move closer to the Wahnfried sanctum although it was nearly four decades before he joined the family. Still in Switzerland, he was pumped full of fascinating fact and fiction about Wagner by (ironically) a Jew from Vienna. He missed the *Ring* at the first Bayreuth festival in 1876 but caught up with it in Munich two years later, just after his marriage to Anna. Impressed by the sound and spectacle, he promptly joined the *Allgemeine Bayreuther Patronatsverein* (Bayreuth Patrons' Society) and submitted an essay to its house journal, *Bayreuther Blätter*. The piece was rejected by the editor, Baron Hans Paul von Wolzogen, a Prussian aristocrat, who went on to maintain in an article of his own that only Germans could really get to the bottom of Wagner. And indeed Chamberlain still held a view anathema to Wahnfried; that the world of art was one thing, the more precise realm of ideas quite another. He even (cogently) argued that, if put to the test, the *Ring* could be held to justify wholly opposite philosophies of life and death. No wonder the ultra-orthodox Wolzogen felt impelled to make a 'Germans are deeper' response, although he had to phrase it carefully to avoid offending wealthy foreigners who might help boost Bayreuth's flagging finances.

Two things above all caused Chamberlain to change his mind. One was his first visit to Bayreuth with Anna in 1882. They attended six performances of *Parsifal* and Houston, at any rate, was bowled over. He spotted Wagner in the distance but was too shy to approach him and (despite repeated claims to the contrary ever since) there is no evidence that they ever met or corresponded. Nonetheless, after *Parsifal* Chamberlain began to talk about Bayreuth as the only source of true culture and agreed there really was a link between music drama, philosophy and religion after all. During his ill-fated spell juggling finance in Paris, he even became representative there of the Patrons' Society and won new recruits for Wagnerism – quite a feat little more than a decade after the French humiliation in the war with Prussia. In Bayreuth Chamberlain had found a cause and, although he did not yet know it, a future home.

The second revelation on the long road to Wahnfried came not in Bayreuth but in Dresden, stamping ground of that younger, revolutionary Wagner whom most conservative followers of the Master were now doing their best to forget. Chamberlain had moved to the Saxon capital after his post-Paris breakdown and there, nursed by Anna and still backed by family funds, he recovered enough to read widely and to write articles – including his first ones in German. One such article, about the tricky relationship between Wagner and his father-in-law Liszt, caught Cosima's eye and won her gratitude. Liszt had died in Bayreuth in 1886 at the age of seventy-four amid charges from his fans that Cosima had paid more attention to running the festival than to tending her father, who had expired in a house just across the street from Wahnfried after contracting pneumonia. The charges were far from groundless. Cosima's treatment of Liszt had latterly become increasingly cold, if not callous, as though she were belatedly paying him back for her unhappy childhood. But Chamberlain claimed that the Master, and by implication Cosima, had always given Liszt the honour he was due, both as a composer and as one of the firmest backers of the festival from the start. No wonder the Mistress of Bayreuth asked to meet the author of this accolade when she visited Dresden in 1888. They hit it off right away – the intense but soft-spoken Englishman and the widow of French-Hungarian birth, both self-exiled in Wagner-land. Chamberlain thought he found in Cosima the embodiment of all that he had come to revere in the Master and she believed him to be 'an aristocrat through and through in the finest sense of the word'.[2] Later she claimed Chamberlain had English courage and tenacity that, combined with German spirit, could guarantee society what she regarded as a civilised future.

There was more to this relationship than deep, largely misplaced, admiration. Naturally Cosima was always on the lookout for 'suitable young men' for her unmarried daughters, and when she thought she had found one she used all her guile to try to haul him in. Her letters to the up-and-coming Richard Strauss, for example, were notably affectionate until he, scenting her net closing around him, bolted for (relative) freedom and married the shrewish Pauline de Ahna. But from the first Cosima's contacts with Chamberlain were on another level, as though she saw in him not so much a potential match for a daughter as a soulmate for herself. Marriage was, of course, out of the question, not just because Chamberlain had a wife already (not an insuperable obstacle) nor because Cosima was eighteen years his senior. More to the point, by remaining simply Wagner's widow Cosima retained a mystique she would largely have lost by becoming someone else's wife. Still, every year she and Chamberlain solemnly recalled the day they first met and scores of their surviving letters to one another (many were destroyed) are intimate in tone. With her eyesight failing Cosima had to dictate her correspondence, including *billets doux*, to her daughter/secretary Eva, who in turn read her Chamberlain's responses, which were always handwritten although most of his other letters were typed. Evidently Eva began to identify with the sentiments her mother expressed and to feel herself the main object of the eloquent replies. At any rate, over the years she slipped out of her role as a mere go-between and began to correspond with Chamberlain directly and often. That helped bring them closer and they finally married, but it is hard to avoid feeling that, for Chamberlain, the daughter remained to the end something of a proxy for the mother. Cosima seems to have thought so too. 'Greet Houston for me,' she told Eva years after the wedding. 'I don't even need to see him. We are always together.'[3]

That first meeting between Chamberlain and Cosima came at a key moment for both of them. Five years after Wagner's death, the festival was an artistic success and the circumspect von Gross was tending the still shaky business side. What Wahnfried lacked was an effective publicist for its regeneration ideology; an intellectual who combined devotion to the Master's works, and to his widow, with a persuasive tongue and a fluent pen. Nietzsche had once been seen by Wagner as a suitable evangelist, as well as a likely tutor for his son, but the former pilgrim of Tribschen days had long since deserted the faith. A brilliant young philosopher, Heinrich von Stein, might have filled the gap and did, indeed, become Siegfried's tutor at Wahnfried – but he died in 1887. Heinrich (Henry) Thode, a Dresden-born art historian of broad learning, seemed another possibility. In 1886 he had married Daniela, the eldest daughter of Cosima and von Bülow, who had for years sadly served as messenger between her divorced parents. But although Thode proved useful to Cosima on several occasions, he finally disappointed her as a Wahnfried propagandist and (still more) the luckless Daniela as a husband.

That left Wahnfried with Wolzogen and his *Bayreuther Blätter* as the principal means of spreading the word. If the utmost devotion and diligence had been enough, Cosima could have rested easy. Born in Potsdam in 1848 and grandson of the great Prussian architect Karl Friedrich Schinkel, Wolzogen had been drawn so strongly as a young man both to religion and to Wagner that the two became for him indivisible. On his honeymoon in 1872, he visited Bayreuth and stood in silent homage before the huge hole in the ground which, at that stage, was all that could be seen of the festival theatre. Five years later when Wagner finally decided to go ahead with his long-mooted scheme to found a journal, it was Wolzogen who got the editor's job. He lacked the intellect and literary style of a Stein, let alone of a Nietzsche, but even Cosima expressed awe at his utter dedication to Wahnfried's cause. For the next six decades Wolzogen popped up in one family photo after another, his walrus moustache growing whiter, his gaze usually fixed beyond the camera as though towards some Wagnerian utopia just over the rainbow. Imperial Germany collapsed, the Weimar Republic came and went, the Nazis moved in, but Wolzogen ground on with his beloved *Blätter* from the first issue in 1878 to the last in 1938. All in all he wrote more than four hundred usually muddled and bombastic articles himself, and edited some twenty thousand pages of text, in which ultra-conservatism and racism went hand in hand with the worship of German art – especially, of course, Wagner's.

During its first five years, while the Master was still alive, the *Blätter* largely lacked political content. That was no surprise. Wagner had long since concluded that it was up to art, not politics, to transform society – a conviction bolstered by the lack of support he had received from 'Berlin', above all in the person of Bismarck. Besides, at the start only members of the Patrons' Society received the journal and they looked to it mainly for monthly news about the Master and the future of the festival. It is not clear how often they read the *Blätter*'s accompanying pieces on philosophy and aesthetics, although they surely did mull over the perplexing 'regeneration' essays on art, religion, race and the Jews that were published there by Wagner himself. Cosima's diaries show her husband felt the journal often fell short of his ideal and that he even toyed with shutting it down, although he never got round to doing so.

After the Master's death, the *Blätter* subtitled itself *Deutsche Zeitschrift im Geiste Richard Wagners* (German Journal in the Spirit of Richard Wagner) but it soon began to carry content its founder would have deplored. Backing was urged not just for Bernhard Foerster's Paraguayan Neu Germania project that Wagner had spurned but also, indirectly at first, for the political right. Racism in general and antisemitism in particular featured ever more often although rabble-rousing prose, felt inappropriate to the 'Bayreuth idea', was usually avoided. Foerster himself contributed a dozen articles until his suicide in 1889; Ludwig Schemann, founder of the German Gobineau Society, produced forty-eight; Karl Grunsky, a Jew-hating musicologist who became an early favourite of the Nazis, wrote more than two hundred – many of them favourable reviews of other antisemitic material. Depressingly for Wahnfried, though, circulation was small. After briefly reaching a peak of more than 1,700 copies per issue during Wagner's lifetime, it sank to around five hundred and stayed there. The *Blätter*'s influence was surely greater than that modest figure would seem to imply. The core of devoted subscribers came above all from the wealthy, educated bourgeoisie – academics, writers, lawyers and other professionals well placed to pass on the gospel to their peers. Even so, the journal's 'regeneration' aim far outstripped its reach.[4] Flanking support was badly needed from a 'true believer' with bestseller flair and Chamberlain, *mirabile dictu*, floated in to over-fill the bill.

Nothing illustrates Chamberlain's special talents and his value to Wahnfried better than the turbulent 'Praeger affair'. Ferdinand Praeger was a German musician and writer who had settled in England and who had often met Wagner during his London stay in the winter of 1854–5, and on other occasions. The two of them had even trotted off together to the Adelphi Theatre in the Strand to see a Christmas pantomime pot-pourri of *Mother Goose*, *Little Red Riding Hood* and *Cinderella* that Wagner called 'in every respect excellently mounted and played' – praise he rarely bestowed on performances of weightier fare, including his own. Armed with much personal anecdote, Praeger completed a lively but in part inaccurate book called *Wagner As I Knew Him* shortly before he died in 1891. It was published in English and German the following year and at once sent the Wahnfried circle into fits of fury. Praeger had not just failed to pass over the Master's less majestic foibles, such as his 'childish, petty fits of anger' and his dyspepsia-generating habit of gobbling his food. Far worse, the author noted that Wagner had mistreated Minna and that he had played a highly active role in the 1849 revolution, both accusations that ran directly counter to the revised, official, Wahnfried version of the Master's life.

Chamberlain launched two attacks on Praeger's book, the second of which proved deadly, in Germany at least. In a first article issued in July 1893, he drew attention to discrepancies between the English and German editions and noted that some of the letters allegedly by Wagner that Praeger had quoted were not written in the composer's usual style. By dwelling on details Chamberlain managed to cast doubt on the book as a whole, a familiar critical device of which he was a master. Still, he had no proof. Accordingly he made one of his rare visits to England and, thanks to help from influential members of his family, managed to worm his way into the country home of Lord Dysart, a Wagnerian who possessed most of the Master's original letters to Praeger. Working mainly overnight, when the rest of the household was asleep, Chamberlain made copies of Wagner's texts, bore them away in triumph and published a second article in early 1894 documenting where Praeger's version differed from the originals.

Chamberlain had long since made his peace with Wolzogen, who had refused his first essay on the *Ring* well over a decade before, and both the Praeger articles were first published in the *Blätter*. But unlike most of the journal's pieces they reached a broad public, partly because Chamberlain could write persuasively without pomposity, partly because he turned out to be an effective string-puller. For all his seeming diffidence he made useful contacts easily and kept them – in Geneva, Paris, Dresden and later Vienna. Even in the England he deplored he initially worked closely on the Praeger affair with William Ashton Ellis, a writer with much influence among Wagnerians despite his cumbersome translations (still, sad to say, widely used) of the Master's already opaque prose. In France he drummed up backing from the small but fervent band of the faithful he had nurtured through the Patrons' Society. In Germany it was not just ultra-nationalist and antisemitic circles that rallied to his support. Even balanced journals like the *Hamburger Nachrichten* carried commentaries praising Chamberlain for his energy in uncovering the 'real facts' and the persuasive way he had argued his case.

As a result of the hullabaloo Praeger's book was swiftly withdrawn from the German market, to the special delight of Cosima who felt handsomely confirmed in her immediate belief that Chamberlain was a godsend. Sadly for the Bayreuthians, though, the book survived and thrived in England. The juicy scandal over it, with Lord Dysart hitting back at Chamberlain's 'underhand' tactics, served to spark interest among people whose eyes might otherwise have glazed at the mention of Wagner. Most critics and readers alike concluded that however correct Chamberlain might be on this point or that, much in Praeger's account about the Master's excesses in life and love 'rang true'. British Wagnerites fumed, of course. Typical was the reaction of the writer George Ainslie Hight who, after confessing he had never read the book, charged that 'more than any other single work' it had been responsible for disseminating false views about Wagner. 'Sensuality, that is in the morbidly sexual sense of the term, was no part of Wagner's character,' opined Hight with the blinkers of the true disciple.[5]

Although the Praeger affair caused a special stir in Wagnerian circles and even beyond, it was only one bitter skirmish in the campaign of revisionism and distortion being run from the Wahnfried headquarters. The key aim, as Cosima and her loyal troops saw it, was to 'cleanse' Wagner's life of all elements that might be 'misunderstood' and therefore harm the 'regeneration' faith being proclaimed from the 'fortress on the hill'. This was a huge task although the Master himself had made a firm start on it with his (naturally) biased autobiography. Still, in Cosima's view even the latter's manuscript needed a spot of cleansing and she had stretches of it (including the one mentioned in chapter three detailing the start of her affair with Wagner) cut or revamped before the first publication in 1911.

Impossible though it was to get rid of all correspondence that in her view could compromise Wagner or herself, Cosima did her dogged best. All the letters she had received from Nietzsche went into her incinerator. So did those to Wagner from Peter Cornelius, one of the Master's more forthright comrades in arms, several from von Bülow and all those from Mathilde Wesendonck that Cosima could lay her hands on. She had, in fact, begun a drive many years earlier to bring as much evidence as possible of the Wagner–Mathilde link under her control. Back in the early days of her affair with Wagner in Munich, Cosima had written to demand from Mathilde the return of the Master's literary manuscripts that she still possessed (quite a lot of them, many with fond dedication), on the grounds that King Ludwig wanted them for publication. Mathilde had sent a reply as prompt as it was piquant direct to a dumbfounded and, for once, embarrassed Wagner. She was sure he knew of the request, she wrote, and was glad to learn he was well and surrounded by those dear to him. *Touché.*

Cosima's example in destroying or suppressing material was followed by other members of the family. Eva, for instance, later burned most of Wagner's letters to her mother and blacked out or pasted over parts of his early diary known as the 'Brown Book'. But in Wahnfried's orgy of obfuscation it was Chamberlain who emerged as the leading spin doctor. Not for him mere suppression of evidence, although he did plenty of that too; the past had to be creatively reshaped to meet the perceived needs of the present. He cut his teeth with that favourable gloss on Liszt and the Wagners that had first impressed Cosima; he produced a stream of articles arguing fluently but implausibly that the festival was being carried on exactly as its founder would have wished; and he wrote a book claiming, still more implausibly, that the Master's music dramas all stemmed from an unchanged philosophy of life.

Chamberlain's biggest contribution to the creation of a new, squeaky-clean Wagner came in 1895 when he published his 'short' biography of the composer[6] – a mere 526 pages compared with the six-volume colossus later laboriously erected by Carl Friedrich Glasenapp, the Master's official biographer.[7] Even Cosima admitted that Glasenapp's opus was tough going and praised Chamberlain for devising something 'appropriate' with more popular appeal. This he did by producing what he called in the introduction a 'sketch' unsullied by an excess of facts that would cloud the 'real' Wagner and his spiritual world. In practice this meant tricky questions like the Master's paternity were largely ignored; that his role as a political (as opposed to an artistic) revolutionary was denied and that his excesses, monetary and otherwise, were portrayed as the inventions of a hostile press. According to the author, Cosima's adultery (not, of course, specified as such) had been inspired by a 'higher calling', Minna had played only a very modest role in Wagner's life and Mathilde Wesendonck next to none. As usual, Chamberlain's near-chatty style made for a smooth read and the book sold well – but another work, far greater in scope, was already welling up in him and it was to make his name far beyond Germany.

Chamberlain once vowed that 'if it was of any use to Bayreuth, I would without hesitation let myself be roasted on a slow fire.'[8] Fortunately he made the pledge to the good-humoured Siegfried, not to

Cosima, who might just have taken him up on it. But despite his undoubted devotion to Wahnfried, Chamberlain kept astonishingly much on his mind beyond Wagner. In 1889, only a year after that first meeting with Cosima, he and Anna abandoned Dresden and set up house in Vienna. In his memoirs Chamberlain says he made the move not just because the Habsburg capital was blessed with much culture (true) and better weather (arguable), but also because it was the home of Julius Wiesner, a professor of botany whose work had intrigued him while he was studying in Geneva. The latter argument is not as spurious as it may seem. Chamberlain was now well into his thirties and uncomfortably aware, as his letters show, that he was still much dependent on the largesse of relatives and one or two rich admirers. He thus seems to have reluctantly concluded that it was time to make another stab at qualifying himself and earning a living. Accordingly he enrolled at Vienna University and took up work again for a doctorate, probing what caused the movement of sap in plants. He failed to finish his studies, typically casting his net ever wider so that what began as a limited investigation became a quasi-philosophical hunt for the essence of life itself; but doctorate or not, the city with its sweet-sour charm would not let him go. Chamberlain finally stayed there for all of two decades, usually in the closest touch with Bayreuth and often visiting the festival, but gradually winning an intellectual independence all but unknown in Wahnfried's inner circle.

It is easy to see why Chamberlain loved Vienna. His spacious apartment was only a few minutes walk from the wide, tree-lined Ringstrasse, encircling much of the city centre and built by special command of Emperor Franz Joseph a few decades before to match the boulevards of Paris. The Court Opera, the grandest building on the Ring, offered fine performances that reached stellar heights after the fiercely uncompromising Gustav Mahler became director in 1897. Theatres, museums and libraries equalled any in the German-speaking world and the ubiquitous coffee houses offered an ideal combination of club and second home for rich and poor alike. Besides, as Chamberlain gleefully noted to a French friend, the city abounded in pretty women of easy morals. Despite his long-standing ailments and intense intellectual pursuits (not to mention his marriage), Chamberlain had found time to philander even before his arrival in Vienna. Once there he became involved in new affairs, including a lengthy one with an actress called Lili Petri whom some of his friends thought he might one day marry. But in the end it was the attraction of belonging to the Wagner clan that Chamberlain found irresistible.

What Chamberlain most loathed about Vienna is plain too: its Jews. Hitherto his antisemitic comments had been intermittent and, despite the influence of Bayreuth, usually marked more by disdain than hatred. In Dresden he had actually claimed to feel real sympathy for Jews after hearing brutish charges made against them there at a tub-thumping rally. But he soon began to change his tune in fast-growing Vienna, focus of the social and political unrest seething throughout the multinational empire. Jews were more visible there than in most German cities, thanks to the often poverty-stricken *Ostjuden* with their distinctive dress and habits who (to the embarrassment of many already-established brethren) streamed in from the east to find work. Moreover, although they made up less than a tenth of the population of greater Vienna, Jews already accounted for nearly a third of the students at the university and, in some faculties like medicine, almost a half. They were prominent in music even before Mahler took over at the Opera and highly active in the press and publishing. To the hypersensitive, intellectual newcomer from Dresden, the Jewish influence that had seemed an irritation started to loom as a threat.

At first Chamberlain's growing hostility was directed largely at Jews, not at other groups from all over the empire that helped people Vienna. He even said he was elated to live amid such a colourful mix of Magyars, Poles, Czechs, Slovaks, Slovenes and the rest. But that feeling gradually changed too. During his long trip on horseback with Anna through the Balkans in 1891, Chamberlain began to be obsessed with race – comparing what he regarded as degenerate Slavs with pure, fair-haired Serbs. He also joined the *Neuer Wagner-Verein* (New Wagner Society), a group that had broken away from Vienna's main Wagner association and which, unlike the parent body, flirted with nationalist politics – even with proto-fascists like Georg von Schönerer, leader of the (Austrian) empire's pan-Germans. Chamberlain despised Schönerer and had become involved with the 'new' society mainly because the old one had increasingly criticised Cosima's imperious rule in Bayreuth. But the more he came into contact with nationalist circles and observed the Jews and Slavs around him, the more he began to see history in terms of racial conflict – with the Germans the highest strain, but gravely endangered. When his Munich publisher Hugo Bruckmann, delighted with the success of *Richard Wagner*, urged him to turn his hand to a new work of greater scope, Chamberlain was only too happy to commit his analysis to paper – at length.

What emerged was a preposterous but seductively well-written racist view of civilisation across the centuries, published in 1899 in two volumes totalling more than 1,100 pages and called *Die Grundlagen des 19en Jahrhunderts* (The Foundations of the Nineteenth Century). Chamberlain had originally planned this hotchpotch of fact and fiction about religion and philosophy, science and the arts as only the first of three parts, but happily he never got round to the other two. He might well have done so since he dashed off *Die Grundlagen* in less than two years, shutting himself away in his study for days on end and preceding each new session at his desk with a prayer to God for guidance. It was during this period that his marriage, shaky ever since the Dresden days, began to slide irretrievably towards breakdown, although the final split did not come until 1905. Unable (at any rate unbidden) to share in his work, merely tolerated by his passionately Wagnerian friends and probably aware of his dallying with other women, Anna began to have the kind of nervous disorders that her husband had so often suffered. Chamberlain agonised between a sense of duty to look after his wife, as she had him, and a yearning to be free of her at last – a dilemma he hinted at by letter to Cosima and hence, inevitably, to Eva. The Mistress of Bayreuth left no doubt where she stood. 'In my view, men are not born to nurse,' she replied, backing her words with a reference to Schopenhauer. 'That is woman's work.'[9]

The main contention of *Die Grundlagen* is that there is no such thing as 'humanity', only races of different backgrounds, physiognomy and ability. All that is best and noblest stems from Aryans, whom Chamberlain from time to time also confusingly labels as Indo-Europeans, Nordic peoples, Teutons and Germans. Everything that is most harmful originates with Semites, although the author hits out at all sorts of targets ranging from Africans to Jesuits, from Peruvians to Napoleon, as well as at those he pinpoints as Jews. History, according to Chamberlain, is comprehensible only as a titanic struggle between these two main forces. Greece and Rome, the sources of true art and law, had gone down to racial degeneration and in the chaos that followed Jews had further spread their evil influence. If there was any hope for civilisation, and Chamberlain evidently thought there was, then it had to be pinned on Aryans (i.e. Germans and the like) emerging supreme at last.

One of the countless drawbacks to this breathtakingly, to many readers irresistibly simple thesis involved the British. In principle Chamberlain's countrymen were Aryans too, yet he found them despicably shallow and commercial – more or less Semitic, in fact. He never really resolved this issue beyond hoping that repeated doses of Germanic culture would drive out the non-Aryan infection to which the British had somehow fallen prey. A much bigger problem was posed by Jesus Christ. Chamberlain had worshipped Christ since childhood (his 'only friend' at school) and stressed in *Die Grundlagen* that he regarded Christ's birth as the greatest event in history. Yet Christ was generally held to be a Jew. Chamberlain therefore concluded that the general view must be wrong and devoted much space to arguing that Christ was really Aryan, coming as he did from Galilee where, unlike Judaea, Jews were relatively rare. His main point, though, was that since Christ was goodness itself and Jews were intrinsically bad, then Christ could not possibly have been Jewish. Thanks to similarly ludicrous logic Chamberlain also managed to 'prove' that the great figures of the Italian Renaissance were Aryan. In view of their genius, there was nothing else they *could* be.

This, then, was the book that quickly became a bestseller such as other Bayreuth scribes could only dream of (and that naturally delighted Bruckmann, who became one of Hitler's first wealthy backers in the 1920s and later published much Nazi-oriented material). Some hundred thousand copies of the German version alone were sold in ten editions before the First World War and translations soon emerged in English, French and Czech. All but unknown a decade earlier, Chamberlain suddenly emerged as a celebrity guru whose racist bible people with intellectual pretensions needed to have a view about, even if they had not actually ploughed through it. One person who not only ploughed through it but reread it so often that he could quote long passages verbatim was Kaiser Wilhelm II, who swiftly became Chamberlain's most highly placed fan. Not content with extolling *Die Grundlagen* to government members and pressing free copies into the hands of influential visitors, Wilhelm summoned the delighted author to his country seat and lined up the whole household, including servants with blazing brands, to greet him at the door. 'It was God who sent the German people your book and you personally to me,' he told Chamberlain in a long letter written on New Year's Eve 1901. Recalling how inadequate he had felt his education to be for the mission facing him in the new Reich, the Kaiser went on, 'Then you come and with one magic stroke you bring order into confusion, light into the darkness; [you reveal] aims to be striven and worked for; an explanation for what was dimly sensed; paths that should be followed for the salvation of the Germans and hence of mankind.'[10]

This letter, signed 'Your true thankful friend,' was only one of a series between Wilhelm and Chamberlain that spanned more than two decades, lasting until well after the Kaiser went into Dutch exile in 1918. In their often ecstatic tone the exchanges recall those between Wagner and King Ludwig and, as with that correspondence, it is often hard to tell when the participants are being serious. In the case of the Kaiser that was never easy anyway. Vain and unstable, much given to phrase-mongering by turns drastic and flowery, he tended to treat the world as a stage on which he could strut in his favourite costume, a military uniform, against his preferred backdrop, a parade ground. The ruthless but rarely reckless Bismarck rightly called him a balloon that needed to be held on its string or it could drift just anywhere. But after the young Wilhelm, newly crowned, dismissed the long-serving chancellor in a show of muscle in 1890, no one adequate was available to keep that string tight. As a grandson of Queen Victoria, whose daughter – also called Victoria – had married Crown Prince Frederick of Prussia, Wilhelm was fascinated by England and obsessed by its armed forces. One of his proudest moments came when he personally commanded more than a thousand German marines, goose-stepping past his grandmother at a parade on the Isle of Wight – just a short boat trip, as it happens, from Chamberlain's birthplace of Southsea. Was there any good reason why a united Germany, increasingly predominant economically, should not have military might and colonies to match Britain's? Wilhelm thought not and, as a first step, gave orders to build a battle fleet that would be at least the equal of the Royal Navy. Chamberlain had little interest in military hardware but his hopes for his adopted country were no less ambitious. 'Germany can achieve complete control of the world,' he wrote to the Kaiser in 1902, 'partly by direct political means, partly by indirect methods of language and culture, only if it succeeds in taking a new direction, which means bringing the nation to a final break with the Anglo-American ideals of government.'[11]

Like *Der Untergang des Abendlandes* (The Decline of the West), Oswald Spengler's dismal hit after the First World War, *Die Grundla-*

*gen* caught a national mood and fostered it with a vast display of pseudo-erudition. But whereas Spengler spoke to a desolate, defeated nation, Chamberlain addressed a boisterously unstable one – flattered to be told with such conviction, moreover by an Englishman, that the future of civilisation lay largely in German hands. Common to both audiences, though, was a widespread loathing of those comparatively new German citizens, the Jews. Not that this animus was much evident in parliament itself at the time Chamberlain was writing. Antisemitism was shunned by the Social Democrats, who were going from strength to strength as rampant industrialisation bolstered their working-class clientele; and new parties with a specifically antisemitic agenda, often badly organised and internally divided, had little success at the polls. But none of that meant envy and hatred of Jews were evaporating, simply that they were coursing mainly through extra-parliamentary channels. Antisemitism was, for example, part of the *raison d'être* of a plethora of newly founded nationalist pressure groups. These included the *Flottenverein* (Naval League), set up to back the Kaiser's aim to rule the waves, which eventually numbered around a million members; the *Bund Der Landwirte* (Agrarian League), hostile to free trade and especially influential in the Conservative Party; and the *Alldeutscher Verband* (Pan-German Association), born in chauvinistic rage over the 1890 deal with Britain, under which Germany swapped its claims to Zanzibar for control of the North Sea island of Helgoland.

With *Die Grundlagen*, Chamberlain made this dangerous brew of nationalism and antisemitism seem palatable – especially to a middle class that felt proud of Germany and hostile to Jews but that, on the whole, abhorred extremists and rabble-rousers. The intellectual ground had been prepared by publications like the *Bayreuther Blätter* and by influential writers such as Paul de Lagarde, a biblical scholar obsessed by the danger he felt Jews posed to German unity and European peace. But it was Chamberlain who most caught the public imagination with his seeming mastery of many fields and his ability to draw a clear racial message from a bewildering mass of material. Many genuine experts rightly saw this feted all-rounder as an inspired dabbler with easily challengeable logic; but even they could not gainsay the effortless style, the beguiling sweet reasonableness, with which he made his nonsense palatable to a wide audience. In *Die Grundlagen* Chamberlain often seems to criticise the Jews more in sorrow than anger, actually deploring in the introduction a 'perfectly ridiculous and revolting tendency to make Jews the general scapegoat for all the vices of our time'.[12] Yet later he refers to Jewish existence as 'a crime against the holy laws of life' and rounds off the first volume with a warning that where the struggle with Jews 'is not conducted with cannon balls, it takes place noiselessly in the heart of society . . . More than others, precisely this silent struggle is a struggle of life and death.'[13] Did the author fail to notice a certain lack of consistency in his approach? Indeed he did not. When Cosima objected to one or two favourable references to Jews in *Die Grundlagen*, Chamberlain boasted that he had inserted them to make his negative comments seem more credible.

It may seem strange that a work so attractive to Wilhelminian Germans should also prove popular with the French (hardly pure Aryans), the British (vilified as conceited mongrels) and even the Americans (given short shrift). But in all three countries Chamberlain was widely praised for his learning and the clarity of his writing, even in translation. His stance on the Jews excited relatively little reproof, further evidence that antisemitism was far from being confined to the German-speaking world alone. In France, wracked by the Dreyfus affair, *Die Grundlagen* fell on especially fertile soil. In Britain, the book's success owed much to the efforts of the first Lord Redesdale, grandfather of the Mitford sisters – two of whom, Unity and Diana, became notoriously close to Hitler in the 1930s. It was Redesdale who revamped the initially poor translation of *Die Grundlagen*, wrote a fulsome introduction and pressed it on influential friends. Like *The Times Literary Supplement*, which called *The Foundations* 'one of the rare books that really matter', the noble lord did in fact chide Chamberlain for his antisemitism while implicitly admitting that he felt the author had a point.

In America the former President Theodore Roosevelt took a similar line in a long review. Although critical of Chamberlain's 'foolish hatreds' against Jews among others, Roosevelt concluded: 'Yet, after all is said, a man who can write such a really beautiful and solemn appreciation of true Christianity . . . a man, in short, who has produced in this one book materials for half a dozen excellent books on such diverse subjects, represents an influence to be reckoned with and seriously to be taken into account.'[14] It was, however, the Nazis who took the author most 'seriously into account', especially their pernicious ideologist Alfred Rosenberg, who paid implicit homage to Chamberlain in the title as well as the content of his main racist work *Der Mythus des 20. Jahrhunderts* (The Myth of the Twentieth Century), published in 1930.

Ironically, one person who did not join in the jubilation over *Die Grundlagen* was Cosima. In principle Wagnerians everywhere and at Wahnfried in particular should have been able to bask in the reflected glory of so noted a Bayreuthian. Indeed, much in the book might have been written by the Master himself; the call to preserve an 'essence of religion' that had been lost to the church; the homage paid to Christ while questioning his Jewishness; the antisemitism that one moment seemed to offer the hand of friendship and the next brandished a clenched fist. But for Cosima that was just the trouble. She felt Chamberlain had taken over many of Wagner's ideas without making adequate acknowledgement. Nor were Wagner and the 'fortress on the hill' given what she regarded as their proper place at the pinnacle of Aryan civilisation – even allowing for the fact that *Die Grundlagen* was meant to be only the preface, as it were, to a much longer work in which this 'failing' could be made good.

This was not the first occasion on which Cosima and her usually adored 'Houston' had found themselves at odds. In Vienna, Chamberlain had given a lecture claiming that Wagner, although an unmatched artist, had never fully understood the philosophers he most extolled. Cosima was not amused. Chamberlain had also constantly pressed her to receive the young and brilliant Swiss stage designer Adolphe Appia, whom he had met in Geneva and who had become a close friend. Chamberlain felt that Wagner's music dramas would be enhanced by Appia's sophisticated use of colour, light and shade – as indeed they were when Wieland Wagner adopted similar techniques on the Bayreuth stage half a century or so later. But Cosima would not hear of it, though her son would be more receptive. Where Appia's notions were correct, she decreed, they were already being put into practice in Bayreuth; where they were not, they were simply childish.

Cosima felt that with *Die Grundlagen*, Chamberlain had become altogether too big for his boots; that although he laudably reproduced much of the Wahnfried gospel, he was also implicitly issuing a personal declaration of independence. In this she was largely right. Intellectual modesty was no feature of Chamberlain's character. With a decade of successful propaganda and a bestseller behind him, the former disciple saw himself – not Wolzogen and others under Cosima's firm thumb – as the truest interpreter of the Wagnerian message. He continued to venerate the Mistress of Bayreuth and to adore the Master's music dramas, but he swam free of the belief that everything Wagner had written was above criticism, or even invariably made sense. Naturally Cosima could not stand for that and detailed her art historian son-in-law Henry Thode, fiercely jealous of Chamberlain for years, to launch a counter-attack. Thode accordingly produced a long review in 1900 lauding *Die Grundlagen* for its scope but arguing that parts of it were derivative and/or misconceived. Chamberlain, incensed, hit back at Thode without mentioning him by name. He even skipped attending the festival and for a few years his correspondence with Cosima became merely polite, although it was never wholly broken off.

That might just have marked the end of Chamberlain's specially close relationship with the family, had it not been for Siegfried. Wagner's composer/conductor son, seemingly the soul of equanimity, had been on good terms for years with 'the sage of Bayreuth' and had stayed firmly on the sidelines during the scrap over *Die Grundlagen*. After his mother suffered a heart attack in 1906, Siegfried took over the festival and begged his old (and useful) friend to return to the fold. Chamberlain in turn made his peace with Cosima, without giving much if any ground on the views he had expressed in his book, when she visited him in Vienna during a trip south to recuperate. Things then moved quickly. Chamberlain's divorce from Anna finally came through and the hitherto sporadic correspondence he had exchanged with Eva became a torrent. In summer 1908 he returned to the festival at last and on 26 December, two days after Cosima's birthday, he and Eva were married. 'After arduous years,' he wrote to the Kaiser, 'first an intolerable conjugal life, then a period that, although it enriched my soul, was often one of aching loneliness, my life's ship now glides into friendlier waters.'[15] As so often, Chamberlain was wrong. For him, the Wagners and Germany the worst was yet to come.

# 7

# Odd Man Out

On the face of it the Wagner clan had much to be grateful for in 1908, exactly a quarter of a century after the Master's death. The festival was going strong, the leadership had passed more or less smoothly from mother to son and, thanks to Adolf von Gross, the family was not just debt-free but seriously rich. Eva had finally married, the last of the four daughters to do so, and Siegfried was widely regarded as one of Germany's most eligible bachelors – although there was naturally speculation about just why he still *was* a bachelor at the age of thirty-nine. '*Nun danket alle Gott*' (Now all give thanks to God), Cosima exulted as she surveyed the family situation in a letter to a friend on New Year's Eve.

The *Hohe Frau* (Exalted Lady) was now seventy-one, she had suffered a heart attack and she was half blind; but she was still clear-minded enough to know that, whatever the public image that she did her best to polish, privately much was far from well with the Wagners. The Italian branch of the family by this time gave least cause for worry. More than a decade after the tragic death of her husband Biagio, Blandine was settled comfortably in Florence, rather to the envy of Siegfried whose inborn love of all things Italian waxed as the years passed. The brightest of her sons, Manfredi, became a top diplomat, to whom no problem seemed intractable; none, that is, until 1929, when he was appointed High Commissioner to Danzig, the Baltic port city placed under the auspices of the League of Nations after the First World War. He died three years later aged only forty-nine, vainly trying to reduce tension there between Germans and Poles. Another son, Gilberto, felt irresistibly drawn to Bayreuth, where Siegfried fostered his musical gifts as conductor and flautist, even composing a tuneful but tricky concerto for him in 1913. With his mischievous smile and seemingly inexhaustible stock of brightly coloured bow ties, Gil – as he was popularly known – became a kind of mascot around Bayreuth right into the 1970s. Latterly he had a vital but inglorious role giving curtain cues during performances at the festival theatre; rather a comedown for one who had earlier won acclaim as an orchestral conductor, even in Vienna. But evidently that did not bother Gil. He seemed almost childishly happy simply to belong to the clan. A rare bird.

Unlike Blandine, Daniela had much of her father von Bülow's short temper and sharp tongue. From whom she had inherited her odd eyes, one grey-blue and one brown, was anyone's guess; likewise of mystery origin was the swarthy complexion that earned her *Mohr* (Moor) as a third nickname (after *Lulu* and *Lusch*). Her talents brought her little joy. A fine pianist, she tortured herself trying and naturally failing to match the brilliance of her maternal grandfather, Liszt. A skilled costume designer for the festival, she rarely seemed content with her work but took umbrage at criticism. Her sudden bursts of fury were terrible to behold – but then, thanks not least to her husband Henry Thode, she had much to be upset about. Like Chamberlain in his pursuit of Eva, Thode seems to have been fired not so much (if at all) by yearning for Daniela as by the ambition to marry into the Wagner clan. That aim achieved, he left his wife almost wholly unkissed and unembraced, according to family gossip – at any rate Daniela, like Eva, had no children.

Ironically it was Cosima who, by engaging the famous – not to say notorious – American dancer Isadora Duncan for *Tannhäuser* in 1904, contributed mightily to Daniela's marital misery. The *Hohe Frau* had already shocked the prudes back in 1891 when she first produced the work with its opening Venusberg bacchanalia within the 'sacred walls' of the festival theatre. But clearly she felt the orgy as staged failed (as it usually does) to match the eroticism of Wagner's music; hence her bold appeal for new choreography from the twenty-six-year-old Miss Duncan, whose sensuous writhing in often-scanty costume, defying most of the rules of classical ballet, had already set pulses racing in theatres across Europe. After taking over a mansion called *Phillipsruh* (Phillip's Rest) on the outskirts of Bayreuth, and swapping all the chairs for couches, Cosima's exotic new 'catch' set to work recreating the Venusberg offstage as well as on. That, at least, was the view of the locals who watched open-mouthed as all sorts of famous male visitors – seemingly unmindful of scandal – padded to the door by night and scuttled away at dawn. One of them was the ruling Prince (and later Czar) Ferdinand of Bulgaria, a Bayreuth festival regular for decades; another was a tenor of legendary skill and stamina – yet another was Henry Thode, whom Isadora first invited in after spying him under a tree gazing ecstatically at her lighted window.

In her memoirs, Isadora scornfully rejects claims of orgies at Phillipsruh and, in particular, swears that during his many nocturnal stays Thode never made love to her, preferring instead to read aloud from his new work-in-progress on St Francis of Assisi. She does, however, admit that he was seized with terror when, about to leave after one all-night literary session, he glimpsed Cosima stalking up to the mansion like an avenging angel.[1] That early visit turned out to have nothing to do with Thode but of course his liaison, platonic or not, could not stay a secret for long, especially not from Daniela and the rest of the family. Isadora's Bayreuth career was limited to that single, tempestuous summer and Daniela's marriage took another lurch towards divorce. As for Thode, he wed a Danish violinist but lost the will to work when his villa on Lake Garda, along with his books, manuscripts and art treasures, was confiscated by the Italians after the outbreak of the First World War. The place fell into the hands of the flamboyant, ultranationalist writer Gabriele D'Annunzio (later much admired by several members of the Wagner clan, including Daniela), and Thode died a broken man in Copenhagen.

While Cosima's contribution to the collapse of Daniela's marriage was unintentional, her efforts to drive a wedge between Isolde and her husband were calculated and implacable. The ensuing family tragedy for which, admittedly, Cosima was not solely responsible, will shortly be given a closer look. Suffice it to say here that Isolde, hitherto Cosima's favourite daughter, finally became an 'unperson' whose existence could not be acknowledged in her mother's presence. Even breathing the name of Isolde might, it was feared, give Cosima one of her attacks. The person firmest in insisting that 'Mama's' welfare must not thus be put at risk was her ever-solicitous son, although in this case his action was not wholly altruistic. In principle Siegfried was riding high, as a festival producer/director popular with artists and public alike and as a composer whose very first opera *Bärenhäuter* had been an outstanding hit. He felt threatened all the same, and not only from the

Isolde wing of the family, although to look at him you would hardly have thought so.

'I do not feel like a tragic figure,' Siegfried states at the end of his skimpy but indirectly revealing memoirs written in 1922. 'I rejoice every day that I had the good fortune to have a father such as mine; I rejoice to have had such a mother and grandfather. I love my sisters who give their brother nothing but love and kindness . . . I am happy that I am not quite without talent and have inherited a liberal dose of humour from my parents. Dear reader, do you think that anyone who has so much to be grateful for can be a pitiable, tragic figure? I certainly don't.'[2]

Similar buoyant declarations pop up so often in Siegfried's slim volume that even the least wary of 'dear readers' may feel the author 'doth protest too much'. They may also wonder why someone who calls his life so blissful allows bleak topics like illegitimacy and child murder to dominate his operas, often with witches and similar agents of evil woven into the tale. Of course composers can and often do write sad music when their lives seem outwardly joyful and vice versa, but in Siegfried's case the contrast looks especially crass. Was the sunny public image, maintained through thick and thin, simply show?

Not altogether. Siegfried surely did inherit a lot of humour although, despite his dutiful reference to 'my parents', precious little of it can have flowed his way from his austere mother. His private letters are full of wit, puns and gentle irony, often directed against himself. Much the same is true of the way he ran the festival, even if there was calculation as well as personal inclination behind his relaxed approach. He would often arrive beaming for rehearsals dressed in plus-fours and yellow stockings, as though just dropping by on his way to the racecourse, then stand about chatting cheerfully until everyone was at ease. Siegfried, in other words, in no way belonged to the 'terror works best' school, either as producer or conductor. Once the real business began he was tireless and exacting. But even then his frequent jokes would bolster a discouraged singer or disarm an enraged maestro – and when he could not avoid enforcing discipline among his 'children', as he tended to call the cast, he used a light touch not a bludgeon. 'Performers planning pleasure tours to Nuremberg', he chalked up on a blackboard in the festival theatre after a bout of absenteeism, 'are requested to inform the festival director, not because the aforesaid wishes to join in the trips but because he would like to know if he may dare to schedule a rehearsal.' For good measure, Siegfried noted that in his view further rehearsals were indeed needed because 'unfortunately we can still not pride ourselves on having scaled the highest peak of perfection'.[3]

What a contrast to the 'fortress on the hill' ethos of the Cosima era. Indeed, for hard-line Wagnerians the laid-back style of the new boss, Master's son or not, seemed close to sacrilege; but then Siegfried despised nothing more than hardliners, in music or anything else. Sometimes he railed against supposed allies who were 'more papal than the Pope', but usually he kept his blood pressure down by seeing the funny side of things. He smirked to learn of the woman who chanted '*War das sein Horn?*' (Was that his horn?) from *Götterdämmerung* every time her husband blew his nose; and he wryly reflected that, in view of the unpleasing bulk of some Wagnerian singers, it might be best to ban opera glasses. For all his love of his father's work, Siegfried was only too happy when he could escape to hear some Donizetti, Verdi – even Bizet, a composer shunned at Wahnfried at least since the hated Nietzsche wrote *Der Fall Wagner*, in which he praised the sharp-etched tragedy of *Carmen* at the expense of the Master's 'fogbound' music dramas. More shocking still, on one occasion during a boring supper given in his honour in Nuremberg Siegfried slipped away to a nearby nightclub featuring a jazz band – the last word in decadence for the old Wagnerian guard . Worst of all, he actually enjoyed it.

Balance, irony, tolerance; those are not the first qualities one tends to associate with the name Wagner, let alone an excess of personal modesty. But when Siegfried notes that he is 'not quite without talent' he is being too coy by half, a trait his critics exploited during his lifetime and still more later. Even, for now, leaving aside his compositions – operas, songs and instrumental works – Siegfried's gifts were wide-ranging. Thanks to his photographic memory, as well as a fine sense of colour and design that he bequeathed to his son Wieland, he might have become an architect and until his early twenties that was his main aim. At least those qualities stood him in good stead as a producer; not, it is true, a revolutionary one (which would surely have upset 'Mama'), but a steady, pragmatic innovator whose impact on Bayreuth stagings over decades, culminating in a legendary *Tannhäuser* in 1930, is often underestimated. When Siegfried claimed that his favourite role in the theatre was to direct the lighting apparatus, he was, as so often, half joking. But it is true that by developing the use of light and shade to match the ebb and flow of his father's music, he implicitly adopted the Adolphe Appia approach that Cosima had shunned (and Chamberlain had long advocated). In this respect at least Siegfried helped pave the way for Wieland's productions, hailed and reviled as 'revolutionary', when the festival reopened after the Second World War.

Views differ sharply about Siegfried's conducting. 'Miserable,' snapped Richard Strauss – the finest composer-conductor of the day, alongside Mahler – after hearing the Bayreuth *Ring* in 1896. That judgement seems plausible on the face of it. Siegfried was only twenty-seven and he was making his festival debut (a single act of *Lohengrin* apart two years before) in the most taxing of all operatic marathons. He was also wielding the baton with his left hand, an oddity some players found confusing and which he later 'corrected'. But then Strauss had recently fallen out with Siegfried – for reasons unclear, although still-embryonic rivalry may have played a role – and he was fed up with Bayreuth in general: a 'pigsty to end all pigsties', he called it in a letter to Pauline, his fiancée.[4] Other critics were usually friendlier about Siegfried's skill on the podium but they were rarely ecstatic, at least not in Germany. When the young maestro appeared at London's Queen's Hall, though, George Bernard Shaw – no less – compared him favourably with Richter and Mottl and declared himself 'touched, charmed, more than satisfied'.[5] What aural evidence there is, about a dozen pieces Siegfried recorded in his last years, tends to support the view Shaw had expressed decades earlier. That goes in particular for the deft, lucid interpretation of the *Siegfried Idyll* played by the London Symphony Orchestra in 1927, which is worlds away from the sentimental approach one might have feared from the dedicatee. On the whole the swift tempi and the clarity of the inner parts (insofar as the dim recordings allow one to hear them) match reports of the Master's own conducting, which Siegfried witnessed as a boy on at least three occasions.[6]

A far from 'pitiable, tragic' figure, then, but for one crucial element that Siegfried naturally does not mention directly; his dread that his bisexuality might be exposed, ruining him and disgracing the family. That Siegfried did not abhor women, nor they him, is plain enough. While married, he fathered four children and long before that he may well (the evidence is mixed) have sired a son in a brief affair with a Bayreuth pastor's wife that was quickly hushed up. His letters also reveal regular but fleeting allusions to a liaison with a Romanian-born singer, Marguerite de Nuovina, that lasted for years. Siegfried seems first to have met her in Paris where she was performing at the Opéra-Comique; they spent holidays together in Italy and on one trip to the French capital he gave her address as his own. When she came to Hamburg in 1905 for the premiere of his fourth opera, *Bruder Lustig* (Brother Merry), Cosima took tea with her and judged her a 'fine, charming' woman' who 'loves Siegfried tenderly' and who 'pleases me uncommonly well'.[7] Praise indeed from 'Mama', who no doubt felt it was high time her son produced an heir and who even seems to have considered Isadora Duncan as a possible match until Thode butted in. But Marguerite finally faded out of the picture. Did she realise she had male rivals for Siegfried's affection?

Even in pre-Freudian days (just), it needed no great insight to see that the young Siegfried might well have trouble establishing his male identity – as an ultra-sensitive only son who for years had next to no contact with lads his own age, with a dominant mother and four doting sisters so protective that, in early photos, they seem almost to engulf the forlorn little brother in their midst. Just six months after Siegfried's birth, his father warned that the boy would later have to be sent away 'to meet other people, to get to know adversity, have fun, and misbehave himself; otherwise he will become a dreamer, maybe an idiot, the sort of thing we see in the King of Bavaria'.[8] Leaving aside that shabby jibe about his greatest benefactor, Wagner's paternal instinct was no doubt correct, but he left most of the children's care to Cosima and died when his son was barely an adolescent. Aged thirteen, Siegfried suddenly became the only man in the family – far from an idiot but surely a dreamer, and idolised nearly to death. When he finally got away from home for a longish spell in 1889 it was at his mother's behest and then only to stay with more family – Henry and Daniela Thode, who at that time lived in Frankfurt.

Cosima planned that Siegfried should take music lessons several times a week from Engelbert Humperdinck, a composer and Bayreuth disciple who lived not far from Frankfurt in Mainz. She repeatedly claimed to all and sundry that her son was free to study architecture later if he really wanted to; but she naturally hoped that under Humperdinck's influence he might yet change tack and opt to join her in running the festival, eventually taking it over. He had, after all, also been named *Helferich* (little helper), meaning that in his parents' view he would do all he could to further the Master's work, an implication of which Siegfried was all too aware. Cosima's hopes were handsomely fulfilled, as the lessons went splendidly. Siegfried began to compose seriously, subsequently learned conducting technique from Felix Mottl and abandoned his dream of becoming an architect. To Cosima's delight, he also won a wider circle of influential Frankfurt friends, including the banker and music patron Edward Speyer (later a key backer of the London Promenade Concerts) and a wealthy young English musician called Clement Harris. 'Mama' would, however, have been perturbed to learn that her son, in the course of the colourful entertainment offered at the Speyer house, sometimes dressed up and performed as a *prima ballerina*.[9] And she almost certainly never realised, despite many hints, just how much the young Englishman really came to mean to Siegfried.

Born in Wimbledon in 1871 into a family of ship-owners, Clement Hugh Gilbert Harris was a man of many talents; artistic (he painted probably the finest portrait of the young Siegfried), literary and above all musical. At seventeen he became one of the favoured few accepted for piano lessons in Frankfurt by the legendary Clara Schumann and at twenty-four his symphonic poem *Paradise Lost* was premiered to critical acclaim before an audience that included the Prince of Wales and the King of Belgium. In Germany his titled admirers included Alexander Friedrich, Landgrave of Hesse, who joined him in piano duets and took him on a tour of the Middle East. In the London of the late 1880s and early 1890s he was a protégé of Oscar Wilde, then at the height of his fame, to whom he performed Wagner transcriptions and talked about 'the most marvellous of all things; painting, music, love'.[10]

Wilde was one of those who referred to the rare aura of the young pianist, confessing indeed that he was sometimes scared by the intensity of his playing. Some even claim that from boyhood on, Harris had hypnotic powers above and beyond his riveting skill at the keyboard. Whatever the truth of that, his gifts, good looks and connections seemed to cut him out for an outstanding career. His aim, he confided to his diary, was to further 'the regeneration of English music' and after his early success as a composer he briefly seemed well set to achieve that; rather more so, in fact, than his older compatriot Edward

Elgar, who was still struggling for recognition. But in April 1897, three months before his twenty-sixth birthday, Harris was killed – apparently shot while fighting for Greek independence against the Turks in the mountain battle of Pente Pigadia. The exact circumstances of his death remain unclear to this day.

When Harris first met Siegfried at one of the Speyers' soirées he was just a highly promising music student of eighteen, but he fascinated his new acquaintance right away. Although two years younger than Siegfried, he seemed far more worldly-wise. The broad-minded, international outlook of his family had rubbed off on Clement early on, just as it had on his elder brother Walter, a journalist, author and adventurer who spent much of his life in his beloved Morocco. This openness extended to music too, arousing mixed feelings in Siegfried. Along with his love of Wagnerian music drama, Clement favoured the work of Robert Schumann (and not just because he was studying with the composer's widow) as well as that of Brahms. To true Bayreuthians, admiration for the – in their view – vastly inferior Schumann and Brahms came close to heresy; indeed the doctrinaire Thode had already squabbled over the issue with Speyer and his soprano wife Antonia, one of the finest interpreters of both composers' songs. In principle the Master's son, of all people, should have been shocked by Clement's sad lack of discrimination, and no doubt he tried to be; but then he too had long felt tempted by siren sounds shunned by hard-line Bayreuth. Even as a child, Cosima reported in her diary, he had sung 'a kind of Turkish music' in his sleep.[11]

Clement and Siegfried quickly became close friends though not exclusive ones. Letters and diary entries by both, often written in a comical mix of misspelled English and German, reveal some friction, because each had other male fans. But after a summer both spent in Bayreuth, Clement, who was feeling nervous and restive, proposed that they take a trip together to the Far East free of charge on one of his father's ships. Siegfried loved the idea and since he was now twenty-two Cosima could hardly say no, though her letters show she had great qualms. For the first time her adored son was travelling beyond even her long reach – who could tell what that might mean for Bayreuth's future? Anyway, Siegfried joined Clement in London in early 1892 and – after a couple of breathtaking encounters with Oscar Wilde, who extolled all the French things usually deplored at Wahnfried – the pair embarked on a voyage that was to last nearly six months. They turned out to be the only passengers aboard the far-from-luxurious merchant ship *Wakefield*, albeit joined during the trip by a growing number of pets including canaries, a monkey and a Chinese dog.

Of the 173 pages of memoirs that Siegfried produced in total three decades later, no fewer than 103 are devoted to that voyage with Clement Harris. Clearly, then, this was a crucial half-year for him, and his lively, often hilarious account of it makes for an easy read. We are told almost more than we might wish about eating pieces of cat and dog in Canton; we are left in no doubt about the joys of nude bathing on a deserted Malayan beach; and we learn how the two young travellers, lying in (Siegfried indicates) separate beds in a Philippines village, are serenaded by a lovely harpist from an adjoining room. There are occasional swipes at British colonialists, American tourists and Jews, but Siegfried directs his fiercest fire at his own countrymen: 'atrocious, noisy, apelike', a clear vindication of Darwin's theory, he calls a group of Germans in a Singapore hotel. And everywhere, whether sweltering on his bunk in the Red Sea, visiting a Buddhist temple or watching the teeming throng in Hong Kong, he has his sketchbook to hand.

Despite all that, much – one is tempted to say most – about Siegfried stays hidden, not just in his memoirs but usually also in the more detailed notebooks he filled during the trip and that were published privately only after his death. Once or twice he lets deeper emotions show through; how his heart almost stops when he unexpectedly hears a Bach chorale wafting from a building half a world away from home; how his blood nearly freezes when he learns, on a trip to a Chinese jail, that a young murderess as beautiful as a Giotto madonna will be hacked to pieces for her crime. But for the most part he offers us no more than a snapshot travelogue and even implicitly admits as much. Of a visit to the Alhambra in Granada with Clement he reports that, precisely because the experience means so much to him, 'I really cannot speak and write about it, as [I cannot] about all things inviolable.'[12] What applies to his account of the voyage is also true of the remaining seventy pages of his memoirs. Siegfried has a knack of claiming that it 'should not be necessary' to say more just when more is exactly what we would love to know. Like the Cheshire Cat, he often lets us see his smile but rarely his substance.

So it is that we learn little of depth about Clement Harris. Obviously Siegfried owed the young Englishman a lot. Thanks to Clement, he came into direct contact with cultures he had only read and dreamed about, and it may be that under Clement's influence he began to question the antisemitism he had imbibed from his parents. It is at least on record that the Harris family deplored remarks against Jews and that Clement gave short shrift to Adolf Stöcker (the antisemitic chaplain at the Imperial Court) when he happened to meet him in Bayreuth. Clement surely helped strengthen Siegfried's regard for composers who did not bear the Bayreuth seal of approval; perhaps he was even behind his friend's decision, abruptly taken in Hong Kong, to drop architecture and plump for a life in music after all. Typically, Siegfried himself gives no explanation for this momentous change of heart beyond insisting that it was not caused by pressure from his mother. For a time on board the *Wakefield* Clement and Siegfried were composing more or less simultaneously. While the former sketched themes for his *Paradise Lost*, the latter began to plan the structure of a symphonic poem of his own called *Sehnsucht* (Yearning), based on a poem of Friedrich Schiller. In 1895 the works had almost simultanenous premieres, Siegfried's in London and Clement's near Frankfurt.

Only once, at the end of their trip together, does Siegfried briefly drop his emotional guard. The *Wakefield* has reached the decidely unromantic stopover of Port Said and Siegfried, keen to get back to Bayreuth for festival rehearsals, has decided to join a faster boat. 'My dear Clement accompanied me on board where we said goodbye,' he writes in a notebook entry not reproduced in his memoirs, 'superficially in as English a way as possible because lots of people were milling around us, but in our hearts with that affection and intimacy with which we had learned to love one another.'[13] Five years later Clement was killed. Siegfried made no recorded comment on the loss, but then silence (his music apart!) was his refuge if faced with the deepest emotion. When three decades later he composed his second and last symphonic poem entitled *Glück* (Happiness), he evidently dedicated it in private to the dead friend whose picture never left his desk. For all his other emotional entanglements, male and female, much suggests that in Clement Harris Siegfried found and lost the love of his life.

Natural reticence was not, of course, the only reason for Siegfried's discretion. As 'the love that dare not speak its name', homosexuality could bring personal and social disaster even to those simply accused of it, let alone sentenced in court. If Siegfried had had any doubt about the risks involved, he lost them at the latest when he came to London to give the premiere of *Sehnsucht* on 6 June 1895 in Queen's Hall. Twelve days earlier, after a second trial for sodomy during which his private letters were read out in evidence, Oscar Wilde had been sent to jail for two years' hard labour. The judge called the case the worst he had ever tried and regretted that in his view the sentence, the maximum the law allowed, was 'totally inadequate'. There is no record of how Siegfried reacted to the trial, but it is inconceivable that he was unaware of it and the events leading up to it. Deserted by most of his friends and family, unable even to rent rooms, the scintillating Oscar, who had been the toast of London and who had dazzled Siegfried just three years before, plunged into a black hole.[14]

The Master's son naturally took care to cover his tracks, thus helping his family – expert erasers of unwelcome facts in any case – to keep the topic for the most part safely sealed. Blackmailers who got wind of Siegfried's sexual escapades are said to have been bought off by the ever-faithful Adolf von Gross, although written evidence of this is unsurprisingly lacking. Only once did a really serious threat loom in the person of Maximilian Harden, feared and fearless editor of the weekly *Die Zukunft* (The Future), who had already caused a national storm with his charges of homosexuality in circles close to the Kaiser. Harden despised the Wagners and his indirect reference to Siegfried's sexual orientation in an article in 1914 suggested he was planning a campaign to bring down family and festival lock, stock and barrel. He might even have succeeded. The Wagners were already reeling under the impact of another scandal that had burst into the open after simmering behind the scenes for years. This one focused not so much on Siegfried, though he was deeply involved, as on his sister Isolde and her ambitious, errant husband.

Mention Franz Beidler nowadays and even keen Wagnerians may be hard put to place him. Didn't a Swiss conductor of that name lead a few performances in Bayreuth early in the last century, and wasn't his son in some way linked with plans to restart the festival on a new footing after the Second World War? Indeed, but there is more to the tale than that. Twice over, the Beidlers came close to playing a key, perhaps decisive, role in Bayreuth. That they failed was due partly to their own bad judgement as well as bad luck; but they were also out-manoeuvred from the start by Wahnfried incumbents ready to use every weapon, including lies and deceit, to defend their patch.[15]

Beidler, born in 1872, was no mean conductor, but his career would almost certainly not have prospered so well at the start, or failed so abjectly later, if he had not first won entry to the ranks of Bayreuth's 'royal family'. At any rate his professional fame soared after he wooed and won the loveliest of the Wahnfried daughters, the proud and impetuous Isolde, who was seven years his senior. Cosima was not happy with the match, no doubt feeling that Isolde of all her daughters deserved a paragon with the fire of a Tristan and the status of a King Mark. But she did not prevent it and probably could not have done so (although she had managed to thwart a budding romance of Isolde's years before). So the two were married in December 1900 and went to live in an idyllic manor house near Bayreuth where, ten months later, their son Franz Wilhelm was born – an event of which the *Hohe Frau* really did approve, at least at the time. Isolde, she gushed to a friend, was an incomparably beautiful and caring mother, just like a being from paradise. Even Beidler came in for belated praise. After poring over the score of *Tristan und Isolde* with her new son-in-law, Cosima concluded that he was a better musician than she had thought, 'excellent' in fact.[16]

For all that, Beidler did not slot into place at Wahnfried. His blunt talk, his disinclination to bow and scrape, were among the traits that had first endeared him to the similarly direct Isolde, but they did not go down well with others at Cosima's court. For the inner circle, family and acolytes, the burly newcomer with the thick Swiss accent was and remained an interloper, unwilling even to master the art of kissing the hand of the *Hohe Frau* with adequate reverence. Nor did his success on the podium as far afield as Moscow and St Petersburg win him friends at home. Quite the opposite. Thanks to Cosima, he conducted a *Ring* cycle at Bayreuth in 1904, well enough by most accounts, and two performances of *Parsifal* in 1906. But when he tried to insist on being given a third *Parsifal*, the *Hohe Frau* flew into a rage that probably contributed to her heart attack late the same year and her subsequent withdrawal from the festival leadership. In a letter of truly Wagnerian intensity, she told Beidler that he was not a really fine conductor – let alone a good husband – and that to become one his whole nature would need to be reborn. Unless and until that happened, Cosima thundered, 'we are divorced.' If asked, she would urgently advise

Beidler's 'pitiable wife' to separate from him.[17]

Clearly there was more behind this fury than a family member's desire, in principle laudable, to conduct the *Bühnenweihfestspiel* more often. The truth is that by 1906 at the latest, Beidler was emerging as a rival to Cosima's adored son, and in his bumptious way he was making that plain. Like Siegfried in 1876, he had begun his Bayreuth career with the toughest possible assignment, the *Ring*, and now he seemed to be laying special claim to the Master's 'holiest' work. That alone did not mean Beidler could displace Siegfried as heir apparent to the festival, but it presaged a likely power struggle once Cosima died or stepped down. Looking still further ahead, Isolde and her husband already seemed to hold a trump card – namely their son – in any future battle for the Bayreuth succession. Blandine and Daniela were 'only' von Bülow's daughters, not Wagner's, and anyway Daniela was childless. Eva was surely sired by Wagner but she was baptised von Bülow, was still unmarried and was getting too old to produce an heir. Siegfried was still a bachelor and even those unaware of his sexual habits had begun to assume that he would remain so. That left little Franz Wilhelm Beidler, born on 16 October 1901, sound in mind and limb and already with an evident ear for music, as the Master's only grandson.

The boy's status depended, however, on the assumption that Isolde, born in Munich on 10 April 1865, really was Wagner's daughter; that she had been conceived at the Master's villa by Lake Starnberg in the summer of 1864, most probably during the week or so when Cosima was present without 'poor Hans', her husband. Wagner had no doubt that he was Isolde's father. Evidently Cosima had none either, referring to Isolde on at least one occasion as her 'first child of love'. Still, legally speaking Isolde was a von Bülow and on the advice of von Gross, keen as ever to ensure a clear line of succession at Wahnfried, she had accepted her share of the estate von Bülow left on his death in 1894. In other words Isolde's true paternity was an open secret that most insiders, including for a time Isolde herself, found it convenient to deny or ignore. Sometimes, though, even the best-trained disciples became a mite confused. When he produced his sycophantic two-thousand-page biography of Cosima in 1928, Richard Graf Du Moulin Eckart referred to Isolde as 'v. Bülow' in the index to the first volume and as '*geb.* Wagner' (born Wagner) in that to the second. By this time, though, Cosima was in little state to care.

Some two decades earlier, she had cared intensely. It is not clear whether Cosima wrote her 'divorce' letter wholly independently or with Siegfried's collusion, but the aim was plain enough; to defend her son's position by driving Beidler out of both the festival theatre and the family. She only half succeeded. Beidler never again conducted in Bayreuth and his later career, in Manchester among other places, proved a flop. But true to type, Isolde stuck to her man. In 1909 she and Beidler wrote to Cosima admitting errors and begging forgiveness but the letter never arrived. Seemingly Siegfried intercepted it. At the very least, he knew of its contents and warned the authors never to try to make such an approach again as it might lead 'Mama' to suffer a relapse. By this time, though, the Beidlers and to some extent Siegfried himself faced a challenge from yet another source – the newly wedded Chamberlains.

Houston and Eva had long been hugely influential at Wahnfried in their separate roles; he (albeit often *in absentia*) as publicist, racist guru and friend of the Kaiser, she as the conduit through which virtually all correspondence to and from Cosima passed. But once together, living in or close to Wahnfried and with direct access to every scrap of inside information, they became all but dominant. Eva remained her mother's secretary and close confidante – so close, in fact, that Cosima put all the diaries detailing her life with Wagner into her daughter's care. Hosts of friends and foes would have loved to scour the intimate contents of these twenty-one handwritten volumes, but Eva made sure that next to no one got the chance. She did the job so well that the revelations of the *Hohe Frau* only became generally available to scholars and the public in the 1970s.

While Eva took charge of the diaries, her husband at Cosima's behest prepared the Master's unfinished autobiography *Mein Leben* for its first issue to the general public. Decades earlier Wagner had sent copies of a private printing to King Ludwig and a few friends but Cosima had managed to claw back most of this material after his death. Now the work was to be made generally available in a 'suitable' form – with seventeen passages deleted or rewritten mainly on the grounds that they reflected poorly on people still living, including Cosima, or on the Master himself. Given the wholesale distortions in Chamberlain's own Wagner biography written a few years earlier, it is something of a surprise that *Mein Leben* did not suffer a still more thorough editorial mangling before it reached the market in 1911.

Daniela, for one, later said she wished additional embarrassing passages of the original had been chopped. Intact and unsullied editions of Wagner's original text finally *did* emerge – but only from 1963 onwards.

Apart from his work on *Mein Leben*, Chamberlain was active as never before – writing a book about Goethe, planning a sequel to *Die Grundlagen* and using his influence to make the *Bayreuther Blätter* still more nationalist and antisemitic in tone. Bit by bit he was abandoning the view, held by Wagner in his later years, that it was in the first place up to art, not politics, to change society. Foreign-policy setbacks, the rising power of organised labour and the 'muckraking' by Maximilian Harden involving the Kaiser's friends – all this helped persuade Chamberlain that Germany faced threats too urgent to be countered by 'regeneration through art' alone. In advocating a firmer political stand against what looked like a far-flung conspiracy to deny the country its rightful 'place in the sun', Chamberlain reflected and intensified the feelings of a growing number of Germans. As usual, Jews (among them the Jewish-born Protestant convert, Harden) were widely blamed for the *misère*. All too few of the grumblers acknowledged that it was not least Germany's own bungling diplomacy since Bismarck's departure, worsened by the Kaiser's hamfisted intervention, that had brought the country more foes than allies.

Far from all of those who trekked to Bayreuth for the festivals were dyed-in-the wool nationalists, but the hardening of the mood in the years before the First World War was unmistakable. Ever more publications appeared linking the festival to 'true German-ness' and carrying Chamberlain's thesis about Aryans as makers and saviours of civilisation to still more absurd extremes. It was in this context that a new drive was launched to try to keep performances of *Parsifal* legally restricted to the Bayreuth stage alone. But despite much lobbying and a petition that won eighteen thousand signatures, parliament failed to act – yet another sign to most of the backers that politics was subject to sinister influences behind the scenes. To such people Chamberlain was a hero and at Wahnfried he had no real rival. His old enemy Thode was disgraced; Wolzogen was intellectually outclassed and Siegfried was on the whole a benefactor who had helped haul Chamberlain back to Bayreuth after the tiff with Cosima over the *Grundlagen*. Siegfried was admittedly in a strong position as son and heir so long as his private life stayed strictly private; but he got on with his

1 Cosima with Richard Wagner. 'I shall come to you and seek my greatest and highest happiness in sharing the burdens of life with you,' Cosima, just turned 31, pledged in her diary on New Year's Day 1869. 'What love has done for me I shall never be able to repay.'

2 Protected or trapped? Richard Wagner's only son Siegfried, aged about 4, encircled by his sisters Isolde (Loldi) and Blandine (Boni) at the rear, Eva and Daniela (Lulu) at the front.

3 Young Wagners clutch an old friend. Eva, Isolde, Siegfried, Daniela and Blandine (left to right) with Hans Richter, long close to the family and conductor of the first 'Ring' cycle at Bayreuth in 1876.

4 Dandies on parade. Siegfried (right) enjoys a joke in front of the Festival Theatre with his brother-in-law Heinrich 'Henry' Thode (left), a historian, and Karl Muck (centre), a martinet of a conductor who rarely looked as jolly as here.

5 The thwarted heir. As Richard Wagner's grandson who went into Swiss exile from the Nazis, Franz Wilhelm Beidler (1901–81) was invited to return and put the Hitler-tainted festival on a new footing after 1945. In the event, the Bayreuth branch of the family managed to retain ownership and management (left). 6 Evangelist of Race. English-born Houston Stewart Chamberlain (1855–1927) adored Germany, married Wagner's daughter Eva and decisively influenced the family circle at Wahnfried for many years. His chauvinistic, anti-semitic writings were deeply admired by Kaiser Wilhelm II and Adolf Hitler.

7 Bayreuth's new Master and Mistress. Siegfried and his English-born wife Winifred, married in 1915 when he was 46 and she 18, take one of their regular strolls through town (left). 8 Averting eruption. The ever-affable Siegfried chatting with the explosive Italian maestro Arturo Toscanini before the Festival Theatre in 1930. Soon after this picture was taken Siegfried collapsed during rehearsals and died in hospital, aged 61. He never saw his 'dream production' – *Tannhäuser* with Toscanini at the helm.

9 Free at last. Siegfried's eldest daughter Friedelind, hunted by the Nazis and interned by the British, arm-in-arm with her 'second father' Toscanini at Buenos Aires airport in 1941. The maestro had pulled many strings to ensure his charge could cross the Atlantic from war-torn Europe to safety.

10 Winifred's Bayreuth team. From the bottom (clockwise), the inscrutable Heinz Tietjen (producer, conductor and eminence grise), Wilhelm Furtwängler (conductor), Paul Eberhardt (lighting) and Emil Preetorius (stage design). The photo was taken in 1936, six years after Winifred took over as festival director and three years after Hitler came to power.

11 Warrior maiden. Frida Leider, here shown as Brünnhilde in *Die Walküre*, was one of the greatest dramatic sopranos of all time. She sang key roles in Bayreuth until 1938 when her Jewish-born husband had to flee abroad and she suffered a nervous breakdown (right).

12 Happier days. Frida Leider cuddling lion cubs at the Berlin zoo. Privately, Frida was a close friend of Friedelind Wagner who admired her artistry, humour and sheer style. It was the fate of Frida and her husband that finally turned Friedelind against the Nazis for good.

13 Hitler snapped with the Wagner daughters. Verena (left), the youngest of Siegfried and Winifred's four children, stayed in Germany and married an SS officer. Friedelind (right) fled abroad, took U.S. citizenship and fiercely condemned the Hitler-Bayreuth connection – above all in her autobiographical *Heritage of Fire*.

14 Hitler with the Wagner sons. Wieland (left) as the eldest child was regarded as heir to the Bayreuth 'throne' and specially dispensed from war service. After his brother's death in 1966, Wolfgang (right) ran the festival single-handed until well into the next millennium.

15 The 'Führer' greeting the crowd from a window of his favourite theatre in 1940. His Bayreuth visits, he told his staff during the war, were his happiest times. When they were over, he felt as he had done when the decorations were pulled down from a Christmas tree.

16 Fascist Parthenon for Bayreuth. On Hitler's orders, the architect Rudolf Adolf Mewes designed this grandiose complex for the 'Green Hill', into which Wagner's festival theatre (seen at the rear) was to be subsumed. Construction was stopped after the war began.

manifold artistic work and left the ideology to Chamberlain, just as he left money matters to von Gross.

Only the Beidlers loomed as a problem. Chamberlain, it seems, had shown an interest in Isolde many years before and may therefore have been jealous of the graceless young Swiss for whom she finally plumped. That aside, he and his wife stood to be sidelined if Isolde were re-admitted to the family fold with a confirmation of the glorious paternity that she now chose to claim. Perhaps, indeed, it was Eva who first intercepted the Beidlers' begging letter to Cosima. She was ideally placed to do so. Can it be that she and Chamberlain subsequently influenced the reply sent by Siegfried? There is no proof but it is striking how the tone of Siegfried's letter, full of bitterness and threats, matches next to nothing else in his available correspondence. Not that Siegfried would emerge with any glory even if it could be shown that he 'merely' gave his name to a document largely formulated by others. Besides his surely genuine concern for 'Mama's' health, he was at least as aware as the Chamberlains of how much there was to lose if the Beidlers gained direct access to Cosima and managed to 'unfreeze' her. If not the main string-puller, he was among the puppeteers – then and later. In 1911 a rash of reports swept through the German press falsely claiming that the Beidlers had divorced and stressing that Isolde was not, as many people believed, Wagner's daughter. The source for this particular fiction was not given, but those who attributed it to 'Wahnfried circles' were surely close to the mark.

Finally realising that she was getting nowhere, Isolde decided – for her son's sake at least as much as her own – to get her true lineage established once and for all by taking her mother to court. She was already suffering from the tuberculosis that was to kill her but she went ahead in 1913 all the same, convinced that her cause was just. No doubt it was but, to cut short the tale of a long legal battle, she lost. After months of deliberation and reams of often gloating press coverage, the Bayreuth court ruled on 19 June 1914 that Isolde had not proved her case and ordered her to pay costs. As the law stood, a wife's sexual intercourse was assumed to be 'exclusive' throughout her marriage; ergo, Cosima's then husband – von Bülow – was automatically deemed to be Isolde's father. This presumption could be overruled only if convincing evidence to the contrary were produced and the court decided that Isolde had not done so. She had been born during Cosima's marriage to von Bülow, she had been baptised a von Bülow and she had accepted a share of the von Bülow estate. Hence she could not, under law, be considered Wagner's daughter. Cosima could have turned this result on its head by swearing that she had made love only with Wagner throughout the period during which Isolde must have been conceived – but of course she swore no such thing. She was not even called to give evidence under oath.

By the time the verdict was announced, poor, doomed Isolde was already undergoing treatment for tuberculosis in Davos. There she remained like a character from Thomas Mann's *Zauberberg* (Magic Mountain), fighting vainly to regain her health, surveying the outbreak of war far down on the 'Flatland' – and, it seems, passing on the background to the trial in every nasty detail to her teenaged son. Was she aware that her husband was meanwhile having an affair with an opera singer and that the two had a daughter (who incidentally as Eva Busch became one of Germany's most famous left-wing cabaret singers)? Probably not. Numbed by growing doses of morphium her spirit broke, then her body, and she died on 7 February 1919 – two months before her fifty-fourth birthday.

This tale has a bizarre postscript. Isolde was buried in Munich where her widowed husband now lived, but that was not her final resting place. Beidler later married his Bavarian housekeeper, Walburga Rass, with whom he had a daughter, Elsa. She in turn married a writer from Söcking, a village close to Lake Starnberg. Many years after Beidler's death in 1930, Isolde's corpse was exhumed and reinterred with his at the cemetery on a hilltop above Söcking. As the crow flies, Isolde's remains thus now lie only a few miles from the spot where she was conceived – that villa made available to Wagner by King Ludwig to which Cosima sped ahead of von Bülow in 1864. After Beidler's second wife Walburga died in 1975, her body too was placed in the selfsame grave. Whoever formulated the inscription on the brown wood memorial there decided to play it safe. Cosima's 'first child of love' is comprehensively identified as 'Isolde Beidler *geb.* von Bülow-Wagner'. Of all the family victims in the history of the Wagners, Isolde is arguably the saddest.

In retrospect, Isolde stood little chance from the start of winning her court battle, but it seems that Cosima and her troops themselves were not sure of that. While the trial was still going on, Siegfried dropped a bombshell, apparently believing that this could induce a wave of public sympathy for Cosima's cause. He suddenly announced a plan to turn over the whole of the Wagner legacy, including the festival theatre and its grounds, Wahnfried and its archive, to a national foundation 'in perpetuity'. He and his mother, Siegfried declared, had decided that the 'Bayreuth of Richard Wagner . . . belongs not to us but to the German people.' What largesse! Maximilian Harden, for one, smelt a rat and said so in an article in which, besides taking an indirect swipe at Siegfried's private life, he scorned the whole clan for pious posing and wearing 'a mask of lies'. Harden was right to be suspicious. Siegfried claimed that the foundation plan had been concocted in mid-1913 and that it could already have gone some way towards implementation. The implication was that by going to court and putting a question mark over the Wagner legacy, Isolde was 'selfishly' delaying the bestowal of cultural riches on the German nation and, if she got her way, might block it altogether. But in fact Cosima had drawn up a will in the second half of 1913 and there was not a word in it about a foundation. On the contrary, she left everything to her son. Once the trial was over little more was heard of the scheme, at least not for sixty years. Then a national foundation really was set up, although those who believed this would mark the end of the Wagners' rule in Bayreuth soon found they had to think again.[18]

Isolde's decision to go to court, the end of copyright on the Master's work, the failure to confine *Parsifal* to Bayreuth; all that made 1913 an awful year for Wahnfried. If anything it seemed still more vile because the family had to go through the motions of celebrating the centenary of Wagner's birth. Speeches were made, choruses sung, even more flowers than usual were placed on the Master's grave, Wolzogen composed a sonnet his fans thought profound. Siegfried was made an honorary citizen of Bayreuth and he was present when a white marble bust of his father was reverently placed in Walhalla, an incongruous Doric temple built decades before on a perch above the Danube. But he understandably looked far from his usual buoyant self that year. It was hard to believe that 1914 could bring anything worse but it did. Nine days after the Isolde trial ended to sighs of relief at Wahnfried, Archduke Franz Ferdinand, the heir to the Habsburg throne, was assassinated in Sarajevo and the old European order moved a big step closer to collapse. The festival went ahead, but as international tension grew the ranks of the foreign pilgrims thinned and of twenty planned performances only eight were held. The final one – *Parsifal* – was given on 1 August before a half-empty house. The same evening Germany ordered general mobilisation.

Although the truncated season meant that the festival made a loss of 360,000 marks, the outbreak of war did not seem an unmitigated disaster at Wahnfried, at least not at first. It spared the Wagners unwelcome questions about when the promise of a foundation would be made good and also, probably, a renewed attack from Harden in *Die Zukunft*. Besides, Chamberlain for one felt war might be the only way for the noble Germany he believed in to renew itself at home and humble greedy, superficial foes – especially Britain. He pinned up a map on the wall at Wahnfried with flags to mark the (soon-stymied) German advance, and produced a stream of rousing pamphlets that won him the Iron Cross in 1915. A year later he took German nationality. The only surprise is that he did not do so sooner. But as the troops stayed bogged down and victory prospects faded, Chamberlain began to complain that the state with its corrupt and squabbling politicians was not worthy of its brave, disciplined army. Lots of Germans felt the same. So was born that disastrous 'stab in the back' legend – that Germany was not defeated but betrayed by cowardly string-pullers in Berlin, not least Jews. Next time, many people swore, things would be different.

Siegfried also wrung his hands over the war and increasingly over the break in the festival that was ultimately to last all of ten years; but he had other things on his mind too. At the age of forty-six he took a step which by that time astonished almost everyone, including perhaps himself. He got married. His bride was no opera singer, no noblewoman, but an eighteen-year-old English-born girl, orphaned as an infant, called Winifred – 'rather boyish-looking' some observers knowingly claimed. Boyish or not, she soon bore Siegfried four children, consolidating the clan but opening the way for new battles a generation hence over the Wahnfried succession. Winifred made her mark in quite another way too. Far more than her husband and no less than her fanatical brother-in-law, Chamberlain, she became devoted to Bayreuth's most notorious visitor – Adolf Hitler.

# 8

# Wolf at the Door

'Much esteemed and dear Herr Hitler,' the fan letter from Bayreuth began.

> You are not at all as you have been described to me, a fanatic. The fanatic inflames the mind, you warm the heart. The fanatic wants to overwhelm people with words, you wish to convince, only to convince them . . . You have immense achievements ahead of you, but for all your strength of will I do not regard you as a violent man. You know Goethe's distinction between force and force. There is the force that stems from and in turn leads to chaos, and there is the force that shapes the universe.[1]

Although Chamberlain was responsible for this fatuous panegyric, over which the recipient reportedly rejoiced 'like a child', he did not physically write it himself. Since the war years the 'seer of Bayreuth' had been close to paralysis with an illness never diagnosed for sure, and his speech was so slurred that the devoted Eva was one of the few who could still understand him. It was she, long her mother's secretary and now her husband's too, who acted as his interpreter to visitors and who painstakingly took down his copious correspondence, including this particular letter dated 7 October 1923 to the up-and-coming leader of the Nazi party. At the end of it, Chamberlain confessed that his hopes for his chosen nation had been at a low ebb until Hitler's visit to Bayreuth a week earlier. Now though, 'at one blow you have transformed the state of my soul. That Germany in its hour of greatest need has given birth to a Hitler is proof of vitality . . . May God protect you!'

A few weeks later, on 8–9 November, Chamberlain's supposed espouser of non-violence tried to stage his Munich 'beer hall putsch' –

planned as the prelude to a march on Berlin to seize nationwide power. The bid failed and Hitler was subsequently jailed. This was less of a setback for the Nazis than it seemed, if indeed it was a setback at all. Hitler used his trial as a propaganda forum and his time in Landsberg prison (he served only nine months of a five-year sentence) to rethink his strategy, during which he produced the first part of the book later called *Mein Kampf* (My Struggle). Chamberlain, for one, remained convinced that Germany's saviour had emerged at long last even though all too many Germans, in his view, sadly failed to realise their good fortune. In a letter dated 1 January 1924 and later widely publicised to mark Hitler's thirty-fifth birthday on 20 April, he compared the Landsberg jailbird to Martin Luther in his 'courage' and 'holy seriousness' and, not least, in his antisemitism. 'He (i.e. Hitler) finds it impossible to share our conviction about the pernicious, even murderous, influence of Jewry on the German *Volk* and not to take action,' Chamberlain observed. 'If one sees the danger, then steps must be taken against it with the utmost despatch. I daresay everyone recognises this but nobody risks speaking out; nobody ventures to extract the consequences of his thoughts for his actions; nobody except Hitler.'[2] Under 'nobody' presumably Chamberlain included himself. Like most 'intellectual' antisemites he did not care to describe, let alone try to initiate, concrete steps to solve the 'Jewish problem'. Hitler, evidently, knew what to do.

Deeply misguided, painfully ill, seemingly close to death (though he lived on until 1927) – Chamberlain was all those things, but he was anything but irrelevant. Among those members of the Wagner clan rooting for Hitler in those days, he was easily the most influential. It was Chamberlain who had produced the by now near-legendary *Grundlagen des 19en Jahrhunderts*; Chamberlain whose patriotic wartime essays had sold up to a million copies; Chamberlain who served as a model for a new generation of racist writers, ranging from the relatively genteel scribes of the *Bayreuther Blätter* to the brutal Artur Dinter – later Nazi Gauleiter in Thuringia – whose *Die Sünde wider das Blut* (The Sin against Blood) became a runaway bestseller. That Chamberlain had for years been a confidant of the now-exiled Kaiser Wilhelm merely added to his prestige – at least among many of those who despised or despaired of the newborn Weimar Republic with its struggling, squabbling politicians. Chamberlain had stayed personally loyal to the Kaiser, and he had gone on extolling the pedagogic value of Wagner's music dramas. But he had finally concluded that Germany could be saved neither by the monarchy nor from the stage – even Wagner's stage. What the nation needed, he declared, was an 'iron broom' to sweep it clean.

Hitler was well aware of Chamberlain's reputation and had evidently dipped into his works; indeed parts of *Mein Kampf* read like an inelegant crib from *Die Grundlagen*. But when he came to Bayreuth on 30 September 1923 it was not, in the first place, to visit either the racist guru at Nr 1 Wahnfriedstrasse or the rest of the Wagner clan round the corner. It was to address a German Day rally – one of a series at which he was trying to drum up support throughout Bavaria and at which, the available evidence suggests, no member of the Wagner family was present. That evening, with the main business of the day behind him, Hitler at his own proposal paid a call on Chamberlain and then went on to a nearby hotel reception hosted by two of his richest sponsors, the piano manufacturer Edwin Bechstein and his wife Helene. Winifred Wagner, who had known the Bechsteins for years, was also present at the party (evidently without Siegfried) and she invited the guest of honour round for breakfast the next day.

Was it love at first sight? It is hard to say what love may have meant to Hitler, if anything; but he clearly took to the twenty-six-year-old 'mistress of Wahnfried' (if not, yet, of the Bayreuth festival) and henceforth, for nearly two decades, he repeatedly sought her company. As for Winifred, she surely did fall right away for the blue-eyed charmer eight years her senior who talked so stirringly of his aims for Germany and his passion for (Richard) Wagner. She was not, of course, alone in that. Hitler's erotic allure is well documented, for instance in those countless newsreels showing women shedding tears of ecstasy at the approach of the Reich's most desirable and least attainable bachelor. But Winifred remained more or less infatuated to the end and, what's more, she did not care who knew it. As late as 1975, five years before her death, she visibly brightened up during a long filmed interview when the talk turned to Hitler. Her devotion was of a different type to Chamberlain's, but it was not a whit less absolute.

Winifred Marjorie Williams was born on 23 June 1897 in Hastings, a Sussex seaside resort located, as it happens, only a shortish drive along the coast from Chamberlain's Hampshire birthplace. It seems likely, though, that these two arch-Bayreuthians (who always conversed with one another in German) rarely talked about their southern English origins and certainly never did so with pleasure. Like Chamberlain, Winifred from the start lacked a real home; like him she went through agonies of loneliness and rejection; like him she only won a sense of belonging when she went to Germany. No doubt all that helped forge the fierce and uncompromising attachment of both outsiders to their adopted country – a passion extreme even by the standards of most native-born, patriotic Germans. The same was surely true of the Paris-bred Cosima with her usually absent French–Hungarian parents and, in part, of the Austrian-born, pan-German Hitler who suffered abject failure and poverty as a young artist in polyglot Vienna. All four of these rootless souls found a physical home at or next to Wahnfried (Hitler, admittedly, only sporadically), and an emotional one in music, above all Wagner's.[3]

Winifred never knew her parents. Her Welsh father, a writer, died of a liver disease before she was two and her mother, an actress of Danish descent, succumbed a year later to typhus. By her own account, the little girl was pretty wild. No one seemed to want her for long and as a result she became wilder still. Decades later she still recalled with awful clarity the privations of her East Grinstead (Sussex) orphanage where kids found guilty of fibbing had their tongues smeared with mustard. That treatment did not make the adult Winifred more tolerant of youthful foibles, at least not consistently. She notoriously often let her own brood run riot as though no discipline was good discipline. But she also fought a fierce battle of wills that lasted for years with her elder daughter Friedelind, who was at least as rebellious as the young Winifred herself had been. The more her mother applied pressure – forcing her to eat what was 'good' for her until she vomited, sending her away to 'learn sense' at a cheerless boarding school (shades of the orphanage!) – the more the girl dug in her heels. Friedelind, it is true, was a special case but, in general, Winifred was not accustomed to taking children in her arms or showing sympathy for 'cry babies'. No doubt she thought she was acting for the best and did not mean to be cruel, but she lacked real warmth. Where, indeed, would she have learned what warmth was?

Perhaps at the home of the Klindworths, the old couple near Berlin who cared for her for eight years; but when Winifred first arrived on their doorstep in April 1907, supposedly for a stay of only six weeks, she was aged nearly ten and was already emotionally damaged goods.

The visit might easily have been a flop for all concerned. While still in England Winifred had contracted a bad skin complaint that was probably psychologically induced. She urgently needed to convalesce but no one could be found to take her until the orphanage, in near despair, finally won guarded assent from Henriette Klindworth, a distant relative of Winifred's mother married to a German musician. Henriette was then seventy, her husband Karl seventy-six. Childless, they lived in a modest country house, pottered in the garden and dreamed of the good old days when Karl had studied piano with Liszt and had been a friend of Richard Wagner. Indeed, he had produced fine piano versions of the Master's scores and still kept in regular contact with the Wagner family, especially Cosima. But times were hard, Karl had to give piano lessons to help make ends meet and neither he nor his wife was in the best of health. In short the Klindworths seemed anything but suitable candidates to take on the challenge of a problem child and a sickly one at that.

Unexpectedly, though, the old people quickly became devoted to Winifred and she to them. The six-week deadline came and went but no move was made to send the little girl back to England, and anyway, no one there was clamouring for her return. So the Klindworths became Winifred's foster parents and eventually adopted her. Karl taught her the piano, giving her first German lessons at the keyboard, and Henriette showed her the basics of housekeeping and gardening. They even abandoned their beloved country retreat and moved with their charge to a flat in Berlin when this seemed better for her schooling; the move gave her access to a wider circle of contacts, including the wealthy and influential Bechsteins. Naturally Wagner's music was among the first Winifred heard in the Klindworth home and, by her teens at the latest, it had become her passion. She dreamed of the Master's heroines – for a time she even signed her letters 'Senta', nicknaming herself after the Flying Dutchman's obsessed and selfless saviour.

She did not, however, get much if any chance to see Wagner staged. Old Klindworth, for all his personal kindness to Winifred, was a nationalist and antisemite who regarded Berlin productions as the new-fangled abominations of an increasingly Jewish-dominated theatre. For him, as for most 'old school' Wagnerians, the Bayreuth festival was the only spot where the world of the Master was still more or less in order. Despite his creaking limbs, he loved attending Bayreuth dress rehearsals at Cosima's special invitation and in 1914 he won permission to bring along Winifred, then aged seventeen. There she was introduced to Siegfried. The cultivated festival director with the smooth-skinned, almost babyish face was nothing like the haggard, driven 'Dutchman' of her dreams, a role Hitler later filled much better. But he was, undeniably and irresistibly, a Wagner – one, moreover, with a kindly voice that Winifred later confessed she instantly fell for.

As for Siegfried, he had once or twice remarked that *if* he were to marry, his bride would have to be poor and without a family. No doubt, consciously or not, he was keeping at least one eye open for a girl in no strong position either to clash with 'Mama' or to make a fuss about his bisexuality. Suddenly there she was (or seemed to be) and just in the nick of time. Although Isolde had lost her court case that summer, the affair had emphasised the vulnerability of the Wagner dynasty so long as Siegfried produced no heir. Siegfried was well aware of that himself, but the family kept reminding him anyway, especially sister Eva who sent him a long letter stressing it was high time he found his '*Katerlieschen*' (little kitten). To cut a long story short – shuttle trips by Siegfried to Berlin, engagement, a bureaucratic battle to win Winifred German nationality despite the outbreak of war – the two were married in Wahnfried on 22 September 1915. The Klindworths were too ill to attend and Karl died the following year.

The house that Winnie (as family and friends called her) now entered was no cosy nest. Built in massive sandstone as though to withstand a siege, Wahnfried featured a bust of King Ludwig in the front garden, a single heavy slab marking the Master's grave at the back (with space ready and waiting for Cosima) and a Wagnerian frieze linking tragedy, myth, music and youth above the entrance. Inside next to nothing had been changed since the Master's death more than three decades before. Cosima spent much of her time in her quarters upstairs, gazing out to the grave from her balcony, receiving old friends like Adolf von Gross and dictating to Eva her (by now dwindling) correspondence. Sometimes she would drift about the house in black, flowing robes, switching to white on special occasions to please Siegfried, checking on the servants and – after the marriage – seeing that Winnie did the dusting properly. The *Hohe Frau* did not believe that a young wife should be under-employed. If Winifred knew much English literature, which is uncertain, she may well have felt transported into a world combining the odder features of *Jane Eyre* and *Great Expectations*. A more sensitive creature would have felt daunted from the start; but Winifred had been toughened in a hard school, as her hapless sisters-in-law and ultimately Cosima herself came to realise.

Eva had taken the lead in pressing Siegfried to marry but she had not expected that the 'little kitten' she urged him to find would have such sharp claws. Before the wedding, she insisted on choosing 'suitable' dresses and shoes for Winifred, who scornfully changed them or gave them away. Eva also tried to advise on housekeeping but Winifred, thanks to Frau Klindworth and a 'domestic science' course in Berlin, already knew a lot more about that – and showed it. Siegfried was called upon to intervene but, true to type, he managed to pass off this or that domestic crisis with a joke and fled to his 'bachelor quarters' – the cottage next to Wahnfried where he composed and met his own (usually male) circle of friends. Poor Eva! Even the parrot seemed against her, as Winifred later maliciously recalled, pecking at her papers and rudely burping whenever she entered the room.

Daniela, too, tried to upstage Winifred, for instance by taking up most of the stool when they played piano duets. But bit by bit she and her sister were sidelined, decisively so when Winifred handsomely fulfilled the main role expected of her and produced four babies in four successive years. Wieland, the eldest, was born on 5 January 1917 – an event so shattering in the long-frozen Wahnfried world that Cosima actually floated down to play a few bars of the *Siegfried Idyll* on the piano. Family legend has it that she had not touched the instrument since Wagner's death and never did so again. It was, in fact, a difficult birth. The baby emerged blue and failed for a while to utter a sound, as though unsure whether the world it had entered was worth the effort (a question the mature Wieland, too, found desperately hard to answer). Friedelind came next nearly fifteen months later on 29 March 1918 – a Good Friday, which was felt to be some sort of omen. Wolfgang followed on 30 August 1919 and Verena on 2 December 1920. Winifred, it seems, was raring for more offspring but Siegfried, who (jokingly?) called his constantly pregnant wife 'Mrs Globus,' was definitely not. He felt he had already done more than his dynastic duty.

By the time Wolfgang and Verena were born the war was over but life even for the relatively well-placed Wagners got harder still. That rarely fazed Winifred who, far better than her husband and in-laws, knew what it was like to go without. The tougher things became the more she seemed to bloom. Ignoring accusations of 'sacrilege' from local fogeys, she had turned Wahnfried's lawn into a vegetable patch during the war. Later, as heating fuel became ever scarcer, she squeezed most of the family (bar Cosima and her nurse) into Siegfried's cottage, where Verena was in fact born. When her husband went on conducting tours to raise funds, she packed him food to save on restaurant bills and urged him to bring back what he failed to eat. She also dealt with correspondence on his behalf, signing herself at first 'Frau Siegfried Wagner'. Later she tended to drop the 'Frau', an omission that, to this day, much vexes archivists, dealers in historic memorabilia – and biographers.

Despite Winifred's thrift and Siegfried's earnings, there was barely enough cash to cover the family's day-to-day spending, let alone to allow resumption of the festival. Inflation gradually decimated not only what was left in the festival kitty after the truncated season of 1914, but also the proceeds of a new fund-raising scheme launched by ultra-orthodox Wagnerians in Leipzig in 1920. One result of the financial woe was growing friction between Wahnfried (Cosima apart) and Adolf von Gross. Siegfried, happy to ignore money matters in pre-war days, now blamed his ex-guardian for having kept funds in '*beschissene Staatspapiere*' ('crappy state securities') instead of shifting them into value-retaining property.[4] Von Gross in turn accused Siegfried and his wife by letter of diverting sums intended for the festival into speculative investments without informing him. Clearly wounded, he went on to recall that he had looked after the family's interests for more than five decades – 'not without success'.[5] A typical understatement – what the Wagners, especially Cosima and her son, owed the old man was inestimable. Nonetheless Siegfried, whether he liked it or not, should long since have been prepared for the business responsibilities he now tried in his fifties to shoulder willy-nilly. Von Gross faded away to the wings as an adviser although, for old times' sake, he remained a regular visitor to Wahnfried until his death in 1931.

Lack of funds, food and fuel; uncertainty over when or even whether the family 'business' would be re-launched – the Wagners suffered all that. But at least in Bayreuth, as though in the eye of the storm, they were spared the worst of the violence sweeping Germany, especially the cities. Small wonder that the Weimar Republic – hated by far left and far right alike, distrusted by the masses who yearned for peace but felt they had been betrayed of victory in war – was more or less stillborn. The real surprise is that it managed to survive until 1933, even beginning to look quite healthy once or twice. Back in the early post-war years the question was not so much whether this or that government would last as whether the country itself, united barely fifty years before, could avoid disintegration. Bands of armed *Freikorps*, disaffected soldiers back from the front without jobs or hope, roamed the country offering their deadly services – also to the central government that lacked resources to keep order. *Spartakisten*, immediate forerunners of the communists, sought to drum up revolution in Germany as the Bolsheviks had done in Russia in 1917. Even in once strongly monarchist Bavaria, a Soviet-style republic was briefly proclaimed until *Freikorps* units intervened to smash it. Politically motivated assassination became routine. Karl Liebknecht and Rosa Luxemburg, radicals (and henceforth martyrs) of the left, were among the victims. So was Walther Rathenau, foreign minister and one of the Republic's few mainstays.

Only one thing, it seemed, united all sides, and that was resentment of the Versailles Treaty that had stripped Germany of territory, restricted its armed forces and given it sole blame for the war. Reparations were set at 132,000 million gold marks, to be paid to the victors in annual instalments, a burden bound to prove economically crushing and to foster political extremism. Wise foreign observers like John Maynard Keynes pointed that out, but their warnings went unheeded for years by political leaders, especially those in a vengeful France still smarting from the Prussia-led drubbing of 1871. Germany, that had begun to feed inflation by printing money to finance the war, now created hyperinflation by printing vastly more to try to meet the near-intolerable demands of peace. As the crazy paper chase accelerated, what a hundred marks had bought yesterday, a thousand could not buy today and a billion might not buy next week. With the exchange-rate of the German currency going into free fall, Lord D'Abernon, the statistically adept British ambassador in Berlin, worked out in 1923 that he was able to obtain as many marks for a single pound sterling as there had been seconds since the birth of Christ.

Some, like his lordship, did not immediately suffer from the crisis. Those with goods and property could sit tight; exporters won new markets with dirt-cheap products; the national debt that had seemed such a burden in weighty old pre-inflation marks marvellously lightened when expressed in gossamer new ones. But millions of people nonetheless faced ruin; pensioners, civil servants, 'blue collar' workers – all those relying on paper savings and paper wages. Next to no one understood the cause of the calamity although as usual Jews were widely blamed, as they were for a variety of other ills including the 'stab in the back' in 1918 and the 'Bolshevik threat' from Moscow. Jews apart, the French seemed the main tormentors, especially when they marched into the Ruhr industrial area in early 1923 on the grounds that Germany had failed to pay reparations on time. Months of strike and more or less passive resistance followed, further crippling the economy and the currency. Secession began seriously to loom in the Rhineland and Bavaria; communists and Social Democrats, usually fierce rivals, joined forces to control Thuringia and Saxony; the end of the Republic seemed at hand.

Such was the chaos when Hitler first met the Wagners in the autumn of 1923, although of course, they had heard about him for years. Back in 1919, Wagnerian friends in Munich had told them of the fiery young corporal, war-wounded and holder of the Iron Cross, who was creating such a stir at meetings of the newly formed *Deutsche Arbeiterpartei* (German Workers' Party). But at that stage the DAP was just one more ultra-nationalist group, so puny that it pathetically began numbering its members at 500 (Hitler was number 555) to try to look bigger. That soon changed. Even before he formally won control in 1921, Hitler lashed the DAP into measures that would boost its appeal. At his instigation, it renamed itself *Nationalsozialistiche Deutsche Arbeiterpartei* – NSDAP (National Socialist German Workers' Party), largely as a gambit to win working-class backing. It also turned out a twenty-five-point programme full of populist demands: abrogation of the Versailles treaty, acquisition of more territory to form a 'greater Germany', a ban on immigration and the denial of equal rights to those already present but not of 'German blood', specifically Jews. All non-German immigrants who had entered the country after the start of the First World War were to be expelled forthwith. People keen to know with some precision what Hitler and the Nazis stood for did not have to wait for *Mein Kampf*. They simply had to read this programme made public at a rally in the Munich Hofbräuhaus on 24 February 1920, although at that stage even the far-right press did not take much notice of the event.

Almost any crackpot could have put such things on paper and got next to nowhere, but this one subsequently went from strength to strength. Why? Obviously Hitler's near-matchless demagoguery and ruthlessness (not least towards over-ambitious fellow Nazis) against a background of mounting national desperation had much to do with it. Less manifest but also crucial was the sheer charm that won him backers among wealthy families, like the Bechsteins (music) and the Bruckmanns (publishing), who would never normally have let such an ill-bred upstart into the garden, let alone the salon. For the ladies involved, Hitler's very awkwardness seems to have added to his attraction. Both Helene Bechstein and Elsa Bruckmann evidently loved the challenge of teaching etiquette to a guest who seemed keen to learn but who would thrillingly appear at the front door equipped with a whip and a pistol. Such seemingly genteel circles were more than ready to overlook the brutality of the Nazi quasi-militia of stormtroopers, the SA (*Sturm-Abteilung*) or – if forced to acknowledge it – tended to argue that one naturally had to defend oneself against leftist ruffians who upset one's rallies. Hitler's nationalist heart, they claimed, was in the right place, and anyway 'things cannot go on as they are'. As for the antisemitism he trumpeted, that was anything but new. It had reared up in fresh forms after the emancipation of the Jews more than half a century before, but then it had lacked a leader able to tap it right across class barriers and sensibilities. Now, in the wake of the Versailles humiliation and amid the despair of Weimar, it got one.

The Wagners, especially Chamberlain and Winifred, fell for the same charm and had an added reason to do so. Hitler had been enthralled by the Master's music ever since his first *Lohengrin* as a youth, had drunk it in at one splendid performance after another in Vienna conducted by (ironically enough) the Jewish-born Gustav Mahler. So it was that when he entered Wahnfried for the first time, on the morning of 1 October 1923, Hitler seemed awed to tread on what was probably the nearest thing for him to sacred ground. As Siegfried and Winifred led him through the great entrance hall, the music room and the library the Nazi leader found himself oddly short of words. Later he stood alone for several minutes in the garden before the Master's grave, then returned to the house to promise the family (vainly as it proved) that should he come to power then *Parsifal* would again become Bayreuth's exclusive property. Hitler met the children but apparently did not see Cosima, although he must have yearned for the honour. Perhaps the *Hohe Frau*, now nearly eighty-six and largely confined to her upstairs room, was simply too weak to receive him. Or maybe she felt the sallow young man with awkward manners and lowly pedigree was not the sort of person with whom she cared to associate – despite all that Houston and Winnie might say in his favour. Whatever the truth, Cosima took it to her grave.

Just over a month later, on 10 November, Siegfried was due to conduct a concert in Munich that included the premiere of his joyful new tone-poem *Glück*. He and Winifred arrived a day or two early for rehearsals and thus witnessed the collapse of the putsch after an exchange of fire between Hitler's followers and the (far outnumbered) police in front of the Feldherrenhalle in the city centre. More than a dozen of the insurgents were shot dead: others were injured, including Hitler himself and Hermann Göring, the former wartime flying ace who later became the most flamboyant of Nazi leaders. The concert was shelved. Back in Bayreuth Winifred gave her version of the Munich events to the local branch of the (now outlawed) Nazi party and a few days later she drew up an open letter of support for Hitler, apparently on behalf of the whole Wagner clan.[6] In the next few months she collected clothes and money for the families of jailed Nazis and helped organise a local petition that won ten thousand signatures demanding Hitler's release. Winifred seems never to have visited Hitler at Landsberg, though those of his Party friends who did so claimed they had never seen their leader looking better – healthy, rested and enjoying the obvious admiration of his jailers. However, she did provide him with various creature comforts including writing paper. Helene Bechstein, not to be outdone, sent him a gramophone and, after his release, a Mercedes.

That is about as close as one can come to pinning down how the paths of Hitler and the Wagners began to cross, but the facts have become obscured by a fog of legend that, if anything, gets thicker as the years pass. For this the family is much but not solely to blame. Unsurprisingly, Winifred played down her own role to denazification authorities shortly after the Second World War, although she played it up later, especially when reminiscing to her still Hitler-besotted friends. She publicly conceded that she had sent 'masses of paper' to the jailed Hitler but scorned the very idea that she was therefore indirectly responsible for the birth of *Mein Kampf*. In that, at least, she had a point. Hitler dictated his text to fellow prisoners, above all to his close aide Rudolf Hess, and history does not record how much, if any, of Winifred's supplies they may have used. That has not, however, harmed circulation of the tale that Hitler set down his grotesque best-seller on Wahnfried notepaper. A related claim has it that the author called his book *Mein Kampf* to forge an obvious link with the adored Wagner's *Mein Leben*. But Hitler's original title was *Viereinhalb Jahre Kampf gegen Lüge, Dummheit und Feigheit* (A Four-and-a-Half-Year Struggle against Lies, Stupidity and Cowardice). His publisher Max Amann understandably found that less than catchy (and much of the text itself a disappointingly turgid read). He thus proposed *Mein Kampf* instead.

It is sadly true that the plucky Friedelind, who fled Nazi Germany before the Second World War, also contributed to the confusion. In her pungent biography called *Heritage of Fire*, first published in America in 1945, she wrote that her mother had met Hitler in Munich even before he came to Bayreuth. There is no evidence to support this and next to none to back up another of her colourful claims, often repeated since – namely that Siegfried visited the wounded and impoverished Göring in Austria immediately after the putsch, paid all his bills and arranged for him and his wife to stay in Venice for a year free of charge. Friedelind also undermined her credibility by wrongly naming May, not October, as the month when Hitler was first shown round Wahnfried – a small point but one that has made it easier for her foes inside and outside the family to cast doubt on the rest of her account. Where Friedelind sticks to her own observation and does not repeat hearsay she is nearly always credible. But when Hitler first came to Wahnfried she was only five years old.

Did Hitler discuss his projected putsch with the Wagners? It has often been suggested that he did, but the claim gains no greater credibility through repetition. A coup was surely 'in the air' in 1923 but Hitler did not go about chattering to outsiders (or even to brand-new friends) of his hazardous and constantly changing plans. Chamberlain, for one, clearly knew nothing or he would not have extolled Hitler in his letter of 7 October for his 'non-violent' intentions. Siegfried's tone-poem *Glück* is sometimes offered as circumstantial evidence of collusion. It is alleged that the premiere of the piece was timed to coincide with and celebrate the putsch; or even, as one contemporary German author amazingly suggests, that the putsch was timed to coincide with the premiere.[7] Had there been such a plan the composer would hardly have gone ahead – as he did – and given the work its delayed first hearing in December in Munich, a stone's throw from the spot where Hitler's bid to seize power had ended in a hail of bullets just a month before. Siegfried did, it is true, complete his first draft of *Glück* (the full score took him another few weeks) on 20 April 1923, Hitler's birthday, but that is no proof that he was implicitly honouring a politician he had not then even met. More plausible is the claim of the late Gertrud Strobel, for many years keeper of the Wahnfried archives, that when Siegfried composed *Glück* it was his long-dead friend Clement Harris, not Adolf Hitler, that he had in mind. But naturally Siegfried could not afford to risk tongue-wagging by making that connection plain in public.[8]

Leaving aside myth and conjecture, what did Siegfried *really* think of Hitler and his programme, not least its racist component? The answer is far from straightforward. Unlike his wife and sisters, Siegfried never joined the Nazi party and, unlike Chamberlain, he was not obsessed with its ideology – or, indeed, any ideology. Winifred reported on one occasion that 'even Fidi' was reading *Mein Kampf*, thus confirming (perhaps unwittingly) that it was not her husband's favourite kind of book. Siegfried nonetheless shared the general conviction that Germany was in dire need of a 'new broom', if not necessarily the 'iron' one Chamberlain advocated; and at least at the start, he evidently felt that if Winnie's new Wagner-loving friend filled the bill then so much the better. 'My wife fights like a lioness for Hitler. Splendid!' Siegfried wrote to a friend in late 1923. At least he seems to have done so. The original letter has gone missing and only a transcript remains available, but on balance the text is probably authentic.[9]

Moreover, a few months later Siegfried joined with Winifred in a bid to extract what could have been crucial financial backing for Hitler from Henry Ford, the fiercely antisemitic car king in the United States. Although themselves in America on a (largely luckless) tour to seek cash for Bayreuth, the Wagners managed to win an introduction to Ford for Kurt Lüdecke, Hitler's main fund-raiser and wheeler-dealer abroad. Lüdecke had high hopes of the meeting, noting that 'with one rasp of his pen' the American multimillionaire could solve the Nazis' money problems and allow them to push their programme ahead 'like a battering ram'. In the event, though, he drew a blank. Ford was becoming wary of stirring up more problems for himself with America's Jews, and while he gave the emissary a sympathetic hearing he did not offer any cash.[10] Evidently Hitler did not hold that against him. In *Mein Kampf* he referred to Ford as a 'great man' and saw to it in 1938 (when the Reich's business ties with America were still close and, indeed, economically vital) that he received the highest award the Nazis could bestow on a foreigner.

The Lüdecke affair shows that, in early 1924 anyway, Siegfried was ready to help Hitler if he could, as the Nazi boss clearly realised. In a letter to Siegfried from Landsberg in May, he thanked both the festival director and his 'lady wife' for their support and stressed that Bayreuth lay on the 'line of march' from Munich to Berlin, a comment notable not just for its geographical accuracy.[11] It may also have been thanks to Lüdecke that the Wagners were given an audience in Rome by Hitler's fascist crony Benito Mussolini on their way home from America – a further sign that at this stage Siegfried was ready and perhaps even eager to hobnob with the far right. A year later though, in the summer of 1925, things were starting to change. Hitler, out of jail and back in action, went to the Bayreuth festival for the first time and heard everything on offer –the *Ring*, *Meistersinger* and *Parsifal*. But he attended privately at the invitation of the Bechsteins, not as a guest of the festival or the Wagners, although he did meet Winifred and gave her a copy, hot from the press, of the first part of *Mein Kampf*. After that he did not return to the festival until the summer of 1933, a few months after he had become chancellor of the Reich and three years after Siegfried's death.

Hitler later claimed he had abstained for so long with regret, despite repeated pleas from Winifred, because he did not want to drag the Wagner shrine into political controversy. There may be something in that. More to the point, by 1925 Siegfried had markedly cooled towards Wolf – the Nazi leader's well-chosen pseudonym – and wanted him on the prowl neither at the festival nor, in principle, at home. Hitler, however, was not so easily kept at bay – at least not in private. He took to flitting into Wahnfried, usually by night and often unannounced, delighting the lady of the house and thrilling the children with bedtime tales about his (real or imagined) adventures. Sometimes, if he were in the neighbourhood but could not drop by, Winnie would drive out into the country to see him if only for a few minutes. Leaving aside the aged Cosima, it would seem that the only member of the Wahnfried clan not overjoyed to clap eyes on Hitler during Siegfried's lifetime was Siegfried himself. Even Straubele, the family schnauzer who normally snapped at strangers, is said to have nuzzled up to Wolf from the start.

Winifred's correspondence shows that Siegfried repeatedly tried, with precious little success, to stop her attending Hitler's public rallies; but he seems early on to have resigned himself to the private contacts between his wife and the Nazi leader. 'Unfortunately Wolf present,' Siegfried noted gloomily in his diary after he and Winifred had arrived at a Munich hotel to find a beaming Hitler in the lobby.[12] He left the happy pair to spend the evening together and went off alone to the theatre. On another occasion he actually took Winifred to a restaurant where she was due to lunch with Wolf, then went off to eat elsewhere. Was Siegfried simply incapable of putting his foot down? Or could it be that he and Winifred had reached a more or less tacit understanding; that he could have his own private life, artistic and sexual, and she could have hers? If so, that need not imply that Winnie actually slept with Wolf. For what it is worth, she later denied having done so. Besides, the trickle of real evidence (as against the floods of rumour) suggests that despite all his outward allure Hitler's involvement with women – from the domineering Helene Bechstein and the headstrong Unity Mitford to the vulnerable 'Geli' Raubal (his niece) – tended, for whatever reason, to stop short of the bedroom. Even Eva Braun, his long-time companion, seems to have been not so much a mistress as a mascot, at least if heavy hints later dropped by Hitler's housekeeping staff are to be believed. All that said, the fanatical adventurer who came and went like the wind clearly offered the hyperactive Winifred thrills her husband could never deliver.

Something of the highly charged emotional atmosphere at Wahnfried in those days emerges from a staccato account given by Joseph Goebbels, later Nazi propaganda minister, after he visited the Wagners in 1926. Like Hitler on *his* first pilgrimage, Goebbels was awed by the Master's heirlooms and grave and, also like Hitler, he was much drawn to Winifred. 'They should all be like that,' he wrote of her in his diary. 'And fanatically on our side. Sweet children. We're all friends right away. She pours out her sorrow to me. Siegfried is so spineless. Yuck! Shame on him before the Master. Siegfried is there too. Feminine. Good-natured. Somewhat decadent. Rather like a cowardly artist. Does such a thing exist?' At the end of his stay, Goebbels found it hard to tear himself away and stood around chatting with Winifred in the hall and the garden. She was crying. 'A young woman weeps,' he recorded, 'because the son is not as the Master was.'[13] Hitler evidently had a similar view of 'Fidi's' person and character but when he raised the topic years later it was more in sorrow than anger. Siegfried, he mused aloud to Goebbels in May 1942, had been compromised by his homosexuality and 'made to marry in a hurry' (presumably a reference to the threatened press revelations of Maximilian Harden).[14] A few months earlier Hitler had even described Siegfried to other leading Nazis as a personal friend – albeit 'politically passive. The Jews would have wrung his neck; he could not do anything else.'[15]

Had Siegfried not been the Master's son, the Führer would surely have been much nastier about his record. When August Püringer, an antisemitic newspaper editor and leading Wagnerite, demanded in 1921 that Jews be barred from the festival in future, Siegfried sent a long letter of reply stressing that Jews (and foreigners) had often supported Bayreuth when 'supercilious Germans' had failed to do so. 'If the Jews are willing to help us that is doubly meritorious,' Siegfried added, 'because my father in his writings attacked and offended them. They would, therefore, have – and they do have – every reason to hate Bayreuth. Yet in spite of my father's attacks, a great many of them revere my father's art with genuine enthusiasm . . . On our Bayreuth hill we want to do positive work, not negative. Whether a man is a Chinese, a Negro, an American, an Indian or a Jew, that is a matter of complete indifference to us.'[16] Siegfried later repeated these views in an exchange of letters with a Bayreuth rabbi, although there he drew a distinction between patriotic Jews and revolutionary 'Marxist' ones who, he claimed, wanted to overturn all that true Germans held dear. The rabbi rejected the 'Marxist' connection and said Siegfried had much to learn about Judaism; but he added that he was glad to find his correspondent did not share the intense antisemitism of some in the Wagner family. He specifically mentioned Chamberlain.[17]

Even if Hitler was unaware of these texts, at least at first, he can hardly have missed seeing an open letter in similar vein that Siegfried issued to the press in February 1925. In it the festival director announced that he had done all he possibly could to ensure that the coming season (i.e. the one Hitler then attended 'privately') would be free of political overtones. Everyone, he pledged, 'whatever religious belief or race he may have, is welcome in Bayreuth . . . No one need worry that any unpleasant incidents will occur'[18] – a reference to vileness that had marred the previous year's festival. In the heart of town,

Nazis and other extremists had spat on visiting Jews, thrust antisemitic leaflets into the hands of passers-by and daubed swastikas on buildings. At the festival theatre itself, most of the audience had risen at the end of *Meistersinger* to intone *Deutschland über Alles*, drawing from Siegfried the ironic aside that if things went on like that the *Ring* would soon be supplemented by public renderings of *Die Wacht am Rhein* (The Watch on the Rhine) – a patriotic song much favoured by German soldiers during the Franco-Prussian war. Making use of a quote from *Die Meistersinger*, he had notices pinned up urging an end to such demonstrations on the grounds that '*Hier gilt's der Kunst*' (Here it's art that counts). When the public in 1925 nonetheless burst into song, Siegfried had the lights turned off.

All that, though, still does not amount to proof that Siegfried was either politically liberal or racially tolerant. His objection to 'audience participation' might have been mainly aesthetic. In the 1930s Hitler himself insisted that no sounds other than Wagner's, not even the most stirring Nazi chorus, should echo through Bayreuth's hallowed hall. Besides, in 1924 the flag of pre-Republican Germany was hoisted above the festival theatre, Erich Ludendorff (the general who had most propagated the 'stab in the back' legend and who had taken part in Hitler's failed putsch) was among the favoured few invited to attend the general rehearsal, and a book issued to mark the reopening was filled with ultra-nationalist material. Busy though Siegfried was trying to ensure the festival would take place at all, it would be naive to imagine he was unaware of these things. Indeed, like many Germans, Siegfried regarded Ludendorff as a great patriot and was shocked that the old man had been among those shot at by police during the putsch.

As for Siegfried's letters, might they not simply have been ploys to try to ensure that vital Jewish support for Bayreuth would not evaporate? No doubt that is partly what Hitler had in mind when he claimed that Siegfried had been forced to act as he did or Jews would have 'broken his neck.' That interpretation also seems to be backed by the chronology. Siegfried's rebuff to Püringer was issued in the context of the first major drive after the First World War to raise funds to restart the festival. As for the 'everyone is welcome' declaration in 1925, that came when the festival was in business again but still shaky. A year earlier the Wagners' US tour had yielded a profit of only eight thousand dollars, not least because American financiers, especially Jews, had looked askance at Wahnfried's contacts with the Nazis. Then came the summer and the antisemitic outrages on the sidelines of a festival that anyway looked more nationalistic than patriotic, let alone international. Siegfried surely had cause by the end of 1924 to try to reassure Bayreuth's wealthy foreign and Jewish friends.

On the other hand, Siegfried's stance cannot solely be explained by his need to drum up cash. The more firmly he came out in favour of Jews, for whatever reason, the more likely he was to run foul of Bayreuth's German nationalist allies, especially in the Richard Wagner associations, who were themselves striving to raise funds for the festival. The same circles also deplored Siegfried's engagement of Jewish artists like the baritone Friedrich Schorr, an outstanding Wotan, and the bass Alexander Kipnis, an unsurpassed interpreter of Gurnemanz in *Parsifal*. Hitler, in particular, squirmed through his first Bayreuth *Ring* because he felt that having Schorr portray the ruler of the gods amounted to 'racial desecration'. Why hadn't Bayreuth instead booked Munich's Wilhelm Rode (later a fervent Nazi), the Führer rhetorically demanded years afterwards of his no doubt nonplussed entourage?[19] To which Siegfried would have had a simple answer: Schorr was finer. 'I must admit that one can really work much better with Jews,' Siegfried wrote to a friend in 1930. 'They are far more intensive and ambitious in their work, and once they have learned something they have got it for good.'[20]

This manifest admiration was far from free of envy. Siegfried often pointed out that Jews achieved particular success because they stuck together and supported one another. If only, he lamented, his own work and that of Bayreuth could enjoy the same kind of solidarity from Germans generally! Siegfried surely spoke from the heart. Over more than two decades he had composed, on average, one new opera every two years, but none had been a hit like *Bärenhäuter* – his very first stage piece, which bubbles along to a happy ending although unpromisingly set during the Thirty Years War. Siegfried's post-*Bärenhäuter* frustrations did not emerge simply because his work was found wanting compared with his father's, nor because his style was considered archaic. Cosima did her son no service when she called *Bärenhäuter* the finest comedy since *Meistersinger* but – remarkably – at the turn of the century it was the opera most often performed on German stages bar none. Mahler himself took it up in Vienna, albeit with cuts.

Had he gone on in the same lightish vein, Siegfried might have carved out a niche for himself not least *because* he offered a contrast of programme to the daunting dramas of his papa. Instead he confounded the expectations raised by his debut with a stream of works that were either ambiguous like *Bruder Lustig* (1904), or that dealt with deeply troubling themes such as child murder in *Schwarzschwanenreich* (The Realm of the Black Swan, 1910), suicide in *Sonnenflammen* (Flames of the Sun, 1912), adultery in *Der Heidenkönig* (The Heathen King, 1913) and, constantly, illegitimacy. Even his brief cantata *Das Märchen vom dicken fetten Pfannekuchen* (The Fable of the Thick, Fat Pancake, 1913) is more macabre than playful, telling of a pancake that flees the women cooks who want to gobble it up but finally sacrifices itself to famished children. Siegfried did not, of course, try to explain how far personal experience played a role in his choice of material; perhaps he did not always know, or want to know. At any rate he disappointed many erstwhile fans and raised questions his embarrassed family was not keen to have bandied about – then or later.

Although he too suffered some grave setbacks even before the First World War, Siegfried's old rival Richard Strauss was in a much stronger position. He did not have to bear comparison with a genius father nor was he subject to blackmail because of his private life. But in a Weimar world throbbing to the likes of Schoenberg and Weill, Krenek and Hindemith, both Siegfried and Strauss (not to mention an arch-conservative like Hans Pfitzner) were increasingly viewed as 'old hat', especially by the young. Even the work of the Master himself was felt by some to be out of tune with the times, despite gripping new productions and the enthusiasm of fine conductors – especially Jews like Bruno Walter, Otto Klemperer and Leo Blech. Siegfried usually failed to show despair but that is surely what he felt; despair at eternally composing 'for the bottom drawer', at having to conduct, year in year out, in one provincial centre after another at home and abroad for fees far less than the commercially adept Strauss commanded. All that he tended to pass off with a wave of the hand and an ironic remark, noting on one occasion that the best thing about conducting was that one could get to visit Italy more often. But once in a while the truth broke through. 'God grant that my children be protected from the wish to be artists,' he wrote in 1920 after a setback in Dresden. 'They should rather become town clerks than go through all the disappointments that are mine.'[21]

Much of this recalls the ambivalence of the Master himself; the esteem for Jews and jealousy of them; the patriotic feelings mingled with resentment that Germans for the most part failed to offer more support. To that extent Siegfried was indeed Richard's son. What he wholly lacked was his father's often ferocious passion and inner compulsion to tell the world of every twist and turn in his thoughts and feelings. On the contrary, in Siegfried's view the less the world knew about him (above and beyond what he indirectly revealed in his music) the better. 'Spineless', Goebbels harshly called him, which is right to the extent that Siegfried strove to avoid conflict even when he might have done better to stand and fight. Typically, he passed off his own lack of obvious heroism with irony, although he could not resist giving himself a modest pat on the back too. 'My parents named me Siegfried,' he noted in his memoirs. 'Well, no anvils have I smashed, no dragons have I slain, no sea of flames have I traversed. Nonetheless I hope I am not wholly unworthy of the name, since fear at least is not in my nature.'[22]

Fear perhaps not, but utmost caution – even in his last years, when Siegfried must at least have sensed where Germany might plunge if the Nazis were to win control. For a dinner in 1929 to celebrate his sixtieth birthday, Siegfried placed on every guest's plate the libretto of his new opera *Das Flüchlein das Jeder Mitbekam* (The Little Curse that Everybody Bears). Nothing special about that, apparently, except that one of the nastiest characters in the piece is a robber baron called Wolf. Is that how Siegfried saw Hitler and how, by this time, he wanted others to see him? Probably. He did not live to complete the music for *Flüchlein* but even if he had done so it seems doubtful that the Führer would have been keen to see the piece staged. On the other hand, Siegfried had two years earlier produced an opera called *Die heilige Linde* (The Sacred Linden Tree), which seemed tailor-made to appeal to the Nazis and their fans. Set in the third century AD, it pits mainly worthy Germans against tricky foreigners, it is full of mythology and (supposed) heroics, and it ends with massed choral appeals for a fatherland cleansed of 'evil spirits' for the next millennium – a 'thousand-year Reich', as it were. But whatever the apparent message of the libretto, easily the finest music goes to those ideologically on 'the wrong side' – the Italians – who thus emerge as far more intriguing folk than the tub-thumping Teutons. It is hard to believe that Siegfried was unaware of this. Anyway, the work was never given under the Nazis and, indeed, had to wait more than seventy years for its premiere.

A few months before that birthday party at which he made public the *Flüchlein* libretto, Siegfried drew up a will. Strictly speaking it was the joint will of his wife and himself, but it seems that Winifred only saw the full text when called upon to sign it before a lawyer. Sign it she did, although not every element of it can have pleased her. Siegfried stipulated that should he die first Winifred would be his sole heir and take over the direction of the festival, but that if she later remarried she would have to give up the direction and would lose most of the inheritance, which would then be divided equally among the four children. He also specified that only works by his father should be performed in the festival theatre. On the face of it that was a self-evident condition, but it was not one that the Master himself had formally imposed; indeed (as outlined in Chapter 4) he had at one time indicated otherwise. Siegfried, however, tried to leave absolutely nothing to chance. By pinning down not only how the inheritance was to be handled *after* the Winifred era but also just what the festival theatre was always to be used for, he cannily helped cement the family's future claims to 'its' festival. This point took on special weight after the Second World War when plans were afoot to dispossess the Wagners and to use the theatre for performances of non-Wagner works.

As for that clause about remarriage, did Siegfried really have Hitler specifically in mind when he drew it up? Perhaps the elements in his work mentioned above might just be coincidence, not covert warnings. As usual, interpreting 'Fidi' is like questioning the sphinx. All in all, though, it seems likely that having failed to keep Wolf out of Wahnfried, let alone openly oppose his march to power, Siegfried did try to stop his abhorrent rival from making the festival his own. If that was his intention he only half succeeded. Winifred never married the Führer or anyone else, but the festival became firmly identified with Hitler all the same.

# 9

# Three Funerals and a New Broom

Of the old Wagnerian guard still entrenched when Hitler and his cronies began to pay court at Wahnfried, Chamberlain was the first to die. 'Shattering scene,' the tireless chronicler Goebbels scribbled in his diary in 1926 a few months before the end came. 'Chamberlain on a couch. Broken, mumbling, with tears in his eyes. He holds my hand and won't let it go. His great eyes burn like fire. Greetings to you, our spiritual father. Trail-blazer, pioneer! I am deeply stirred. Leave-taking. He mumbles, wants to speak, fails – and then he cries like a child! Farewell! You are with us when we are close to despair.'[1]

That Goebbels, like Hitler (and indeed the Kaiser), felt near-religious awe for Chamberlain comes as no surprise. More striking is the fear he hints at that the Nazi movement, for all its initial success, might have no more of a future than the ailing figure on the couch. Against all the odds, the Weimar Republic had begun to seem almost healthy for the first time since the war. Inflation had been brought under control, a somewhat better reparations deal with the allies had been negotiated, the occupation of the Ruhr had ended and the country was close to admission to the League of Nations. In sum, prospects for extremists looked bleak, especially for the Nazis, with Hitler still widely banned from making political speeches although long since out of jail. Goebbels himself faced the task, seemingly hopeless at the time, of bolstering the party in hostile, strongly Social Democratic Berlin. In fact, the country's new-found relative stability was fairly soon to be smashed, especially by the stock-market crash of 1929 and subsequent recession. But naturally the ratty little Nazi with the club foot and silver tongue had no inkling of that when he made that depressing pilgrimage to the party's gradually expiring 'spiritual father' in Bayreuth.

When Chamberlain died at last, on 9 January 1927, the Nazi leadership milked the event for all its propaganda worth. In a long obituary the party newspaper, the *Völkische Beobachter*, contended that the deceased had passed on an inexhaustible stock of spiritual weapons for the struggle for 'the coming Third Reich'. As for the funeral itself, the Nazis simply stole the show, although plenty of notables were on hand like Prince August Wilhelm, a son of the Kaiser, and the exiled Czar Ferdinand of Bulgaria, that staunch Wagnerian who had been one of Isadora Duncan's nocturnal visitors in Bayreuth more than two decades before. One group of brown-shirted stormtroopers bore the coffin from the morgue to the hearse and another, carrying a huge swastika-bedecked wreath, led the mourners tramping through the streets. Black flags fluttered everywhere. Hitler, present with Rudolf Hess, seemed so overcome with emotion that his words of tribute were barely audible.

All the adult Wagners were on hand apart from Cosima, who was in no physical state to attend and was anyway barely able still to distinguish between the dead and the living. Long largely blind and now suffering frequent hallucinations, she nonetheless remained queen bee in her upper chamber at the Wahnfried hive. 'Greet Houston for me,' she urged the still-grieving Eva two years after Chamberlain's funeral, 'we are very close – I think we met before on another star.' On other occasions she asked where Liszt and Loldi (Isolde) were, even whether Richard Wagner were alive – to which Daniela diplomatically replied 'Yes Mama, *he lives*!' Sometimes she would cry out in the night, relive her battles to achieve worthy stagings of Wagner's works, lament Jewish 'hatred for the German character'. Sometimes she would break into French, loudly complaining that '*Je suis d'une grande mélancolie, je suis d'une grande mélancolie.*' Just once, in 1929, she confessed that 'I want to die.' But she lived on another year.

It wasn't all gloom. The four children loved to scamper upstairs to their grandma and 'play doctor', pretending to take her temperature with a pencil, feel her pulse and comb her still-thick, silver hair. Then they would wheel her chair onto the balcony where she could bask in the sun and listen to the birdsong. Daniela and Eva took it in turns to sit with her throughout the day and, when he was at home, Siegfried came up for a chat every afternoon. Cosima particularly enjoyed Fidi's attention, once exclaiming with apparent innocence that 'you are more like a daughter to me than a son.' In those last years she also seemed in part to come to terms with her past. Of Marie d'Agoult, the mother who shelved her, she admitted that, after all, 'there was something heroic about her,' and of Hans von Bülow, the husband she deserted, that he would have been 'the only competent' person to work with her in Bayreuth. It is sometimes said that when the end came, on 1 April 1930, Cosima's last words were 'Forgive, forgive,' uttered with Hans in mind. That is false, if the notes of Cosima's remarks diligently taken by the two daughters are anything to go by. According to Eva, Cosima muttered 'As God wills' and 'Wonderful' before breathing her last; according to Daniela, in this case perhaps a cooler chronicler, 'Mama' followed up 'Wonderful' with 'Pain' thrice repeated.[2] Whatever the truth about that, the statistics of Cosima's remarkable life are not in doubt. From her birth as an illegitimate child in a Como hotel room to her death as the *Hohe Frau* of Bayreuth, she survived for ninety-two years and three months. After Wagner expired in Venice, she stayed a widow for just over forty-seven years.

Ironically Siegfried, the ever-solicitous son, was not on hand when his mother died. Unable to resist the temptation to work at La Scala, Milan, Italy's finest opera house, he had accepted an invitation to produce and conduct the whole *Ring* cycle there in March. Siegfried well knew that soon afterwards he faced specially taxing preparations for the summer festival in Bayreuth, but he reckoned that in the wake of the Milan exertions he would be able to take a break to recover in Greece. He never got the chance. Alarmed by a cable from Wahnfried saying Cosima's condition had worsened, he and Winifred scrapped the Greek trip and took a night-sleeper home. They arrived too late. 'Mama' already lay surrounded with flowers on her bier, hair combed, hands folded and looking, as Siegfried put it in his diary, 'young and beautiful, as [she had done] thirty years ago'.[3] After the funeral ceremony at Wahnfried a hearse bore the body briefly to the festival theatre, the house Cosima had exulted and suffered over so much longer than the Master who built it, and thence to cremation. 'A fine ceremony there too,' Siegfried noted, 'despite an annoying, albeit well-meant, speech from a somewhat drunken enthusiast. Around an hour with friends in hotel, then journey home.'[4]

From his unimpassioned, near-offhand, comments you might think Siegfried took his mother's death almost in his stride. A photo snapped soon after the funeral could give the same impression; Winifred dressed all in black, from her driver's cowl to the tips of her elegant shoes, Siegfried in light-coloured jacket and plus-fours, a cigarette dangling from his fingers. But all that simply serves to confirm an old rule – that the deeper Siegfried's emotion, the less he was inclined to show it or able to express it in words. Equable as ever throughout those dismal April days, he nonetheless looked, as one prescient eye-witness put it, 'as pale as death.'

Italy helped, as usual. By the end of the month, Siegfried had made off again over the Alps to relax in his favourite way; hobnobbing with Blandine, Manfredi and other members of the Wagner clan's Italian branch, dining well but not wisely and revisiting art and architecture he had loved since childhood. In an admission that would probably have gone too far even for his Italophile father, he claimed that on hearing parts of *Lohengrin*, *Tristan* and *Tannhäuser*, he saw pictures in his mind's eye by Raphael, Titian and Correggio. *Götterdämmerung* he linked to the work of Tintoretto. Left to himself, perhaps Siegfried really would have made good the threat he uttered in his latter years to 'close the shop' and emigrate to Italy for good. But there were the children to consider, Winifred too, although she was well able to look after herself. Besides, in 1930 he was at long last set to realise his greatest festival ambition – to create and present a new production of *Tannhäuser*.

With its theme of the artistic outsider struggling between the demands of the flesh and the spirit, with its near-Italian lyricism and with the special challenges it posed to stage – from the orgy on the Venusberg to the great crowd scenes at Wartburg castle – *Tannhäuser* was the Wagner opera that Siegfried found easily the most intriguing, albeit not the most fully realised. But because of the problems and especially the cost involved, the work had not been given at Bayreuth since that turbulent summer of 1904, when Isadora Duncan had choreographed the orgy and Siegfried had conducted all five performances. In 1924 there had barely been enough cash on hand to restart the festival with tried and tested productions, let alone to risk a new *Tannhäuser*. Siegfried pencilled in the work for 1927 but then regretfully substituted the less costly *Tristan*. By 1930, though, the money had been raised – thanks above all to Winifred, who organised a special *Tannhäuser* appeal and presented her husband with the proceeds of 100,000 marks for his sixtieth birthday.

Siegfried could thus go ahead and in so doing he dropped nearly all his familiar caution, engaging an avant-garde choreographer (Rudolf von Laban) and a notably international cast: Sigismund Pilinszky (Hungarian) as Tannhäuser, Maria Müller (Czech) as Elisabeth and Ivar Andrésen (Swedish) as the Landgrave. Above all he booked Arturo Toscanini, the first foreigner (Isolde's Swiss husband apart) ever to conduct at Bayreuth. The latter decision enraged hard-line Wagnerians and especially Karl Muck, that fine but fiercely jealous conductor who had first appeared in Bayreuth in 1901 and who regarded his own interpretations as uniquely close to the Master's wishes. Muck, now seventy, stormed and intrigued against Toscanini (as he had in 1924 against another top conductor, Fritz Busch, who never returned to Bayreuth), but Siegfried refused to budge. He had admired the Italian maestro ever since hearing his *Tristan* in Milan decades before, but he had hitherto bowed to pressure from traditionalists who argued that the Bayreuth pit was no place for a non-German – not even for the most famous conductor of the day, which Toscanini by this time surely was. Now he stood firm, as though aware he would not get another chance if he buckled this time.

Siegfried was already hard at work with the singers at Wahnfried even before official rehearsals began at the festival theatre in June, but his troubles really started when Toscanini arrived in a blaze of (mainly adulatory) publicity to take on not just *Tannhäuser* but *Tristan* too. Muck, booked as usual for 'his' *Parsifal*, felt more than ever sidelined and had constantly to be soothed by Winifred, who had a real way with the old man, to stop him making good threats to resign. Meanwhile Muck's similarly choleric new rival threw tantrums from his very first rehearsal, incensing the players with charges of incompetence and unsettling singers who could not match his swift tempi. Siegfried was all diplomacy, smilingly asking the '*caro maestro*' to remember that a 'rough German' text could not be handled like a 'flexible Italian' one, quietly switching one or two of the less deft instrumentalists and trying to ensure that the eager but ailing Pilinszky did not sing himself out before the first night. Up each day from seven a.m. until well after midnight, snatching snacks between crises, chain-smoking and subject to sporadic asthma attacks, Siegfried finally collapsed clutching at his heart during a *Götterdämmerung* rehearsal in mid-July. A few days later the festival began with the first of five performances of *Tannhäuser* that were widely hailed as among the greatest triumphs in Bayreuth history, partly because of the singers (the strenuous Pilinszky largely excepted) but above all thanks to the conductor and producer. Siegfried saw none of it. He died peacefully in hospital on 4 August aged just sixty-one, exactly four months and three days after his mother. At a memorial concert on 8 August Muck and Toscanini for once collaborated, the former conducting the funeral march from *Götterdämmerung*, the latter the *Siegfried Idyll* – that birthday present 'with Fidi birdsong and orange sunrise' for Cosima from 'her Richard', premiered on the staircase at Tribschen sixty years before.

It is tempting to see a direct link between Cosima's death and Siegfried's, to surmise that the son just could not live on without the mother he adored, but that explanation is too simple by half. In the course of his adult life, Siegfried wrote the music and librettos for fourteen complete operas and began work on several more; he conducted sixty-two performances at Bayreuth alone (including eleven complete *Ring* cycles) and countless others in opera houses and concert halls elsewhere. He acted as a vocal talent scout with a fine ear for subtlety as well as power, and as a producer with an artist's eye for staging. He ran the festival after Cosima stepped down in 1906 and got it going again six years after the war. At the end, with failing health, he was doing more than ever. A multi-talent with a deceptively casual air, then, who worked himself to death – is that the verdict? Not quite, because as the Master's son he also bore the burden placed on him of unfulfillable expectations, and as an active bisexual he faced the ever-present threat of scandal. He gave few hints of inner tension but tension there surely was; all the more searing, no doubt, because bottled up and only partly released in his (frustratingly ill-acknowledged) compositions. That element too, unquantifiable though it be, belongs to the diagnosis of the workaholic who so swiftly followed his mother to the grave.

Prolific composer though he was, Siegfried was largely out of step with his time although Arnold Schoenberg, no less, praised him in 1912 as 'a more profound and original artist than many today who are more famous'.[5] Rather backhanded praise, perhaps, but praise all the same. Sometimes too long, often with over-intricate plots, unexpectedly hard to perform, Siegfried's operas at their best can nonetheless bring an audience cheering to its feet – on the rare occasions, that is, when the works are given at all. As a producer Siegfried was hardly 'the greatest of his time' (Friedelind) but he was good enough to win admiration from the most talented of peers like Max Reinhardt. Siegfried's *Tannhäuser* is widely, probably rightly, hailed as his finest stage achievement but his *Lohengrin* and especially *Meistersinger* – both before the war – were bolder steps forward for Bayreuth in the immediate post-Cosima era than is often acknowledged.

Nor is it true, as is sometimes claimed, that the festival was becoming a shambles under Siegfried until Toscanini arrived to lick it into shape. That the Italian indeed achieved great things is clear from the near-complete recording of *Tannhäuser* made at Bayreuth in August 1930 (the month Siegfried died) – fully prepared by Toscanini although conducted, for contractual reasons, by the younger and far less renowned Karl Elmendorff. But the Bayreuth recording of much of *Tristan* made two years earlier, also under Elmendorff, is orchestrally exemplary, and renderings of excerpts from *Parsifal*, conducted in 1927 by Muck and Siegfried, are among the finest ever committed to disc – flowing, dramatic but never superficial. Reopened Bayreuth had its cash troubles, dowdy sets and in large part deplorably nationalistic public; but in the main it offered, on the evidence available, performances of high rank. The signs are that by 1930 Siegfried was trying to make a firmer declaration of independence, both artistically and, via his will, vis-à-vis Hitler (who came neither to Cosima's funeral nor her son's). Might Bayreuth, then, have played a different role in the Nazi era if Siegfried had lived? Perhaps – but not, all things considered, a *very* different one. Taking on Wolf eyeball to eyeball came to Fidi no more naturally than slaying dragons.

The morning after Siegfried died, Winifred went straight to his office and issued her first orders as the new festival director. There seemed no doubt about her right, indeed her duty, to take over – at least according to the will her late husband had drawn up and that he and she had signed just a year before. Besides, she was already deeply involved in festival affairs, well beyond mothering awkward artists like Muck and dealing with reams of correspondence on Siegfried's behalf. The success of the *Tannhäuser* appeal showed her ability to orchestrate fund-raising on a big scale, and she had even been aiming to take half a year off to study business management. Instead, Siegfried's sudden death meant she had to 'learn on the job' and, with an energy that drew gasps of fury and respect, she started to do just that. Parts of the festival theatre and restaurant were revamped, a kind of press department was set up (for 'propaganda', Winifred privately explained) and the basis of a proper archive was laid. Siegfried's 'bachelor house' next to Wahnfried was also converted, the better to receive important guests – not, initially, Hitler though he regularly stayed there later.

Old-guard Wagnerians hated changes anyway, even the ones gradually made by Siegfried, but he at least had been the Master's son and almost until his death he had basked in the aura of the enfeebled but revered *Hohe Frau*. His widow enjoyed no such protection. Foreign-born, she was seen by the hardliners as fitted neither by blood nor talent to act as chief guardian of the Bayreuth grail. Exactly these charges had been levelled at Cosima after the Master's death nearly half a century before, but that was an inconvenient fact the critics chose to ignore. Winifred, anyway, showed no more willingness to back down than her late mother-in-law had done. When the town of Bayreuth with unseemly haste proposed that Wahnfried be turned into a museum and the family moved to 'alternative accommodation', she scornfully refused and underlined her independence by paying for her husband's funeral. Strictly speaking the town should have footed the bill because Siegfried had been an honorary citizen.

Inevitably Eva and Daniela, known to the children as 'the aunts' and to many Bayreuthers as '*die Dynastie*', were among Winifred's fiercest foes. The two of them had long been at loggerheads with their sister-in-law but they had proved indispensable all the same, for years visiting Wahnfried every day (and many nights) to look after their mother. Now, within months, they lost both their key nursing role and the backing of their brother (who incidentally had helped boost their incomes with 'perks' from festival funds, a practice Winifred soon stopped). Daniela remained the festival's costume designer and wardrobe mistress, the job she had held for more than two decades, but it seemed plain that she too would eventually be swept away by the new broom on the Green Hill. In a bitter note written in 1932 that found its way into the Wahnfried archive, she charged that the festival had been gripped by a spirit of commercialism from the moment Siegfried had entered his grave. Respect, piety, tradition; all that, Daniela bewailed, now counted for next to nothing. The new building work ruined the look of the theatre and (a dig at Winifred as mother) the children clambered all over the place like hooligans. Worse still, Daniela and Eva later learned to their horror that a new staging of

*Parsifal* was projected for 1934. In principle, a planned revamp of the *Bühnenweihfestspiel* ought to have been good news. The sets, virtually unaltered since the 1882 premiere, looked almost comically tatty and were even dangerous. But 'the aunts' insisted that no change whatever could be made to a staging 'on which the Master's eye had rested' and organised a petition that attracted more than a thousand signatures.[6] Their campaign failed, but naturally it brought still frostier relations with Wahnfried's new mistress.

Winifred pushed on regardless of the hostility she faced from the start, scoring what looked like a great coup as early as 1931 when she signed up Wilhelm Furtwängler – acknowledged as Germany's foremost conductor despite much strong (not least Jewish) competition. The Berlin-born son of a famous archaeologist, Furtwängler had reached the peak of his profession in 1922 at the age of only thirty-six, taking over the Berlin Philharmonic Orchestra from the legendary Arthur Nikisch. Although a champion of modern music with more than 180 contemporary works in his concert repertoire, a fact barely reflected in his recordings and now usually forgotten, it was above all for his searching, seething renderings of the Austrian-German classics that Furtwängler was renowned. By hauling him aboard as Bayreuth's 'music director', Winifred seemed to win a near-guarantee of the festival's long-term success, not least at the box office. All the more so since she simultaneously appointed the multi-talented Heinz Tietjen, who already ran a bewildering number of opera houses and theatres in and beyond Berlin, as Bayreuth's 'artistic director'. Tietjen in fact turned out to be the far more vital, indeed fateful, catch but at the time it was Furtwängler who grabbed most of the headlines.

Briefly, things went well. Although, like Tietjen, booked to take on his full role only two years later, Furtwängler happily agreed to make his Bayreuth debut with *Tristan* in the coming 1931 season. As Toscanini was returning to conduct *Parsifal* (taking over from Muck who had stumped off in a huff and never returned) as well as *Tannhäuser*, Wagnerians could look forward to a 'dream festival'. All the more so since the two conductors made for a study in contrasts – the Italian with his precise beat and insistence on the letter of the score, the German with his bizarre but miraculously effective baton technique, all flutters and jerks as though a water-diviner were being employed to find hidden treasure beneath the notes. Bayreuth audiences would not be able to see what was going on in the covered orchestra pit, but they were clearly in for a feast of comparative interpretation of the highest class. That, indeed, is what they got, but not quite in the way expected. Furtwängler opened the festival with a lithe, translucent *Tristan*; superb in its way but, thanks to the singer-friendly Bayreuth acoustic, less crushing orchestrally than fans of the conductor were used to elsewhere. Meanwhile Toscanini, often thought a speed merchant, produced a ruminative *Parsifal* that to this day ranks as the slowest in Bayreuth's history.

Then the trouble started. The two conductors, along with Elmendorff who was in charge of the *Ring*, were due to give a benefit concert in memory of Siegfried. At the last moment Toscanini pulled out in a rage and left town, returning to give the rest of the festival performances for which he had been booked but swearing never to conduct at Bayreuth again. Just why he took such umbrage remains unclear. It is claimed he was furious because an audience had been present against his wishes at a rehearsal, but there was surely more to it than that. He was suffering great pain in his right (conducting) arm; as a fierce anti-fascist he had been roughed up by Mussolini's blackshirts during a recent concert tour in Italy; and – probably above all – he was more than irritated by the presence of Furtwängler as Bayreuth's new, much-fêted 'music director in waiting'. A year earlier the (positive) festival news had been all Toscanini, now it was mostly Furtwängler – thanks not least to the brilliant management and publicity skills of the German maestro's long-time personal assistant Berta Geissmar, a Jewess later forced by the Nazis to flee the country.

Furtwängler saved the concert by taking on Toscanini's part of it as well as his own (he had originally wanted to conduct the whole thing anyway), but he made trouble too. Winifred was ready, even eager, to seek the best possible help but as Siegfried's successor she felt she had the right to the last word. Furtwängler, though, was anything but a 'team player'. He was often nervous and indecisive in business (and political) affairs, hence the huge influence of Frau Geissmar who once struck a pen from his hand when he was about to sign a contract she judged unwise. But when it came to making music he was filled with a near-Bayreuthian sense of 'holy mission' and regarded compromise as heresy. Besides, neither he nor Winifred was the soul of diplomacy. When she tried to tell him how far he could go as director and muttered in passing that 'no one is indispensable', he wrote a haughty letter in early 1932 telling her that, on music, she was frankly an amateur. Since she nonetheless reserved the right to overrule him, he felt unable to take up the director's job as foreseen. Clearly incensed, Winifred (the former 'Senta' Klindworth, after all!) retorted that she had worked closely with Siegfried for fifteen years under Cosima's eye and that she knew her Wagner very well, thank you. 'With the expression of regret, I therefore release you, as desired, from your promise,' she pronounced. 'Perhaps a way will be found all the same for you to conduct in Bayreuth.'[7] A way *was* found, but not until four years later.

Winifred's plight seemed all the worse because the errant Furtwängler was not just Germany's favourite conductor but Hitler's. How would 'Uncle Wolf', who had already thrown a tantrum in 1931 on learning of Muck's 'treachery', react to the news that his Winnie had let such a great catch slip through her fingers? Fortunately for her, she got a chance to put her side of the story during a long car drive in early May 1932 and Hitler took it well – in part, no doubt, because the outing included a jolly reunion with the Wagner children. The Nazi leader had been unable to see them for nearly a year and he greeted them, as usual, as though they were his own.

That pleasure aside, Hitler had other reasons to be upbeat. Although he had recently lost the race to become Germany's president against the octogenarian incumbent (and ex-field marshall) Paul von Hindenburg, he had polled more than thirteen million votes compared with his opponent's nineteen million. His whistlestop election campaign had made him even better known (there sometimes seemed to be half a dozen Hitlers simultaneously on the stump) and his party was well set to become much the strongest in the Reichstag. For many Germans Hitler now offered the 'last chance' – as Nazi placards plastered everywhere put it – to give the country international clout again and deliver it from crushing unemployment. Some change for the ex-jailbird of Landsberg and for his Nazis who four years before had scraped together only 2.8 per cent of the national vote! Hitler's post-putsch change of strategy (from armed struggle to a superficially legal 'march through the institutions') was paying off handsomely at last, helped by the opportunism of monied conservatives who thought they could use the Nazi boss's charisma for their own ends.

Goebbels, also present at that May get-together with Winifred and her children, was at least as buoyant as his boss. He even speculated that by the summer of 1933 when the next festival was due (1932 was a performance-free year), the Nazis might already be in power. That turned out to be right. In the meantime, though, Winifred was still in dire need of a star conductor. Toscanini saved the day, or seemed to, by finally yielding to her entreaties and agreeing to return after all to conduct *Meistersinger* as well as *Parsifal*. The notion that Toscanini would in effect replace Furtwängler was hard for Bayreuthers to take; but they contented themselves with the thought that, thanks to his services to the Master, the Italian was more or less an honorary German anyway. Anyway, hadn't Chamberlain himself decisively shown that the great figures of the Italian Renaissance were pure Aryans?

Alas for Winifred, when the Nazis came to power in 1933 and persecution of the Jews began in earnest, the outraged Toscanini called off his festival plans – despite a letter from Hitler saying how much he was looking forward to seeing the maestro in the summer. Three years after Siegfried's death, the new mistress of Bayreuth faced a debacle; no Muck, no Furtwängler, no Toscanini, a Führer livid because he had been rebuffed and, thanks mainly to the artistic uncertainty and political upheaval, precious few ticket sales. But Winifred still had a trump card in the person of Tietjen – a wily, hugely influential figure who deserves a close look here, or at least one as close as his enigmatic personality allows.

Heinz (Heinrich Vivian) Tietjen was, according to Bruno Walter who worked with him in the 1920s at Berlin's Städtische Oper (Municipal Opera), 'one of the strangest persons with whom life has ever brought me into contact. In spite of our meeting almost daily for four years, I cannot say that I ever came to know this impenetrable man.' In his memoirs, written some two decades later, Walter goes on to describe Tietjen as 'of medium height, with drooping eyelids, a constant sideways look of his bespectacled eyes, a narrow-lipped and tightly compressed mouth, and a nervously twitching face. Never a spirited or spontaneous – to say nothing of an interesting – word came from his lips.'[8] Hardly a flattering portrait, but that is no surprise. Walter finally dropped his job as music director at the Opera because he felt that Tietjen, the general manager, was plotting behind his back (which was probably true) and making promises he never meant to keep. And yet, along with all his bitter words, Walter could not help acknowledging the 'self-sacrificing spirit' with which Tietjen strove 'to have all my artistic wishes fulfilled, though they must frequently have been inconvenient to him'. He concluded that 'I am not angry with him. I like to recall the minutes of his frankness and am ready to forgive the hours of his opacity.'[9]

Walter's confessed inability to identify 'the man behind the mask' was almost universally shared. Was Tietjen a Social Democrat, as some top Nazis charged, or a Nazi sympathiser, as many – not just left-wingers – claimed? Was he a traditionalist because of his dominant role in Bayreuth, or was he a modernist because he backed contemporary opera, especially in Berlin? Was he pro-Jewish because he worked closely for years with artists like Walter and Klemperer, or antisemitic because he (in the main) stood by when the Nazi persecution began in earnest? In old age, Klemperer recalled that when he went to Tietjen in 1933 to say he was fleeing the country that very day, he got no reaction from his long-time colleague and boss beyond conversation about health and diet. 'Imagine,' Klemperer snorted, 'this man knew I didn't have a penny in my pocket and that I would never come back. And he was only interested in diets. Terrible, terrible.'[10]

Even the question often put in jest by theatre folk – 'Did Tietjen ever (really) live?' – is not wholly straightforward to answer. To close associates, including Walter, a fleeting smile and a few warm words showed that the man could indeed 'come alive' once in a while. Some women, Winifred among them, found him utterly charming. To a less favoured circle, though, Tietjen seemed a phantom figure; nondescript in appearance, near-impossible to pin down in conversation and extraordinarly adept at covering his tracks. So much is sure. Tietjen became the grey eminence of German theatre during the Weimar Republic, he stayed at the top throughout the Nazi era despite intermittent harassment, he sailed through post-war denazification and then pursued his career even (very briefly) in Bayreuth. Yet his tale has received nothing like the attention it deserves (an omission far more painful than that involving von Gross, a key figure for Bayreuth but hardly beyond). Perhaps the challenge of pinning down a phantom, even one so potent, has proved too daunting – or perhaps those most involved felt they would compromise themselves by telling what they knew.

At least a few clues can be dredged from Tietjen's own brief autobiographical essay, slanted and full of holes though that is.[11] His skill at slipping out of tight corners no doubt came from his father, a widely travelled diplomat, and much of his aptitude for music from his British mother, who taught him the piano. Precious little colour seems to have rubbed off on him from the exotic cities of his early years, Tangiers where he was born in 1881 and Constantinople where he was partly raised; but he did pick up languages easily, even Arabic, and at first wanted to become a diplomat like his father. Instead he plumped for music, partly thanks to a chance meeting with the legendary Nikisch, partly because serious eye trouble forced him to lie in the dark for months, reflecting on his future and becoming still more sensitive to sound. In his twenties he was already accomplished enough to put on an entire *Ring* cycle as conductor and producer in the provinces, and ambitious enough to write to Cosima telling her he yearned to do the same in Bayreuth. It took him nearly three decades more to achieve his aim but this was a man well able to wait – and to pounce when the time was ripe.

Contemporary reports and his few recordings suggest Tietjen was an efficient rather than an inspired maestro, but his productions won widespread praise for superb organisation and (much more surprising) imaginative flair. One great admirer was Siegfried who was bowled over by the *Lohengrin* Tietjen put on in Berlin in 1929. Siegfried in any case believed that it took producers equally at home on stage and in the orchestra pit, like himself, to draw the most from his father's works. On seeing the Berlin *Lohengrin*, original in concept but never betraying the flow of the music, he felt his view handsomely confirmed. Should anything happen to him, he advised Winifred, then Tietjen would make an ideal artistic adviser at Bayreuth – at least until the children were grown. Did it cross Siegfried's mind that Tietjen of all people might be able to offer an effective defence against the voracious 'Wolf'? If so, it was an inspired thought.

Alike though the two men of the theatre were in some ways, Tietjen had attributes Siegfried sadly lacked (or could not be bothered to develop); administrative skill amounting to genius and an ultra-sensitive nose for power. To read his memoir you would think that Tietjen rose to the top mainly because important people begged him to take on one difficult job after another in which he then happened to be able to shine. He was, he claims, amazed to be appointed as a young man to direct the smallish opera in Trier close to the border with Luxembourg, he later slipped into the top job in nearby Saarbrücken, he had a wonderful time running the opera in Breslau (now Wroclaw in Poland) and gave that up only with reluctance to go to the Städtische

Oper in Berlin-Charlottenburg. It was not long before he was also in charge of the more prestigious Staatsoper (formerly the Court Opera) on the Unter den Linden avenue, and finally he became manager of all Prussian State Theatres (not opera houses alone), thus extending his influence far beyond Berlin. He has warm words for Walter, Klemperer and, not least, Max von Schillings, whom he replaced, sadly he says, at the State Opera. He also pats himself on the back for ensuring that the Jewish conductor Leo Blech was able to draw a full pension after being driven into exile by the Nazis. Tietjen surely did help Blech and others, but just as surely his career and motives were murkier than he suggests. No doubt it would be naive to expect more frankness, even in an account compiled and published long after the Second World War.

Few things better illustrate Tietjen's knack of 'running with the hare and hunting with the hounds' than the brief, tumultuous history of Berlin's Kroll-Oper at the Platz der Republik. Strictly speaking the Kroll was an offshoot of the Staatsoper and was financed out of the latter's budget, but Tietjen kept it on a long artistic leash which Klemperer, the music director, used to the full. Daring, uncompromising, and massively persuasive, Klemperer even managed to attract Alexander Zemlinsky, Schoenberg's brother-in law and a distinguished composer in his own right, to the Kroll team 'merely' as an assistant conductor. For four years from 1927 audiences were treated to (or sickened by) a rich diet that mixed Schoenberg, Stravinsky, Hindemith, Krenek, Janácek and other 'moderns' with bold productions of classics including Wagner. Traditionalists and, above all, the Nazis loathed the Kroll but Tietjen stuck to his guns until 1931 (two years *before* Hitler came to power) when the house was closed for good, officially for lack of finance. Later Klemperer claimed the action had been taken because he was a Jew. Tietjen disagreed, saying that Klemperer's 'whole political and artistic direction' had been responsible.[12] That Tietjen himself had long seemed to identify with that very same direction caused him trouble with the Nazis but not lasting harm. By 1931, anyway, he had slipped into yet another fascinating role – advising Winifred and, bit by bit, coming to dominate her.

It was Tietjen who had first encouraged Winifred to get Furtwängler to Bayreuth while warning her that the conductor was nothing if not a prima donna. What role he may have played in Furtwängler's subsequent extended absence from the Green Hill is (as so often with Tietjen) far from clear. According to Friedelind, Tietjen had the confidence of both Furtwängler and Winifred (but never of Toscanini) and shuttled between them telling tales that strengthened his own position with each. That account seems plausible; at least it fits what is known of Tietjen's tactics elsewhere. On the face of it, therefore, Furtwängler's withdrawal in high dudgeon from the festival seems to cast doubt on Tietjen's skill as diplomat and go-between – but does it really? With Furtwängler gone for years, and then returning more or less as a 'guest', Tietjen was left without a real rival at Bayreuth in artistic matters, let alone administrative ones. That might not have been his firm aim from the start; but he already knew his Furtwängler inside out from long experience in Berlin, and he surely sized up Winifred quickly enough to see that she and her prospective 'music director' would soon be on a collision course.

Tietjen must have been vexed when Toscanini bolted for good in 1933 but he had evidently been expecting it and had sounded out Fritz Busch as a possible substitute. No doubt in the circumstances Busch looked a near-ideal candidate; neither foreign nor a Jew, long-time music director in Dresden and ranked by Hitler not far behind Furtwängler as a conductor. Unfortunately for Tietjen, Busch despised the Nazis and had fallen so foul of the local Saxon branch that, despite the Führer's admiration, he had been driven out of his job. He promptly took his family abroad and stayed there, like his similarly principled musician brothers Adolf and Hermann, despite repeated bids to get him back. In his memoirs, he recalls a conversation in Italy in May 1933 with a deeply distressed Toscanini, who showed him Hitler's 'looking forward to seeing you' letter. Busch wrote:

What was depressing Toscanini, from his youth closely attached to the art of Richard Wagner, and its greatest interpreter, was anxiety for the future of the Bayreuth Festival. Feeling thus he asked me, 'What will Bayreuth do if I refuse?' 'Then they will invite me, Maestro,' I said. Toscanini was speechless. 'That is to say, they *have* invited me. Tietjen, who expects your refusal, has already taken steps.'

I was delighted at his astonishment and added with a laugh, 'Of course, I will refuse, like you.' Toscanini shut his mouth, which had remained open from astonishment, and purred, in his warm, melancholy, voice, '*Eh, caro amico*!' We were both silent and a feeling of great sorrow came over us.[13]

With so many top conductors either sulking, already in exile or simply 'unacceptable' (a word in ever-increasing use), Bayreuth seemed doomed to hold its first festival in the Nazi era without a single baton star. Tietjen, though, did not give up. Suppose Bayreuth could secure the services of Richard Strauss, the 'grand old man' of German music, for at least part of the programme; what a coup that would be, albeit one inordinately tricky to bring off. Strauss, remember, had not conducted at Bayreuth (that 'pigsty of pigsties' as he had called it) since 1894, when he gave five performances of *Tannhäuser.* As a composer he had been a rival to Siegfried and, partly because of that, he had fallen foul of the *Hohe Frau.* Still, Siegfried and Cosima were now dead and Strauss revered Wagner's music at least as much as ever. Moreover, he seemed less than squeamish when it came to acting as a high-level stopgap for colleagues who fell foul of the regime. In March, Bruno Walter had fled Germany after being threatened by the Nazis and barred from conducting a concert with the Berlin Philharmonic Orchestra. As Walter drily noted in his memoirs, his place on the rostrum had been taken by 'the composer of *Ein Heldenleben*' (A Hero's Life) – Richard Strauss.[14] Later the agent who had arranged the concert claimed Walter had, in fact, proposed that Strauss step in so that the event could go ahead and the orchestra be paid. Like so much else from those years in particular, the exact circumstances are no longer verifiable. At least there is no doubt that Strauss conducted and that he donated his fee to the Philharmonic.

Finally Strauss stepped in for Toscanini, 'for the sake of Bayreuth' as he put it, just as he had done for Walter, supposedly 'for the sake of the orchestra'. Tietjen (later the dedicatee of Strauss's opera *Die Liebe der Danae*) prepared the ground with the utmost finesse and Winifred clinched the deal when, hand-wringing as it were, she visited the composer at his home at Garmisch in the Bavarian Alps. Strauss agreed to conduct *Parsifal*, in the event shaving some forty minutes off Toscanini's timing from two years previously, as well as a celebratory performance of Beethoven's Ninth Symphony with its choral finale extolling the brotherhood of man. Thanks to Hitler, who attended the festival for the first time in eight years and backed it in cash and kind, the erstwhile blocks of unsold tickets were snapped up after all. The Führer, it was claimed, had saved Bayreuth. It would be at least as correct to say that Tietjen had done so. It was he who had pulled the strings to get Strauss, who had drawn in vital staff and artists from his Berlin Staatsoper team (some, admittedly, already active at Bayreuth in Siegfried's time) and he who had conceived the new productions of the *Ring* and *Meistersinger*, working hand-in-glove with his celebrated stage-designer colleague Emil Preetorius. As though that did not keep him busy enough, Tietjen also made his Bayreuth debut as a conductor, taking over several performances of *Meistersinger* from Elmendorff.

'It would have been a pardonable error on the part of any casual visitor to Bayreuth to have mistaken this year's Wagner festival for a Hitler festival,' reported Walter Legge, correspondent of the *Manchester Guardian* in August 1933.[15] Legge was not referring only to the china plaques of the Führer and the copies of *Mein Kampf* filling shop windows all over town, but also to the audiences which, he felt, gave the impression that 'since Hitler likes Wagner's music, we are here too' – an observation especially accurate, as it happens, with respect to most of the Nazi grandees in the Führer's entourage. The British critic complained that Strauss and Elmendorff were inferior to Toscanini as interpreters (he even compared Strauss to an American tourist who sees everything in record time and feels nothing), but he nonetheless found both the orchestral playing and choral singing 'electrifying'. Above all he praised the staging as far beyond anything to be seen at Covent Garden, claiming that 'even those of us who have watched with interest the development of Emil Preetorius as a scenic artist and of Heinz Tietjen as a producer have been astonished by the dramatic strength and stark realism of these Bayreuth productions.' The two Germans, Legge enthused, 'give dramatic truth, and Wagnerian dramatic truth will outdo any other form of theatrical art.'

Legge was a perceptive critic with a fine ear. He also had a persuasive tongue and a keen, not to say ruthless, business sense – attributes most fully displayed after the Second World War when he founded the Philharmonia Orchestra and, as a record producer of genius, got Furtwängler to London to put the whole of *Tristan und Isolde* on disc. There is thus every reason to take seriously his report on the 1933 festival, including that special praise for Tietjen and Preetorius who henceforth dominated production and staging at Bayreuth. By no means everyone judged their work with such favour. Many of the old guard like 'the aunts' saw the creations of Berlin's 'terrible twins' as newfangled, even heretical. Less hidebound Wagnerians, on the other hand, often felt Tietjen's massed crowd scenes to be 'over-produced' – that is, too busy and cluttered. A kowtow to abominable Nazi taste perhaps?

Hardly. Long before the Nazis came to power Tietjen had shown how he loved arranging masses of people onstage – as many as his budget would permit and arguably more than was always good for the piece in hand. Even so his work was and remained a world away from the pompous tub-thumping and overstrained pathos of a Nazi producer like Benno von Arent (who staged nothing on the Green Hill). The truth is that in Bayreuth, as in Berlin, Tietjen and Preetorius usually managed to offer enough stage evidence to underpin Wagner's story, but not so much that it would smother the allegory behind it. That was the case for much of their *Ring*, as well as for their new *Lohengrin* from 1936, their *Tristan* from 1938 and to some extent for their *Holländer* from 1939. When the artists were also up to scratch, as they clearly were in that *Lohengrin* conducted by Furtwängler with Franz Völker in the title role and Maria Müller as Elsa, the result was unsurpassed by any stage anywhere.

Much of that was registered – or at least foreshadowed – in Legge's report of 1933. Even so, the English critic cannot quite have realised how all-pervasive Tietjen's influence really was nor, perhaps, have appreciated the full irony of the situation; namely, that at Bayreuth's first 'Hitler festival', the biggest accolades were deserved by a producer and a stage designer who were regarded with the utmost suspicion by most Nazis and who (like Furtwängler) never joined the party. For insight into all that, Legge would have needed to uncover intimate details about Winifred's relationship with Tietjen, which at that stage was far less widely remarked upon than her long-standing ties with 'Wolf'. He would also have had to seek clarity on a matter at least as opaque – the real roles played by Wagner and Bayreuth in the power structure of the 'Third Reich'.

# 10

# All the Reich's a Stage

Although the Nazis put on many viler propaganda shows than the one dubbed the 'Day of Potsdam' that they staged on 21 March 1933, none was ever better managed or more crushingly effective. For Hitler the success of the event was not just welcome but badly needed. At that time he had been chancellor of a coalition government for nearly two months and his party had emerged stronger from the nationwide election of 5 March. Nonetheless, despite their terror tactics during the campaign, the Nazis had still won 'only' 43.9 per cent of the vote (after 33.1 per cent in the previous poll just four months before) and hence remained well short of an absolute majority in the Reichstag.

In other words, the new chancellor looked far from dominant. Many people thought he would soon fail like his two immediate predecessors, Franz von Papen and Kurt von Schleicher, each of whom had lasted in office for only a few months. Liberals, Social Democrats and communists naturally loathed Hitler and the churches were wary of him. The officer corps looked down on him, a mere ex-corporal, while fretting that the Nazis' 'private army' of SA stormtroopers, close to half a million strong, was emerging as a real rival to the regular army. Business and industry were now pumping more cash into Nazi coffers after a slow start, but many bosses still worried about what the 'socialist' component of 'National Socialism' might mean for private enterprise and profit. As for the conservative partners in the coalition, they thought that having helped Hitler to power they would be able to pull the strings to which he would dance – or rather, as vice-chancellor von Papen more graphically put it, to push him into a corner until he squeaked.

It was, as we now know, others who were soon forced to squeak –

and worse. But in mid-March Hitler's position was still shaky even within his own party, rent by personal and ideological rivalry barely visible to a public used to near-ceaseless displays of unity by brownshirts on the march. The 'Day of Potsdam' changed much of that, although the Führer had to wait rather longer to crush or slaughter his Nazi rivals like Ernst Röhm, the SA boss who was looking dangerously autonomous. Organised down to the last detail by Goebbels, newly appointed minister for 'Public Enlightenment and Propaganda', the Potsdam spectacle was officially billed as an inauguration ceremony for the Reichstag elected a fortnight before. In the event it bolstered Hitler's backing among conservatives, further neutralised his leftist opponents (hundreds of whom were already being jailed and/or murdered), disarmed many middle-of-the-road sceptics and heralded the end of parliamentary democracy in Germany for sixteen years.

From the Nazi standpoint, Potsdam was a perfect choice. As a military centre and long-time residence of the Prussian kings, including Frederick the Great, it gave Hitler the ideal stage on which to woo monarchists and the army with a display of reverence for their kind of tradition. Exit the grubby, howling revolutionary, enter (however briefly) the very model of a stable statesman, spick and span with top hat, white scarf and morning coat. Miraculously, Hitler even managed to look humble when, at the Garrison Church (site of the Prussian royal tombs), he shook the hand of old Hindenburg who had bested him in the presidential race a year before. Scores of veterans from several wars looked on, eyes moist, medal-bedecked breasts swelling. So did Crown Prince Wilhelm, eldest son of the exiled Kaiser, present in uniform and seeming implicitly to offer royal benediction. Everyone was aware that exactly sixty-two years ago to the day, on 21 March 1871, Bismarck had convened the first Reichstag of the newly united Germany. That 'Second Reich' (presumed successor to the centuries-old Holy Roman Empire of the German Nation) had gone down ignominiously in 1918. For the assembled old-timers, let alone the Nazis, a new and more glorious 'Third Reich' was long overdue.

The churches figured prominently in the Potsdam show, offering services for the assembled notables before the inauguration proceedings began. Two Nazi ministers, Hermann Göring and Wilhelm Frick, were among those who attended the Protestant ceremony; Heinrich Himmler, the SS leader who was already busy setting up the country's first concentration camps, went to the Catholic one. Prayers for government and parliament were offered up at both. Hitler and Goebbels attended neither but ostentatiously paid homage to 'fallen comrades' at a local cemetery. Bands played, bells pealed, thousands cheered. Microphones dotted all over town at Goebbels' behest carried the joyful sounds and pathos-soaked commentaries, minute by minute, hour by hour, to a nation long sick of deepening economic misery, ineffective government and seemingly endless wheeler-dealing in Berlin. Nazi excesses were indeed deplorable, so mused many so-far uncommitted 'solid citizens', but (that fateful, ever-stronger 'but') hadn't there been serious provocation, especially from the communists who seemed linked to the burning of the Reichstag building on 27 February? And was it clear that Hitler himself, rather than over-zealous underlings, had been responsible for the brutal backlash? He had been appointed chancellor by 'grand old' Hindenburg and he certainly seemed to be cutting a confidence-inspiring figure in Potsdam. Perhaps he really was the man to get things done in Germany at last.

Indeed he was, and henceforth with such speed that there seemed barely time to draw breath. Two days after the Potsdam show the Reichstag, amid tumult, passed an enabling act (comfortingly called the 'Law to Remove the Distress of People and State') that gave Hitler the constitutional basis for dictatorship. Since the Reichstag building itself had been gutted, the drama was enacted instead in the Kroll opera house, that former bastion under Klemperer of all the Nazis hated most in modern music. Social Democratic deputies, to their lasting credit, were the only ones to vote against the proposed law; the communist ones were already in flight, under arrest or dead, the Catholic ones of the Centre Party backed Hitler – believing his claim he would leave their church alone. By the end of March the regional German states were being stripped of their power; in April a boycott of Jewish business was organised and the Gestapo founded; in May independent labour unions were dissolved and books of 'unacceptable' authors publicly burned. In November a *Reichskulturkammer* (Reich Chamber of Culture) with seven divisions was inaugurated to bring all the arts into line with Nazi doctrine. Richard Strauss was appointed president of the music chamber, an 'honour' he held for less than two years but to which he responded at the time with a song dedicated to Goebbels, overall boss of the new organisation. When yet another national election was held that same November the Nazis won ninety-two per cent of the vote, hardly a surprise since theirs was the only legal party remaining. Simultaneously ninety-five per cent backed a plebiscite endorsing German withdrawal from the League of Nations.

What did the rest of the world make of all this? There was much huffing and puffing and many democrats were genuinely shocked. On the other hand, so a popular argument ran, perhaps the chaotic Weimar experience proved that Germans more than others needed a 'firm hand' at the top. Besides, Europe needed a bulwark against Soviet communism and the Nazis seemed to offer that. The anti-communist aspect surely counted for much with the Vatican when it concluded its Concordat with Hitler in July, giving him his first major diplomatic success. As for Germany's Jews, lumped together with 'the Bolsheviks' by the Nazis as part of a 'world conspiracy', they had few effective advocates abroad. When the Nazis organised the boycott of Jewish shops in April, they stuck antisemitic posters written in English as well as German on many windows to test world opinion. The world reacted, on the whole, with a shrug. One could not, it was widely argued, interfere in Germany's admittedly unpalatable internal affairs and besides (a pernicious addition often made 'behind the hand'), perhaps the Jews needed taking down a peg anyway. The Holocaust, of course, was still years away and inconceivable to most people – even, no doubt, to most of those aware of Heine's century-old warning that 'those who start by burning books will end by burning people.'[1]

That is jumping on a bit, and a last ritual on that symbol-laden 'Day of Potsdam' still needs recalling – a gala performance at the Berlin Staatsoper of *Meistersinger* conducted by Furtwängler, produced by Tietjen and attended by all manner of Nazi grandees. It would be easy to dismiss the event as a postscript (admittedly a long one) to the day's 'real business', but for Hitler and his master choreographer Goebbels it was surely an integral part of it. At Potsdam the Austrian-born demagogue with artistic pretensions, jailed after a failed putsch exactly a decade before, presented himself preposterously but somehow persuasively as the true heir to Germany's monarchical and military tradition. Hours later at the opera he used a work by his beloved Wagner under his favourite conductor to identify himself, only slightly less preposterously, with Germany's cultural and social heritage. Originally Richard Strauss's *Elektra* had been billed but it was dropped at Hitler's wish in favour of *Meistersinger*, with its idealised vision of community life in old Nuremberg and its rousing finale hailing Germany's (artistic)

Masters. Goebbels for one could hardly contain his enthusiasm. 'The evening closes with a magical performance of *Meistersinger* at the Linden opera,' he recorded in his diary. 'Everything is submerged in music. Now the joyous "Awake!" chorus regains its meaning.'[2] In other words, for Goebbels the true spirit of Wagner's uplifting music drama and of Hitler's newly stirring Germany were one and the same. Many in the 'special' audience that evening, particularly Hitler himself, surely thought likewise.

The 'Day of Potsdam' that began with a striking display of politics as theatre thus ended with one of theatre as politics; or rather the two fields, close cousins anyway in every place and era, merged to such an extent that it became near-impossible to tell them apart. Probably those most deeply involved did not feel the need to try. As Goebbels put it, National Socialist politics was not just a technique needed to govern but the 'noblest and truest of the arts' – a means of fashioning the masses as a sculptor did a slab of stone or a composer did notes. Hitler evidently felt the same, only more so, as a frustrated painter-turned-Führer and an actor with a seemingly limitless ability to hypnotise himself as well as others. Did he actually believe the lies he uttered and the humble gestures he made with such seeming sincerity in Potsdam? No doubt he in effect became his role while playing it so that the question of belief barely arose. Did he identify himself with Hans Sachs, that most creative and far-sighted of Wagner's Mastersingers, acclaimed by the adoring populace on the meadow before Nuremberg? It is hard to believe he did not, not least because year by year he addressed Nazi rallies of overwhelming theatricality on the fringe of the very same city.

On other occasions, Hitler may well have seen himself as Lohengrin, the mystery knight in shining armour, or as Rienzi, the tribune of implacable will with the (doomed) mission to make Rome powerful again. We know from *Mein Kampf* that *Lohengrin* was the first opera he ever saw – in his home town of Linz when he was only twelve – and that he was 'captivated at once'.[3] A few years later, according to the memoirs of a youthful pal named August Kubizek, Hitler saw *Rienzi* and promptly went into a kind of trance from which he emerged convinced he would lead Germans to greatness. Like the accounts of many claiming intimate knowledge of Hitler's doings and motivation, much in Kubizek's book is suspect; but there is enough independent evidence to suggest that at least the core of the *Rienzi* tale is probably true.[4]

Even leaving aside such doubtful sources, Hitler's passion for and knowledge of Wagner's music dramas is well documented. The love affair that began in Linz soon intensified when the budding artist with big dreams and empty pockets reached Vienna and somehow inveigled his way night after night into the Court Opera. No wonder he felt bewitched. At least one of the Wagner performances he attended was conducted by Mahler to stage designs by Alfred Roller, one of the greatest teams in the entire history of opera. The future Führer does not seem to have been unduly fazed by the fact that Mahler, a convert to Catholicism, was Jewish-born. As for Roller, an influential professor of fine arts as well as one of Mahler's closest collaborators, Hitler was simply in awe of him; so much so, he later confessed, that although he had a letter of introduction to the great man in his pocket he felt too shy to make use of it. By the time he made his first visit to Wahnfried in 1923, Hitler could probably have hummed his way through many of the Master's works from memory and he had firm ideas on how they should be staged. Just over a decade after that, his memories of Vienna still vivid, he persuaded Winifred to engage the aged and ailing Roller for the new Bayreuth *Parsifal*, a less than happy experiment, as it proved.

If Wagner is still widely thought of as the 'house composer' of Nazi Germany, this is thanks mainly to Hitler's mania for the Master, made manifest even to the casually interested in often re-run film footage showing a beaming Führer greeting delirious crowds during the Bayreuth festival. But of course Wagner's music regularly thundered or wafted through the Reich even when the spotlight was not wholly on Hitler. *Meistersinger* was the frequent opera of choice on 'gala' occasions and was the cultural high point, in theory at least, of the programme on the sidelines of the Nuremberg rallies. The *Walkürenritt* (Ride of the Valkyries) was used to accompany wartime newsreel of German air attacks; part of the *Rienzi* overture often heralded solemn pronouncements in Nuremberg and elsewhere; an abrupt radio broadcast of the funeral march from *Götterdämmerung* would signal that some notable had died – in 1945 Hitler himself.

Alongside such 'bleeding chunks' hacked from the Master's music dramas, the Reich was awash with works either popularly thought to be by Wagner or at any rate vaguely identified as 'Wagnerian'. The latter, near-endless category included pieces like Liszt's melodramatic tone-poem *Les Préludes*, used to herald radio bulletins on the war in the east, and the background music (only a scrap of it by Wagner himself) to Leni Riefenstahl's notorious propaganda film *Der Triumph des Willens* (The Triumph of Will) about the 1934 Nuremberg rally. Not that 'Wagnerian' automatically meant 'ear-splitting'. It surely covered the solemn Adagio of Bruckner's Seventh Symphony that was regularly used to precede statements by the Führer on culture (and was another of the pieces broadcast at his death). In this case the term even had a certain justification since the Adagio was in part composed in the Master's memory and makes use of Wagner tubas.

Several false conclusions can be, and often are, drawn from all this. It is, for example, widely assumed that under the Nazis the Master's works became still more popular and that, thanks especially to the Führer's example, they must have been played more often than those of supposedly 'less Teutonic' composers. Precisely the opposite is in fact true. In the repertoire for the 1932–3 opera season, largely mapped out before Hitler came to power, four of the six works most frequently performed throughout Germany were indeed by Wagner. Bizet's *Carmen* easily took top place with Weber's *Der Freischütz* second, but these were followed by a strong quartet from the Master – *Fliegende Holländer*, *Tannhäuser*, *Meistersinger* and *Lohengrin*. By 1938–9 the ranking had changed greatly, but not as one would expect after years of Nazi music policy rammed home via Goebbels' *Kulturkammer*. Only one Wagner opera still appeared fairly near the top of the rankings: *Lohengrin* at number twelve. The most performed German work of the season was an undemanding 'opera for young and old' called *Schwarzer Peter* (Black Peter) by Norbert Schultze, a contemporary composer and sometime cabaret performer later to win vastly greater fame with his song 'Lili Marleen', especially after it was taken up by Marlene Dietrich. *Schwarzer Peter* took fourth place in the popularity stakes, just ahead of Albert Lortzing's light-hearted perennial *Zar und Zimmermann* (Tsar and Carpenter). And the top three positions? They all went to Italy: Leoncavallo's *Pagliacci* at number one closely followed by Mascagni's *Cavalleria Rusticana* (two shortish works nearly always given as a double bill on a single evening), with Puccini's *Madama Butterfly* rolling in third.

The above might be construed simply as a temporary setback for this or that piece by Wagner, but the overall statistics tell a different story. After the Nazis came to power, the total number of performances of Wagner's works fell pretty steadily – from more than 1,800 in 1932–3 to just over 1,300 in 1938–9. The latter figure still narrowly left the Master as the most performed opera composer in the Reich, but that was soon to change. In the war years Verdi moved into top place. Even Puccini and Lortzing came to be staged more often than Wagner.[5] The question is why. The particularly strong showing by Italy cannot plausibly be ascribed to a surge of German enthusiasm for Mussolini's fascist state! Puccini and – to some extent – Verdi are less complex and costly to stage than Wagner and this no doubt played a role, especially in the war years. But even that explanation does not get to the root of the matter.

The truth is that Wagner's popularity was already in *relative* decline during the Weimar Republic and simply fell further, more quickly, under the Nazis. During the last years of the Kaiser's Germany (and despite the cost and privation of the First World War) the Master's works were still hugely popular, accounting for over eighteen per cent of all opera performances, a share no other composer came close to matching. By the mid-1920s, though, the figure had dropped to around fourteen per cent. That is not quite the setback it seems at first sight. Wagner was by then being performed even more often than during the war years, but the competition had become hotter, notably from the Italians but also from contemporary composers despised by traditionalists and especially by the Nazis. In other words, with more opera overall being performed Wagner was still on top but less dominant than before. Hitler in particular railed against 'unnatural, Bolshevik, Jewish' trends in music and looked to the day when he would be able to steer things in a 'healthier' direction. Once in power he moved swiftly to try to make good his threat; but neither the witch-hunt against Jews, atonalists and (harder to define) 'unacceptable modernists', nor the drive to boost the work of 'pure German' composers past and present brought a Wagner renaissance. On the contrary, the Master's works were performed less often and his 'market share' finally plunged to well below ten per cent.[6]

As early as 1911 Thomas Mann, locked throughout his life in a love-hate clinch with Wagner, had pointed out that the *Zeitgeist* was not working wholly in the composer's favour. In an article entitled '*Sinkender Stern*?' (Sinking Star?), written appropriately enough in Venice where the Master had expired nearly three decades earlier, Mann poured scorn on Wagner's theoretical writings. No one, he firmly (and not quite accurately) claimed, would take the prose seriously for a moment were it not for the greatness of the music – but even the latter was in the meantime being treated with suspicion or simply ignored by many young people. Mann found this development far from surprising. Wagner was 'nineteenth-century through and through'; the trend in the current century was towards a 'new classicism' that sought to make its impact more with coolness and logic, less with sheer size and emotional frenzy. Mann indicated that he felt this to be no bad thing, but typically rounded off his piece by confessing that he only had to hear a spot of Wagner to fall under the old wizard's spell again.[7]

The terms 'new classicism', 'neo-classicism' or 'new objectivity' (*neue Sachlichkeit*) certainly do not cover all the music being written around 1911, the year Mahler died, and Mann's argument does not take account of the rise of the Italian school, including the melodramatic *verismo* of Leoncavallo and Mascagni. Still, with composers like Ravel, Debussy and Stravinsky also increasingly to the fore, and Schoenberg in firm retreat from the gigantism of his early *Gurrelieder* phase, it is easy to see what Mann was thinking of. He was surely right to note that a new generation was far from ready automatically to sit at the Master's feet, even before the First World War during which the 'old world' came crashing down. That point was later stressed by Hans Heinz Stuckenschmidt, twenty-six years younger than Mann and one of the most perceptive of German musicologists and critics. Writing in 1928, Stuckenschmidt recalled that, 'We who were born around 1900 no longer went through the narcosis of Wagner-mania. The idol of the nineteenth century was for us a composer of the past, almost like any other.' For a time it had even been quite common to ridicule Wagner, Stuckenschmidt wrote, but that period had now passed. What remained beyond idolatry for Wagner and reaction against him was simply 'a great German musician. A person who eminently widened the musical horizon (like every Master) and paved the way for the revolutions in music that still shake us today.'[8]

Not everyone shared (or shares) Stuckenschmidt's balanced view. Indeed, with a Weimar generation increasingly drawn to the fascinating thrills and spills of new music, or at least to novel presentation of traditional opera, old-guard Wagnerians felt even more impelled to extol the 'true German virtues' of the music dramas and to insist on stagings exactly as the Master had specified. Bayreuth naturally became still more of a 'fortress on the hill' for the latter group, with Siegfried caught in the middle, under 'moral' pressure not to modernise from his mother and sisters as well as the Wagner societies, but knowing full well that some change was unavoidable, indeed desirable. 'Something unbelievable has happened,' wrote another music critic, Bernhard Diebold, within months of the above piece by his colleague Stuckenschmidt. 'Since the war the educated public of the political right has raised Richard Wagner to its special God of art and culture. Lacking creative spirits of their own, the men of the right have chosen the revolutionary, the refugee and decades-long exile from 1848–9 to be fulfiller of their nationalistic needs.' In Diebold's view leftists and liberals also bore responsibility for this trend because they had shown 'a no less fatal thoughtlessness towards the spiritual phenomenon that is Wagner'. Repelled by the reactionaries of 'Haus Wahnfried' and by 'Herrn Chamberlain', Diebold charged, the left had lost sight of the real essence of Wagner and abandoned the field without a fight.[9]

The rightist embrace of Wagner did not, of course, start only after the First World War and the Master had, *nolens volens*, himself embraced the right when it seemed likely to back him with cash and clout. But Diebold put his finger on a key point all the same; for conservatives Wagner's role as revolutionary was a severe embarrassment – best ignored or, failing that, explained away. Cosima and Chamberlain, prime obfuscators, showed how. For the Nazis, superficial appearances notwithstanding, the revolutionary Wagner was still more of a headache. They could and did present themselves as 'Socialists' of a kind, committed as the Master had been to overturning a supposedly corrupt and unjust order. But the anarchic dreams of the author of *Art and Revolution* were devilishly hard to square with the Nazi resolve to control and transform national life at every level. Nor did the content of most of Wagner's music dramas offer much encouragement to the self-styled builders of a Third Reich, particularly not that of his 'flagship' composition, the *Ring*. However one interprets the latter's fire-and-flood ending, the course of the cycle as a whole shows how disaster strikes those spurred by greed and lust for power. The truth of this 'message' was, indeed, never better confirmed than by the Führer and his gruesome movement, but that was surely not their intention.

As for *Tristan und Isolde*, described by Hitler as the greatest Wagner opera,[10] its doomed, treacherous lovers were anything but role models for a Reich urging increased production by dutiful families of bouncing (Aryan) babies. *Parsifal* was an even bigger headache; indeed the Nazis more or less banned it at the outbreak of war although it could sometimes be heard after that, at least in excerpt. For those who interpret *Parsifal* as a paean to racial purity, the quasi-suppression of it on the eve of the Holocaust must seem illogical to say the least. But then, whatever its racial content may be, the work is undeniably shot through with anguish and the Nazis may have rightly judged that the *Volk* would soon be getting quite enough of that anyway. Besides, Parsifal himself saves the Grail community after shunning weaponry and learning compassion, never a course associated with Nazism and particularly not after 1939. Goebbels, anyway, had always disliked the work. *Parsifal*, he wrote in his diary in 1936, was simply too pious. If its stage presentation were not modernised it would not, in the long run, be able to keep its place in the repertory.[11]

At least, one might think, *Meistersinger* was tailor-made for the Reich – especially its last act with that rousing '*Wach' auf!*' (Awake!) chorus that so pleased Goebbels, and with Sachs's forceful warning in the closing minutes ('*Verachtet mir die Meister nicht*' – Do not disdain the Masters) about threats from abroad. One can argue about whether the latter is the most appropriate ending and Wagner was long in two minds about it himself. But *what* Sachs sings is hardly bellicose – that should Germany fall under foreign rule, it would only be in art as preserved by the Masters that the true spirit of the nation could survive. As for '*Wach' auf!*' this could give a boost to Goebbels and his like only if ripped out of Wagner's context. Sachs, to whom the chorus is directed, promptly responds with an admonition – that the people too easily bestow great honour on one not fit to receive it. This, the music tells us, is no show of false modesty but deadly serious. Wagner here harks back to the great '*Wahn*' (Madness) monologue at the start of the act, in which Sachs reflects on the endless capacity of human beings to 'torment and flay each other in useless, foolish anger'. Even when this madness seems to halt, Sachs mourns, it is only gaining new strength in sleep – and once awoken 'then see who can master it'. If Nazi leaders had listened carefully and pondered what they heard, they would have found it hard to avoid classing Wagner's real 'message' as subversive.

Evidently few top Nazis (let alone the rank and file) were disposed to do any such thing. One interesting exception was Alfred Rosenberg, long regarded as the party's leading ideologist, who really did know his Wagner and tied himself in knots trying to reconcile his personal doubts about it with the official, Hitler-inspired jubilation. For Rosenberg, the real Nazi model was Beethoven who 'took fate by the throat and acknowledged force as the highest morality of man . . . Whoever understands the essence of our movement knows that there is a drive in us all like that which Beethoven embodied to the highest degree.'[12] Rosenberg claimed that Wagner too revealed the strength of the 'Nordic soul' but, such party-line poppycock aside, he felt compelled to criticise the Master's work in detail, especially the *Ring*. In the latter, he asserted, 'the inner harmony between word content and physical conduct is often hindered by the music . . . An attempt to wed these arts forcefully destroys spiritual rhythm and prevents emotive expression.' Rosenberg hastily added that 'these remarks are in no way intended to denigrate Wagner's work', but in fact they hit at the very core of the Master's *Gesamtkunstwerk* approach. For good measure, Rosenberg also charged that the stage demands in the *Ring* were so huge that they could never be met properly. In sum, his criticism is not so much ideological as technical – that Wagner, as he put it, 'frequently gets in his own way'.[13]

Not many of the Nazi 'elite' would have known or cared whether these arguments had substance. Goebbels, who saw Rosenberg as a rival and quickly outmanoeuvred him once the Nazis were in power, does seem to have had a certain affinity for Wagner. At least he claimed in his diary to have been stirred in his youth by the music and he visited Bayreuth with apparent pleasure; but he reveals no special insights on the works in his private jottings (witness that 'Day of Potsdam' entry), let alone in his public speeches. The similarly powerful Göring stumped along to Bayreuth when the Führer was there but there is every sign he would have preferred to go hunting instead. He did indeed pour much effort and money into bolstering Berlin's Staatsoper, over which he jealously kept control. But that had far less to do with a love of opera, let alone Wagner, than with his fierce rivalry with Goebbels, who yearned to bring every cultural bastion, including the Staatsoper and Bayreuth, under his thumb. He never quite succeeded, but that was not for lack of trying. Albert Speer, Hitler's personal architect and later also his armaments minister, was another Bayreuth regular motivated by duty rather than personal interest. The Führer, he noted in his memoirs, often discussed Wagner with Winifred and seemed to know what he was talking about. Evidently Speer himself did not know enough to be sure.[14]

The truth is that many Nazis, in high and low places, were bored to tears by Wagner. There is nothing very odd about that. Lots of people past and present who may well have a certain interest in other music will run a mile to escape a seemingly interminable evening with the Master. Too few tunes, too many scenes in which people stand about for ages apparently doing nothing much. The point is only worth stressing here because the Nazis are reputed to have had a special affinity to Wagner's music. The evidence suggests this was simply not so. Speer is only one of those who give the 'inside story' on those 'gala' performances of *Meistersinger* on the sidelines of the Nuremberg rallies. In 1933 so few of the invited party 'faithful' were present when the work began that Hitler in fury sent out patrols to the brothels and beer gardens to round up the truants. The next year the house was well filled from the start on Hitler's orders, but many of those present fell asleep or clapped in the wrong places. After that the Führer gave up his bid to 'educate' his errant flock and the performances were thrown open to Wagner fans generally (who had to pay for their seats).[15] *Tristan und Isolde* seems to have had a similarly soporific effect on top Nazis – at least if an account by Hitler's secretary, Traudl Junge, is to be believed. On one occasion, she recalled, a member of the Führer's entourage was rescued in the nick of time after he nodded off and began to fall forward over the railing of his box. The rescuer himself had been asleep until a moment before. Another in the group, blissfully unaware both of the little drama nearby and the big one on the stage, simply snored his way through it all.[16]

It wasn't all Wagner, at least not quite. Hitler rarely went to concerts though he had some time for symphonies by Beethoven and, latterly, by Bruckner. But what he loved most (the Master apart) was operetta – a genre he had publicly scorned as inferior in the 1920s but which he came to adore when in power. His favourites seem to have been *Die lustige Witwe* (The Merry Widow) of Franz Lehár and *Die Fledermaus* (The Bat) of Johann Strauss, both choices that caused much head-scratching among the Reich's guardians of 'pure German art'. Lehár had been born in Hungary, his wife was Jewish and he had worked closely throughout his career with Jewish artists like Richard Tauber, who fled from the Nazis to London and died there. Strauss was in principle even more of a problem. After the *Anschluss* with Austria in 1938, the Nazis came across evidence showing the composer was of Jewish descent. Goebbels quickly had the records doctored and hushed up the whole affair. It hardly did to make a fuss about darlings of the Führer. Anyway, Goebbels himself was keen to promote 'lighter' music, even jazz in limited doses, if it helped raise the spirits of the *Volk*.

Wagner and operetta thus emerged as the main ingredients in Hitler's hugely indigestible 'musical evenings' – events dreaded by most of those forced to take part. At least the Führer's similarly interminable 'movie evenings' might, amid all the sentimental dross, throw up a foreign feature of passing interest not shown in public cinemas. No such novelty could be expected on those occasions when Hitler trapped his unhappy guests around the turntable, notably at his *Berghof* Alpine retreat perched high above the small Bavarian town of Berchtesgaden. As one recording of the Master's works succeeded another, the Führer would amuse himself, if no one else, by trying (usually successfully) to guess the identity of the singer. Bit by bit many of those present would tiptoe away to drink and chat in another room until, their absence noted with displeasure, they had to slink back for the rest of the programme, mainly jolly ditties by Lehár and Co. According to Frau Junge the marathon would usually be rounded off in the early hours with the 'Donkey Serenade' – a surprising but, all things considered, not inappropriate choice.[17]

Just what was it about Wagner that so attracted Hitler? This is a simple question that, on the face of it, ought to have an easy and plausible answer. We know that from early adolescence Hitler was 'captivated' by the Master's works, that he studied them voraciously and that he went to countless performances of them. Since he talked near-incessantly about almost everything under the sun including the arts, one would think that the reasons for his Wagner-mania must be exhaustively documented. Even if one discards much-touted but suspect reports of Hitler's private remarks, like those of Kubizek or of Hermann Rauschning, a self-important and mendacious Nazi official who wrote up hobnobs he claimed to have had with the Führer, a mountain of well-authenticated material remains. Oddly enough, though, ploughing through the public and private sources for insights on the Hitler–Wagner connection yields slim pickings.

Sticking for a moment to the sparse facts, Hitler demonstrably 'loved the noise' Wagner made and he was drawn irresistibly to all the visual and technical paraphernalia of theatre. He beamed while listening to *Meistersinger* and trembled when he heard *Tristan*. On one occasion he stated that the Master's music raised people up out of the daily grind into the pure air, on another he claimed to hear in it the 'rhythms of the primeval world'.[18] Beyond such banalities he had little of substance to say about the scores themselves, though he had a good ear and could pick out – say – when an oboe was out of tune or a tenor missed a bar. Productions and staging absorbed him at least as much as the music, perhaps more – hence his special request to Winifred that his youthful idol Roller be engaged for Bayreuth. He adored going behind the scenes to view lighting and scenery, he could spew out statistics about opera houses all over Europe and he spent hours poring over stage designs of his own. Not that he was content with stage concepts alone. Aided and abetted by Speer, he went on to concoct monstrous 'real-life' schemes, most of them happily unrealised, for vast buildings and new cities such as the world had never seen. He thus belatedly picked up those threads of a career in the visual arts that had snapped decades before in Vienna. As Nazi leader he had near-unlimited means to do so and his abiding love of Wagner's stage works surely spurred him on – so much so that most of his entourage, especially his general staff, came to bewail the inordinate amount of time he 'wasted' on art.

Isn't all that, though, missing the wood for the trees? For many people the explanation for the link between Führer and Master is (dangerously) obvious; that a fascist, fiercely antisemitic leader with artistic pretensions is pretty well bound to be drawn to a fascist, fiercely antisemitic composer. 'There is much Hitler in Wagner,' as Thomas Mann put it with, for him, rare pithiness in a letter in 1949.[19] This was not the first time Mann had said something of the kind. His long-standing doubts about the composer's work, which he could not help loving all the same, grew stronger after he went into exile in 1933 and observed Hitler's embrace of the Master from afar. He even wrote in America in 1940 that with its '*Wagalaweia* and its alliteration, its mixture of roots-in-the-soul and eyes-toward-the future' Wagner's music was 'the exact spiritual forerunner of the "metapolitical" movement today terrorizing the world.'[20] Still, Mann is a dangerous witness for Wagner fans and foes alike. He frankly admitted to his ambivalence, telling a friend in 1942 that today he could write one way about the composer and tomorrow another. Sure enough in 1951, four years before his death, Mann pops up again enthusing about *Meistersinger* as 'a splendid work, a festival opera if ever there was one . . . that awakens enthusiasm for life and art.'[21]

If Wagner's works really were 'the exact spiritual forerunner' of Nazism, surely the Führer of all people would have drummed that point home ad infinitum. But one looks to him in vain not only for fascist interpretation of the music dramas but, stranger still, for direct references to the theoretical writings. There is, indeed, surprisingly little evidence that Hitler read Wagner's prose works, though he evidently did borrow some from a library before he rose to power and the wording of some of his speeches indicates that he imbibed at least *Das Judentum in der Musik*. Why then did he not use the Master more clearly as an ally, especially in his antisemitic cause? In *Mein Kampf*, for instance, he notes that his early hostility to Jews owed much to the example set by Karl Lueger, the antisemitic mayor of Vienna. He also praises Goethe for acting according to the spirit of 'blood and reason' in treating 'the Jew' as a foreign element. He pays no similar tribute to the Master, indeed he only mentions Wagner by name once in the whole book (although he refers elsewhere to the 'Master' of Bayreuth).

Even when Hitler complains in another context that allowing Jewish artists to perform in Bayreuth amounted to 'racial desecration', and that this had marred his first festival visit in 1925, he does not go on to say something like 'the Master who so rightly despised the Jews must have been turning in his grave.'[22] By this time, moreover, his antisemitism had become still more intense, probably because of the injuries he had suffered, especially from gas attack, in a war that he felt had been lost through 'Marxist-Jewish' treachery. In a chilling foretaste of the 'final solution', Hitler wrote in *Mein Kampf* that, 'If at the beginning of the War and during the War twelve or fifteen thousand of these Hebrew corrupters of the people had been held under poison gas . . . the sacrifice of millions at the front would not have been in vain.'[23] Yet he never directly called on the Master he near-worshipped as a witness against the people he most loathed.

The likeliest explanation for this reticence is that Hitler realised, better than Goebbels for instance, that with Wagner he was on tricky ideological ground. After all, the Master had himself engaged Levi, albeit unwillingly, to conduct *Parsifal* and he had had lots of Jewish friends, however badly he treated them. As for the solution he had proposed in *Judentum* to the 'Jewish problem', that amounted to total assimilation and hence could not have been further from what Hitler aimed for. It is true that in his later version of the essay Wagner raised the question of whether Jews might be expelled, thus coming closer to a stance of which Hitler would have approved; but he hardly did so with a conviction that made the comment useful for Nazi propagandists. Besides at the end of his life Wagner, twisting and turning on the issue, seemed to raise the prospect that Jews could be saved through 'Christ's blood' – conversion. All in all, Hitler may have failed to cite Wagner's prose not because he knew little of it but because he had read too much and felt it wiser to cry off.

Ambivalent though his brand of antisemitism was, Wagner served as a model for Hitler all the same. What kind of model? The answer emerges pretty clearly when Hitler makes that single reference to the Master by name in *Mein Kampf*. At this point in his wearyingly prolix tale, Hitler is not directly discussing antisemitism or music or drama but what he calls 'marathon runners of history' – great and solitary individuals who work for the future, doomed to be largely misjudged in their own day but ready 'to carry the fight for their ideas and ideals to their end'. As examples, Hitler mentions just three names – Luther, Frederick the Great and Wagner – but he obviously reckons the list could be extended to include himself. Of this trio, Wagner was easily the closest to Hitler historically, and the fate of many of Wagner's stage heroes came near to matching that of the 'marathon runners': Rienzi the tribune who went down in flames, Lohengrin and Tannhäuser the misunderstood 'outsiders' – even wise old Sachs, the widower who wins public acclaim but sentences himself to continued solitude by renouncing Eva and helping her beloved knight win the Master's prize. Isn't this how Hitler saw himself: lonely, struggling, heroic? Grotesque though it may seem, Wagner's life and works were almost certainly mirrors in which the Führer thought he saw himself reflected – at least in broad and, to him, imposing outline.[24]

No wonder Hitler was moved when he visited Wahnfried for the first time on that autumn morning in 1923 and stood before the Master's grave. All the more so since he suddenly found himself at the centre of what was apparently a happy, close-knit family – for an often-penniless drifter, war-scarred veteran and great hater a rare experience. If Siegfried seemed to Hitler a bit of a softie, he was nonetheless the Master's son and he was striving to get the festival back on its feet again. Besides, there were the lively children, the grand old granny upstairs, the ailing 'sage' Chamberlain round the corner and, above all, the adoring Winifred. Nearly two decades later, reminiscing at his *Wolfsschanze* (Wolf's Lair) headquarters in East Prussia, Hitler spoke emotionally of that first day and of how the family had stood by him when he was at his lowest ebb. 'I love these people and Wahnfried!' he confessed, adding he saw it as a special stroke of good fortune that, by saving the festival from financial collapse when he came to power in 1933, he had been able to make good the Wagners' early support for him. His regular Bayreuth visits, he said, were always his happiest times and when they came to an end he felt as he did when the decorations were pulled down from a Christmas tree.[25]

After Siegfried's death, and despite his will, there was much speculation that Hitler and Winifred would marry. Their long-standing liaison was widely known, even down to reports (naturally embellished) about 'Wolf's' lightning nocturnal visits. By 1932, at the latest, when the Nazi leader ostentatiously sent a huge bouquet of flowers to Wahnfried, the local press had concluded that an engagement was in the offing. But the flowers were, in fact, to mark the confirmation of Wieland and Friedelind as full church members, and an engagement never came. '*Mei Mudder mecht scho, aber der Onkel Wolf mecht halt net*,' Friedelind is reported to have said. The ineffable flavour of her patois is lost in translation but the meaning is clear enough: 'My Mother wants to all right, but Uncle Wolf simply does *not*.'[26] That is probably correct. Hitler left it very late to marry, whether because he felt the need to 'save himself for the German people' or for more intimate reasons – or a mixture of both. Notoriously, it was 29 April 1945 before he tied the knot in his Berlin bunker with his long-time companion and presumed mistress, Eva Braun. The next day the newlyweds took their lives.

Whether despite or because of the absence of marriage bonds, 'Winnie' and 'Wolf' stayed in constant and friendly contact for years, although the link between them did loosen during the war. He wrote to her regularly, not least when he was down in the dumps or even deeply depressed (as he evidently was after the mysterious gunshot death of his pet niece 'Geli' in his Munich flat in 1931). Winifred did her best to cheer him up and bubbled like a schoolgirl at every sign of affection. 'I'm over the moon with delight and thanks,' she confessed after he sent her a portrait of himself. The picture was, she claimed, 'a masterpiece of accuracy and ability' that 'now graces my little house with the blessing of your constant presence. Endless thanks to you, spender of such nameless joy! In faithful friendship, Your Winnie.' [27]

On the practical side, of course, Winifred as festival director had far more to thank her 'Wolf' for. For one thing, he swept away Bayreuth's money troubles as no benefactor, not even King Ludwig, had quite managed to do before. Admittedly much of the cash did not come direct from him or even, in every case, from other Nazi bodies simply bowing to the Führer's obvious wish. At the start Goebbels was particularly active in his support for Bayreuth, perhaps thinking he could buy his way into decisive influence there. In 1934 alone, his propaganda ministry bought up more than 11,000 tickets for 364,000 marks (around a third of the whole Bayreuth budget). The same year the *Reichsrundfunk* (state radio service) spent 95,000 marks for festival broadcasting rights and continued to pay weighty (albeit lesser) sums annually thereafter. But overall, in the pre-war years up to and including 1939, Hitler's *Reichskanzlerei* (chancellery) was the biggest backer, putting up a total of more than half a million marks for Bayreuth tickets and new productions. Incongruously, from a financial standpoint, things became still simpler for the festival during the war years (1940–4). On Hitler's orders a Nazi leisure organisation bought up all the tickets and paid nearly all the bills, doling out on average more than a million marks annually.[28]

Besides flourishing under this rain of cash, Winifred also knew that she could call on Hitler when she felt her position as festival director was under threat – from jealous local Nazi functionaries, for instance, or from the ever-acquisitive Goebbels. Thanks to Hitler's protection, she was often able to take on or retain artists she badly wanted but who would almost certainly have been lost to her under a strict interpretation of the Reich's odious political/racial rules. One case in point was the *Heldentenor* Max Lorenz, a practising bisexual with a Jewish wife, whom Winifred engaged year after year for key roles including Siegfried, Tristan, Parsifal and Walther von Stolzing. Another example was Franz von Hoesslin, a conductor with Jewish links by descent and marriage, who was shunned by other German opera houses during the Nazi era but who continued to appear regularly at Bayreuth. Not that Winifred always had to appeal direct to her 'Wolf' for help; the mere knowledge of her link to the Führer was frequently enough to keep otherwise obstreporous Nazi bureaucrats at bay.

To that extent Bayreuth from 1933 was a 'Hitler festival' rather than a 'Nazi festival.' That does not mean it was in some way morally 'better', as some over-zealous post-war apologists have sought to imply. Nor does it mean that the Führer always got his way when it came to choices on performers and stagecraft. He surely played a key role in the engagement of Roller for *Parsifal* and in the return of Furtwängler to Bayreuth in 1936, and he concocted a plan, only partly realised before war began, for a giant new festival complex in which the existing theatre would have been subsumed. But for the most part Winifred managed deftly to field his wishes while effectively defending her own, especially that the Heinz Tietjen/ Emil Preetorius duo be given something close to carte blanche. Not that her reasons for so arguing were purely professional ones. By 1933 at the latest Winifred had become emotionally dependent on her 'Heinz' – more so, in fact, than she was on the still-desirable but seemingly unattainable 'Wolf'. For the children, now in their teens, Hitler remained the largely benevolent uncle but Tietjen had emerged as a substitute father. It was a role that could and did cause untold resentment.

# 11

# Dissonant Quartet

Shortly before they first met him in 1931, the Wagner youngsters pored over press photos of Heinz Tietjen and pronounced his face to be like that of an orang-utan. This unflattering but not wholly inaccurate comparison rather vexed the festival's new artistic director designate when he got to hear about it, as he did about most things, but it should hardly have surprised him. Almost from the time they could trot, Wieland and Wolfgang, Friedelind and Verena had been notorious for sheer cheek and much mischief. Some visitors to Wahnfried in the 1920s, Hitler and Goebbels firmly included, found the Master's grandchildren diverting, even adorable; others snarled more often than they smirked at the little terrors and their doings. A few of the local old folk could still ruefully recall the near-perfect manners of the five offspring the Master and the *Hohe Frau* had brought to town decades before. What a contrast, they groaned, to the loud and dissonant quartet produced by the all-too-amiable Siegfried and his foreign-born wife. That such behaviour could be allowed even at the Wagner shrine was just one more sign that the Fatherland was going to the dogs.

The kids did tend to go a bit far – wrestling on the Master's grave, turning the carefully tended front lawn into a muddy football pitch, scaring guests they disliked with a makeshift 'ghost'dangled into the entrance hall from the gallery above. Pudgy Friedelind, inappropriately nicknamed 'Maus' or 'Mausi', was easily the noisiest child, with the quickest and often most wounding repartee. 'My elder sister ruled the roost and held the floor,' Wolfgang bitterly (enviously?) recalled years later. 'As I see it, Friedelind's contrary, rebellious attitude was a way of life in itself.'[1] Winifred thought much the same. Whenever she discovered evidence of some domestic misdeed, she tended to assume that Friedelind was the culprit and reacted with a noise level even her daughter found hard to match. Her wrathful cry of 'Mausi' could be heard, it was said, far into the Hofgarten behind Wahnfried's back gate.

Put down most of these 'sins', though, to high spirits and the presence of extraordinary temptation. Above all there was the festival theatre, Bayreuth's Disneyland, to scamper through; not during the performances themselves of course, when the four boringly had to try harder to behave, but in those thrilling months of preparation when carpenters banged, painters splashed and singers strutted about in fancy dress, cooing, bellowing and – with luck – dispensing chocolates to hopeful urchins. There was a real magic dragon to be wary of and a wonky 'wave machine', built for the undulating Rhinemaidens in the *Ring*, to mount for a ride – at least until Papa or giddiness put a stop to the fun. Back home, dressed up as four *Nibel-jungen* in miniature *Ring*-robes and winged helmets designed by Aunt Lulu (Daniela), they would chase one another squealing through the garden, to the mingled delight and vexation of Wagnerians come to view the Master's last resting place. For a few coins, the gang would draw visitors from gate to grave in a handcart. Heinrich Himmler was one of those who took the trip. Years later he still enthused about it.

Siegfried's death brought a drastic change, especially for Friedelind. She had always thought of herself as her father's favourite and that was probably true. He loved her wit, happily put up with her pranks and dried her tears when she came running after yet another brush with Winifred. When he was away on conducting trips she felt lost and vulnerable; when he was composing in his 'bachelor cottage' she would crawl under a piano there and watch him for hours. On one of their long walks together she even offered innocently to marry him, evidently seeing herself as a more than acceptable substitute for her mother. He graciously explained to the crestfallen Maus why he could not take up the offer, but it seems he did tell her several times that one day it would be up to her to carry on his festival work.[2]

Siegfried probably did not believe that his eldest daughter ever could or should run things alone; his will, after all, treated the four children as equal heirs after Winifred. But spurred by her father's well-meant words, Friedelind for many years (perhaps, in her heart, always) saw herself as the 'crown princess' of Bayreuth. She slaved to improve her pianism, pored over scores and stage models of the music dramas and, sooner than her siblings, began to treat the festival theatre more as training ground than playground – often to the mild unease of the artists she shadowed, drinking in their every word and gesture. The great soprano Frida Leider recalled that while resting in her dressing room between acts of *Parsifal* 'a little girl with long blonde plaits appeared, sat down opposite me, folded her hands and stared questioningly at me without saying a word. We began to make conversation and finally got on very well . . . Eventually I had to kindly but firmly send her away as she showed no signs of leaving.'[3] The year was 1928; Friedelind was aged ten, Frida had just turned forty and was one of the greatest singers of her time or, indeed, of any time – especially in Wagner. As one connoisseur ideally put it, she had a tone of 'perfect character, existing at that rarely achieved point where the heroic has not become inhuman, and where the human does not undermine tragic dignity'.[4] From that unlikely start in the Bayreuth dressing room and despite the age difference, a close friendship was to emerge – and to deepen in the late 1930s when both women had special cause to despise and fear the Nazis.

Whatever Siegfried's view of the festival's future, Friedelind's youthful dream of winning the Bayreuth throne one fine day was not inherently absurd. Cosima had shown that a woman could well take charge, whatever jealous males might mutter, and anyway neither of Friedelind's brothers seemed to be raring for the job. Quick-witted but moody Wieland was initially far keener on painting and drawing than on music, just as his father had been until well into his teens. There were, it is true, early claims – repeated with embellishment abroad – that he was developing into a 'young Liszt'; but these were based on no more solid evidence than the press report of a school concert at which the supposed *Wunderkind* had picked out a carol on the piano. The only notable feature Wieland had inherited from Liszt were his hammer-toes; it was Friedelind who got the long and sensitive fingers. As for Wolfgang, easy-going and practical, he felt drawn to the festival more as artisan than as artist or musician. Intrigued by all the trappings of stagecraft, he set up a workshop of his own in the cellar at home where (shades of the *Rheingold* Nibelungs) he battered and sawed away for hours on end. No fool when it came to money matters, indeed imbued with a farmer's canniness and sense of thrift, 'Wolfi' also raised chickens and sold the eggs to Winifred at the going market price. His pragmatism and business nous paid off handsomely much later when he became festival director, but as a boy he seems never to have dreamed that he would one day run the show. If anyone had first refusal, he believed, it was the so-far hesitant Wieland. In those days at least, Wolfgang looked up to his elder brother with fondness and some awe. Finally there was bonny little 'Nickel' (Verena), the pet of the family. She was well able to pout and wheedle to get her own way, useful attributes both, but no one saw her as a future boss on the Green Hill.

When Siegfried died after those hugely taxing *Tannhäuser* rehearsals in 1930, Friedelind lost not just her adored father but, as she believed, her greatest ally. Only Toscanini, that demon of a maestro with a soft heart, came anywhere near taking Siegfried's place in her affections. He went out of his way to comfort the children in that sad summer and later gave Mausi decisive help when she was down and almost out – hence the dedication of her 1945 book *Heritage of Fire* 'To my two fathers, Siegfried Wagner and Arturo Toscanini'. The omnipresent Tietjen she saw as no kind of an emotional substitute, and in due course she painfully concluded that he would not help her to the top at the festival either. He did, indeed, humour her for a while, writing her flowery letters and letting her give a hand at rehearsals, but that seemed as far as he was ready to go.

Winifred, at least, made plain whom she thought must head the festival one day and it was certainly not the obstreperous Maus. Friedelind was exiled to an isolated boarding school in the wilds of Brandenburg to 'learn discipline', and sent to clinics to diet because she was no longer just plump but downright fat. None of that worked, of course. For all her own unhappiness as an orphan, Winifred seems not to have realised that her daughter's behaviour and weight problems were the outward signs of deep inner loneliness and disappointment. Or if she did realise it, she simply felt at her wit's end and decided to get Mausi out of the house for as long as possible, come what may. Despite Friedelind's obvious fixation on the festival and her already thorough knowledge of the music dramas, Winifred saw Wieland as the clear heir apparent – however reluctant he might currently seem to be and whatever Siegfried's will might say. She even appealed to her old friend Wolf to allow the will to be changed specifically to give precedence to the eldest son. Hitler too favoured Wieland, giving the youth a special (and specially remunerative) concession to take official photos of top Nazis and presenting him with a Mercedes, no less, when he got his driving licence in 1935 at the age of eighteen. But the Führer was not prepared – even for Winnie – to permit any tinkering with the last will and testament of the Master's son, however critical he might feel of its contents.

Unlike Friedelind, Wieland seemed not to suffer much, if at all, from Siegfried's death. According to a much-repeated family tale, he had once remarked years earlier that he wished the thrilling 'Uncle Wolf' were his real father and Siegfried his (usually absent) uncle.[5] Even if the boy did not say exactly that, he and his father were plainly never close. Despite their common passion for visual art, they were of almost opposite temperaments; the sociable Siegfried with his humour, patience and immaculate manners; his stand-offish first-born more often sulking than smiling, and liable (throughout his life) to fly into sudden rages that just as suddenly blew over. Over the years, one photo after another shows a grumpy-looking Wieland staring at, or often past, the camera as though inwardly growling 'Who the hell are you?' or 'What am I doing here?' At school the girls were liable to scatter at his approach because he would kick a football at them and mutter insults – which treatment, mark you, did not stop quite a lot of the victims finding their tormentor weirdly attractive. Good-natured Wolfgang they could treat as a real chum; Wieland spelled excitement, danger.

With his father dead Wieland became for a time the 'man of the house' if hardly, at age thirteen, the 'master' of it. Long aware that he was Winifred's favourite, as Friedelind had been Siegfried's, he now sought to meet her every wish almost before she asked, plundering his savings to buy her presents and putting her for a time at the centre of his new hobby, photography. With all-too typical boorishness, he told his girlfriend (and future wife) Gertrud Reissinger that they could never be wed because he would only marry someone as lovely as his mother.[6] No wonder Tietjen's arrival caused him inner turmoil no less radical than Friedelind's – not, admittedly, at the very start when the odd-looking newcomer with vast theatrical experience seemed something of a blessing, but soon thereafter when 'Heinz' began to haunt Wahnfried still more regularly than 'Uncle Wolf' had done.

For all the children, but especially for Wieland, it was disturbingly clear that more linked their increasingly preoccupied mother to the new director than festival business alone. The usually steady and resolute Winifred began to switch with bewildering speed from a mood of near euphoria to one of gloom and vice versa; she monitored her weight with furrowed brow and hung with rapt attention on Tietjen's every word, however commonplace. In short she had fallen in love – again. The new object of her infatuation possessed no 'kindly voice' like Siegfried's nor hypnotic blue eyes like Hitler's but he had a persuasive tongue and an air, usually justified, of being able to control the trickiest situation. Although he was sixteen years her senior Winifred surely saw that as no drawback; on the contrary, experience showed that in the main she felt attracted to older men, her late husband and Wolf included. Perhaps she was unconsciously seeking the father she never knew; at any rate she was, as her private letters show, consciously seeking a husband.[7] Unlike Cosima, she was far from disposed to play a widow's role for around half a century although, despite her best efforts, she ended up doing just that. When Siegfried died she was only thirty-three and had good reason to feel she was getting a second chance, but unfortunately for her Tietjen already had a wife (though he lived apart from her). He promised to obtain a divorce and eventually kept his word but then, soon after the war, it was a ballet dancer he married – not the 'Mistress of Bayreuth' he had kept dangling for years.

Like Hamlet, Wieland resented his mother's new attachment and was plagued by indecision. In contrast to Mausi, he remained far from sure that he wanted to devote his life to Bayreuth – yet his mother, not to mention Hitler, seemed to take it for granted that he would do so. Not surprisingly most of the rest of the Wagnerian world did so too. Time after time at official gatherings it was Wieland who was seen to be closest to Winifred's side, and when the Führer was snapped arm in arm with the two sons it was naturally Wieland that he placed on his right. For all that, Tietjen carefully worked to keep the succession issue open, sometimes seeming to favour one brother, sometimes the other, temporarily at least encouraging Mausi but also flattering the ever-prettier Verena. Was this a policy of sensible even-handedness in the spirit of Siegfried's will or one of 'divide and rule'? Perhaps both. Tietjen may genuinely have felt that it was too soon to earmark any 'greenhorn' for a job that demanded so rare a combination of artistic talent and management skills. At the same time he clearly had a vital interest in securing his own role on the Green Hill for the indefinite future. For Tietjen, Bayreuth was an added insurance against harassment and worse by his many foes among the country's new rulers, Goebbels in particular. In Berlin, he was protected by Göring who wanted to ensure that 'his' Staatsoper stayed the best; in Bayreuth he had Winifred as a powerful advocate with Hitler, who distrusted Tietjen but was prepared to set aside his doubts in the interests of the festival.

Tietjen could not afford to be seen placing obstacles in Wieland's path, all the same. That would have risked too much strife with Winnie and besides, there was no gainsaying the ever more evident talent for visual art of her adored eldest son. Much encouraged and influenced by Franz Stassen, an artist friend of his father's, Wieland honed his painting skills and began constructing models of stage sets that showed real promise although still in firmly traditional mould. From models he soon moved on to the real thing, designing scenery for productions of three of his father's operas – *Der Bärenhäuter* in Lübeck and Cologne, *Sonnenflammen* in Düsseldorf and *Schwarzschwanenreich* in Antwerp. Above all, in 1937 Tietjen finally let him wholly redesign the sets for *Parsifal* that Roller had concocted three years before and that most people (a disappointed Hitler included) agreed had been unsuitable. This was surely a challenge and an honour for a young man just turned twenty, even for a clearly gifted Wagner heir, but Wieland was anything but grateful. Years later he still claimed that he had had to fight hard to extract the commission from Tietjen at all; besides, he had also designed costumes of which (for whatever reason) few were used. After a long period of indecision he now wanted more from Bayreuth and quickly too – or nothing. When Tietjen offered him an eight-year 'learning the ropes' course in production and management at the Berlin Staatsoper, he turned it down with a snort. With the *Parsifal* achievement behind him, eight years of training seemed to Wieland a lifetime – as Tietjen had no doubt expected. Sure that he was being baulked by an interloper of an inheritance that he alone had the right to take up or spurn, he stomped off to Munich to study painting. Long seething, his dislike of Tietjen now erupted into hatred.

When Wieland left home in the autumn of 1938 for an atelier in Schwabing, Munich's bohemian quarter, the 'thousand-year Reich' was little more than five years old. In that brief span the Nazis had worked to transform Germany at giddy speed as though rightly sensing that they did not have a millennium of power before them after all.

Foul though they were, the events of 1933 like the burning of books, the 'coordination' of culture and the (only partly effective) boycott of Jewish shops were just the first steps down a trail of blood and terror. Others quickly followed. In 1934 Hitler consolidated his power in the 'night of the long knives', using the regular army and SS to crush the SA, the near-independent stormtrooper force of his rival and erstwhile friend Ernst Röhm. Röhm himself was murdered along with scores of other alleged 'traitors' – some unconnected with the SA but (like ex-chancellor Kurt von Schleicher) thought ripe for elimination anyway by Hitler and his main accomplices, Göring and Himmler.

A year later new action was taken against Jews, already chased from the civil service and for the most part from the professions and the arts. Under the 1935 'Nuremberg Laws' that notoriously claimed to define Jews by race rather than religion, they were now deprived of their civic rights and marriages were forbidden between them and 'citizens of German or kindred blood'. Tens of thousands emigrated but, disastrously, many stayed put for years until the trap snapped shut on them. When Hitler came to power Germany's Jews had totalled some half a million (less than one per cent of the population) and despite every villainy, most of them continued to look on Germany as their home. Besides, the cost of leaving was high and the prospect of being welcomed elsewhere with open arms small. After each new stage of persecution Jews tended to believe the nadir had been reached and each time they were wrong. In 1936 they were indeed harassed less overtly because the Nazis did not want to revolt foreigners visiting the Olympic Games in Berlin. But once the Games were over hostility mounted again, reaching a new but far from final peak of violence on 9–10 November 1938, the so-called *Kristallnacht* (literally 'crystal night' or 'night of broken glass'), when hundreds of synagogues were gutted countrywide and thousands of Jewish homes and shops ransacked. Close to a hundred Jews were murdered and up to thirty-five thousand others thrust into concentration camps, raising the number of inmates to around sixty thousand in one swoop. Four months earlier, at the United States' behest, a thirty-two-state conference had been held in Evian, France, to address the plight of Jewish refugees. It took no firm action.

Although Jews were the main targets they were not, of course, the only ones to suffer. Real and imagined foes of the regime were hounded down, tortured and slaughtered; 'inferior elements' including gypsies, homosexuals and the mentally handicapped were sterilised or used as 'guinea pigs' for odious medical experiments. The web of concentration camps spread steadily, culminating in the creation of extermination camps like Auschwitz-Birkenau and Treblinka in Poland after war began. How much of all this were ordinary Germans aware of, despite the Goebbels-induced clouds of propaganda emitted via the 'coordinated' press and radio? Many knew enough not to want to know more. Besides, the Gestapo and its army of informers seemed everywhere. 'Awkward' questions, let alone criticism, even within the family, could spell denunciation, sudden arrest and disappearance, perhaps for good.

For all that, the Nazi era seemed to many Germans not so much a 'reign of terror' as a stunning success, at least until the first big setbacks of the war. Thanks above all to public-spending programmes (not directed, at the start, mainly towards an arms build-up), unemployment that had peaked at more than six million at the end of the Weimar era had all but vanished by 1938; indeed in some sectors there was a serious shortage of skilled labour. The efficacy of what became known as 'Keynesian economics' was thus being demonstrated in practice in Nazi Germany even before Keynes got his *General Theory of Employment, Interest and Money* down on paper in 1936. Moreover a lot of good jobs and affordable dwellings became available because Jews were booted out of them or left the country, a circumstance that evidently gave few of the beneficiaries a bad conscience. On the contrary, many of those who deplored physical violence against Jews nonetheless welcomed the practical benefits that were being siphoned off at last to 'true Germans'. In this respect lawyers and judges, presumed guardians of justice, were no different to other professionals and intervened just as rarely on behalf of wronged Jewish colleagues – although some *did* intervene. In many fields there were individuals who shunned opportunism and tried to help the victims – but such bold and principled spirits were the exception, as they usually are in every place and era. Meanwhile the masses were enjoying cheap vacations, theatre trips, sports events and the like offered by *Kraft durch Freude* (Strength through Joy), a Nazi organisation that was meant to boost morale and demonstrably did so.

As for foreign policy, Germans happily noted that Hitler seemed able to thumb his nose at the rest of the world and get away with it, especially by reneging on the hated Versailles treaty. He ordered troops into the demilitarised Rhineland in 1936, gobbled up Austria in the *Anschluss* of 1938 and soon afterwards tore the mainly German-speaking Sudetenland away from Czechoslovakia with the connivance of Britain, France and fascist Italy. No wonder most Germans felt that '*Wir sind wieder wer*' (We're somebody again) after the drift and humiliation of the Weimar years; all the more so since an impressive array of foreigners clearly felt the same. One such fan was David Lloyd George, British prime minister from 1916 to 1922, who after visiting Hitler in 1936 extolled him as 'the George Washington of Germany – the man who won for his country independence from all her oppressors'. It was true, he conceded, that Hitler's methods were not those of a parliamentary democracy; nonetheless, Germany was now 'full of hope and confidence, and of a renewed sense of determination to live its own life without interference from any influence outside its own frontiers'.[8] Lloyd George was no fascist, though there were plenty such in Europe, including Oswald Mosley's blackshirts in Britain. Nor was he, at heart, either a coward or an appeaser. He was simply dazzled by the Führer and, like the mirror image of so many western democrats praising Stalin's nightmarish Soviet Union as a socialist paradise, he was endlessly naive.

What did the Wagner children make of all this? When the Second World War began in September 1939, Wieland was twenty-two, Friedelind twenty-one, Wolfgang just twenty and Verena nineteen – all old enough, in principle, to have views of their own. During Hitler's rise to power they had, of course, been too young to be fully politically aware even if their Bayreuth environment at home and school had encouraged a critical interest in politics, which it had not. Their father apart, they had been surrounded mainly by Nazi sympathisers like Winifred and 'the aunts', not to mention 'Uncle Wolf' with his singular entourage on his lightning visits. After Siegfried's death, Wahnfried became an even firmer pro-Nazi preserve with the coming of Lieselotte Schmidt, a busybody of a young woman who was engaged 'temporarily' as a children's coach-cum-secretary but who stayed for years. Her letters and diary entries gush with admiration for 'Wolf' (although her special idol was Hans Frank, Hitler's lawyer and a frequent Wahnfried visitor, whom she vainly hoped to marry) and are shot through with near-hysterical antisemitism. In 1933, for instance, we find her claiming that Jews had inspired a 'real witches sabbath' against Bayreuth with a campaign of lies and dirty tricks, but that happily the newly ensconced Führer had driven back the 'forces of darkness' in the nick of time.[9] The children tended to resent Lieselotte, not (with the later exception of Friedelind) because of her antisemitism but because she tried too overtly to play 'mistress of the house' when Winifred was away. On the other hand she readily helped them with their homework and cooed over every jot of talent they displayed. So she became a semi-permanent member of the household.

Although Hitler's achievement of power was an obvious boon for the festival itself, it at least temporarily caused a protocol dilemma for the Wagners. How if at all do you raise trickier matters of (Nazi) state – like plots, pillage and murder – with a Führer you have known for years as a close family friend? Specially alive to this problem after the Röhm purge in the summer of 1934, Winifred told the children to be tactful when 'Wolf' arrived a few weeks later for the festival. She need not have worried. Hitler himself broached the matter right away, claiming that not more than seventy-seven people had been executed, although unavoidably, several had been shot by mistake. According to Friedelind, her mother expressed understanding for the action, noting that the 'poor Führer' must have had a terrible shock 'to find himself betrayed by his best friend'. And the children? There is no good reason to suppose they reacted very differently, not even Friedelind at the time. Although she later related the incident in her book with a general air of condemnation for Hitler, back in 1934 Mausi was still an innocent in more ways than one. When she was told in a shocked whisper that on his arrest Röhm had been found in bed with a man, she retorted: 'But imagine how embarrassing it would have been if they had found him with a woman?'[10]

Four years later Winifred seems to have been genuinely horrified by *Kristallnacht*, probably because she had the nasty evidence thrust under her very nose. In Bayreuth Nazi thugs mishandled Jews, pillaged their homes and laid waste the four remaining Jewish businesses (from more than thirty when Hitler came to power) that had not already been 'appropriated' by 'Aryans'. It may be that Winifred played a role in preventing the synagogue from being burned down, although it was ransacked. The details are murky. But it is a fact that the synagogue immediately adjoins that superb Margravian opera house the Master had loved but found too small for his festival needs, and that if the former had been set alight the latter would almost certainly have been gutted too. That would have been an awful loss for the town, and particularly so for a Wagner.[11] Anyway, according to a report by the mayor, Winifred was appalled by the violence and resolved to complain to Hitler when he was next in Bayreuth. She seems to have kept her pledge but that does not mean she blamed him personally. On the contrary, to the end of her days, Winifred held 'Wolf' responsible for all she felt was good about the 'Third Reich', and his treacherous, incompetent underlings for all that was bad. Naturally Hitler encouraged this approach. According to Wolfgang, when he and Wieland expressed 'indignation' over *Kristallnacht*, the Führer replied that the affair had been an independent initiative launched by Goebbels. He, Hitler, had not known about it in advance – a claim that the evidence, including Goebbels' diaries, unsurprisingly fails to support.[12]

Despite their 'indignation', the brothers evidently did not conclude that they lived under a regime that was evil to the core. On *Kristallnacht* Wieland was already living in Munich, the so-called *Hauptstadt der Bewegung* (Capital of the [Nazi] Movement), where the plunder was far worse than in Bayreuth and synagogues were indeed burned. His girlfriend Gertrud recorded that the two of them picked their way round the shattered glass on the streets, neither supporting the action nor trying to stop it. 'One simply looked on,' she wrote. 'Wieland found it bad.'[13] The pair seems to have reacted just as passively a year earlier in Munich on visiting the notorious exhibition of so-called 'degenerate art', some 650 paintings, drawings and sculptures by avant-garde masters like Nolde, Kirchner, Schmidt-Rottluff and Klee whose work the Nazis banned. If, as a budding artist himself, Wieland felt any empathy for these works despite (or because of) the official censure, there is precious little sign of it. For years afterwards his style stayed heavily traditional – at least up to his last recorded picture during the Munich era, an unfinished portrait in oil of his chief patron, the Führer. When questioned by the brothers about 'degenerate art,' Hitler was once again evasive. The offending works, he pointed out, had not actually been destroyed. Some had been sold abroad and Old Masters bought for German museums with the proceeds.[14]

Wolfgang, it is true, presents himself in his memoirs as having been anything but a fan of Nazism. He states that, unlike Wieland, he never joined the party, that he left the Hitler Youth movement and its 'swindlers' in dudgeon after only three months and that he repeatedly spoke his mind to nincompoop Nazi officialdom. Unlike his brother and sisters, Wolfgang says, he 'largely refrained' from cultivating the official connections that could have been his too, and stresses that he never accepted Hitler's hospitality in the capital.[15] That claim about Berlin seems odd since all the children are on record as having visited the Führer there both before and, Friedelind apart, during the war. Moreover all of them, not just Wolfgang, got away with insubordination to Nazis high and low precisely because they were Wagners and well known to have Hitler's blessing. Still, when Wolfgang expresses distaste for the party in general and many of its representatives in particular there is no good reason to doubt him.

Not that Wieland's attitude was much different. Although it is a fact that he joined the party, he signed up only belatedly – in 1938, after Hitler put him on the spot by asking whether he was already a member. Wolfgang, who was present at the start of this uneasy chat, promptly made himself scarce to avoid being faced with the same question.[16] Evidently the Führer did not subsequently ask about him, or if he did he could not be bothered to follow up the matter. Wieland he regarded as the 'heir' – entitled to privilege, yes, but more or less behoven not to stand aside from the party indefinitely. The little brother was, at best, 'the spare'. Wolfgang plainly suffered later from being treated as Bayreuth's second string in talent as well as age, but in the pre-war era (not to mention during post-war denazification) his less exposed role proved largely a blessing. Free of the burden of high expectations that his brother struggled with, neither arrogant nor specially ambitious, he made friends easily at school and got on happily with his hobbies.

Neither then nor later was Wolfgang much given to critical reflection. The title of his autobiography *Lebens-Akte* (perhaps best translated in this case as Action Man) suggests as much, no doubt unintentionally. He surely did, though, have a fine eye for the ridiculous. When a firework display in the garden at Wahnfried went wrong, engulfing a livid Führer and festival artists in clouds of smoke, young Wolfi was tickled pink. He found it no less hilarious to have to rescue the broad-beamed 'Hermann the Magnificent' (i.e. Göring) from a narrow chair in which he had become hopelessly stuck.[17] Such incidents offered rare but welcome relief to the strains of having Hitler around as a summer house guest for several days at a time rather than as a fleeting visitor. The Führer's reputation as a 'night owl' was all too well deserved. After festival performances, he would receive fawning guests in the Wahnfried annexe and deliver himself of protracted monologues until the small hours of the morning. After most visitors had gone home and even the weary Winifred had retreated, the children (or at least some of them) were required to stay up and keep 'Uncle Wolf' amused. Sometimes it would be close to dawn before he too decided to trudge off to bed. Until he awoke in mid- to late morning, everyone had to go around on tiptoe, the dogs were kept indoors, and the car was rolled by hand out of the garage to the distant street. As Friedelind noted, entertaining a Führer – even one so well disposed to his hosts – was 'not all roses and champagne'.[18]

Perhaps it was 'baby Verena' – already emerging as an attractive young lady when Hitler came to power – who suffered least from this wearying summer schedule. With her refined dress sense, slim figure and come-hither smile, Nickel was the toast of virtually all male visitors to Wahnfried, especially of Wolf and his bustling coterie. When he held forth in the annexe she was often at his side and, with a bat of her eyelids, could even get away with an occasional, semi-irreverent interjection. It was hardly a surprise when, during the war, she married a top Nazi official. Her spouse was old enough to be her father but then, after Cosima and Winifred, that was something of a family tradition. Her less comely but more talented sister, on the other hand, took a course that could not have been more different.

## 12

# Mausi at Bay

Of Siegfried's and Winifred's four children, it was Friedelind who finally emerged as the one heroic rebel. Thanks largely to her independent mind, critical eye and what even her mother admitted to be her 'enormous sense of justice', she alone made a clean break with the 'Third Reich'. By thus following the example of her idols like Toscanini and (another fiercely anti-fascist conductor) Erich Kleiber, Mausi incensed such noted Wahnfried visitors as Goebbels and Himmler and, it seems, rendered the Führer uncharacteristically speechless when he was told of her 'treachery'. Even for one who was unhappy at home and felt baulked of the artistic inheritance she craved, her choice of self-exile at a time when Hitler's power was at its height showed principle and guts. That she of all the Wagners should then – in post-war Germany – regularly have been dubbed the 'black sheep of the family' is a peculiarly shabby irony.

Friedelind was no saint all the same. As a child she could be a real little beast, jealous and wounding. It was she who first brought her school chum Gertrud Reissinger home to Wahnfried and hence ultimately into the arms of Wieland; but when she felt she was starting to lose her girlfriend to her brother, she stole and made public compromising photos that she vainly hoped might force the pair to split. Not much early 'sense of justice' there, even if the affair can be passed off as a fit of spite (albeit far from the only one) by a boisterous but at heart lonely adolescent. Nor, despite her habitual love of the forthright, is Friedelind wholly candid in her memoirs and passes over the fact that, in her late teens, she had still not fully shaken off either her racial prejudice or a certain admiration for Hitler's Germany.

From her account in *Heritage of Fire* one might well conclude that

Friedelind had been against the Nazis and sympathetic to Jews almost from the moment Hitler came to power in 1933. A rather different picture emerges from private sources including her correspondence with Eva and Daniela – 'the aunts' with whom she continued to have close relations because they were her beloved father's sisters and hostile to Winifred. The letters show that Friedelind was still going out of her way to defend the 'new Germany' in 1937 during one of her lengthy stays in England and that she was making snide remarks about Jews and blacks even in early 1938.[1] Memoirs are anyway not the place to look for relentless self-criticism, but in this case Friedelind had special cause for caution. She wrote her book in English while in wartime exile, starting it in Britain and finishing it in America where it was first published. In neither country would such unsavoury revelations about her fairly recent history have gone down at all well. As it was, the revelations she *did* make about her family, Bayreuth and the Nazis were anything but welcome in her home country – although most people there long knew of them only from press reports and hearsay. A German translation, not an original German text written by the authoress, called *Nacht über Bayreuth* (Night over Bayreuth) was published in Switzerland as early as 1945; but this was very hard to come by for decades in Germany itself and only found a publisher there well after Friedelind's death in 1991.

For all her childish nastiness and sins of omission, the fact remains that Friedelind finally *did* see through 'Uncle Wolf's' awful Reich and drew the consequences, unlike her siblings, let alone her appalled mother. Ironically Winifred was partly responsible for her daughter's slow but sure conversion. By shunting her off to boarding schools and letting her spend ever longer spells abroad, she helped Mausi gradually win a perspective on Wahnfried and the Nazis that was denied the rest of the family. Arguably the process began as early as 1930 when Friedelind, then barely twelve, was assigned to a school at Brighouse in Yorkshire. For Mausi it was a sad time because first Cosima and then Siegfried died within months of one another, but she liked the school itself – certainly far more than the ones in Brandenburg and Berlin to which she was subsequently propelled. A few years later, after more bitter rows with Winifred, she was back in England again – this time at a school near Arundel in Sussex, not far, in fact, from the birthplaces both of her mother and of her late uncle Chamberlain. Not that Mausi felt an urge to make a pilgrimage to either spot or, indeed, to spend much time mulling over her books. Repeatedly, she skived off to London for meetings with Frida Leider who was singing Wagner at Covent Garden and for a happy reunion with her 'other father' Toscanini whom she had not seen for years.

Thanks partly to these contacts Friedelind gained new friends who henceforth stuck by her as she flitted in and out of London, increasingly at odds with her homeland and usually all but out of cash. One of the closest of them was Isabella Wallich, a brilliant young pianist and niece of Fred Gaisberg, the near-legendary gramophone pioneer who had already recorded extensively at Bayreuth. Indeed, it was 'Uncle Fred' who had signed up Siegfried Wagner to record the *Siegfried Idyll* in London in 1927. Small wonder the two young ladies hit it off – despite a row at their very first meeting when the often bossy and possessive Mausi, invited by Toscanini to one of his rehearsals, questioned Isabella's right to be there too. The incident shows well enough how Friedelind could be her own worst foe, but in this case her sharp tongue did not abort the birth of a lifelong friendship.[2] Decades later when Isabella herself became a record producer with her own company, she and Mausi were to collaborate in a bold but fraught venture that brought some of Siegfried's works (among other rarities) to disc.

Another stalwart during Friedelind's London years was Berta Geissmar, Furtwängler's former private secretary who had taken on the same role for Beecham, Britain's leading conductor, after being chased from Germany because she was Jewish. Whatever prejudice Friedelind still had against Jews in general at that time, she liked Berta and helped her with odd jobs at Covent Garden. The feeling was mutual. 'Maus was in many ways the image of the great Richard,' Berta wrote in her book *The Baton and the Jackboot* in 1944. 'She was gifted and courageous; but she was not an easy character, and has gone her own way in life.'[3] Although far from well-off herself, Berta invited Friedelind to stay with her and naturally slipped her opera tickets. On one occasion during the 1938 season, she recalled, Maus happened to share a box with Gustav Mahler's sculptress daughter Anna, who had just fled Austria and had also approached Berta for a free ticket. How much those two independent-minded ladies would have had to say to one another: Friedelind the Master's granddaughter, Anna the only surviving child of that great composer and conductor of Jewish origin whose Wagner at the Vienna Hofoper had so thrilled Hitler. Sadly, it seems the chance was missed.

The presence of a Wagner daughter in London was not just a matter of interest to music fans in general and Wagnerians in particular. As a member of a family that had enjoyed regular and intimate contact with Hitler for years, Friedelind naturally came under the close scrutiny of British (and later American) officialdom. She notes in her book that at the start of the war 'I had already put myself at the disposal of the English government which considered me of "unique propaganda value",' and broadly speaking that seems true.[4] Although she mentions no names, her main backer in London was, in fact, Beverley Baxter, a Canadian-born Conservative MP who was also an influential writer and journalist. He in turn brought Friedelind's case to the attention of powerful contacts – notably Sir Samuel Hoare, the then Home Secretary, Sir Robert Vansittart, from late 1937 chief diplomatic adviser to the government, and R. A. (Rab) Butler, under-secretary of state at the Foreign Office. According to Baxter, all four of them agreed that the Wagner girl could be 'of use'. Whether they actually saw her as of 'unique' value is another matter.[5]

Meanwhile in Berlin, Hitler had apparently been pumping Friedelind about her impressions while in England and did not like what he heard. She claims that at a private lunch in the Berlin Chancellery around Christmas 1937, she told the Führer that Joachim von Ribbentrop, the German ambassador in London, thoroughly misjudged the British and that his lack of diplomatic finesse was making unnecessary foes in high places. The Austrian ambassador, she added, was far more popular and respected. Hitler, it seems, angrily rejected this analysis, although Ribbentrop's blunders (like giving the Nazi salute to the Royal Family) were notorious even in Berlin. But he calmed down after taking a pill and a glass of water.[6]

It is perfectly possible that Friedelind did indeed see Hitler when she says she did. Mausi with her big mouth and puppy fat was surely never Hitler's favourite Wagner – but a Wagner she was and hence, like all other members of the family, almost under orders to pay the Führer a visit when in Berlin. It is also more than likely, in the circumstances, that England would have been discussed even though the details Friedelind gives are unverifiable. On the list of Hitler's obsessions Britain with its empire ranked high – an object of fury but also of wary admiration, as repeated allusions not least in *Mein Kampf* make clear. For the Führer as for (Houston Stewart) Chamberlain the British were Aryans, and hence natural racial relations of the Germans, who had gone tragically wrong under Jewish influence. But what had gone wrong, in Hitler's view, could and should be put right. Nazi Germany was showing how!

Nor did the Führer lack for signs, mixed though they were, to back his hunch that Britain was an ally-in-waiting. Hadn't the London government largely acquiesced in his muscle-flexing foreign policy; didn't Lord Rothermere's press empire busily issue one pro-Hitler paean after another (like that George Washington comparison made by Lloyd George); weren't many of the 'upper class' in particular wooed by the Nazi ability to 'keep order' and (apparently) to stand firm against Soviet communism? The British visitors who beat a path to Hitler's door included the Duke of Windsor, who had abdicated as King Edward VIII in 1936 and who made little secret of his sympathy for the Reich. Hitler did not put much faith in Oswald Mosley's fascists as a force for change in Britain, feeling they were too close to foreign brands – notably Mussolini's blackshirts – to win credibility at home. Had he been starting such a party there, Hitler once mused, he would have taken Oliver Cromwell as his model and probably called his followers 'Ironsides'. He did, however, hugely admire Mosley's scintillating, aristocratic wife Diana, one of the Mitford sisters, who had first been married to the wealthy Bryan Guinness (later Lord Moyne). When Oswald and Diana wed in Berlin in October 1936 the Führer devoted much of his day to them – throwing a Chancellery supper in their honour as well as attending the registry-office ceremony and a subsequent lunch offered by Goebbels at his Wannsee villa. Amazingly, the event itself and the attention given it by the Nazi leadership stayed hidden from the public for two years.[7]

For Hitler, Diana and her still more fervently pro-Nazi sister Unity seemed handsome proof that the finest Aryan stock still flourished among Britain's 'top people'. They were, as he was well aware, daughters of the ultra-conservative Lord Redesdale whose own father had done so much to promote Chamberlain's racist bible *Foundations of the Nineteenth Century* in England three decades or so before. Both Mitford girls accompanied Hitler to Nazi rallies and to the Bayreuth festival; indeed for a time Unity was so often on hand that she became known as *Mit-fahrt*, a pun hinting both at her role as political fellow traveller and as the Führer's frequent companion. According to her diary, she met and conversed with Hitler on 140 days over the five years between 1935 and 1939, a claim that other accounts suggest is not exaggerated.[8] When the land of her birth finally declared war on her beloved Nazi Germany in September 1939, Unity was so distraught that she went to the Englischer Garten, Munich's biggest park, and shot herself in the temple. If she had really meant to kill herself she botched the job. Critically injured, she was taken to a local clinic where Hitler visited her, paid her bills and packed her off to England. There she lived on as a brain-damaged invalid for almost another decade.

In those pre-war years, Hitler pumped both Unity and Diana for word on the mood in Britain and made comments 'in confidence' that he evidently assumed would be passed on to influential circles in London. Perhaps he tried to use Friedelind in a similar way. If so he chose the wrong person at the wrong time. It was almost certainly in 1938, and thanks in particular to her friendship with Frida Leider, that Mausi became fully aware of the iniquity of the Nazi regime. Frida was married to a Jew, Rudolf Deman, who hitherto had been protected by two things: his Austrian nationality and his key role as concertmaster (leader) of the orchestra at the Berlin Staatsoper, valued and protected by Tietjen. When the Nazis came to power Frida had considered making her career in America but Tietjen, keen to keep both artists, told her all would be well and offered her a stellar salary. For years neither Deman nor (by association) his non-Jewish wife suffered direct threat despite ever-more virulent antisemitism, but that changed in 1938 when Austria was drawn into the Reich. In one fell swoop Deman lost his Austrian nationality and Frida, sick with worry, came close to a nervous breakdown. In the summer she went to Bayreuth but had to cancel a performance, to the fury of Tietjen who felt she was well enough to sing (and of Winifred, who looked askance at the close ties between Frida and Mausi). Deman, seeking to defend his wife, had a dispute with Tietjen so heated that the shouts resounded through the corridors of the festival theatre. A few months later Deman fled to Switzerland. Frida stayed behind, fearful that she would be unable to start a new career in exile at the age of fifty and hoping that the worst might soon pass. But she never sang in Bayreuth after that 1938 season and it was nearly eight years before her husband could return to Germany.[9]

Since that first encounter in a Bayreuth dressing-room a decade before, Friedelind had witnessed Frida's triumphs in London and Paris as well as Germany; she had met her scores of times privately and had come to admire her talent, her spirit and her taste (not least in clothing). Above all she was able to pour out her heart to her as she almost never could to Winifred; indeed Frida came close to being the mother Mausi felt she had never really had. Friedelind had overheard the Deman–Tietjen row, she saw her beloved friend brought low, physically and spiritually and she knew what was at the back of it – Nazi racial laws, in this case combined with Hitler's march into Austria. She reacted with pain and revulsion.

Although the Frida–Deman affair was evidently the key event on the road to Friedelind's final break with the Nazis, it was not the only one. That same summer, she attended the newly created Lucerne festival, backed largely by artists who either could not or, on moral grounds, would not perform in the Reich (which now included Austria). Winifred dismissed the festival as 'anti-German' but, with great self-exiled artists like Adolf Busch and his brother Fritz making music there with Jewish colleagues, Friedelind knew better. All the more so since Toscanini was on hand to welcome her and to pay special homage to Wagner with a performance of the *Siegfried Idyll* in the garden of Tribschen. The next year Friedelind was back again and this time she stayed, occupying rooms at Tribschen long since made available to members of the Wagner family. What more fitting spot could she have found to rest and reflect on her uncertain future than the villa where her father had been born and where even her explosive grandfather had found something like peace for a time? 'You will see where your Hitler is leading you, namely into the abyss, into ruin,' she told her mother in a letter around that time.[10] Recalling that warning nearly four decades afterwards Winifred paused as though a bit nonplussed, then belatedly conceded, 'Unfortunately she was right about that.'

Once war broke out, Winifred made a single, desperate bid to extract her 'prodigal daughter' from her refuge and bring her home before her presence abroad caused real propaganda harm to the Reich. With Hitler's approval and clutching a visa personally issued by Himmler, she crossed into neutral Switzerland in February 1940 and spent two days and nights trying to make Friedelind see the error of her ways. But the Maus was not to be trapped.

The fraught encounter took place neither at Tribschen nor at nearby Lucerne but, at Winifred's proposal, in Zurich – a lot closer to the

German border. In *Heritage of Fire*, Friedelind says she had grave doubts about making the trip, fearing the Gestapo might have plans to kidnap her; but she went all the same – drawn to her mother despite everything and anxious for more news of the family. As it happens the two of them stayed at the Baur au Lac, the lakeside hotel where nearly nine decades earlier the newly exiled Master had given the first public readings of his *Ring* text, but naturally neither was in the mood to discuss music drama or family history. Over long hours in restaurants and hotel rooms Winifred sought with all manner of arguments – the brothers' shame over their errant sister, the failing health of 'the aunts', the Führer's intense vexation – to persuade Mausi to come to heel. Finally, as the time for parting neared, she told her daughter she faced a stark choice – to return to the Reich or to go to a neutral country and keep quiet for as long as the war lasted. If she failed to comply, 'the order will be given; you will be destroyed [*vertilgt*] and exterminated [*ausgerottet*] at the first opportunity.' Friedelind wrote that she felt the blood leave her face, not so much at the threat itself as the language her mother used. 'Destroyed' and 'exterminated', she noted, were surely Hitler's terms or Himmler's.

Friedelind's account of the Zurich meeting, especially that last chilling phrase she attributes to Winifred, is easily the most notorious part of *Heritage of Fire*. It was seized on avidly by the press when the book was published and it helped put Winifred still more on the defensive immediately after the war. How credible is it? Since no one seems to have overheard what the two women said to one another (though Friedelind reports that she looked under her bed for a spy) the memoir is the only detailed report available.[11] Not surprisingly Winifred declared the whole book to be full of holes and errors, a claim backed among others by Wolfgang, who specifically called the 'destroyed and exterminated' quote an anathema 'worthy of the Old Testament'. That does not prove the words were never uttered. Winifred was surely convinced her daughter was in mortal danger and perhaps, when she saw her mission was failing, she did indeed parrot a brutal remark she had heard only recently in Berlin (more likely from Himmler than from her 'Wolf'). According to that interpretation, the 'threat' would really have amounted to a dire warning issued as a last resort by an anguished mother.

A few weeks after the reported 'showdown' Mausi sent her mother a letter from Tribschen that she does not mention in her book; indeed the memoir ends with Winifred's departure by train for Germany wailing 'Do come home, Mausi. Please come. I need you.' In her letter, Friedelind described the recent get-together as 'worthwhile', pledged to do 'nothing unconsidered' and signed off 'heartfelt thanks for all your kindness, your Maus'.[12] On the face of it those affectionate words cast doubt on the harsh account of the selfsame meeting given in *Heritage of Fire*, but there is more to the tale than that. The letter is dated 29 February (no slip of the pen since 1940 was a leap year). The very next day – on 1 March – Friedelind left Lucerne, crossed France (three months before the German invasion) armed with a transit visa and finally arrived in Britain for which she had another visa, evidently thanks to the pressure applied on her behalf by Beverley Baxter. In other words, when she wrote so warmly to her mother she knew she was about to turn her back on the Reich and enter enemy territory for good – or at least for the foreseeable future. Almost certainly, therefore, her letter was meant to put the Gestapo off her track (which, for a while, it evidently did). Friedelind was well aware by this time that her correspondence was being intercepted; and if she had had any lingering doubts about the danger she faced as a self-exiled Wagner in wartime, the Zurich meeting with her mother must have put paid to them.

Friedelind had yet another reason to be ultra-cautious, of which next to no one was aware at the time. In *Heritage of Fire* she briefly refers to a 1938 summer holiday she spent in Lucerne, Venice and other spots with an 'attractive young Austrian' and his mother, 'a dashing Viennese baroness'.[13] Winifred, she says, backed the trip, vainly hoping her unruly daughter would marry the young man, an assistant at the Bayreuth festival, and thus be off her hands for good. Although Friedelind named no names, it was not hard from her description to identify the couple as Gottfried von Einem, later one of Austria's most noted composers, and his mother Gerta Louise von Einem, the German-born wife of an Austrian nobleman. 'Dashing' the baroness certainly was – a woman of striking beauty and countless affairs (Gottfried was the product of one of them with a Hungarian count), and also a spy whose tangled activities during the Nazi era have never been fully unravelled. Suffice to say here that she survived arrest by the Gestapo as well as death sentences from both German and French courts, and passed away peacefully in her bed in 1964.

Friedelind admits that she and the 'young Austrian' spent much of their free time together, but in his 1995 autobiography, appropriately entitled *Ich hab' unendlich viel erlebt* (I Have Had a Boundlessly Eventful Life), Gottfried von Einem goes further. For a time, he says, he and Mausi were 'in a way even engaged' and when they went to hotels together they took care to take adjoining rooms with an unlocked door between them.[14] After war broke out, Gottfried managed to get into Switzerland (he does not reveal how), withdrew all his mother's valuables from her bank accounts there and passed them on to Friedelind before she left Tribschen for England. In other words he (and presumably his mother) did not feel Switzerland would be a safe haven from the Nazis for long and decided to use Mausi as a courier. He even claims he accompanied her across the border to France. At least part of this tale is suspect. According to Gottfried, an ebullient, larger-than-life figure with a tendency to exaggerate, the valuables included all his mother's Swiss money, jewels and 'a considerable quantity of gold'.[15] It is hard to see how Friedelind could possibly have carted such a Fafner-like hoard through so many controls, in wartime at that. There is no doubt, nonetheless, that she *did* take von Einem jewellery with her from Switzerland at Gottfried's behest, and that this had repercussions after the war.

No wonder Mausi was keen to hide her real plans when she wrote to her mother on that last day of February 1940. For a while thereafter she seemed to vanish into thin air. Winifred desperately tried to discover her whereabouts, but she and the family only learned the truth in May when Friedelind began writing articles in the London *Daily Sketch* that filled Goebbels for one with growing fury. 'The little fat Wagner is writing disclosures against the Führer in London,' he noted in his diary on 4 May. 'This could become embarrassing.' A day later he reported that Wieland had been called in by Hitler to be told of the 'serious disgrace' caused by his 'fine little sister'. Finally the propaganda minister abandoned any pretence at irony and charged in his entry of 10 May that 'This fat beast is committing wholesale treachery against her country.'[16] The particular cause of that outburst was a piece in which Friedelind detailed snide remarks she claimed Hitler had made in private about Mussolini. By this time Winifred must have been not just worried but truly alarmed. 'Of course if we hadn't been members of the Wagner family, the whole lot of us would have been put in a concentration camp,' she reflected years later – a remark more revealing than she seems to have realised.[17]

Unfortunately for Friedelind, the 'unique propaganda value' she claims to have had for the British did not protect her for long from being treated as an 'enemy alien'. She had arrived in London during that period of relative calm known as the 'phoney war' – before the retreat from Dunkirk, the Battle of Britain and the Blitz – but even so her friends were dumbfounded when she popped up unannounced in their midst. Isabella Wallich recalled her jaw dropping when she peered out of her window one day and saw Mausi, of all people, dressed in a black cloak and approaching the house 'like a ship in full sail'.[18] Isabella and several others did what they could to help, but once the war began in earnest Friedelind was arrested, bustled off to Holloway prison in north London and thence to internment in the Isle of Man. She stayed under lock and key for nearly nine months, from 27 May 1940 to 15 February 1941, when she was packed off to Argentina.

It may seem odd that Mausi should have been thus treated – given those friends in high places who had helped her enter the country in the first place. But by the end of May at the latest Britain was manifestly in grave danger of invasion. German troops had just sliced through Holland and Belgium and, skirting the supposedly impregnable 'Maginot Line', were advancing on Paris. British forces on the continent were in retreat and about to be evacuated willy-nilly from Dunkirk, leaving their equipment behind. Neville ('peace in our time') Chamberlain had resigned and been replaced as Prime Minister by Winston Churchill who told Parliament he had nothing to offer but 'blood, toil, tears and sweat'. Such were the circumstances in which tougher steps were demanded – and in part implemented – against around seventy-five thousand men, women and children in Britain who were of German or Austrian nationality or descent. In the event some thirty thousand of them, mostly refugees from Hitler and many of them Jews, were interned or shipped off to distant parts of the British empire.[19]

This policy of mass internment was far from undisputed even within the government itself, let alone in the country at large. Both the Home Office and Foreign Office long argued against locking up people many of whom had already suffered at Nazi hands and who could well prove useful to the British war effort. But the War Office and especially MI5 claimed that allowing so many 'enemy aliens' to run free posed a grave security risk, and their view prevailed – at least for a time. By the summer, though, the internment policy was being fiercely debated in Parliament and contested as a grave injustice by part of the press. Eventually it was largely reversed – a striking show of democracy still working even at a time of great national peril. But in the meantime thousands of innocent people were swept up by it – including Friedelind, despite the seemingly firm anti-Nazi credentials she had displayed to all and sundry in her *Daily Sketch* pieces.

Ironically, it was in part those very articles that told against her. At first only a few people were aware that Mausi was back in London, but her subsequent press attacks on the Nazis naturally put her in the limelight and aroused decidedly mixed feelings. Some readers praised her evident pluck, others – including people who had known her personally – expressed strong doubts over whether her professed 'conversion' was genuine. One couple, for instance, warned police that Friedelind had once told them she believed Britain would be better off under a dictatorship. An ex-mistress at the Yorkshire school Friedelind had attended in 1930 told how her charge had constantly given the Nazi salute, much to the mirth of fellow pupils. Another woman recalled how Friedelind had boasted at school that she was 'a personal friend of Hitler'. One of the odder reports to the authorities came from a woman professing to be a distant relative of Tietjen (who, as noted earlier, had a British mother). She asserted that around 1937 Friedelind – 'unquestionably very much under Hitler's influence' – had sought her help at the request of Tietjen, who wanted to trace his British ancestry and prove that he was, for the Nazis, a 'true Aryan'.[20]

These and similar claims that flowed in from citizens worried about a 'fifth column' in England were very likely true. Mausi's final 'conversion' evidently did come pretty late and then for a reason – the fate of Frida Leider and her husband – that next to no one in England knew about. In any case such accusations served to bolster doubts at official level about the 'Wagner girl' (variously called, Friedelinde, Friedland, Friedlen and Mausie), as files first released in 2005 by the security service make all too clear. One British source reported home from (neutral) Lisbon that Friedelind worked for the SS, another claimed she was one of a small group of agents personally sent abroad by Hitler in 1938 'with ample funds', yet another noted that while in England she had met Franz von Rintelen – a master spy for the Germans during the First World War who had settled in Britain after apparently disowning his homeland. A police report concluded that 'she could prove to be a singularly dangerous woman.'

Those trying to collate such material in London were far from convinced that Friedelind was a spy; still less did they believe the rumour, apparently first put about by the Gestapo in Paris, that she had become the mistress of Anthony Eden, Foreign Secretary until 1938 and again from 1940. But they did feel there was enough cause to put her where she could do no harm – and keep her there. When Friedelind applied in September from her detention camp in the Isle of Man for a visa to leave for South America, she was refused forthwith, although in the meantime Toscanini, hearing of her plight, was pulling strings from the US on her behalf. Her case was also raised in Parliament, but this too brought no change. The breakthrough came only in December when Beverley Baxter wrote a stinging article in the *Sketch* charging, with some exaggeration, that the treatment meted out to Friedelind reflected badly on Britain 'in the eyes of the world'.[21] First officialdom had dragged its feet over allowing her into the country, he claimed, so that her 'damaging anti-Hitler propaganda' had come somewhat late. Then she had been locked up and her request to go abroad rejected. Baxter conceded that Mausi was 'obstinate, opinionated and tactless. If these are crimes instead of misfortunes then she is guilty. But Richard Wagner was her grandfather and he, too, was all these things.'

Baxter might have added that Friedelind resembled her grandfather in yet another way – her strong propensity to run up debts. Several documents make that plain, including a solicitor's letter arguing that if 'Miss Wagner' were to be released she should first be brought back from the Isle of Man to London (as indeed she was), not least because she had many creditors pressing for payment. According to the letter, Friedelind had not so far received a cheque for £150 that had been sent on to her for the *Sketch* articles, and she seemed to have no other resources in Britain apart from (a possible reference to the von Einem 'hoard'?) 'certain jewellery of no great value'. It is not clear from the letter whether the missing £150 would have been enough to pay off the outstanding bills, and as a self-exile – let alone as an 'enemy alien' – Mausi was bound to be hard-pressed for funds anyway. But she had, in fact, earlier received a hefty advance in Britain for a book that she had started but (unsurprisingly) failed to deliver, and just a month before her detention another sum from an undisclosed source had been credited to an account for her in London. She evidently used the latter for, among other things, the hire of a Steinway piano. Not that Friedelind spent money simply on herself, either in London or elsewhere. Friends over many years testified to her spontaneous, even wild, generosity. But it is plain that when she did come into funds, which was not often, they tended to slip through her fingers like sand.

Following publication of the Baxter article, it was decided to grant Friedelind an exit visa after all and she was brought back to London en route for Buenos Aires. Toscanini had fixed her up with an invitation to work at the city's famed Teatro Colón, where he was himself due to appear, and the exiled Erich Kleiber – also a regular conductor in the Argentinian capital – put in a word for her too. But despite the backing of these two noted anti-fascists, British officials still had lingering doubts about Friedelind and were not inclined to let her go without further scrutiny. On 24 January 1941, she had an hour-long visit in London from a man who told her he was an anti-Nazi writer interested in her work but who, records show, was working for the security service. In his account of the meeting, he described Friedelind's comments as politically naive – including, surprisingly, her claim that as late as 1937–8 Hitler had still wanted to be friends with Britain – and concluded 'the remote possibility remains that Miss Wagner may secretly be a Nazi propagandist'.[22]

This informant, identified only as 'source 32a', was soon to change his tune. A few days later he reported that he had now had a chance to examine the contents of Mausi's suitcase and had read the incomplete manuscript of 'her book on Hitler' (clearly an early draft of what became *Heritage of Fire*). The latter he regarded as so important that he – vainly – recommended it for immediate publication even in 'abbreviated form'.[23] But it was evidently letters he found in the suitcase, above all ones from Winifred warning her daughter what she risked by turning her back on the Reich, that finally persuaded him Friedelind was genuine. 'If Miss Wagner were an agent,' he concluded, 'then Hitler would know it. If Hitler knew it, the mother would know it. If the mother knew it she *could* [emphasis in original] not have written these letters.'[24]

Thus Winifred unwittingly proved of service to her 'errant child' after all. Little more than a fortnight after '32a' had rummaged through her luggage, Friedelind was taken from London to Glasgow under Special Branch escort and put on the SS *Andalucia Star* bound for Buenos Aires. The crossing was rough, not to mention dangerous, with German U-boats about, and Mausi was often seasick; but there is no hint of that or of her previous long months of privation in a photo taken after her arrival – unless it be that she had, to advantage, manifestly lost weight. Sporting an elegant outfit topped by a huge round hat like an over-emphatic halo, she stands beaming with obvious relief, arm in arm with Toscanini, her 'second father'.

Mausi spent only a few months in Argentina before winning entry to the United States, again with Toscanini's help. On arrival in New York she was questioned by the Office of Strategic Services, the predecessor of the Central Intelligence Agency, but such information as she had to give did not bring her special privileges – nor, it seems, did she seek any. Rashly determined to stand on her own two feet, she eked out a meagre existence for years with a string of jobs including waitress, dish-washer, secretary and market researcher. Between times she tried to get on with her book, although some material for it that had been retained in England and was later sent on to her apparently got lost in transit. Fatefully, when she was all but skint, she pawned the von Einem jewels and was later unable to raise the cash to get them back. The items were therefore sold and passed beyond Friedelind's reach, let alone the von Einems', for good.

Despite her chronic shortage of funds, the Maus somehow managed to keep up with her music. She took singing lessons from the peerless baritone Herbert Janssen, a refugee friend from Bayreuth festival days, and mulled over plans to found an opera troupe to tour the US in better times – a dream that years later nearly came true. Meanwhile, she did not have to miss out on exemplary renderings of her grandfather's works. Hitler or no Hitler, New York's Metropolitan Opera continued to give much of the Wagner canon with casts (including Kirsten Flagstad, Kirsten Thorborg, Helen Traubel, Lauritz Melchior, Alexander Kipnis – and Janssen) rarely matched at any time anywhere – even in Bayreuth. One case in point was the *Tannhäuser* under Erich Leinsdorf given at the Met in February 1942, just two months after America entered the war, to mark the anniversary of Wagner's death. Friedelind was present, of course, and during one of the intervals she broadcast to her homeland. 'It was not easy for me to leave Germany,' she declared, 'and I only did so when the murderous intentions of the current German regime became plain.' Wagner 'loved freedom and justice even more than he loved music', she added, and 'Alberich–Hitler' blasphemed him by making him his favourite.[25]

One may doubt whether Wagner really loved anything more than music, particularly his own. On that his defiant granddaughter-in-exile, not quite twenty-four years old, was probably a mite too idealistic. But in comparing Adolf Hitler – Germany's Führer and Wahnfried's 'Wolf' – to the *Ring*'s power-hungry, lethal Nibelung she was surely bang on target.

# 13

# War – At Home and Abroad

While Friedelind was still digging in her heels at Tribschen and Wieland toiled at his easel in Munich, Wolfgang had to go to war. He evidently went on leaden feet but his combat duty did not last long. During the invasion of Poland in September 1939, his patrol was caught in a hail of machine-gun fire. One bullet smashed through his hand and wrist, another through his thigh. Bleeding badly, he was briefly taken prisoner by the Poles, then dumped in a cart and returned to the German lines. Thanks to an operation by a top surgeon at the Charité, Berlin's finest hospital, Wolfgang's arm was saved but his fighting days were over. After a long spell of recuperation he was listed as disabled and discharged from the army in June 1940, two months before his twenty-first birthday.

According to Winifred, the Führer visited the invalid in hospital – even brought him flowers and told his own doctor to keep an eye on the case. Special treatment for a Wagner?[1] Wolfgang rejects the very idea, putting down the tip-top care he received at the Charité to 'the unpredictable workings of a kindly providence'.[2] Be that as it may, big brother Wieland had no need to rely on mere 'providence' to evade wounds or worse. As 'heir' to Bayreuth, he was one of a few lucky young men personally exempted from call-up by Hitler on the grounds that their survival was specially vital to the Reich. And what was Wieland doing in his Munich studio to prepare himself for his great calling while Wolfgang vainly sought to dodge bullets at the front? At first not much – indeed in the wake of his rejection of Tietjen's training offer it seemed doubtful whether he would take up the reins at Bayreuth at all.

That began to change in the course of 1940. It was clear to Wieland that although his artistic ambitions met with the Führer's benevolent interest, more was expected from him in return for his release from military service. Besides, his brother unexpectedly started to emerge as a pretender to the Bayreuth throne. Just before the war Wolfgang had, in fact, raised the prospect that he might help run the festival one day, arguing it was unlikely that Wieland would be willing or able to do everything himself. It is unclear whether Wieland took that portent seriously at the time, but even if he did he must have largely discounted it when Wolfgang left for the front. A year later, though, things looked different. Out of the army and seeking a career, Wolfgang was offered a training course at the Berlin Staatsoper by Tietjen and, unlike his brother back in 1938, he accepted it. By the autumn he was starting to learn the ropes at arguably the finest opera house in the Reich and, for a time, he lived in Tietjen's flat. He even saw Hitler now and again and discussed the festival's future. From being a happy-go-lucky 'second string' in the provinces, Wolfgang began to look – and feel – like an upwardly mobile professional at the heart of the action.

It was hardly mere chance that in that same autumn Wieland began to take music lessons in Munich from Kurt Overhoff, a Viennese-born composer and conductor. Overhoff later ascribed his engagement to a meeting at Wahnfried at which he had played extracts from *Rheingold* on the piano and analysed the technique the Master used to make emotional and psychological points. Wieland, he said, then bitterly complained that his mother and Tietjen were deliberately holding him back and begged the visitor to become his long-term tutor.[3] No doubt Overhoff did not need much urging. Although he had for years been music director in Heidelberg, a prestigious post in its provincial way, he was only thirty-eight and looking for a change when Wieland made his appeal. By becoming mentor to the Bayreuth 'heir' in matters musical, he must have hoped to land a key job at the festival at the latest when his (presumably grateful) pupil took over. Instead he walked, more or less blindly, into a snakepit – albeit one where he was greeted with anything but venom by a deeply relieved Winifred. Far from holding Wieland back, she was delighted that her eldest son seemed to be showing a real interest in music at long last. She promptly negotiated Overhoff's release from his Heidelberg job and put him on the Bayreuth payroll.

What was it that turned Wieland from being a notable dabbler into one of the finest producers in the history of theatre? Clearly he inherited his father's talent for painting and something of his grandfather's instinct for drama, but up to the start of the 1940s neither his pictures nor his stage designs hinted at real originality, let alone genius. Besides, he had no special knowledge of music, and had it not been for Hitler's Bayreuth expectations and Wolfgang's growing aspirations perhaps he would not have moved to acquire it. Happily he alighted on Overhoff, a practical musician with the rare ability to make the paraphernalia of counterpoint, key relationships and tone colour seem quite riveting and, in opera, to relate it all to the composer's dramatic aim. From him, Wieland gained the technical wherewithal to plumb the most complex of scores, above all his grandfather's, and even to conduct an orchestra, although he only needed to try the latter once to realise it was 'not his thing'.

Overhoff had no easy time of it. Although Wieland claimed to be desperate to learn he at first resented the hours lost to his painting, telling his exasperated tutor that as a means of expression 'it is colour and form that count, not words and music'.[4] It took him a while to acknowledge that, of course, they all counted. For an aspiring 'compleat' opera producer aiming to recreate the Master's *Gesamtkunstwerke* something else counted too – the ability to match onstage action to music and text. For Wieland, at least at the start, that was a real problem. Colour and form he knew much about, the mysteries of music and libretti he could unlock with Overhoff. But for all his artistic skill and imaginative insight, he did not have a feel for the rhythm and movement that could give life to the stage pictures he saw in his mind's eye. Luckily, though, he was very close to someone who had just the gift he lacked.

Gertrud Reissinger, Wieland's dark-haired, lissom girlfriend since Bayreuth schooldays, was born to dance. At home she swayed and pirouetted to music almost before she could walk, at school she much preferred gym to books. Where she got this urge to perpetual motion was a mystery; certainly not from her father Adolf, an authoritarian schoolteacher who revered Hitler, nor from her long-suffering mother Luise, nor from her uncle Hans, an opportunist architect who slipped easily from designing bombastic piles for the Nazis to proffering humbler structures to post-war clients. Hans's *Haus der Deutschen Erziehung* (House of German Upbringing), a Nazi temple whose converted remnants can still be spied in the heart of Bayreuth, drew the exclamation 'Really lovely!' from Hitler when he toured the forbidding interior in 1936. Neither Gertrud's family background, nor her schooling, nor her Wahnfried connection turned her into a keen Nazi, but she was no critic of the regime either. Her world was dance. All else, including her boyfriend, was secondary. When her family moved to Munich in 1934, she went along eagerly although she was then seventeen and had been linked to Wieland for years. In the Bavarian capital she had the chance to join the Dorothee Günther dance school, one of the country's finest, and that counted most. Desperately short of cash, she was taken on at a reduced fee because of her manifest talent.

Despite their separation, Wieland and Gertrud stayed in contact and when he too moved to Munich in 1938 (to a studio close by the Günther school) they picked up more or less where they had left off in Bayreuth. The relationship had changed all the same. Gertrud was still happy to sit as Wieland's model, but she was now a young woman with four years in the 'big city' behind her and good career prospects. She was anything but domineering by nature and when it came to arguments with Wieland, as it often did, she usually got the worst of them; but in her own beloved field, and especially in the art of choreography, she had a passion and flair hard to resist. In spite of himself, Wieland digested what she said, saw how she made a musical phrase visible in movement, even, at her behest, reluctantly learned to dance. At times his studio became a miniature ballet school, with Gertrud inviting up her girlfriends to waft about to records of Ravel and Debussy (two of the many composers disdained at Wahnfried) while Wieland looked on with mingled irritation and fascination.[5]

Spurred by his own gifts and ambition, as well as by Overhoff's teaching and Gertrud's example, Wieland became increasingly impatient to try his hand as a fully fledged producer, not as a stage or costume designer alone. He was surely influenced too by what he saw at the Nationaltheater in Munich, a house with a Wagner tradition that went back to the Master himself and King Ludwig. Invited to rehearsals by the fine if flamboyant music director, Clemens Krauss, Wieland admitted later that the experience showed him there were other worthwhile ways of staging Wagner besides Bayreuth's. Since Munich's productions were far from daring that hardly seems a revolutionary remark – though no doubt it caused the arch-conservative aunts Daniela and Eva, who died in 1940 and 1942 respectively, to turn in their graves. But coming from the Master's eldest grandchild, it did suggest that before long a wind of change might be blowing through the corridors of the Festspielhaus.

Much firmer, and to old-school Bayreuthers more troubling evidence emerged in 1943–4 when Wieland finally made his debut as a producer with the toughest possible challenge, an entire *Ring* cycle. Astonishingly enough, for over a year he worked on two different productions of the tetralogy more or less simultaneously. One of them, in Nuremberg, was grand, costly and for the most part traditional, but not quite complete: war pressures forced the house to shut before *Rheingold* could be staged. The other production at Altenburg, a smallish town in Thuringia, included all four parts of the cycle and was far more intriguing. Dark, spare, almost skeletal, it foreshadowed Wieland's mature style in paring away clutter to aid concentration on the core of the drama. Then, as later, some critics were scandalised, which did not seem to bother the producer one jot – rather the opposite. Just how Wieland came to take that imaginative leap forward in Altenburg is hard to say. He later claimed he had been forced to adopt a novel approach because the modest house lacked resources, but that cannot be the whole story. Plenty of cash was available, thanks not least to Goebbels, who had fixed Overhoff's appointment as music director in Altenburg so that the Bayreuth 'heir' could gain practical experience there. No doubt the propaganda minister thought that by so doing he would eventually be better able to extend his influence to Bayreuth itself, still effectively the preserve of Tietjen and Winifred. Instead, by indirectly helping Wieland find his way as a producer, he unwittingly did the post-war festival a big favour.

By now Wieland and Gertrud were married – a natural outcome, one would think, for two young people with complementary talents who had felt drawn to one another for more than a decade. Wieland, though, did not give up being single without a struggle. In the months before the wedding he was even testier than usual and flirted still more blatantly with other girls (including a fetching blonde Wolfgang brought home to Wahnfried) as though challenging Gertrud to break with him, which at least once she nearly did. As for the ceremony itself, it was held – with a bare minimum of celebration – not in Bayreuth but at a registry office in Nussdorf, a sleepy nest on the shore of the Bodensee (Lake Constance) where Winifred had bought a holiday chalet years before. On the day, 12 September 1941, Wieland turned up in an open-necked shirt and afterwards demonstratively pulled the ring off his finger. Might he, in fact, not have married Gertrud at all had it not been for intense pressure from his mother? Winifred did indeed yearn for grandchildren and made it mighty clear that she felt it was time for her eldest son to face up to his dynastic responsibilities. She may even have feared that, like Siegfried, Wieland might be sexually drawn to men and that for safety's sake he should therefore be propelled post-haste into fathering an heir. If that really *was* her concern, no reliable evidence has come to light showing it was justified. Besides, for all his bad grace and fear of commitment Wieland surely knew better than anyone what he had in Gertrud and what he stood to lose if she slipped away. In the event she bore him four children and played a key role in his productions starting with that first *Ring* in Altenburg, sometimes as choreographer and always as his closest ally and critic. Although he by no means invariably acknowledged her contribution later, he was far from unaware of it. 'I don't need to tell you', he wrote to her during a period of enforced separation in 1946, 'that without you I would never have found my way to the theatre. You have helped me so much and can help me a lot more.'[6]

A few weeks before that unspectacular wedding in Nussdorf, the doors of the Festspielhaus had closed on Bayreuth's second 'war festival'. Not surprisingly fewer works than in peacetime had been on offer – 'merely' *Holländer* under Elmendorff and the *Ring* conducted by the ubiquitous Tietjen (his last appearance in the Bayreuth pit apart from a brief, astonishing comeback in 1959). The striking thing is not that the programme was shorter but that the festival was still being held at all. Back in early 1940, Winifred had told Hitler that with so many musicians and technical staff already at the front or on a war footing, there was no way performances could go ahead in the summer. The Führer, though, insisted that Bayreuth must not suffer closure as it had during and after the First World War, and pledged that essential personnel would be made available. When Winifred retorted that, even so, there would be next to no audience, Hitler agreed to fix that as well. He too, he joked, could not perform to an empty hall.[7]

So it was that for five summers, from 1940 to 1944, tens of thousands of fighting men, factory workers, medical staff and the like were shuttled into town by the *Kraft durch Freude* organisation to imbibe the Master's works (and attend compulsory lectures about them) on the Green Hill. Despite her initial worries, Winifred soon came round to this handy arrangement. The festival itself was freed of bother over transport, lodging or even of the need to sell tickets. *Kraft durch Freude* saw to all that. Besides, decades later Winifred still enthused about the special quality of those wartime audiences with their many 'plucky soldiers and officers', lots of them crippled and unable to struggle to the Festspielhaus without aid. These were no random conscripts to the Bayreuth cause, she stressed with pride, but true Wagner fans who had earned the right to seats thanks to their special contribution to the war effort.[8] Nazi propagandists had often spouted in similar vein. Inspired by a festival public that had looked death in the face, they claimed, singers and players rose to still greater heights and in turn fired those who heard them with new courage. The 1941 film *Stukas*, praised by Goebbels for its 'wonderful air footage', rammed the point home by showing how a dejected dive-bomber pilot regained the will to battle after a strong dose of Wagner at Bayreuth. On a rather more sophisticated note, it was argued that with audiences now being drawn from all sections of society and (thanks to the largesse of the Reich) attending free of charge, the festival was at long last matching the Master's original high-minded vision.

Most of this was rubbish. Naturally those who streamed or hobbled to the 'war festivals' were glad to get out of the line of fire or off the production line for a while, and some of them surely liked what they heard. Whether even the Wagnerites among them preferred to devote their precious free time to the Master rather than to friends and family is another matter. At any rate this was anything but the kind of public – enlightened pilgrims in a kind of neo-Hellenic society of the future – that Wagner had dreamed of a century or so before. Nor would he have thought much of a Bayreuth programme from which both *Parsifal* and *Tristan und Isolde* were excluded in advance, the former because the Nazis found it 'problematic', the latter because the spectacle of the dying hero in Act III was felt too dispiriting. Finally, in 1943 and 1944 *Holländer* and the *Ring* were dropped too and *Meistersinger* alone was programmed. By that time Bayreuth's civilian resources were running thin even with the Führer's backing and members of the SS's 'Wiking' division, decked out in medieval costume for the occasion, had to be drafted in to swell the ranks of mostly jolly Nurembergers onstage.

Against this bizarre, not to say macabre, background a struggle for control of the festival erupted that in ferocity and duplicity surpassed any that had gone before, even the ones at the start of the Cosima and Winifred eras. Since those involved in it included Nazi leaders as well as Wagner family factions and their various backers, many details are naturally murky, but the main cause of the conflict is plain enough: Wieland's resolve to make Bayreuth his future after all, and quickly too. That meant dislodging the Tietjen–Winifred duo and, incidentally, Preetorius as well, whose stage designs Wieland felt wrongly conceived. This would be a tough task, but then the Bayreuth 'heir' did not lack allies. Among them were the erudite Otto Strobel, director of the Wagner archive, and his wife Gertrud who ran to Wieland with chapter and verse whenever Tietjen–Preetorius productions deviated even a jot from the instructions handed down by the Master. The unhappy Overhoff was urged to collect similar ammunition and soon found himself not just caught in family crossfire but embroiled in a seemingly unfathomable intrigue. For a brief span he was even called up for military service, a shock Wieland ascribed to string-pulling by Tietjen to deprive 'the heir' of his music tutor. As a result it came to a shouting match, overheard and diligently noted by Frau Strobel, on the lawn at Wahnfried in the summer of 1941. Wieland and Tietjen traded charges while Overhoff and a tearful Winifred stood helplessly by.[9]

What really lay behind Overhoff's sudden call-up and his equally sudden return to his music post? Perhaps just a bureaucratic blunder, but Wieland's suspicions cannot be wholly dismissed. Tietjen had powerful backers in Berlin – above all Göring, his 'protector' at the *Staatsoper*. Wieland on the other hand was favoured by Goebbels, who despised Göring and longed for the day when he could put the Staatsoper, and ultimately Bayreuth too, under his thumb. Although it may seem barely credible that Nazi bigwigs sparred over such matters on the home front while putting to flame much of Europe, the evidence that they did so is overwhelming. In a way, Göring, Goebbels and Co. were simply following in the footsteps of their art-obsessed Führer. The Overhoff affair could therefore have been just one skirmish in the broader campaign for personal aggrandisment through control over culture.

Whatever the truth, thanks to Hitler's special backing Wieland had a unique advantage; at least he seemed to and often talked as though he did. The reality was rather different. He did indeed see his mentor regularly in Berlin right up to the closing months of the war, evidently bewailing what he felt was wrong with the festival and stressing his role as 'heir'. On one occasion he held a long pow-wow with 'Uncle Wolf' at the Chancellery while Tietjen, also hoping to discuss Bayreuth business, waited vainly in an ante-room. That incident alone would seem to show who had the most leverage where it counted. But although Hitler treated Wieland like a son, and even seems to have backed his unilateral demand for a change in some festival plans, he did not yet regard the young man as experienced enough for the Bayreuth throne and did not intervene decisively to put him there. Perhaps Hitler also felt wary of handing Goebbels a clear victory at Göring's (not to mention Winifred's) expense by booting out Tietjen. Of the Bayreuth top trio that had emerged after Siegfried's death, the only one to go before the war's end was Preetorius. Denounced for corresponding with Jews abroad, he was interrogated by the Gestapo in late 1942, forbidden to work and escaped a worse fate only thanks to Hitler's belated intervention. Preetorius suspected that Wieland had acted against him in these machinations, details of which remain sparse to this day.

Meanwhile Wolfgang naturally sought a share of the power in Bayreuth and had cause to feel that he too had backing at the top. In 1942, for instance, the festival's future came up at an 'animated' conversation 'Uncle Wolf' held over lunch with Wolfgang and Verena at the Osteria Bavaria, his favourite Munich restaurant (where he had first met Unity Mitford). According to the official note-taker, Hitler observed that while Wieland was specially suited musically to take on the Bayreuth heritage, Wolfgang promised much on the technical side.[10] It is unclear whether Wolfgang felt altogether happy still to be docketed as a 'second string', but he evidently did not feel that anything was to be gained by seeking to drive out Tietjen precipitously. On the contrary, he had already bluntly warned his brother in the autumn of 1941 that his tactics threatened to leave the festival high and dry, with Tietjen likely to withdraw in dudgeon and Wieland unable to fill the vacant shoes. Half a year later he returned to the attack, accusing his brother of getting Hitler to agree to a change in festival programming without consulting Winifred (or, presumably, Tietjen) – a charge Wieland bitterly rejected as a 'malicious slander' in a letter he drafted but never sent.[11]

Whatever his personal feelings about 'Heinz', Wolfgang's interventions seem hardly surprising. Had Tietjen really been driven ignominiously from Bayreuth, the impact would have been grave not just on the festival but almost certainly on the training course the 'little brother' was pursuing at the Berlin Staatsoper. And that course was going well. Wolfang was not only gaining a thorough insight into the business of running a huge theatre (as Wieland was not) but he was learning plenty on the artistic side too. By 1944 he was ready for his first Staatsoper production, a staging of his father's *Bruder Lustig* – renamed *Andreasnacht* since a cheerful title hardly fitted the mood in the increasingly bomb-scarred capital. That debut was less challenging than Wieland's a year earlier with those *Ring*s in Nuremberg and Altenburg, but Wolfgang carried it off well anyway. He had a further reason to be grateful to the Staatsoper. It was there that he met Ellen Drexel, like Gertrud a pretty and accomplished dancer, and married her in 1943. Wolfgang was thus following closely in his brother's footsteps, professionally and personally. There was a difference though. Unlike Wieland's wedding ceremony, Wolfgang's was held in Bayreuth – at the Siegfried-Wagner-Haus adjoining Wahnfried. It was as though Wolfgang was underlining his attachment to a home and family tradition about which his brother had, at the very least, grave doubts.

Tietjen, meanwhile, bobbed and weaved with his habitual aplomb, aware that he was fighting not just for his jobs in Bayreuth and Berlin but possibly for his life. Just how risky he felt his situation to be emerges from a memorandum he drew up in December 1941 for 'Haus Wahnfried' – in the first place, therefore, for Winifred.[12] In it he proposed three possible ways of ending the tension over who should run the festival, the first being that he would simply resign forthwith. If this occurred, though, he warned that he would make use of a full account he had drawn up for the Führer of all that had happened since he, Tietjen, had become involved with Bayreuth in 1931. He had placed the document in a sealed envelope that, should any ill befall him, would be handed on to Hitler by a person of trust. This scheme, of course, amounted to a threat, since no one knew better than Tietjen the often unpalatable inside story of the festival and the family during the 'Third Reich'. Alas, the account to which he referred has gone missing (assuming it ever existed), like so much material in Tietjen's connection.

Failing that course, Tietjen pledged to prepare the next summer's festival and then request release from his Bayreuth tasks because of work pressure elsewhere. His exit would be described in public as temporary but he and the family would know it was for good. Should that second proposal be found unacceptable too, then Tietjen said he would summon his 'last remaining physical reserves' and stay on despite everything to ensure the festival kept running. 'Naturally' Wieland would be detailed to produce the stage designs for a planned new production of *Tannhäuser* (in the end shelved) and Wolfgang would be included in the team as an assistant. But if that were to happen, a firm line under the past would need to be drawn by all concerned (specifically including 'Dr Strobel', who would have to stop running to Wieland with complaints). Tietjen, at any rate, represented himself as ready for 'reconciliation'.

Few documents better show Tietjen's diplomatic skill, at least matching that of his ambassador father. Although pragmatic in tone and seemingly flexible in content, his memorandum left the Wagners next to no alternative. Course one was surely out of the question. Course two on the face of it amounted to more or less what Wieland was after; but neither Winifred nor Wolfgang felt the 'heir' was ready to take over and Tietjen at least surmised that Hitler thought the same. In other words he was calling Wieland's bluff. That left course three, but this too was not quite what it seemed. Wieland had recently told Winifred angrily that he would not work on designs for a new *Tannhäuser* anyway, so Tietjen was making a 'generous offer' that he must have been aware had already been refused. As for when the brothers would finally take control, that remained as unclear as ever. Tietjen had often said that he and Winifred would step down after peace had come and a vast new building complex – into which the Festspielhaus would be subsumed – had been erected on the 'Green Hill', a scheme much favoured by Hitler. But who could say when that might happen, if at all? The longer the war lasted the less likely Nazi victory seemed.

Outmanoeuvred by his wily adversary, Wieland bit by bit grudgingly backed down – a strategic retreat rather than an admission of defeat. In 1943 he actually managed to swallow his pride and (replacing the ejected Preetorius) cooperated with Tietjen and Wolfgang on *Meistersinger*, the first and last production on which the uneasy trio worked together. A year later Tietjen was still firmly in control and, aware that Hitler seemed to have given up neither on the war nor the Bayreuth festival, he began looking into plans for a 1945 season. In a letter of 17 December 1944, he told Winifred she would be 'astonished to learn' that there were no insuperable material or artistic obstacles to a repeat of the tried and true *Meistersinger*. The wherewithal could even be found for a wholly new production if the Führer so wished although, given the current strains, he did not regard that course as 'morally' justifiable.[13] Tietjen was spared having his moral scruples on that score put to the test. By the following summer the war was over, American troops were in Bayreuth and the festival was shelved for six years.

One might think that Winifred, given her long-standing link with 'Wolf', must have been playing a decisive role in all this, but in fact she was not. Although Hitler had insisted that the festival continue during the war, he only attended once himself – on 23 July 1940 for, prophetically enough, *Götterdämmerung*. That may well have been the last occasion on which he and Winifred met, and it is so described by Wolfgang among others. Winifred herself said the same at her 'denazification' trial in 1947; but decades later she changed her tune, holding that Hitler had, in fact, visited Wahnfried shortly before Wehrmacht officers sought vainly to blow him to bits at his East Prussian headquarters in July 1944. She claimed to recall that on leaving the house on that occasion he had turned to her muttering that 'I hear the wings of the victory goddess rustling' – a remark that at that stage of the war even she found odd and ascribed to pep-up injections he was being given by Theo Morell, his doctor.[14]

Winifred's memory may simply have played her false although (unlike her judgement) it did not often do so. Hitler's comment would have been unremarkable had he made it during what was, without doubt, his last festival visit if not, perhaps, his very last trip to Wahnfried. By the summer of 1940 German troops had already occupied much of Europe from Poland to the English Channel and a tripartite pact was imminent between the key axis powers – Germany, Italy and Japan. At that time the fickle 'victory goddess' did indeed seem to have settled in Berlin, but a year later she began to flutter off for good. In June 1941 the Nazi supremo ordered invasion of the Soviet Union, disastrously opening up another front while still deeply involved in action against the British; then in December, delighted by the Japanese attack on Pearl Harbour and sniffing global victory, Hitler sealed his fate by declaring war on the United States. In 1942 the British smashed Rommel's Afrika Korps at El Alamein; in 1943 the Russians crushed Paulus's Sixth Army at Stalingrad and in June 1944 the western allies launched their D-Day Normandy landings. Small wonder that even the Wagner-doting 'Führer' did not find the time to squeeze in attendance at the Bayreuth festival. Perhaps he did not really feel like going. As the tide of war turned against him, it seems that Hitler selected the Master's works rather less often from his private record collection and lighter fare rather more.

Even if Hitler did make that 1944 visit to Wahnfried, most signs are that during the war his relations with Winifred cooled – and not just, or even mainly, because of the 'Friedelind affair'. The two of them stayed in sporadic touch but no evidence has come to light that the 'mistress of Bayreuth', unlike her sons and Verena, visited 'Wolf' in Berlin after 1940 as she had often done in pre-war days. Apparently her letters did not always get through. She claimed that Hitler warned her that Martin Bormann, his Machiavellian close aide, was intercepting some of them and that in future she should contact him via his doctor. That could be true. Bormann was no fan of the Wagners and had in effect replaced the more amenable Rudolf Hess after the latter fled to Scotland in 1941. On the other hand Hitler might just have got sick of Winifred's frequent requests for help of one sort or another, and sought an excuse for evading more of them. She did, for instance, detest Fritz Wächtler, the brutal Gauleiter of Bayreuth, and vainly pleaded with 'Wolf' to replace him. More in her favour by far, she repeatedly intervened on behalf of Nazi victims, Jews and non-Jews, whom she felt 'worthy' of the Führer's clemency. As usual, she put down the cases of injustice brought to her attention as deplorable but isolated incidents for which Hitler could not be held responsible.

Only once, she maintained, was 'Wolf' really angry with her and that was because she did *not* intervene when he felt she should have done. In 1941 Ulrich Roller, son of Hitler's revered Alfred Roller and himself a talented stage designer who had worked as an assistant at Bayreuth, was killed in action in the east. It turned out that Winifred had meant to ask the Führer to ensure that Ulrich be spared combat but the young man, then serving at a concentration camp, had begged her not to intercede on his behalf. It seems he was so shattered by the horrors he saw at the camp that he preferred to take his chance at the front instead. Hitler regarded his death as a useless sacifice of 'Aryan talent' and at least partly blamed Winifred for it.

For most of the war Wieland was spared the kind of dreadful dilemma that Ulrich Roller faced. The worst battle the Bayreuth 'heir' felt called upon to wage was the one against Tietjen, and although he lost a decisive round of it he continued to believe he would eventually emerge on top. But that prospect began to fade by the summer of 1944, at the latest. As allied forces ineluctably closed in on Germany from east and west all theatres throughout the Reich were ordered to be closed – the decree covered those in Altenburg, where Wieland had recently staged a new production, and Vienna, where he had offered designs (later lost in a bombing raid) for a projected new *Ring*. Key artists and stage workers who had hitherto kept their civilian jobs were now drummed into war service – in the case of Overhoff, for the second time. Even the favoured few who, like Wieland, had been granted special protection by Hitler began to feel vulnerable: all the more so since their status looked bound to count against them should the war be lost. Had it not been for his new brother-in-law, Bodo Lafferentz, who offered him a job in a hush-hush research establishment in Bayreuth, even the 'heir' might have found himself drawn into combat. As it was, Wieland could sit out most of the rest of the war, from September 1944 to April 1945, in Lafferentz's *Institut für physikalische Forschung* (Institute for Physical Research) housed in a former cotton mill at the foot of the Green Hill. It was an enterprise a lot less harmless than its name implies, and it was decades before its real role and that of its restless, inventive founder were widely realised.[15]

For most devotees of the Bayreuth festival the name of Bodo Lafferentz probably rings only a distant bell at best. Those with long memories may recall that he was the man who handled the *Kriegsfestspiele* logistics as head of *Kraft durch Freude*, that he thus got to know the Wagners well and that he eventually married Verena, the 'baby' of the family. The few inclined to delve more deeply may even be aware that Lafferentz (born in 1897) was twenty-three years older than the comely 'Nickel' and that when he met her he was already a married man. In fact his divorce from his first wife came through only a few days before he wed his new spouse at Wahnfried on 26 December 1943, with Wieland and Wolfgang as witnesses. Given the age difference, was this perhaps a 'strategic union' – rather like Chamberlain's marriage to Eva in the very same place on exactly the same day thirty-five years before? Ruggedly handsome and boundlessly ambitious, Lafferentz won entry to a clan that had the Führer's special blessing, and

Verena, with her husband's manifest authority behind her, stood to gain a weight she had hitherto lacked in family counsels. If such calculation was involved at the start it did not bring much of the benefit hoped for, at least not for long. But that question apart, the available evidence suggests the marriage was firm and harmonious. It produced five children and ended only with Lafferentz's death in 1974. Verena never remarried.

More needs to be said about Lafferentz than that, however. Apart from heading *Kraft durch Freude*, he was a senior director of the Volkswagen concern and ran a clutch of research outfits from a base in Berlin. All these activities were, in fact, related. Shortly before the war Hitler had charged Robert Ley, a doggedly loyal associate since the 1920s, with construction of a plant to build a car (the famous VW 'Beetle') that the masses could afford to buy. Ley headed the *Deutsche Arbeitsfront* (German Labour Front), into which independent trade unions had been subsumed in 1933 and of which *Kraft durch Freude* was a part. Hence Lafferentz entered the picture. Indeed, it was he who from a spotter plane pinpointed the site where the VW plant was then built and who became responsible from Berlin for sales of the projected vehicle – initially known as the '*KdF* car'. However, the newly founded company soon went onto a war footing, the 'Beetle' was used for military purposes alone and Lafferentz found himself with an underemployed Berlin team. The *KdF* boss was not a man to stand around idle, let alone to relinquish ground won in the Nazi hierarchy. Impressed by his qualities as a manager and 'ideas man', the SS had already made him an *Obersturmbannführer* (lieutenant colonel) in 1939. Armed with this rank and with contacts that went right up to Himmler and, sporadically, to Hitler himself, Lafferentz reorganised his Berlin operation into a *Forschungs-und Verwertungsgesellschaft* (research and implementation company) that busied itself with all manner of schemes to help the war effort. Later he was awarded the SS's coveted *Totenkopfring* with its death's head insignia.

Was Lafferentz, then, a 'fanatical Nazi' as one contemporary historian of the Bayreuth festival maintains? Certainly he was no Nazi activist from the movement's early years like Goebbels, Göring or – indeed – the notorious drunkard and womaniser Ley. Nor is there any sign that he was an ideologue or racist, let alone that he was personally brutal. On the contrary Lotte Warburg, a woman of Jewish descent who had to abandon her estate near Bayreuth and flee abroad, described Lafferentz almost glowingly in her diary as a pleasant-spoken, 'very good-looking gentleman'.[16] That was the way he seems to have struck most people. A gifted linguist with a degree in economics, he only joined the party after Hitler came to power and it seems that he got to know Ley, who opened the *KdF* door for him, more or less by chance while on a trip abroad. But like so many ambitious managers of the time Lafferentz put his talents wholly at the disposal of a murderous regime and turned a blind eye to the moral implications of his work. Volkswagen, for instance, made use of around twenty thousand prisoners – in part from concentration camps – to boost its labour force in the course of the war; indeed in 1941 Himmler proposed setting up just such a camp next door to the VW headquarters. Although in the end that particular plan was not implemented there is no record that Lafferentz and his fellow directors raised objections to it. Besides, at least two of the research projects in which Lafferentz was involved from Berlin made use of concentration-camp labour. One of them was established close to Auschwitz and sought to extract urgently needed rubber from plants found in the Soviet Union. The other was that Bayreuth institute to which Wieland bolted for around half a year. It aimed to develop a better guidance system for flying bombs and, as such, was part of Hitler's drive for a *Wunderwaffe* (miracle weapon) to snatch victory for the Reich from the jaws of defeat.

It is easy enough to see how Lafferentz came to set up the latter project. Volkswagen had been deeply involved in construction of the V-1 flying bombs, first launched against Britain in mid-1944. Despite their destructive power and the threatening noise they made, the 'doodlebugs' (as the British called them) were too inaccurate and vulnerable to turn the war in Germany's favour. Few can have been better aware than Lafferentz of these flaws, or of the kudos awaiting anyone able to eradicate them on the V-1 and similar weapons. As for the decision to site the institute in Bayreuth, that arguably made strategic sense. The town was (still) relatively far from the front and had almost never been a target for allied bombers, so there seemed a fair chance that work could go ahead largely undisturbed. That apart, Lafferentz was evidently a dab hand at linking 'business' interests with those of himself and his family. One of his research 'firms', for instance, consisted of a single person – Adolf Reissinger, Gertrud's schoolteacher father, who had always fancied himself as something of a natural scientist.

Another project, apparently aimed at developing floating docks for sea-fired rockets, was moved late in the war to Überlingen on the Bodensee – handily close not only to Winifred's summer chalet at Nussdorf but to the possible bolt-hole of Switzerland across the lake. The Bayreuth facility fitted much the same pattern. Set up just ten minutes' drive from the Wagner family seat where Lafferentz and Verena had married a few months before, it soon proved useful, perhaps even a lifesaver, for Wieland.

Just what the Bayreuth 'heir' found to do there is unclear. He had no scientific expertise and although it has been claimed that he was the institute's deputy civilian leader, proof of that is lacking. A few years before he died, Lafferentz told Wieland's English biographer that the young man had spent most of his time constructing stage models and working out lighting systems for them.[17] That could well be true, although Lafferentz was evidently less than forthright to his interlocutor about the institute's real purpose, saying simply that it had sought to devise a tracking system for anti-aircraft defence. Whatever Wieland's role, Gertrud reported that he returned home daily looking ever grimmer – as well he might. His place of work was one of the direct offshoots (*Aussenstelle*, as they were called) of Flossenbürg, a concentration camp hard by the Czech border about eighty kilometres south-east of Bayreuth.

Flossenbürg, it is true, was not designed as an extermination centre like Auschwitz (although some thirty thousand prisoners died there in the course of the war), and conditions at its Bayreuth 'branch'– one of about a hundred such *Aussenstelle* scattered across north Bavaria and Saxony – were less appalling than those at the main camp. They had to be. The eighty-five prisoners there from nine countries were picked for their value to the research effort and, although subject to threats and beating, needed to be kept alive. There is no evidence that either Wieland or Lafferentz personally mishandled inmates; indeed, after the war at least one ex-prisoner testified that the pair had acted humanely, in the ghastly circumstances. Lafferentz was, in any case, rarely on the spot. He still lived and worked for most of the time close to his headquarters in Berlin and turned up in Bayreuth only occasionally. Nonetheless the 'institute' *was* part of the concentration-camp network that spread ineluctably across the Reich year by year, it *was* largely run on slave labour under guard from the SS – and the 'heir' joined in, thanks to his influential brother-in-law's backing, to save his skin.

The *Aussenstelle* offered only a temporary refuge. In April 1945, with American troops streaming ever closer, the plant was abandoned and the prisoners were marched back to the main camp. One of them died on the three-day journey, others did so in a subsequent trek south after Flossenbürg itself was evacuated. The civilian personnel fled – some, like Werner Rambauske, the institute's chief scientist, bearing details of their research that they then made available to the Allies. As a result Rambauske later became one of the hundreds of boffins from Nazi Germany (like Wernher von Braun and his Peenemünde rocket team) who were transferred to the United States to work for the American military.[18] Wieland and Lafferentz made off too, taking with them to Winifred's Nussdorf chalet not scientific blueprints but rare Wagner manuscripts from the Wahnfried archive. A selfless bid, one might think, to ensure that the irreplaceable documents escaped destruction. Wolfgang, who had been drawn into the Bayreuth 'home guard' and did not accompany the fleeing pair, has a less flattering explanation. The manuscripts were removed, he writes, 'not for safety's sake but because of their monetary value, which might help to keep the wolf from the door or provide them (i.e. Wieland and Lafferentz) with the wherewithal to start a new life'.[19]

One explanation does not wholly exclude the other. Possibly Wieland and Lafferentz sought in the first place to preserve part of the 'family silver' (as Wolfgang and Winifred were also doing before American tanks rolled into town) knowing that, in dire extremity, they would have something precious to sell. Whether the proceeds from such a sale would then have percolated through to the whole family is an open question. Plainly, though, the decision to remove manuscripts from Bayreuth was not taken on the spur of the moment. Well before the town was badly bombed the Master's score of *Tristan und Isolde* and his letters to Liszt, among other things, were taken to the Nussdorf chalet – presumably either for eventual transfer back to Wahnfried in 'better times' or for removal abroad. Valuable though this cache of Wagneriana surely was, a still more precious one remained – so near and yet so far – locked up in the bunker of the Reich Chancellery in Berlin. By a roundabout route, Hitler had come into possession of most of those manuscripts (including the autograph full scores of *Die Feen*, *Das Liebesverbot* and *Rienzi*) that the Master had presented decades before to King Ludwig in return for 'services rendered'. Understandably 'Uncle Wolf' was reluctant to give up this treasure trove, valued just before the war at 800,000 Reichsmarks, even to the Wagner family. Wieland and Lafferentz nonetheless made two joint bids to get him to change his mind.

On the first occasion the two of them – accompanied by their wives – got to see the Führer face to face. Invited to 'lunch' in early December 1944 at the Berlin Chancellery, the quartet finally sat down at table with Hitler some time after midnight. It can hardly have been a jolly occasion. Although Wieland later told his mother that their host was, if anything, friendlier than ever, Gertrud for one felt shocked by the grey-faced figure who, she said, talked absent-mindedly, ate nothing and patted his German Shepherd dog with a twitching hand.[20] It seems that Wieland also had a private meeting with Hitler on the sidelines of this grotesque, nocturnal feast, but on neither occasion was a promise extracted to hand over the desired documents. Evidently the Führer felt the treasures could not be safer than with him. Despite his physical condition, much worsened since the bid to assassinate him in July, he still believed in victory and that the Bayreuth festival would go ahead the following summer. Wieland even took away the impression that Hitler expected him, with Wolfgang's help, to take charge in 1945 in place of Winifred and Tietjen. At least, that is what he claimed to his mother in a letter soon afterwards in which he yet again demanded the festival directorship.[21]

Did the 'heir' really believe there was still a chance Nazi Germany might emerge on top, allowing him to take up the Bayreuth job he craved? That hardly seems to square with his efforts to prize those manuscripts out of the Führer's increasingly shaky hands. Besides, there is evidence that around the same time he considered asking Hitler for free passage abroad – albeit no sign that he actually popped the question. The truth probably is that, like thousands if not millions of others, Wieland was desperately torn. A letter he wrote to Overhoff in September 1944, just before he began work at the *Aussenstelle*, indicates as much. In an admission dangerous, perhaps, even for him had the Gestapo intercepted it, Wieland wondered whether life would again be worth living 'even if we are not swept away in the general chaos'. On the other hand, he claimed there was no reason 'yet' to give up all for lost and to draw conclusions that could 'only be interpreted as signs of individual weakness'. There was still hope, he added in a pathos-laden reference to *Parsifal*, 'that the Grail will glow again'.[22]

In the following months, the life-and-death events in the Reich recalled the *Ring* and especially *Götterdämmerung* rather than *Parsifal.* Not that even the Wagners had much time to ponder the difference. In April 1945 in particular, they were barely able to recover from one blow before the next one fell. On the fifth of the month Wahnfried was badly damaged in the first of a series of Allied bombing strikes that, all in all, destroyed more than a third of Bayreuth. Almost miraculously, the whole family escaped uninjured. Verena and Gertrud, in the meantime with three small children between them and both again pregnant, had been packed off to the relative safety of the Nussdorf chalet. Wolfgang's wife Ellen, also pregnant, chose to stay behind. She and Winifred by chance took refuge not in the cellar of Wahnfried itself but beneath the adjoining Siegfried-Wagner-Haus (the so-called *Führerbau* where 'Uncle Wolf' had spent so many happy festival days) and thus escaped the bombs. Neither Wolfgang nor Wieland was at home when disaster struck but both turned up soon afterwards and Wolfgang, ever the handyman, began to shore up part of the roof.

Twenty-four hours later Wieland and Lafferentz set off by car for Berlin on a 'now or never' mission to persuade the Führer to yield his Wagner nuggets after all. Accounts differ on whether the two of them ever reached the capital but it is certain that, in the chaos of the war's last phase, they did not get to see Hitler. On 8 April they made it back to Wahnfried, collected what they could of value from the archive and set off again, zigzagging through waves of refugees, to join their families in Nussdorf. Even Winifred, the 'old warhorse' as Wieland half-affectionately called her, at last beat a retreat. She made off with Ellen, not to Nussdorf but to a more primitive dwelling she owned on the edge of a forest in the hills above Oberwarmensteinach, a village a few miles from Bayreuth. Wolfgang shuttled between Wahnfried, the Festspielhaus and the village transferring and hiding what remained of the Wagner archive. On 14 April American tanks rolled into Bayreuth and that same day Ellen gave birth to a daughter, Eva, by candlelight in Oberwarmensteinach. According to Wolfgang, Winifred proposed a 'hare-brained' scheme (albeit one strongly recalling the plot of *Die Walküre*) to flee into the woods with the baby to escape the wrath of the approaching foe. He talked her out of it.[23]

Down by the Bodensee it was advancing French forces, not American ones, that the Wagner contingent had to fear. At least Nussdorf was better placed than the Bayreuth region for a getaway and, thanks to foresight more than luck, the means for flight was at hand. On 22 April adults and children clutching a few belongings (including Wagner manuscripts) piled into a boat awaiting them at nearby Überlingen, courtesy of Lafferentz's 'marine institute' there, and set sail for Switzerland. At first they were lucky. An occasional dive-bomber flew overhead but took no notice of the little vessel. Once in Swiss waters, though, they were stopped by an armed patrol. Wieland shouted the name of Wagner and waved one of the Master's scores as proof of identity. Either the Swiss failed to understand or they understood all too well. At any rate the would-be refugees were sent back. On reaching the chalet again, they found locals had already partly plundered it.[24]

With the French almost at the gate, the Wagner treasures were hurriedly stashed away. Some of them went into a wooden cavity on the terrace, others were wrapped in rubber diapers, secured with sealing wax and buried in the garden. The occupying troops failed to find them, or perhaps did not look very hard. According to one family tale, a French officer who burst into the chalet with his men promptly saluted and withdrew again with apologies on learning that Wieland was Wagner's grandson. Although such a triumph of culture over coercion may seem unlikely, a strikingly similar event, later authenticated by both sides, did occur at almost the same time in Upper Bavaria at Garmisch. American troops drove up to Richard Strauss's villa with the aim of requisitioning it, but dropped the idea after the master of the house appeared at the door and identified himself as the composer of *Rosenkavalier*.

Eight days after that abortive flight across the Bodensee, the family's once mightiest friend and sponsor took his life in his Berlin bunker. The Wagner manuscripts he had kept 'for safety's sake' probably perished with him. Or at least they vanished, though there is a faint chance the Russians made off with them and may one day reveal their booty. Shortly afterwards Nazi Germany surrendered unconditionally and the war in Europe was over. The Wagners were scattered, Wahnfried largely a ruin, many family treasures gone for good. For Wolfgang, though, there was no need for either he or Wieland to feel accountable, let alone to have a sense of shame. 'Fortunately,' he claimed in his autobiography nearly half a century later, 'neither my brother nor I had any reason to put on sackcloth or beat our breasts in remorse – our past was too short and insignificant for that. We had not done anything criminal and had no need to seek justification for any actions or sins of omission.'[25] Winifred felt the same, only more so. 'History will justify my actions,' she wrote to a Swiss friend in a letter intercepted by the Allies. 'I am very proud of having fulfilled my mission for the last fifteen years by myself. This I did in honour of R. Wagner, the town of Bayreuth and Germany.'[26]

# 14

# New Bayreuth?

Rage, bitterness, frustration; all that and more welled forth from a striking commentary on 'New Bayreuth' that appeared in August 1951 in *Das literarische Deutschland* (Literary Germany), a usually sober intellectual weekly. 'Only six years after an unparalleled material and – still greater – moral collapse,' the author lamented, 'the Bayreuth Festival can be resumed as though nothing has happened; without the slightest sign of a change . . . on the contrary with a proud display of continuity, indeed with pomp and luxury as a social event of the first order.' Those responsible, the writer charged, had speculated, largely with success, on people's short memories. One would do well not just to accept this 'astounding fact' without a thought.[1]

It was easy to pick a few holes in this trenchant tract. Even those who did not attend the festival could hardly fail to be aware, thanks to reams of press coverage, that something new and challenging was happening on the Bayreuth stage. That applied above all to Wieland's dark, spare production of *Parsifal* (with choreography by Gertrud) – loathed by some but adored by others, including the doyen of English Wagnerites, Ernest Newman, who called it the best performance of the work he had ever seen or heard. As for the charge of 'pomp and luxury', ladies with off-the-shoulder dresses could indeed be spied in the audience and caviar could be found (with luck) in the festival restaurant; but the town itself still showed its bomb scars, the hugely overbooked accommodation was usually primitive and the cuisine far from tempting. Nor was the festival a social event quite 'of the first order'. Both Theodor Heuss and Konrad Adenauer, respectively president and chancellor of the newly founded Bundesrepublik Deutschland (Federal Republic of Germany), ostentatiously stayed away. For democratically elected German leaders, the shadow of the Führer still loomed oppressively large over Bayreuth in particular.

Besides, might not Franz Wilhelm Beidler, the author of the scathing piece, simply have been indulging in 'sour grapes'? In a letter to the editor, a reader suggested exactly that. Herr Beidler, he pointed out, was the man from Switzerland who a few years before had proposed setting up an international foundation, in which he would have played a leading role, to run the Bayreuth festival. The scheme had come to nothing, the reader argued (without going further into what had been a very tangled affair), because the festival theatre had remained the property of the Wagner family. Herr Beidler's vaunted 'Swiss perspective' thus seemed personally motivated. Another letter from a Bavarian parliamentarian took no issue with Beidler directly, but it did express confidence in Wieland and Wolfgang as 'realists' and approvingly quoted the former's comment that 'We are no longer interested in Germanic gods, but in man alone. We want to get away from the Wagner cult and closer to the cultic theatre.' Whatever those words might mean in detail, they did seem to suggest that a new and hopeful page was being turned.[2]

Missing from these exchanges, though, was any mention that the irate Swiss scribe was himself a Wagner – or at least, with good reason, considered himself one. For this was the very same Franz Beidler born back in 1901 to the ill-starred Isolde, Cosima's 'first child of love', and her Swiss conductor husband. When Isolde lost her bid in 1914 to be legally recognised as a daughter of Wagner, not of Hans von Bülow, her son's chances of ever succeeding to the Bayreuth throne plunged – all the more so when, soon afterwards, Siegfried married and fathered four children. Franz Beidler Jr. might therefore have faded out of the Wagner saga for good, but for two things. Virtually everyone close to the matter well knew that Isolde really was the Master's daughter, whatever a court of law might rule; and young Beidler (unlike his father) turned out to be a person of high principle and intellectual standing. In particular he despised the Nazis and they, in turn, hated him – both for his left-wing views (he wrote regularly for Social Democratic publications) and above all for his close ties to Jews. At the age of twenty-two he had married Ellen Gottschalk, daughter of a Jewish professor of medicine, and he long worked in Berlin as a close aide of Leo Kestenberg, also Jewish, who was a high-ranking government official responsible for a far-sighted reform of music education during the Weimar Republic.

After Hitler came to power, the three of them joined the droves of refugees fleeing abroad – Kestenberg making his way via Prague to Tel Aviv where he became manager of the Palestine Orchestra (later the Israel Philharmonic), the Beidlers hopping first to Paris and thence to Zurich where they had the right of abode since Franz, via his late father, had Swiss nationality. But although he and Ellen henceforth made Zurich their home, Franz saw himself first and foremost as a Wagner in exile – like the Master, his grandfather, in the same city long before and like Friedelind at Lucerne a few years later. At any rate, outside Germany he emphasised his family roots more than ever. He began to sign articles 'Beidler-Wagner' and when von Bülow's second wife, Marie, died naming Franz her heir, he rejected the inheritance on the grounds that he was not a blood relative. Above all, backed by influential well-wishers like Thomas Mann and Ernest Newman, he toiled away for years on his most ambitious project – a biography of Cosima meant to reveal the 'real truth' about the *Hohe Frau* as Du Moulin Eckart, Chamberlain and other 'Bayreuthians' had manifestly failed to do. Alas, when Beidler died in 1981 his magnum opus was still far from complete, but even the torso of it published sixteen years later turned out to be well worth reading for its psychological insight and elegance of style. Among books about the Wagners (let alone *by* the Wagners), it stands close to the top.[3]

With his background as a leftist Wagner long in exile, Beidler was almost bound to react harshly to much about 'New Bayreuth'. Despite Wieland's new-look *Parsifal* and his partly novel presentation of the *Ring*, the three maestros invited to the Green Hill in 1951 were no strangers to those who had lived through the 'Third Reich'. That applied above all to Furtwängler, the Führer's favourite who, although he found the regime repugnant, had stayed in Nazi Germany almost to the end and had led most of Bayreuth's wartime stagings of *Meistersinger.* After (typically) changing his mind repeatedly about whether to take part in the newly launched festival at all, he finally agreed to do so – not, as in the 'old days', to conduct opera but instead to give a celebratory opening performance on 29 July of Beethoven's Ninth Symphony. The 'festival proper' would then begin the following day with Wieland's tensely awaited new *Parsifal*. That seemed a clever choice. Thoughts would in the first place be directed not so much to recent history as to that occasion, nearly eight decades before, when the Master himself had conducted the 'Choral' Symphony to mark the laying of the festival theatre's foundation stone. On the whole this approach paid off although, even with Beethoven rather than Wagner, Furtwängler could not wholly erase memories of his role in the Reich. Hadn't he led that very symphony to celebrate the Führer's birthday in Berlin in 1942, reaching down from the stage (albeit, as film footage shows, with obvious distaste) to shake hands with Goebbels who had been sitting in the front row?

As for the 1951 opera fare itself, one *Ring* cycle as well as a new *Meistersinger* (in a traditional production by Rudolf Hartmann, a Munich opera stalwart) were in the hands of Herbert von Karajan, already an ambitious rival to Furtwängler prior to 1945. Karajan, now forty-three, had joined the Nazi party not once but twice – first in Austria and then in Germany – not for ideological reasons but (like so many others) to help boost his career after Hitler came to power. That early history set him back a bit after the war, but by 1951 he was on the rise again and using Bayreuth as one springboard towards what would soon be world stardom. Meanwhile the other *Ring* cycle and *Parsifal* were in the intermittently safe charge of the sixty-three-year-old Hans Knappertsbusch (known as Kna), a craggy giant of a man who hated rehearsing but who could usually generate a shattering performance 'on the night'. Given to the bluntest of talk laced with wry and often scatalogical wit, Kna had gained – and long retained – a reputation as something of a hero who had faced the Nazis down. In fact he had served the regime's aims pretty well right from the start in 1933, when he helped instigate a public protest in Munich against Thomas Mann as a 'bad Wagnerian' with 'cosmopolitan-democratic views'. This campaign was the immediate reason, though not the only one, that the Nobel prize-winning writer decided to turn his back on Nazi Germany. That Kna's career did not subsequently prosper as he had hoped was due in particular to the Führer's – wildly inaccurate – view of him as a mere 'band-master'. Though Furtwängler remained Hitler's favourite, he ranked Kna well behind Clemens Krauss, a star of musical life in Berlin, Munich and Vienna during the 'Third Reich' who also briefly popped up in 'New Bayreuth'. He replaced his old rival Kna there for a single season in 1953 but died the year after.

Naturally reasons could be found to justify the Furtwängler–Karajan–Kna lineup. All three conductors had come through post-war vetting by the Allies and all were undeniably fine artists, albeit in very different ways. But were there no excellent maestros around who were wholly untainted by the Nazi era? Toscanini's return would have been too much to hope for, but what of exiles like Fritz Busch, Bruno Walter, Otto Klemperer and Erich Kleiber, or rising stars like Rafael Kubelík (who later made exemplary recordings of *Lohengrin*, *Parsifal* and – especially – *Meistersinger* down the road in Munich)? Busch was the only one of these ever to conduct at Bayreuth, and then for just a single season in 1924. Later he made common cause with Toscanini and resisted Nazi blandishments to return to the Green Hill or anywhere else in the Reich. As a sturdy anti-fascist as well as a peerless interpreter fêted at New York's Metropolitan Opera, Busch might have been the ideal catch for 'New Bayreuth' – at least at the very start. Sadly, he died aged sixty-one only a month after the first post-war festival ended. As for the other possibles, Wieland, it is true, did meet Klemperer in the mid-1950s and got on well with him, despite the veteran maestro's typically caustic greeting: 'What was it like sitting on the Führer's knee?'[4] But plans for the two of them to work together fell through mainly because of Klemperer's failing health.

Beidler's complaint that there was 'not the slightest sign of change' could hardly have applied to the 1951 singers – a largely new team that included, to name but two outstanding sopranos, the Swedish-American Astrid Varnay as a dazzling Brünnhilde, and the German Martha Mödl as a supremely alluring yet pitiable Kundry. He was on rather stronger ground with respect to the 'brown history' of key but less prominent figures. One of them was Gerhard Rossbach, a vital raiser of festival funds and ex-leader of a notorious paramilitary *Freikorps* unit that thirty years earlier had sought to destabilise the Weimar Republic. Another was Hans Reissinger, Gertrud's architect uncle whose career had spectacularly flowered under the Nazis. He was now responsible for the *Meistersinger* décor and also turned his hand to a couple of anodyne articles, one on 'The Beautiful Town of Bayreuth', in the festival's programme book.[5]

Apart from such personnel questions, though, there was a broader issue and it was raised by Wieland and Wolfgang themselves at the very start. In a written declaration, the brothers urged that in 'the interests of a trouble-free realisation of the festival', visitors should 'kindly desist from discussion or debate of a political nature'. On the face of it that request seemed fair, all the more so since it ended with the words '*Hier gilt's der Kunst*' (Here, it's art that counts) – the very words with which Siegfried had sought to block further ultra-nationalist demonstrations in the festival theatre long before. But for Beidler and those who thought like him, 'debate of a political nature' was exactly what was needed in post-war Germany, not least in Bayreuth, a place that stood for much of the best and worst of which the nation was capable. How did the 'unparalleled material and moral collapse' come to happen? Who was responsible? How could any recurrence best be prevented? As for the festival, how come that in democratic Germany it was still in the hands of a family that for years had been closer than any other to Adolf Hitler? Such questions were tricky, of course, but that was no good reason to avoid thrashing them out. Quite the opposite.

On at least three occasions before 1945, a knife had seemed poised over the umbilical cord between the Wagner family and its voracious baby, the Bayreuth festival. In 1883 after the Master died intestate, it had at first been far from clear that Cosima could or should take charge of the infant, even assuming it survived. And Winifred's position in 1930 had initially looked hardly more secure. Although named as Siegfried's heir, in the eyes of many hard-line Wagnerians she was (another) foreign-born 'interloper' with little authority in artistic matters. In between the reigns of these iron-willed matriarchs, Siegfried – fearing a growing campaign by a hostile press against himself and the family – had talked in 1914 of handing over the whole Wagner legacy 'to the German people'. Whether sincerely meant or not, that proposal might even have been adopted had not the outbreak of war taken people's minds off Bayreuth scandal. So it was that thanks to luck, tenacity, canny advisers and latterly the backing of the Führer, the Wagners kept the festival in the family for nearly seventy years.

At the end of the Second World War, though, that long-standing link seemed set to be severed for good. In Germany the clan was scattered between two of the four occupation zones set up by the victorious powers, with Winifred and Wolfgang answering to the Americans and the Nussdorf contingent to the French. Most of the family assets, including the festival theatre and what remained of Wahnfried, had been impounded and it was unclear when – or even whether – they would be returned. Meanwhile in New York more trouble was brewing. Friedelind, like an avenging angel, was publishing her *Heritage of Fire* with its inside story of the close links between the Wagners and

Hitler. Initially the other members of the clan did not know what was in the book, indeed had long heard nothing from Mausi at all, but they naturally fretted about what she might be up to.

It was not even plain in those early days that Bayreuth would ever again host a Wagner festival, with or without the family. What Winifred called 'clueless, coloured' US soldiers poked about for souvenirs in the Wahnfried rubble and jitterbugged in the garden around the grave of the Master and Cosima. The adjoining *Führerbau* did varied service as a counter-intelligence headquarters, an officers' club and, according to Wolfgang, a brothel.[6] At least the theatre on the Green Hill had escaped destruction, though no one seemed sure why. Some claimed that Allied bomber pilots had been keen to spare so famous a cultural landmark, others more plausibly held that the sprawling reddish pile had been mistaken for a brewery. Whatever the truth, Wagnerian costumes and scenery were looted (by desperate Germans as well as trophy-hunting Americans), the sunken orchestra pit was covered over and the place turned over to entertainment for the troops. The 'hallowed hall' that had closed a year before to *Meistersinger*, was soon resounding to performances by the Rockettes from New York's Radio City and to shows including *Ten Little Indians* and (suitably enough) *Anything Goes*. Not for long, though. For the Americans the place proved too vast for its new role and, despite the deployment of around two hundred stoves, too hard to heat in winter. In 1946 the 'white elephant' was dumped on Bayreuth – or, put more elegantly, it was placed in the trusteeship of the struggling, semi-ruined town.

Characteristically, Winifred was unbowed and unrepentant: indeed, like Wolfgang, she claimed to see nothing to be repentant about. When Furtwängler asked her how she could bear to have invective like so many buckets of refuse poured over her by the Allies and hostile Germans, she serenely replied that none of it touched her as she felt guilty of no crime. Like an exiled queen, she issued firm but usually fruitless edicts from her Oberwarmensteinach refuge, ticking off the Americans for installing all those stoves in the highly combustible festival theatre and urging Interpol to be on the lookout for the former Führer's missing Wagner manuscripts. Yes, she repeatedly told allied interrogators, she had long been a close, personal friend of Hitler though, no, she had never slept with him.[7] She had always found him to be charming, humorous and reliable – as well as a real Wagner connoisseur – and she was not going to claim otherwise just because he was now dead and the war had been lost. Their relationship, she insisted time after time, had had nothing to do with politics.

Although Winifred was forthright by nature, it is unlikely that her seeming openness in this case was devoid of calculation. The allied campaign of denazification was already starting to roll – with special impetus in the American zone – and the 'mistress of Bayreuth' well knew that much about her links with Hitler was too well documented to be deniable. Far better, from her point of view, to admit right away what was broadly known, seek to have the most favourable interpretation put on it and draw a veil over the rest. When asked whether she had any letters from Hitler she promptly handed over a few but, as she later noted privately, she kept back many others and the Americans, happy with her seeming readiness to cooperate, did not probe further. Even Thomas Mann's son Klaus, back from US exile and at least as hostile as his father to Hitler, reacted to Winifred with something like awe. After interviewing her for the American forces newspaper *Stars and Stripes*, he reported that he had met only one person in post-war Germany who freely admitted to having been a Nazi – and she was British-born.

Down by the Bodensee, though, Wieland was far from thrilled by his mother's apparent candour, which seemed bound to draw still more unwelcome attention to the family's role, especially his own, during the 'Third Reich'. Happy enough for years to enjoy Hitler's favour, he was now keen to dissociate himself from the Führer and all his works. In a letter, he told his mother she might be surprised to learn that but for his 'understanding' for her in the era that 'thank God lies behind us at last', he would 'a hundred times over' have chosen the course taken by Friedelind.[8] Winifred surely *was* surprised. Although Wieland had latterly considered fleeing the Reich, and had abortively tried to do so at the very end, there was no sign that he had considered exile when Hitler was at the height of his power. But apart from her surprise, if not incredulity, over this particular revelation, Winifred simply felt it behoved Wieland to show more thanks to his late benefactor. As she pointed out years later, Hitler had favoured Wieland 'in every possible way' – had probably even saved his life by freeing him from military service. That her eldest son showed such ingratitude after the war was, she bemoaned, incomprehensible.[9]

It was, of course, nothing of the kind. Although it was not immediately clear at war's end just what penalties the Allies might impose on ex-Nazis, the 'heir' had every reason not to trumpet about his long and privileged relationship with 'Uncle Wolf'. The fact that he had joined the party 'only' at Hitler's personal request was unlikely to be seen as a mitigating circumstance, even given his youth; nor might his constant hobnobs in the Berlin Chancellery almost until the final days of the war be construed simply as harmless contacts in the cause of art. Then there was that brief but potentially damning spell at the Flossenbürg offshoot in Bayreuth. All in all, Wieland had good cause to keep his head down. So did Bodo Lafferentz, who along with his family was a fellow refugee in Nussdorf. Although Lafferentz had not been part of the Wagner clan for long and had had few personal contacts with Hitler, he now looked specially vulnerable thanks to his record as an SS officer and top manager in the Nazi war machine. As best they could from afar, he and Wieland followed the start in November 1945 of the Nuremberg war crimes trial against leading Nazis – among them familiar figures from old Bayreuth days like Hermann Göring, Albert Speer and Hans Frank (Lieselotte Schmidt's former heart-throb, dubbed 'the butcher' during his term as a pitiless Governor General of occupied Poland). In the event, of the twenty-two accused who went into the dock, twelve – including Frank and Göring – were sentenced to death. Lafferentz's former boss Robert Ley was also among the Nuremberg prisoners, but he strangled himself in his cell before the trial began.

Compared with such sharks Wieland and Lafferentz were smallish fish, but that did not mean that they, let alone Winifred, were likely to slip through the net altogether. Under guidelines laid down by the pacesetting Americans and later adopted by the other Allies, Germans faced case-by-case scrutiny and classification into one of five categories according to the degree of support they had shown for the Nazis. All but those in the fifth group ('exonerated') were liable to penalties that ranged from the draconian for 'major offenders' – up to ten years' hard labour and forfeiture of all assets – to little more than fines for 'fellow travellers'. Fair though this procedure may have looked on paper, the guidelines were applied by the Allies in different ways from zone to zone. Besides, German civilian tribunals (*Spruchkammern*) set up under Allied supervision to try suspects, badly lacked qualified personnel and their proceedings were clogged by testimony from shoals of 'witnesses' keen to whitewash former comrades or denounce old rivals.

In their zeal to track down former Nazis and active backers of the regime, the Americans concocted a 131-point questionnaire to be filled out by all Germans over the age of eighteen. Penalties for giving false or incomplete information were high and, on key matters at least, culprits ran a real risk of exposure as full membership lists of the Nazi party and related organisations had early on fallen into US hands. Even so, with millions of more-or-less completed forms flooding in, the resources were simply not available for comprehensive cross-checking. Broadly speaking, the British and French turned out to be less rigorous and instead of trying to chase up every last possible miscreant they tended to concentrate on 'worst cases'. For Wieland and Lafferentz, holed up in the French zone, that was some comfort – but not much.

Life was harsh for the Nussdorf Wagners even leaving aside the threat of denazification. They were surely far better off than the many millions of homeless and wounded in Germany and beyond, especially in the east, but that seemed small comfort. Packed into four rooms of a holiday home never meant as winter quarters, shunned by many locals gleeful that the once-mighty visitors from Bayreuth had been brought so low, they were bitterly cold for nearly half the year, often sick and almost always hungry. By the end of 1945 there were ten of them – five adults (with Elfriede, Gertrud's sister) and five children, including two new babies. Somehow amid the howling, the nappy-changing and the constant hunt for food, fuel and medicine, Wieland found time to look into philosophy and psychology (when he could get hold of the books) and eventually to paint (when his fingers were not too numb to hold a brush). Late at night, when they were not wholly exhausted and the children were in bed, he and Gertrud would sprawl on the floor and argue loud and long over the Master's scores, notably *Tristan.* For a time Wieland even hoped to get over to Garmisch and realise an old ambition to study the whole Wagner oeuvre with Richard Strauss. But Strauss, it turned out, had beaten a retreat to Switzerland and when Wieland got to Garmisch at last it was mainly to resume study with Overhoff, who had been engaged there as music teacher to Strauss's grandson.

Wieland later referred to this period as his 'dark, creative years' – a spell in the wilderness, as it were, that finally formed him for the top job in Bayreuth. There is something in that. For the first time he came across the theories of Freud and Jung, he took a new look at the work of some of those 'degenerate' artists he had previously passed over and he excitedly identified parallels in the *Ring* between Greek and Nordic myth (an obvious connection that, oddly enough, seems not to have struck him before). As a result, although the seeds of his later 'Bayreuth style' had already been sown in the war years, during the 'Nussdorf era' he at least partly rethought his approach to the stage. The trouble was he had no stage to work on and prospects looked slim that he would get one anywhere in Germany, let alone on the Green Hill. For a while he vainly considered trying to establish a Wagner festival abroad – in Switzerland or even Monte Carlo – to be kick-started with funds from the sale of some of the Master's manuscripts.[10] The United States seemed a possible option too. Long before his mother, he made contact with Friedelind who had applied for American nationality and aimed to set up her own opera company. Wieland sent her costume and stage designs – also some of his oil paintings that his sister promised to hang in the foyers of theatres across the US when her company went on tour. The pictures, it seems, were largely ruined in transit.

Wolfgang was livid when he got to hear about this unexpected transatlantic entente, fearing that if Friedelind's scheme were a success (it later foundered for lack of funds) she might use it as a springboard to the top job in Bayreuth – with Wieland's indirect help, at that! Where would that leave him, the 'little brother' who alone of the family had had to fight (however briefly) for the 'Fatherland', who had persevered with the Berlin opera training Wieland had shunned, who had stuck by his mother in and around Bayreuth at war's end and who had daringly spirited away much of the Wahnfried archive for 'safe keeping' from prying American fingers?

Even the dogged Wolfgang seems to have had some doubts whether he or any Wagner would ever return to the Green Hill, once telling Wieland he felt the family was simply 'incapable' of getting the festival on its feet again.[11] Nonetheless, in early 1946 he had moved back to Bayreuth from Oberwarmensteinach with his wife and baby Eva and had set up home in four rooms above the gardener's cottage at Wahnfried. A year later his only son, Gottfried, was born. Of itself, his presence 'back on base' gave Wolfgang no special rights with respect to the festival, but he was better placed than any other member of the clan to resume old contacts and watch for new opportunities. He was also, as he put it, 'entirely devoid of political encumbrances'[12] – which was true inasmuch as he had never joined the Nazi party. Back in 1938 he, unlike Wieland, had managed to slip away when Hitler had raised the question of party membership, and his later contacts with the Führer had been neither as regular nor as intensive as his brother's. Hence if there were to be a festival one day and if any Wagner were to be involved – two big 'ifs' – then Wolfgang looked well placed to play a key role, perhaps even the leading one. This was provided his pesky sister in America did not muscle in: no wonder he was wrathful when she and Wieland seemed to make common cause.

In view of their growing differences, the two brothers agreed in early 1947 to meet and thrash things out on neutral ground – the Strauss villa in Garmisch. It must have been a stormy session with Friedelind's spirit, like Banquo's ghost, haunting the fray. Wolfgang's wrath still shows through in his memoirs, although he wrote them long after the event when both his elder brother and sister were dead. Wieland's 'sudden affection for Friedelind and his participation in her work', he charged, 'might have been understandable from the aspect of pure self-interest, but not when one considered her behaviour towards the family, the non-emigrants who had remained in Europe and whom she despised with all her heart'. By 'selling himself' to his sister Wieland had been in effect 'betraying the rest of us, who were doing our best to preserve Bayreuth'.[13] For 'the rest of us', Wolfgang might as well have written 'me'. Winifred was also much interested in 'preserving' Bayreuth, but in the first place she had to preserve herself. At that time her denazification trial was imminent and she was busy marshalling her defence.

Naturally Friedelind's behaviour could be interpreted far more positively than Wolfgang allowed, and she surely did not despise the whole family – rather the ideology with which its members, in varying degrees, had identified. Apart from her semi-businesslike contacts with Wieland, she had begun to send over food and clothing in CARE packets from which all the Wagners benefited, not least Wolfgang, his wife Ellen and baby Eva. Still, she undeniably *did* represent a threat to the ambitions of the family's 'non-emigrants', albeit not the only one. Already in 1946 the newly appointed mayor of Bayreuth, Oskar Meyer, had appealed to what he called the Master's 'legitimate and politically uncompromised descendants' abroad, to return to Germany and help get the festival going again on a wholly new basis. One of the mayor's letters went to Friedelind in the US who, it seems, failed to respond – at least directly. The other went to Franz Beidler in Zurich.[14] The name meant little or nothing to most Wagnerians but it set warning bells ringing among the scattered members of the clan in Germany. In the dim and distant past, little Franz had for a while looked well in line to succeed to the Bayreuth throne. Was he belatedly going to make it after all?

Small wonder that Beidler felt, as he put it, 'moved and shaken' when he received the mayor's 'momentous letter'. He took nearly a month to reply, saying he judged the omens for a new start in Bayreuth to be poor because 'too much has happened over the years for us ever to be able to erase it from our memories'. But he agreed a try had to be made and just before Christmas he arrived in Bayreuth with a draft plan that was as detailed as it was ambitious. Under its terms, the festival was to be turned over to an independent foundation with a governing council on which representatives of, among others, Bayreuth, the state of Bavaria, UNESCO, Switzerland and a 'future Federal German State' would have seats and voting rights. Thomas Mann was slated as the council's honorary president along with a dazzling array of experts ('only Jews', Winifred inaccurately complained to a friend) ranging from Alfred Einstein, Ernest Newman and Beidler's old Berlin boss Leo Kestenberg to the composers Arnold Schoenberg, Paul Hindemith, Arthur Honegger and Karl Amadeus Hartmann. Much of the 'donkey work' would evidently have fallen to Beidler who suggested himself as first secretary.[15]

Most of the 'big names' did in fact indicate they were willing to take part; even Thomas Mann in his Californian refuge did not quite say no despite his intense reluctance to get involved again in any enterprise on German soil.[16] The proposed foundation would not, therefore, have lacked for prestige, but would it have worked in practice? The structure Beidler outlined looked pretty unwieldy with too many chiefs and too few Indians, but that could – and probably would – have been streamlined. The biggest snag was that, as Wolfgang cuttingly put it, Beidler was 'handing out the pelt before the bear had been felled.' Under the joint will of Siegfried and herself, in 1930 Winifred had inherited the entire Wagner estate – including the festival theatre and Wahnfried – on condition that when she died, or if she remarried, the fortune would pass to the four children in equal shares. In other words, although the festival assets had been requisitioned by the Americans and placed in trusteeship they were still the property of the

Wagner family, as Wolfgang tirelessly stressed to all and sundry in Bayreuth, including his visiting 'cousin Franz'. If the assets were legally to pass to the Beidler foundation or to any other party, the Wagners – in the first place Winifred – would have to be dispossessed. That was no news to Beidler himself, who even argued against offering compensation. Siegfried, he noted coolly, had proposed back in 1914 that the festival theatre and Wahnfried be 'given to the nation' via a foundation.[17] That aim now looked close to being realised, albeit more than three decades late.

In those first post-war years, dispossessing the Wagners (with or without compensation) did indeed seem a real possibility, as Tietjen for one underlined in 1947. Already rebuilding his career and seemingly eyeing a possible return to the Green Hill, the irrepressible 'Heinz' argued that although the festival ought in his view to stay a family business, the military government might use 'the law of the victor' to decide otherwise. In that case, he claimed, the only feasible solution would be an international foundation with an artistic director (Tietjen?) and a governing council that could include some members of the Wagner family. He specifically mentioned Wolfgang and even Beidler but not Winifred and, unsurprisingly, not his old foe Wieland.[18] The Bavarian government, too, for a time toyed with plans for a foundation to replace the Wagners, fearing not least that tourists, especially Americans, might stay away from Bayreuth if so notorious a 'Third Reich' family stayed in control.[19]

Tietjen was right in principle about the 'military government'. But in practice the Americans had by this time largely handed over denazification to German tribunals, although they still kept a weather eye on the proceedings, and no longer directly intervened in the murky affairs of the Wagners. All eyes therefore turned to Winifred's trial, which began before a *Spruchkammer* in Bayreuth on 25 June 1947 – two days after her fiftieth birthday. Accused among other things of being 'one of the most fanatical and loyal supporters of Adolf Hitler' who 'received considerable sums of money' from the Nazis thanks to her 'active role in the party', Winifred faced possible conviction as a 'major offender' – meaning she stood to lose virtually everything, including her freedom. That prospect seems not to have fazed her. Armed with a sixty-four-page defence plea that she simply called her *Denkschrift* (i.e. exposé), and backed by an array of witnesses who testified that she had helped them in the worst of times, the 'exiled

Mistress of Bayreuth' sought to show she had done no wrong and much right. Her main arguments were, by this time, familiar enough: to wit, that her close ties to Hitler had been those of personal friendship based on a love of Wagner's work; that her last meeting with him had been early in the war (which, she stressed, she had firmly opposed); that she had consistently used what influence she had to help Jews and others victims of the party machine; and, last but not least, that the funds the Nazis had ploughed into Bayreuth (peaking at an annual average of more than a million Reichmarks during the war) had gone to the festival, not to enrich her personally.[20]

Much of that seemed plausible, but it was far from the whole truth. Even leaving aside the question of when she had really last seen Hitler (decades later she claimed it had been in 1944), Winifred hedged and contradicted herself over how much she had known about the concentration and extermination camps. Although she had manifestly hoped up to 1939 that the war could be headed off, she then backed it to the bitter end, terming it in a Bayreuth booklet a struggle between 'the world of Western culture and the destructive spirit of the pluto-crat-Bolshevist world conspiracy'.[21] Such antisemitic, anti-Russian jargon might well have come from one of the many tirades of her friend Wolf, and perhaps that is where she had picked it up. As for the Nazi money for the festival, it was true that little of it had gone directly into Winifred's own purse (and also true that the gifts the 'mistress of Bayreuth' received from the Führer were probably worth no more than those she gave him). But wasn't the festival Winifred's private property and main means of livelihood? Didn't it – and therefore she – thrive after 1933 above all because Hitler backed it with his presence and, directly as well as indirectly, with funds?

Behind these matters of detail lay the key question of how far, if at all, Winifred was justified in drawing so firm a line between her private life and its public context; here her friend Wolf, there the Führer; here the family festival, there the Nazi backing for it; here her personal appeals for 'clemency' for those who she considered 'worthy' (as she put it), there a regime incarcerating and slaughtering at whim and will? Where did Winifred's responsibility and guilt really begin? What, indeed, was her crime? The public prosecutor (the 'so-called' prosecutor as Winifred privately called him) was on tricky ground when he argued that the accused had 'placed Richard Wagner's legacy at the disposal of the ideological views of National Socialism'. Had *she* really been responsible for that, even assuming accord could be reached on which 'legacy' was meant and what the Nazis had made of it? The prosecutor had rather more of a point in arguing that the very number of witnesses Winifred had lined up – some thirty of them present and others sending written testimony – backed his case rather than hers. That she had been able to help so many off the Nazi hook who would otherwise have been jailed or murdered, in his view simply went to show how great her clout had been at the very top of a system evil through and through.

Faced with arguments of such scope and complexity the court evidently felt out of its depth and its verdict, handed down on 2 July, unsurprisingly satisfied neither side. Because Winifred had helped 'many people in trouble' and had 'at no time behaved in a brutal and reprehensible manner', it was decided that she should not be placed in the top (i.e. worst) category of offenders. On the other hand, as a 'loyal friend of Hitler's' she was deemed to have 'been a committed supporter of the National Socialist tyranny' and was accordingly classed as an 'activist' (category two). Later Winifred reflected with mingled hilarity and contempt on some of the penalties imposed, such as a ban on preaching or giving radio commentaries for five years. Others, like a commitment to 450 days' community service, were hardly a laughing matter. Easily worst, sixty per cent of her assets were to be confiscated for good.[22] Beidler regarded the latter step as an at least partial victory for all those pressing for a 'New Bayreuth', and urged that in the light of it a quick decision should be made on the festival's future ownership.[23] But that was easier said than done. Winifred, particularly aggrieved at being dubbed a backer of Nazi tyranny, promptly appealed against the sentence. The prosecutor, sure that a 'major offender' was being allowed to slip away, did the same. The matter therefore went back to the courts for nearly eighteen months – crucial ones, as it turned out, not just for the Wagners but for Germany and the wartime victors. Circumstances changed – and circumstances, as the saying goes, alter cases.

Just two years before Winifred went on trial, the war in Europe had ended with what seemed to most people a clear outcome. On the one side were the Russians and the western Allies deliriously celebrating their joint victory over Hitler; on the other were the Germans, crushed in battle and increasingly despised as the full extent of Nazi mass murder began to emerge. Amid that fever of joy and disgust, it was at first easy for many in the west to forget or fail to realise the threat posed by 'Uncle Joe' Stalin's Soviet Union – a dictatorship no less odious than 'Uncle Wolf's' had been. The Russians, it was widely acknowledged, had suffered terribly and fought valiantly. If their troops now occupied much of Europe, including a big slice of Germany – well, that was due to Hitler's initial aggression, not to intrinsic Soviet imperialism. Besides, at the 'big three' conference between the Americans, British and Russians in Yalta shortly before war's end, hadn't Stalin agreed (spuriously, as it turned out) to future free elections in 'liberated' eastern Europe? He had even backed moves to create the United Nations organisation!

Rather soon, though, even the least discerning began to realise that the 'hot' war was being replaced by a 'cold' one in which a former partner was becoming a foe and, more gradually, vice versa. In March 1946 Winston Churchill famously declared that an 'iron curtain' had descended across the continent 'from Stettin on the Baltic to Trieste on the Adriatic'. The Russians, he warned, sought 'an indefinite expansion of their power and doctrines' notably in Germany. Six months later Secretary of State James Byrnes in a Stuttgart speech underlined the US determination to keep Germans as far as possible in the western camp, promising them a free, self-governing and prosperous future (a far cry from the former US 'Morgenthau plan' that had aimed to de-industrialise Germany for good). It was not long before the Byrnes pledge started to be fulfilled, politically and economically. Facing deadlock with Moscow over Germany's future, the western Allies decided a common political order should be established in the area under their control. Accordingly a provisional constitution called the 'Basic Law' was drafted in the summer of 1948 (provisional because Germans in the Soviet zone were not – yet – able to join), and the following May the Federal Republic of Germany (west) was born with the Rhineland town of Bonn as its capital. A few months later a 'German Democratic Republic' (east) was formed in the Soviet zone.

Meanwhile, US Marshall Aid – boycotted as 'American economic imperialism' by Moscow and the states under its thumb – had begun rolling into devastated western Europe, among other things laying the basis for the West German *Wirtschaftswunder* (economic miracle) of the 1950s. At least as vital a prerequisite for the 'miracle', though, was the currency reform of June 1948 in which the enfeebled Reichsmark was scrapped, along with most price controls and rationing, and replaced by the perky new Deutsche Mark. Implemented not only in the western areas of Germany but also in the western sectors of Berlin, a city under four-power occupation although far inside the Soviet zone, the reform brought a swift and drastic backlash from the Russians. They introduced a separate currency in the east and, for nearly a year, cut off all land and waterway links from the west to the two-and-a-half million citizens of west Berlin. In response the western Allies organised an airlift of unprecedented scope, running nearly three hundred thousand flights to shuttle food, fuel and goods to the greater part of a city on which, a few years before, they had been raining bombs. Many Germans saw the pilots as heroes and in much of the west the image of the 'plucky Berliner' tended to replace that of the goose-stepping Nazi. If Stalin had sought to encourage popular support for a new anti-Soviet alliance, he could hardly have found a better way.

In this context denazification almost inevitably ran out of steam. By early 1948 the drive was anyway near-complete in the Soviet zone, thanks to the 'clean sweep' made by the communists as they busily replaced the old dictatorship with a new one of their own. For the western Allies the hunt for the guilty, long beset by problems of personnel and procedure, made ever less political sense as the cold war grew frostier. Whatever the moral scruples about letting old Nazis off the hook, it seemed essential to swallow them and forge a common front against the growing danger in the east. Besides, hadn't scruples already been swallowed in respect of those Nazis – from the rocket expert Wernher von Braun to 'Hitler's top spy' Reinhard Gehlen – deemed of special value to western military and intelligence immediately after the war? It now became a matter of applying similar *Realpolitik* to the far greater number of Germans still in the waiting line for judgement. Not that denazification ground to a halt right away; it limped on until 1950 when the Bundestag (the lower house of the federal parliament) under Chancellor Adenauer more or less buried it – albeit not for good. But as a rule the longer the process lasted the less people caught up in it had to fear – much to the disgust of those who had come before them and been more strictly treated.

Suppose Winifred had been brought to trial a year earlier. Might she indeed have been deemed a 'major offender' with all the consequences, as the prosecution demanded? If so, what would have happened to the festival? Would the four children have taken over, or some of them, or would the Beidler scheme for an international foundation have come into its own? Speculation aside, the fact is that by 8 December 1948 when the appeal court gave its ruling, the Berlin airlift was in full swing, the birth of the Federal Republic was just a few months away and denazification had lost its élan. Winifred had even applied for reinstatement of her British nationality, believing that as a Briton she would stand a better chance of a reduced sentence. Evidently British officials looking into her claim were not impressed by her chutzpah (one noted 'I think there is little doubt she is a bad lot'), and failed to expedite her application.[24] But she did indeed regain her British nationality – while retaining her German one – soon after completion of her 'denazification', under a new law that thoroughly revamped Britain's complex rules on nationality, citizenship and naturalisation. Thus the 'mistress of Bayreuth' re-established the formal link with the land of her birth that she had lost on her marriage to Siegfried more than three decades before.

In a parallel development far more parochial but nonetheless vital for the Wagners, local council elections in Bayreuth in May 1948 brought a new mayor to office. Out went Oskar Meyer of the Christian Social Union, in came the Social Democrat Hans Rollwagen who thought nothing of his predecessor's moves to hand over the festival to expatriates and foreigners. In his first public speech in his new job Rollwagen stressed that although, as he delicately put it, a 'shadow' had fallen over the festival in recent years, the Wagner family's right to run things was 'sanctioned by history and the law'. A few days later he got together to plan strategy with Winifred and Wolfgang in the Wahnfried gardener's cottage (a kind of 'resistance centre', as Wolfgang put it, for organising the defence of family interests) and began to pull what strings he could with the Bavarian government in Munich, which was still undecided about the festival's future. Prospects for Beidler's foundation plan were thus dwindling steadily but, pending the result of the appeal, they had not quite vanished.

Surprisingly in the circumstances, the seven-member appeal court under its chairman, Otto Glück, made a better stab at getting to the heart of the Wagner/Hitler/Bayreuth/Winifred complex than its predecessor had done. Indeed, the twenty-page document it issued explaining its verdict with arguments from history, psychology and musicology remains well worth reading to this day, even if the verdict itself seems in part at odds with the reasons given for it.[25] Rejecting from the start the defence view that in the early years Winifred had been wholly in the shadow of Siegfried and Cosima, the court judged that, on the contrary, it was above all she who had taken the family initiative to back Hitler and to whom the eyes of the public had turned. Later as head of the Wagner dynasty and 'keeper of the Grail' during the 'Third Reich', she had found herself 'in the happy position that her personal, political, artistic and entrepreneurial interests all lay on *one and the same* line' (original italics). By putting 'the weight of one of the most famous names in cultural history in the scales for Hitler' (a more carefully phrased claim than the one about 'Wagner's legacy' made by the prosecution), Winifred had 'without doubt' brought the Nazi leader much extra sympathy and more followers.

Did that imply Wagner's music itself had inherent appeal for those of a fascist disposition? The court agreed that nationalists (it specifically mentioned Kaiser Wilhelm) had tended to identify the music dramas with a 'German military spirit' rooted in myth, but it claimed that this was too narrow an interpretation. *Lohengrin*, the work that had first fired the young Hitler's passion for Wagner, was a case in point. Arguably Elsa's love for Lohengrin was the real core of the piece but Hitler, like many in the Wilhelminian era, had been drawn above all to the patriotic element: a knight in shining armour with a 'divine mission' to save Germany. By the time he made his first 'pilgrimage' to Wahnfried in 1923, the amateur painter of limited talent and unbounded political ambition had long since come to see in all Wagner's works a perfect union between art and nationalism. Beyond that Hitler 'like all usurpers' had sought a veneer of legitimacy and soon realised what nimbus he stood to gain through association with the Wagner family. It naturally made a world of difference whether one was identified mainly as a rabble-rouser or, on the contrary, as a person able to hobnob as an equal with the intellectual and artistic elite. And the strategy had paid off! In an unusually personal aside, Herr Glück and his men recalled with evident bitterness how Hitler's followers had gloated triumphantly over their leader's prestige-boosting relations with Bayreuth and Winifred Wagner.

All that seemed like grist to the prosecutor's mill. The judges even conceded at one point that in principle the importance Winifred's backing had had for Hitler would have justified a more severe sentence. In practice, though, they found extenuating circumstances.

Winifred had surely helped a lot of the Nazis' victims and she had been young and impressionable when Hitler had first burst on the scene. Besides, the court argued (in seeming self-contradiction), her example had probably not induced many Germans to back the Nazis who would not have done so anyway. Had Winifred nonetheless helped deceive foreign governments about the true character of the Nazi Reich because she ran a festival of international prestige regularly attended by the Führer? By no means. Diplomats, the court observed with some irony, were considered clever people with access to much information. They must therefore have known perfectly well what 'the terrorist' (i.e. Hitler) was up to, not least since they often saw him in action at Nazi party rallies. As for the wartime festivals, the judges condemned them as 'hangmen's breakfasts' for 'doomed gladiators and slaves of the arms industry', but concluded (rightly) that it was Hitler not Winifred who had insisted they be held.

It is hard to believe that in the changed conditions of late 1948 Winifred would really have been dispossessed and jailed; but given the balance of the arguments that it marshalled, the appeal court might well have confirmed the sentence passed by its predecessor. In fact it did not do even that. Winifred was re-classed as a 'lesser offender' rather than an 'activist', fined DM6,000 and put on probation for two and a half years. During that time she was to be barred from running, supervising or acquiring a business and, more to the point, from access to any stake she already held in an enterprise as owner or partner. In effect, therefore, the festival assets were to stay frozen and in the hands of a trustee until mid-1951. Just two days after the announcement of this verdict, that is on 10 December 1948, Wieland sailed through denazification with a sentence even his mother regarded as lenient. Judged to have been merely a 'fellow traveller,' the Hitler-sponsored heir to the Bayreuth throne was fined DM100 and ordered to pay costs. He did not have to make a personal appearance in court. Bodo Lafferentz with his SS past was scrutinised more carefully, but in February 1949 he was finally classed, like Winifred, as a 'lesser offender'. Describing him as a man of 'brilliant ability', the court (using an increasingly familiar argument) said Germany could not afford to undermine the future of such people without harming itself. In the denazification questionnaires that they had had to complete, neither Wieland nor Lafferentz mentioned his link with the Bayreuth offshoot of Flossenbürg concentration camp.[26]

Even the relatively mild sentence handed down by the appeal court was not enforced for long. In January 1949 (taking up a suggestion the court itself had made) Winifred cleared the way for early release from her probation by agreeing to refrain henceforth from 'organising, administering or running' the festival. 'In keeping with a long-cherished plan', as she put it in a legally binding declaration, these tasks would in future be handled by her sons.[27] As a result of this pledge, the Bavarian government agreed a month later that the festival assets should be 'unfrozen' prematurely and in April this was done. The process was not, in fact, by any means as smooth as it might seem. Despite denazification and the post-war chaos, Winifred had often toyed with the idea that she might one day re-emerge as festival queen, perhaps with Tietjen at her side again (as artistic adviser if nothing more). Signing herself out of power manifestly cost her dear. The Bavarian government too agonised over its part in the deal. The prime minister, Hans Ehard, grumbled that 'given Frau Wagner's political role' it seemed to him intolerable to treat her better than 'countless individuals far less compromised'.[28] His influential state secretary for cultural affairs, Dieter Sattler, stuck to his view that the shadow cast over the festival during the 'Third Reich' could only be dispelled 'by divorcing Richard Wagner's works from the Wagner family'.[29] All to no avail. In view of the appeal court's decision, the government could not in any case have blocked return of the assets indefinitely.

Verena, too, was deeply unhappy over the outcome – not, of course, because the property was being freed at last but because she felt that she and Mausi were being shunted aside by the brothers. Both girls, she stressed in a letter to her mother, had 'rights' with respect to the festival that Winifred had a duty to defend, and in principle that seemed true. Hadn't Siegfried in his will named all four children as equal heirs after Winifred – evidently aiming to give the girls as much future influence on the festival (or at least the chance of it) as the boys? So he had. But by making the assets that had been returned to her available to Wieland and Wolfgang, Winifred was not breaking the letter of the will even if, arguably, she was acting against the spirit of it. She was 'merely' using her sons as managers – of a business virtually down-and-out at that. The festival theatre, badly in need of repair, remained her property and the brothers subsequently paid her rent for its use. Wahnfried was still in ruins and working capital all but non-existent. On the face of it, therefore, Winifred was not so much doing the boys a special favour as handing them, in true Wagnerian fashion, a poisoned chalice. That they then managed to get the festival up and running in only two years says much for their doggedness and skill. Whether the Bayreuth branch of the family, formal denazification notwithstanding, really deserved to be calling the shots again so soon – or indeed at all – is quite another matter.

# 15

# The Road Not Taken

How different things might have been! Suppose that, with 'Alberich Hitler' dead and his Nibelung-Nazis crushed, Friedelind had sped back to Bayreuth from New York determined to get the festival on its feet again. No one would have been even faintly surprised. The daughter-in-exile had just resoundingly confirmed in *Heritage of Fire* what she had told all and sundry for years – that since childhood she had felt a burning sense of mission to carry on her father's work. She was a more than competent pianist and singer, she had plenty of contacts in the musical world from Toscanini down and, as a long-standing anti-Nazi, she was the only member of her family wholly 'politically correct'. Everything seemed to speak in her favour, not least that she indisputably *was* a descendant of Richard Wagner (unlike 'Cousin Franz' Beidler who had never been legally recognised as such) and a direct beneficiary of Siegfried's will. Yet she delayed her return until 1953 by which time the festival, run by her brothers, was in full swing again and most doors were closed to her. Why?

The answer is far from straightforward. Friedelind herself gave part of it – but no more – in a long letter she wrote to New York's *Musical Courier* in late 1949 responding to repeated queries about Bayreuth's future. She noted that soon after the war she had received invitations to return home and take over 'both from German quarters as well as from American Occupation Authorities', but in those bleak days she had judged the very idea of holding a festival to be inappropriate. Since then things had become little better. It was true that the Bavarian government wanted to see the festival restarted as a tourist attraction and even seemed to have offered a subsidy – subject to the appointment of a business administrator to work alongside the Wagners. But 'the only time in history when a German government took interest in us was under the Nazis,' Friedelind recalled, 'and we could well have done without this kiss of death.' Bayreuth should try to pull through on its own 'with the help of politically and economically disinterested lovers of my grandfather's work'. If the festival were to reopen too soon this might 'prove fatal both to its spirit (if there still is such a thing) and its finances'.[1]

Besides her worry about economic conditions in Germany, Friedelind was increasingly pessimistic about the international situation. In a letter to Winifred a few months earlier, written when the Berlin airlift was still in full swing, she had warned that a still more serious East–West crisis was brewing and that any advance tickets sold for a newborn Bayreuth festival were bound to be returned. 'Even here in the richest country on earth', she added, worry about the future had become so pronounced that she had been unable to find enough guarantors for a 'Friedelind Wagner Opera Company' to tour the US with *Tristan und Isolde*. Perhaps she was, in part, trying to explain away her inability to win adequate backing; but it is a fact that by 1949 fears were indeed mounting of a new 'hot' war and even well-established US cultural bastions like the Met were having more trouble raising funds. Anyway, word that Friedelind's tour plan had foundered was received by most of the Wagners with ill-concealed glee. Winifred and Wolfgang opined that the family's 'pipe-dreamer' had been dealt a salutary lesson and even Wieland, who had originally designed the sets and costumes for the planned *Tristan*, sneered about '*Die Maus Pleite*' (The Mouse Crash)[2]. No doubt he and his brother were still more inclined to *Schadenfreude* because their own plans were initially blocked for lack of finance. During the summer of 1949 they had sketched a skeleton programme for a mini-festival to be held in the following year, but had then had to abandon even that modest scheme as unrealistic. Perhaps that was just as well since in June 1950 communist North Korea invaded the south, redoubling worries that similar, Russian-led, aggression might be in the offing in western Europe and especially Germany. As Friedelind had guessed, it would not have been a good time to try to launch festivities, especially in a town barely an hour's drive from the Soviet zone.

Despite that sombre background, a head of fund-raising steam astonishingly did start to build up in Germany all the same – thanks not least to a newly founded *Gesellschaft der Freunde von Bayreuth*

(Society of Friends of Bayreuth). Wieland was at first sceptical, recalling that in the past such 'friends' had sought to exert artistic influence on the festival in exchange for the cash they raised. He even went so far as to charge that 'this blasted old Wagner club with its cliquish self-importance is getting out of hand again,'[3] but he finally accepted the proffered help because he had to. At this key stage it was Wolfgang, pragmatic as usual, who seized the initiative. He drew up estimates of the funds needed, buzzed around Germany on his motorbike coaxing potential sponsors – and agreed not to prepare a production of his own for the 1951 festival so that he would have more time for the vital but inglorious task of business organisation. Wieland was rarely generous with praise, but in this case he remarked more than once that while the festival could do without him it could certainly not do without his brother. From the business viewpoint that was surely true, especially in those first years of struggle.

From her Manhattan base Friedelind could not, or at any rate did not, keep abreast of all the ups and downs at 'home'. She sent one CARE packet after another to the family and corresponded occasionally with her siblings, notably Wieland; but she did not write at all to her mother until May 1947, one month before the start of the latter's denazification trial. Even then her letter was distant in tone, mainly posing questions about the family estate. Winifred, on the other hand, sent a string of at times anguished appeals to New York stressing that the case against her seemed bound to be drawn mainly from *Heritage of Fire* and that she could well be sentenced to a labour camp. At first she noted that she had not been able to get hold of the book and begged Friedelind to send a copy so that she could prepare her defence.[4] She, Winifred, would pay the costs involved when she could scrape the money together 'in better times'. Later, after obtaining *Heritage* elsewhere, Winifred wrote that she had found errors in it that she would be able to identify as such under interrogation by quoting from Friedelind's own correspondence. Even that implicit threat brought no response; nor did more affectionate letters reporting on family and friends and ending with '*Es umarmt Dich innigst Deine Mama*' (With warmest embraces, your Mama).

From all that, it might seem that an implacably vengeful daughter was simply getting her own back on a domineering mother. But shortly before Winifred was due to appear in court, Friedelind abruptly changed tack. She fired off a telegram to Bayreuth demanding (unavailingly) that the trial be postponed, she pressed (successfully) for the exclusion of *Heritage of Fire* from prosecution evidence, and – hardly less surprising in the circumstances – she promised to phone her mother on 23 June to congratulate her on her fiftieth birthday.[5] She kept her pledge, but in those post-war days of makeshift communication Winifred was unable to receive a transatlantic call in Bayreuth (let alone in the village where she lived) and instead had to trek to Nuremberg for the fifteen-minute chat. It is not clear just what Friedelind said to her beleaguered Mama in their first conversation for seven years, apart from 'Happy Birthday', but evidently Winifred felt the arduous trip worthwhile. Back in Bayreuth that night, she and other well-wishers celebrated with a bottle of champagne somehow drummed up at Wolfgang's home in the Wahnfried gardener's cottage. Mausi's gestures of goodwill, especially her move to head off the use of her book against her mother, seemed a good omen for the imminent trial.

Even if *Heritage of Fire* had been used in evidence it is unlikely that, on the strength of it, Winifred would have been judged a 'major offender' (rather than 'merely' an 'activist') and hence given the toughest possible sentence. Although the book contains many piquant details, they mainly round out a picture of the 'Mistress of Bayreuth' and her close relations with Hitler that the court was able to glean anyway. Friedelind's eleventh-hour intervention, therefore, probably did not much influence her mother's fate – but it surely did raise or bolster doubts about the veracity of *Heritage of Fire* that have persisted ever since, especially in Germany. By urging that the book be barred from use in court the authoress seemed implicitly to admit what Winifred, backed to the hilt by Wolfgang, had argued from the start – that the text was often tendentious and in part pure fiction.

Friedelind, in fact, acknowledged no such thing either then or later. She *did* get some things wrong (about Hitler's first Wahnfried visit, for instance), she *was* guilty of 'sins of omission' (her relatively late anti-Nazi 'conversion') and she *was* arguably unfair in some of her personal judgements; but the bulk of her account is either independently confirmable or at least highly plausible. That goes not just for family details (like Cosima's habits and history, the oddities of the 'aunts', the pranks of the 'gang of four') but for the behind-the-scenes revelations about the festival itself before and especially during the 'Third Reich'. When Frida Leider got hold of the book, in its less than ideal German

17 Bayreuth harmony, 1950. Wolfgang with his first wife Ellen née Drexel, a ballet dancer he met in wartime Berlin and who bore him two children. A retiring and delicate figure, unlike most other members of the clan, Ellen shunned conflict and sought no role in running the festival. She and Wolfgang were divorced in 1976 after 33 years of marriage.
18 Pleading innocence. A typically trenchant Winifred, flanked by her lawyer Fritz Meyer, holding forth at her 'denazification' trial in Bayreuth in 1947. The court found her to have been a Nazi 'activist' (the second highest category of offender) and ruled that she be stripped of 60 per cent of her assets. On appeal, the sentence was largely quashed a year later.

19 What now? Wolfgang (left) and Wieland ponder the future outside their bomb-damaged home *Wahnfried* in 1948. As so often, the practical Wolfgang looks upbeat while his chronically-sceptical elder brother seems to doubt there will be much of a future worth working for.

20 Briefly happy families. Gottfried and Eva (right), Wolfgang's two children, romping in the garden at *Wahnfried* with Wieland's four (from the top of the ladder) Wolf Siegfried, Iris, Nike and Daphne. Later Wolfgang forbade his kids to play with the others, evidently feeling his brother's brood acted like hooligans.

21 In waiting. Wolfgang's little son Gottfried (left) and Wieland's Wolf Siegfried ('Wummi'), four years his elder, pose like prospective 'masters of the house' before *Wahnfried*. Both seemed set to direct the festival one day, stepping into their fathers' shoes. But after Wieland's death in 1966, Wolfgang long ran the show himself, keeping all other claimants at bay.

22 Smile please. Friedelind Wagner (left), on her first postwar visit to Bayreuth in 1953, mounting the steps to the festival theatre with Winifred her mother. Although the two are beaming here, relations between them were usually tense and often explosive. Above all, Friedelind came to despise Winifred's Hitler fixation and finally fled into exile (above).

23 Perfect (Wagnerian) profiles. Friedelind had more in common with her grandfather Richard than a prominent nose and jutting chin. Musical, plucky, forceful with an often biting tongue, she might well have run the festival the 'Master' founded. But she ignored invitations to come back to Bayreuth from US exile immediately after the war, and when she finally did return her brothers were running the show.

24 Checked. The 'outsider' Tannhäuser, as vulnerable as a pawn on a chess board as he faces judgement during the (Act 2) singing contest in Wartburg castle. This scene from his 1954 production helps show how Wieland Wagner with skeletal sets, creative lighting and judicious placing of the protagonists could, time after time, capture onstage the essence of his grandfather's music.

25 Love goddess. Anja Silja, every inch a golden Venus, looking implacably irresistible in Wieland Wagner's 1964 *Tannhäuser*. For Anja, then aged only 24, this was her fifth season in Bayreuth following her sensational debut there as Senta in *Fliegende Holländer*. She was also working with Wieland in other productions across Europe from Berlin to Naples, and the two had long since become lovers.

26 Husband and wife team. Gertrud Reissinger, Wieland's childhood sweetheart, married him in 1941 and bore him four children. A talented dancer and choreographer with a decisive manner, she had more influence on her husband's career than rivals cared to acknowledge.

27 High hopes – dashed. Wieland's trenchant daughter Nike, a fierce critic of her uncle Wolfgang's marathon rule on the 'Green Hill', preparing to make her bid for the festival directorship. With Elmar Weingarten (right), manager of the Berlin Philharmonic Orchestra, she drew up a wide ranging reform plan but it failed to win the crucial backing of the Richard-Wagner-Foundation.

28 Soulmates. Wolfgang's son Gottfried, increasingly repelled by all he gleaned about Bayreuth's role during the 'Third Reich', enjoying New York in 1978 with Lotte Lenya, widow of the German-Jewish composer Kurt Weill (left). 29 Thwarted heiress. Eva Wagner-Pasquier, Wolfgang's daughter by his first marriage, was fomally chosen in 2001 to take over from her father as festival director. But Wolfgang simply refused to cede his place to her at that time.

30 Festive trio. Wolfgang in buoyant mood with his second wife Gudrun (left) and their daughter Katharina, born in 1978. When the board of the Richard-Wagner-Foundation rejected Gudrun's bid in 2001 for the festival directorship, Wolfgang decided to stick to the top job – until his 'Kati' was ready to take over.

31 Time papa, please. Katharina, putative heiress to the festival directorship, deep in pow-wow with her father Wolfgang – master on the 'Green Hill' (initially with his brother) for more than half a century. After hedging her public comments for years, Katharina finally admitted in 2007 that she would like to take on the festival job 'if the conditions are right.'

translation, she read it with 'great interest and joy' and judged it 'very honest'. At least that is what the veteran soprano, who had been through such peaks and troughs in Bayreuth over many years, told her 'dearest Mausi' by letter from Berlin in 1946.[6] It is unlikely that Frida would have gone out of her way to report so positively, even to flatter an old friend, had she really found the book mendacious or gravely error-prone.

As for Friedelind's by turns chilling and hilarious descriptions of Hitler – his theatrical rages and comic imitations, his abrupt switches of mood from charm to venom, his odd nocturnal and eating habits – they may well have seemed fanciful to some readers. But other accounts issued over the years, including the memoirs of foreign diplomats and members of the Führer's own entourage, go far to confirm that the bizarre picture drawn in *Heritage of Fire* is not exaggerated. Nor is it true, as sometimes claimed, that Friedelind's tale became distorted in the course of collaboration with Page Cooper, an American writer who helped prepare the manuscript for publication. Much of what appears in *Heritage of Fire* had already been revealed by Friedelind (albeit in less fluent English), either in the press or to British and American intelligence, well before she got down to completing her book in New York. There *are* a few discrepancies between the account in *Heritage* and the one in the transcript of Friedelind's American debriefing, but they can probably be ascribed to the failure of the intelligence official concerned fully to grasp what he was told.

If Friedelind's intervention did not imply that she was disowning her book, why, then, did she intercede on behalf of her mother at all – and then only at the last moment? Later she referred vaguely to her motive as a disinclination to 'kick a person when she is down', which was no doubt true but hardly goes to the heart of the matter. Mausi, remember, had been at (often violent) odds with Winifred since early childhood. As a young woman she had come to despise her mother's unwavering support for Hitler and – perhaps above all – she resented the emergence of Tietjen as an, in her view, wholly inadequate *Ersatz* for her beloved father. Her resentment was all the greater because she believed, rightly or wrongly, that a far more appropriate suitor had been in the offing after Siegfried's death but that the chance had been missed. In a letter to an American friend, Friedelind claimed that during his Bayreuth days Toscanini had fallen 'madly in love' with Winifred (despite her 'Nazi passion') and later regretted that he had not plucked up the courage to start an affair with her. 'I regret it almost as much or more so,' Friedelind added, 'because things might have taken a different turn in that case!'[7]

Reasons enough, one might think, for a triumphant Friedelind to relish Winifred's post-war plight, with the Führer dead, Tietjen remarried to a ballet dancer and her trial looming. No doubt the daughter who had been through so much for her convictions really did enjoy being proved right at long last – but that was surely not all she felt. Her relationship with her mother was far too complex for that. In one revealing passage of *Heritage of Fire*, Friedelind describes a fierce confrontation just before leaving home in 1938 for what turned out to be years of exile. Before retreating to bed, Winifred accused her daughter of bringing disgrace to the name of Wagner by associating with 'international Jews and traitors' and vowed never to 'let you out of my sight again'. Recalling the scene years later, Friedelind wrote:

That was the memory of her I carried away, beautiful and flushed and unforgiving. At midnight I slipped out of Wahnfried as though I were a thief, not a daughter, and . . . wondered what was this fierce emotion that we aroused in each other. Under the storm and fury there was respect, I knew, and admiration.[8]

Respect and admiration? Perhaps Friedelind was implicitly admitting how similar she and her mother were in strength of will and lack of tact, despite all their differences on politics and people. Indeed, wasn't it exactly because the two were so alike in character that time after time their disagreements blew up into 'storm and fury'? As for Winifred, she surely did feel baffled respect for what she later acknowledged to be the 'enormous sense of justice' of her unbudgeable daughter.[9] Respect, though, was far from enough for Friedelind. She sought the love she had enjoyed for years from her father and that her mother so rarely showed, maybe could not really feel. In her book, Friedelind recalls being embraced on a few occasions when Winifred was distressed and herself looking for solace, but the moments quickly passed and the stage was set for the next row. Mausi's correspondence home tells a similar tale of hopes briefly raised by this or that warm remark from her mother only to be quickly dashed. 'How can you stand by and let your best friends spread slander after slander about me,' she bewailed to Winifred in one letter from abroad just before the war, 'at the very moment when I receive evidence of your motherly affection?'[10]

If Friedelind had loved her mother wholly, without reserve, it is hard to see how she could have gone ahead with publication of *Heritage of Fire* – however strong her belief that the truth about Hitler and the Wagner family ought to be made known. Although the 'Mistress of Bayreuth'emerges from the account not as personally evil but as blinded by her friend 'Wolf', it must have been plain to the authoress that she was – at the very least – doing her mother no service. On the other hand, if Friedelind had simply despised Winifred she would have left post-war justice to take its course. Instead, her feelings were at least as intense and contradictory as ever: fury and frustration on one side, unwilling admiration and the hope of love on the other. Given that inner turmoil, Friedelind's sudden bid to help her mother after so long a silence seems more understandable – but it was not the only reason why she acted as and when she did. Another was her long-protracted uncertainty about her status in America.

In the introduction to *Heritage of Fire*, Friedelind notes that she flew into New York from Buenos Aires with Toscanini on a summer afternoon in 1941 and at 'nine o'clock the next morning I made application for my first American citizenship papers. Again I will belong. How good it is to have a country in which one can work and breathe and live in amity with his neighbours, only those can know who have experienced the other kind of life.'[11] What Friedelind did not make clear when she wrote those evidently heartfelt words is that in 1945 she had still not been granted full US citizenship, despite her manifestly anti-Nazi stance, of which her book was only the latest evidence. Until her papers came through her situation remained shaky. She was odd-jobbing, near-broke and light years away from realising her aim to found a US opera company – a scheme that, if successful, stood to consolidate her claim to the throne in a rebuilt, denazified Bayreuth.

Meanwhile Winifred, with her widely publicised post-war praise for Hitler 'as man and music connoisseur', seemed almost to be going out of her way to confirm the picture of her drawn in *Heritage of Fire*. Small wonder, in the circumstances, that Friedelind did not choose (and perhaps at that stage did not feel the urge) to speak up on behalf of her defiantly unrepentant mother. In a solitary interview with the *New York Times* in April 1947, she even claimed that although she sent her siblings CARE packets, which was true, she had not written to any of them since the war, which was not.[12] Apparently she still sought to avoid even a hint of collusion with those who had not turned their backs on Hitler as she had done. Just two months after that interview, on 9 June 1947, Friedelind became a US citizen at long last.[13] All her efforts on Winifred's behalf came between that date and the start of the *Spruchkammer* hearing sixteen days later.

Suppose those citizenship papers had not come through until later. Would the daughter just have stood by and watched as the mother went to trial? It seems very likely. As the years passed, Friedelind evidently yearned more than ever to become a US citizen and shunned anything that might even remotely have told against her. Despite often menial jobs and chronic lack of cash, she had come to see America as her new home – one could say her 'real home' – and she was determined to be adopted by it, no matter what. With her enthusiasm and lack of guile she won friends (and foes) easily; she found in New York a variety and frisson she had not encountered before, even in London; and she was, she admitted, simply overwhelmed by the quantity and quality of the music-making on offer.

In a (seemingly unscripted) radio broadcast on 'Music in America' that she later made during one of her visits to Germany,[14] Friedelind's words tumbled over one another as she introduced stage works by – among others – Alban Berg and Benjamin Britten, recalled peerless recitals by artists like Rudolf Serkin, Adolf Busch and the late Sergey Rakhmaninov, and extolled orchestral concerts under Serge Koussevitzky, Dimitri Mitropoulos, Eugene Ormandy, the young Leonard Bernstein and, of course, Toscanini. She was critical of the Met – too much a 'society affair', too vast and 'plushy' for the good of singers – but stressed that the regular opera broadcasts from there reached an audience of millions. As for Carnegie Hall, she so often haunted the place for rehearsals as well as performances that the doorman had proposed she move her bed there. 'I'm often asked in Germany whether I really like life in America,' Friedelind noted at the start of her hour-long talk. 'The answer is – I do, madly.' She certainly looked as though she thrived on it, as those who had known her back in the 1930s noted with some wonder. Gone was the plump, moody tomboy; in her place a far slimmer, self-assured blonde with a ready smile and chic apparel that would have turned heads in Berlin, let alone Bayreuth. The sharp tongue, admittedly, was much the same as ever.

Partly through force of circumstance, partly thanks to her own temperament, Friedelind thus became the Wagner family's first real cosmopolitan – or at least the first after grandfather Richard, who had also knocked about a lot, had likewise fled into exile and in his last years, it will be recalled, had pondered settling in America. Whether he would really have taken to the life there and been given the support he felt he lacked in Europe is quite another matter. As for Siegfried, he was drawn to all things Italian but never broke with Bayreuth, and neither Winifred nor her children, Friedelind apart, knew much of the world beyond Germany. While Wieland struggled with less than full success to escape the Bayreuth-centred orbit into which he was born, Wolfgang evidently felt no impulse to try. Verena with her brood down by the Bodensee became a marginally more distant satellite – but a satellite all the same. Would the spirited Mausi, 'on the road' more or less continuously since that first spell at a Yorkshire boarding school in 1930, really have been content to renounce her beloved New York for a life in provincial Germany – even if it had meant fulfilling the role for which she felt her father had destined her? It is hard to imagine. By 1947 at the latest it was manifestly hard for Friedelind herself to imagine. In her *New York Times* interview that year she confirmed that she felt 'an obligation to save' the Bayreuth festival but also stated flatly that she planned to make her permanent home in America.[15]

In other words, Mausi hoped to have her cake and eat it. She must have had at least an inkling that this was unrealistic, but at that stage she did not believe the festival could restart for another decade and in the meantime her top priority was to get an American opera company of her own on the road. Even if, though, she had been right about the Bayreuth timing and her US plan had succeeded, in the long run the festival could hardly have thrived under a director absent for much of the year. Perhaps Friedelind really aimed to share power with Wieland or even with both brothers – she using her international contacts mainly from New York to drum up singers and conductors, they dealing with the production and business side on the spot. On paper that might have looked like a clever solution; in practice, anyone aware of the family's recent history and the abrasive characters involved would have known that such a trio would be unable to harmonise for long. As it was, the Wieland–Wolfgang duo alone had a job to stay in tune.

Family strains apart, Friedelind surely had qualms about how she would react to the shamed and shattered land of her birth and about how most Germans would react to her. Notwithstanding the urgent appeal from Bayreuth's well-meaning mayor to her (and Beidler) to return, she could not expect to be welcomed by all and sundry as the plucky, politically uncompromised young Wagner who had suffered for her convictions and hence deserved the top festival job. More likely she would be looked at askance – not by everyone but very likely by most, as a drifter who had turned her back on her country and who had had the luck to choose the winning side. That the buoyant young lady breezing in from New York had turned out to be right about Hitler would not increase her attraction. Rather, her very presence would seem aggravating to the many who did not want to have their consciences jogged and who felt that they were suffering enough anyway. Officially the 'new Germany' (not to mention the occupation authorities) would be on her side. Unofficially, she seemed bound to run into intense hostility.

A foretaste of what might well await her, and exiles like her, had come immediately after the war in a widely publicised battle of words between Thomas Mann and others – notably writers – who had failed to leave the 'Third Reich' during the Nazi era. What began as a more or less civil exchange, with an appeal from an ex-colleague[16] in an 'open letter' to Germany's most famous living author to return home from America, soon became a bitter shouting match in which neither side gave quarter. Mann, who had for years written and broadcast attacks on the Nazis from exile, did not even try to hide his contempt for those who had failed to take a similar stand. In his long reply sent to an Augsburg newspaper, he argued that if the whole of Germany's intelligentsia – writers, musicians, teachers, and so on – had shunned the regime at the start, had gone on strike or into exile, things could have taken a different turn. As one who had watched 'the witches' sabbath' from afar, it was now hard for him to reach an understanding with those who had danced along with it and 'paid court to Satan'.[17]

That broadside naturally brought a counterblast, especially from writers who argued that they had gone into 'inner emigration' – sticking it out in their benighted 'Fatherland', refusing to produce propaganda and even, so they claimed, taking judicious snipes at the Nazis 'between the lines'. What raised hackles most, though, was Mann's assertion that books printed in Germany between 1933 and 1945 ought to be pulped because they stank of 'blood and shame'. It was all very well, outraged scribes retorted, for the renowned Thomas Mann to adopt a high moral stance from the comfort and security of his home in Pacific Palisades, California. Few other German writers had enjoyed similarly influential foreign contacts and financial means. Besides, some of Mann's own work had gone on being published in Germany for several years after the Nazis came to power. Did it too reek of 'blood and shame'? Maybe it was better if Mann, a US citizen since 1944, did not leave his new homeland after all. As one critic scoffed, the very sight of the rubble in Germany might mark so sensitive a soul for life.

Friedelind was undoubtedly aware of this exchange. She had contact with the Mann family in the US and besides, one person became involved in the conflict whom she had known well years before at 'home' – Tietjen's stage-designer partner in Bayreuth (and Berlin), Emil Preetorius. In that 'witches' sabbath' piece flaying Germany's intelligentsia, Mann had devoted one long passage to music and musicians – a world that he adored almost as much as that of literature, sometimes perhaps more. His sharpest barbs were aimed at conductors (he was surely thinking in the first place, but not only, of Furtwängler) whom he felt were guilty of an 'obscene lie' in claiming they had simply made music and fostered culture, although their actions served the regime's propaganda machine. That Beethoven's *Fidelio*, a work imbued with love for freedom and respect for human dignity, could have been staged and applauded at all in 'Himmler's Germany' he found simply disgusting. Almost in passing, Mann also noted sarcastically that more honourable activities were conceivable than creating Wagner décor 'for Hitler's Bayreuth'.[18] He did not specifically name Preetorius and compared with the rest of his tirade the comment was mild – perhaps because he and the accused had struck up friendly relations more than two decades before. Still, there was no doubt whom he meant.

Deeply hurt, Preetorius wrote a long reply to Mann, thought twice about sending it but finally did so all the same. He pointed out that he had neither joined the Nazi party nor in any way extolled its ideology or leaders, that he had never publicly or privately backed antisemitism and that, indeed, the Gestapo had opened his letters, tapped his phone and interrogated him because of his contacts with Jews. As for Bayreuth, he had first been singled out for work there by Siegfried

Wagner himself and he had made his debut on the Green Hill in 1931 – after Siegfried's death but well before Hitler came to power. Subsequently, in the years before the war, he had been invited to stage works by Wagner in Britain, France and Holland and to address audiences throughout Europe on topics from Chinese art to the origins of French impressionism. Was it likely, he asked Mann rhetorically, that he would have been thus treated had it been felt he was a propagandist for the 'Third Reich'? Preetorius added that he found it 'deeply shaming' to feel forced to frame such a self-defence and realised that, in the end, nothing was to be gained by it. 'Your heart has become hard,' he sighed, 'and your perspective from all too far away is necessarily distorted.'[19]

What Preetorius wrote about his career and his distaste for the Nazis was demonstrably true. Had he wished, he could have mustered a lot more detail to back it up, even raised the question of his betrayal to the Gestapo for which he suspected a jealous Wieland – the 'Bayreuth arsehole' as he called him in a post-war letter to Tietjen – had been responsible. In other words, he seemed to have good reason to reject the snide remark about him from one he had considered a friend. But Mann did not in the first place set out to attack this or that individual, particularly not Preetorius; he argued more drastically that it had been simply impossible to produce untainted work of true cultural value within the 'Third Reich', even for genuinely talented and well-meaning artists, let alone for the mass of blatant propagandists and mediocre opportunists. However fine the painters and writers, however professional the singers, producers and stage designers, their achievements could not help but lend spurious lustre to an abominable system. Indeed, the more accomplished the creators and performers, the more they contributed to the fiction that German humanism not only survived but thrived in Hitler's state. Not that Mann only had members of the 'intelligentsia' in his sights, although in this case they attracted his main fire. In his view everyone was tainted who had helped stabilise the regime. That firmly included not just the active supporters but also those who had shrugged off the crimes – the good citizens who, as Mann implacably put it, went about their business in a seemingly honourable way and tried to ignore the stench of burning human flesh from the death camps.[20]

At odds with all those Germans who deplored his 'distorted' views about the 'Third Reich', Mann – once the embodiment of bourgeois conservatism – ironically also ran foul of the cold war's ever-mounting anti-communism. After visiting Germany in 1949 he was attacked, not least in America, for receiving a literary prize in Weimar, the town that had once been home to Goethe and Schiller but that now lay in the Soviet zone. Shocked by what he called a 'hysterical, irrational and blind' campaign that, fanned by the Congressional Un-American Activities Committee, spread across the US to engulf far more liberals than dyed-in-the-wool communists, Mann finally retreated to Switzerland and died there in 1955. Few other exiles from the world of the arts had a better time of it. Some, like the philosopher Theodor Adorno, did indeed manage to establish themselves in the newborn Federal Republic and others, like the writer and dramatist Bertolt Brecht, settled in the so-called 'Democratic Republic' in the east, although they found life under the Soviet thumb no easy option. But many could not bring themelves to return at all and some of those who did, like the novelist Alfred Döblin, left again in disappointment.

Friedelind was one of those who became a commuter between the New World and the Old. Advance word that she was planning to return to Bayreuth in 1953 for her first visit in fifteen years naturally aroused mixed feelings among the rest of the clan; intense curiosity, some joy (notably in Verena's case) and much foreboding. Would she try to muscle in on running the festival – a particular worry to Wolfgang who already felt that Wieland's wife Gertrud wielded too much influence on the Green Hill as adviser and choreographer? Would she bring up the 'Third Reich' and crow over her role at the expense of her mother and siblings? In the event the family reunion went off well enough, as though everyone, even the trenchant authoress of *Heritage of Fire*, had decided in advance to skirt 'awkward' topics. Cheeks were kissed, toasts were offered, the new generation of little Wagners was comprehensively cooed over by the glamourous auntie who had mysteriously popped up from America. From photos snapped at the time – one in particular showing a beaming, elegantly attired Mausi on her way to a festival performance with a similarly radiant Winifred at her side – you might think that the whole nightmare of the 'Third Reich', of flight and exile, of 'destruction and extermination' had never been.

For Friedelind, though, the full story was far less cheerful than those snaps suggested. Hardly had she settled in at Bayreuth than the vexed affair of the von Einem jewellery she had received in Switzerland and pawned in America came back to haunt her. She had long since told her ex-boyfriend Gottfried what had happened to the jewels and why; but once she set foot on German territory she was promptly served with a demand for full compensation by lawyers for Gottfried's mother Gerta Louise von Einem, that 'dashing baroness' who had also been a *grande dame* of espionage.

Just what 'full compensation' meant was a question that plagued German courts and titillated the press for years. Some speculated that the amount owed could be so vast that Friedelind would only be able to muster it by putting in hock the share due to her of the Bayreuth inheritance.[21] The accused herself maintained that the jewels had netted her no great sum, hence her continued hand-to-mouth existence in New York. She also claimed that before her flight to London from Switzerland in 1940 the von Einems had armed her with a power of attorney, to be used in extremity, over a bank account they had amazingly managed to keep in Britain even in wartime. Friedelind said that she had at no point made use of this freely offered safety net but, despite a search in London in 1954 in which both the police and MI5 became involved, she was unable to dig up documents to back her story.[22] For outsiders, and probably most insiders, the affair of 'Von Einem against Friedelind Wagner' soon became as baffling as most other things in the baroness's chequered history. In the end, Friedelind was sentenced to pay compensation amounting to five thousand US dollars and eighty-two British pounds (with interest) – no fortune, but for the perennially impecunious Maus no negligible sum either.[23]

That marathon legal scrap did not mean the von Einems shunned the Wagner family as a whole (although Gottfried came to do so later). On the contrary, as early as June 1951 the baroness had visited Wolfgang to propose using her manifold contacts in politics and business on the festival's behalf. At that stage she was already aware of the fate of her jewels but, according to Wolfgang, she agreed from the outset that her claims on Friedelind could have 'absolutely no bearing' on her support for Bayreuth. Not surprisingly, her offer was snapped up. Cash for the festival was still desperately short and Friedelind from afar had, in public and private, fiercely opposed raising more by selling off some of the Master's manuscripts – one course repeatedly mulled over by Winifred and her sons. When Wolfgang asked the baroness whether she might even be able to prise aid out of the federal government in Bonn, although public responsibility for cultural matters lay first and foremost with the provincial states, she inscrutably replied 'We shall see what we shall see.'[24] Was it just chance that a year later Bonn made its first (but far from last) grant to the festival – a total of close to a quarter of a million Deutschmarks used to renew the stage lighting system? Whatever the background to that particular transaction, it is sure that the baroness's unsurpassed skill as a puller of strings lay behind a stream of donations for Bayreuth from all sorts of sources throughout the 1950s.

If Friedelind had loved or at least admired what she saw of the Federal Republic from the start, if she had believed that the new state was, even in embryo, the kind of Germany she and other Nazi foes had yearned for, perhaps she would have settled in the 'old country' and fought harder to run the festival after all – her attachment to America and her court battle notwithstanding. Later, indeed, she would constantly return to Bayreuth, mainly to run a series of masterclasses (of which there will be more to say). She got on with Wieland and was close to Verena, who seems to have been the only family member to feel her sister deserved backing in the von Einem affair. But the truth is that, on her every visit, she could hardly wait to leave again – not just her provincial home town but the country as a whole. Her letters make that painfully clear.

'Bayreuth has a crippling impact on the psyche, on the spirit, on the body, really on the whole person,' Friedelind wrote to a friend in America. She elaborated:

> I simply yearn to get 'out' again – I mean from the whole of Germany . . . it is like reliving the bad dream BEFORE my emigration. One is shocked to see time and again that basically nothing at all has changed – least of all the people! That thin veneer of political polish applied thanks to the occupation has long since been washed away by 'sovereignty' – and to have been a Nazi is once more exactly what it was ten years ago, NOT to have been one . . . It is depressing and horrifying.[25]

Harsh words; even harsher than those the outraged Beidler had used about the resumption of the Bayreuth festival 'as though nothing has happened' a mere six years after Hitler, and on the face of it hard to justify. On the contrary, there seemed more to praise than curse about the buoyant new (western) Germany, rising from the ruins with almost none of the inbuilt flaws of Weimar, let alone of the 'Third Reich'. As a federal state with a wisely framed constitution, the fledgling republic enjoyed a thoroughgoing devolution of power that arguably harked back to the regional diversity of the pre-Bismarck era – but without the worst drawbacks. The federal parliament, for instance, was made up of two chambers – the *Bundestag* (representing the nation as a whole and elected by universal suffrage) and the *Bundesrat* (representing the regional *Länder*) – that governed through a more or less amicable tug-of-war. Beyond that, two independent institutions in particular set limits to the ambitions of power-hungry and/or greedy politicians: a *Bundesverfassungsgericht* (Federal Constitutional Court) that stood guard over the Basic Law, and a *Bundesbank* (first called the *Bank Deutscher Länder*) with a mission to keep the currency strong, above all by fighting inflation. Many non-federalists (like the British) wondered how such a confusingly multipolar set-up could work at all, but they comforted themselves with the thought that a German system with too many checks and balances was far more desirable than one with too few.

Moreover, the country seemed lucky from the first with its political leadership: the veteran Konrad Adenauer as chancellor, a shrewd Christian Democrat from Cologne with a strong anti-Nazi record and a special commitment to rapprochement with the old enemy, France; Kurt Schumacher as the main opposition leader, a charismatic Social Democrat who had survived years in concentration camps; and the learned, liberal Theodor Heuss as president, admittedly now a largely ceremonial office wisely shorn of most of the sweeping powers invested in it under Weimar. To say the least, early post-war Germany could have done a lot worse for its 'top trio' of national leaders. Psychologically and symbolically, too, the choice of unpretentious little Bonn as federal capital could hardly have been a happier one. From the start, the mere sight of the 'federal village on the Rhine' helped soothe those foreigners who arrived with qualms that Germany, already resurgent economically, might soon become too big for its boots again. The sleepy charm of the place did, it is true, bring some drawbacks. Once in a while official visitors would come late to appointments with the federal establishment grousing that their cars had been delayed by flocks of sheep on the road. Better that, though, than a punctual arrival under intimidating escort amid the mind-numbing bombast of 'the Führer's Berlin'.

Friedelind, then, was wrong to claim that 'nothing at all' had changed; but she was sadly on the mark with her charge that many Germans still sought to forget, ignore or explain away (not least to themselves) their real roles between 1933 and 1945. Despite all the immediate post-war efforts to mete out justice – like the thirteen showpiece Nuremberg trials of the Nazi 'elite' and the flawed but far-flung 'denazification' drive to punish the rank and file – German society in the 1950s was frankly riddled with ex-servants of the 'Third Reich'. Those who found themselves back with jobs and clout included bankers who had helped finance Hitler, industrialists who had helped arm him, professors who had given intellectual absolution to his racism, doctors who had gone along with the euthanasia of 'undesirables' – not to mention tens of thousands of civil servants who had been removed from office just after the war only to be amnestied a few years later. Adenauer himself drew some ex-Nazis into his cabinet and long employed Hans Globke, co-author in 1936 of a notorious official commentary on the Nuremberg racial laws, as one of his closest aides. As for judges who had handed down shoals of draconian sentences, often death, in dispensing what passed for 'justice' under the Nazis, hardly one of them was called to account in the Federal Republic. Broadly speaking, it was claimed that 'their Honours' had simply been applying the then law of the land – an argument notoriously underpinned in a keynote ruling by the *Bundesgerichtshof* (Federal Supreme Court) in 1956 and only revised four decades later. Ex-victims of Nazi courts might sometimes even find themselves up for trial before the selfsame judges who had sentenced them during the Reich.

Did this have to be? The unpalatable truth is that backing for Hitler had been so widespread, and so ardent at least until the war began to go badly, that it would have been hard indeed to find enough experienced people with a wholly untainted history to run the young Federal Republic. Besides, the new democracy faced challenges from both ends of the political spectrum; from the communists on the far left and from several small but fast-growing parties on the far right, the latter partly drawing support from among the millions of homeless refugees flooding in from the east. By urging an end to denazification – in effect offering a 'second chance' to those with a 'brown past' – Adenauer was able to kill two birds with one stone. He helped draw into the political mainstream (not least into his own Christian Democratic Union) many of those who, had they continued to be punished or shunned, might well have swelled the ranks of the neo-Nazis. That in turn created a sturdier bulwark against the communists, not just internally but vis-à-vis the Russians who claimed to be ready to accept a reunified Germany – but only in return for its neutrality. Adenauer distrusted Moscow's intentions at least as much as the western Allies did, hence his proposal that Germany rearm and place its forces at the disposal of European defence. Whatever qualms the Allies (and indeed many Germans) had about that scheme, the need for a German buffer against Soviet expansion outweighed them. That meant, among other things, making use of those who had served in Hitler's war and whose expertise could now be vital to the proposed new *Bundeswehr* (federal armed forces).

In retrospect, the best argument for this *Realpolitik* (one of those words, like '*Angst*', that came to be widely adopted by non-Germans) is that, against the odds, it worked. From a deeply unpromising start, with much about it that was depressing and even horrifying, as Friedelind said, a mostly prosperous state emerged in which extremists have never won national power, that remained firmly tied to the Western community of nations, and that achieved reunification by peaceful means after decades of confrontation. For all that thanks is fairly due to Adenauer – coolly calculating almost to the point of callousness – and to Allies who, whatever their motives and failings, did not impose crushingly punitive conditions on Germany as they disastrously did after 1918. But there was a price to be paid for this happy result. It is all very well to extol a policy of *Schlusstrich* – of drawing a line under a peculiarly disagreeable past so that people and energy can be freed to mould a better future. The trouble is that the past is not so easily disposed of. Those who leave skeletons in the cupboard should not be surprised when others, especially the inquisitive young, eventually dig them out and start asking tricky questions. That is what happened in Germany and, albeit falteringly, what happened in Bayreuth.

# 16

# Sins of the Fathers

Some time in the autumn of 1956 when his parents were on holiday, Gottfried Wagner, aged nine, managed to pocket a master key to the deserted Festspielhaus and set off alone, heart thumping, to explore the place. With its maze of passages, buried orchestra pit and cluster of outbuildings housing weird and wonderful 'props', the 'fortress on the hill' promised untold adventure to any child, but especially to Gottfried who had been strictly forbidden from playing there by his father, Wolfgang.

After snooping into every nook and cranny of the main theatre, the little boy unlocked the door to the old set-painting workshop nearby, padded up the dusty stairs inside and found himself in a junk-room-cum-archive. He poked into boxes filled with barely decipherable letters in old German gothic script, he recoiled on spying an oil painting of Hitler fondling a menacing Alsatian dog, and he pored over a huge plaster model of what seemed to be the Festspielhaus transformed. Only later did he learn that the model was part of the grandiose design, produced at the Führer's wish, for a kind of monumental, fascist Parthenon on the Green Hill – to be built as soon as Nazi Germany had won the war.[1]

Shortly before that escapade, Gottfried had seen film shots of the Nazi era that showed the Wehrmacht on the march, the mass adulation for Hitler and the corpses piled high at Buchenwald. But when he had sought to find out more, his father had told him he was too young to understand (a familiar chant throughout Germany in those days) and his granny Winifred had dismissed the scenes of mass carnage as American 'propaganda'. It was not until he was sixteen that he realised just how close the link had been between the Wagners and the

Führer. Poking about at home while his parents were again away, he uncovered reels of old film in rusty containers in the sidecar of his father's motorbike. Bit by bit he examined the footage with a magnifying glass and identified one member of the family after another, strolling about happily with Hitler at Wahnfried. As Gottfried recorded in his memoirs three decades later, Wolfgang, Wieland and much of the rest of the adult world suddenly came to seem sinister. He carefully replaced the containers where he had found them, hid the film material in his wardrobe and took to questioning his father with as innocent a face as he could muster about life in the 'Third Reich'. Much had been good about it, the sceptical youth was told, including Hitler's 'idealistic rescue of the Bayreuth *Festspiele*'.[2]

Perhaps in other circumstances – had there been no Hitler, no war and no Holocaust – Gottfried might have ended up as director of the festival, or at least co-director. In principle he seemed destined for the role. Born in Bayreuth in 1947 and raised initially in the gardener's cottage next to dilapidated Wahnfried, he was named Gottfried after the heroine's brother in *Lohengrin*, and Helferich after his grandfather Siegfried. Among the new generation of six Wagner children he and Wieland's son Wolf Siegfried were the only boys – and despite the Cosima/Winifred tradition, not to mention Siegfried's will, it was long assumed that when it came to taking charge on the Green Hill the girls would hardly be in the running. Besides, with his jutting chin, prominent nose and disconcerting tendency to switch from charm to fury in a trice, Gottfried came closer than any other member of the clan to resembling the Master himself. What else could he possibly do other than take over the festival?

The answer turned out to be pretty well anything, from producing opera (but never, one brief spell as an assistant apart, in Bayreuth) to selling shoes in Italy, from working in a Munich bank to writing a dissertation in Vienna on Kurt Weill – the German-Jewish composer of *Die Dreigroschenoper* (The Threepenny Opera), a piece whose aesthetic was light years away from the world of Richard Wagner.[3] In a clinch with his father from the start, shocked by what he uncovered about the Hitler connection, repelled by all antisemitism but especially Wagner's and bored by the provincial world of Bayreuth, Gottfried became a wanderer who until quite late in life lacked a real role. As for the exasperated and infuriated Wolfgang, he finally seemed to shrug off the son of whom, no doubt, he had once had high hopes, and did his best to ignore him. In his more than five-hundred-page autobiography he barely acknowledges Gottfried's existence. He writes little more about his daughter Eva – that baby born by candlelight in 1945 as the Americans marched into Bayreuth – but until his second marriage his relationship with her was relatively friction-free.

The Wieland children – Iris (born in 1942), Wolf Siegfried, known to all and sundry as 'Wummi' (1943), Nike (1945) and Daphne (1946) – had a far easier time of it, at least at the start. Like Winifred's 'dissonant quartet' back in the 1920s, they cavorted shrieking in the Wahnfried garden and clambered about the Festspielhaus more or less at will. At festival time they would be propelled, spick and span, into the family box, but as the day's performance wore on and on the bored little brats would start to whisper, tickle one another and giggle. Once in a while Wieland would react with a brief, fearsome burst of wrath, but in general he tolerated (or failed to notice) his children's antics and did not try to thrust the works of the Master down their throats. When Gertrud with her passion for dance proposed that the kids be given small parts in the music dramas as flower maidens (in *Parsifal*), Bacchic nymphs (in *Tannhäuser*) and the like, Wieland at first said no because the idea smacked of nepotism. In the end Gertrud won her point and the children, partly through their onstage involvement, partly through watching Wieland's rehearsals, gradually concluded that their great-grandfather's stuff was not so bad on the whole. Not that they often put records of Wagner on the turntable at home, and they virtually never did so when their parents were away. More likely, since the 'American way of life' with its petticoats, popcorn and pop music had percolated through even to the *Festspielstadt* in the 1950s, it would be the strains of Elvis Presley or Bill Haley and his Comets that thumped and twanged through the chambers of the house the Master built. Another favourite, something of an ironic choice in the Wagner family context, was German pop singer Heidi Brühl's sentimental ditty '*Wir wollen niemals auseinandergeh'n*' (We Never Want to Part).

As for Hitler and the Nazi era, the topic rarely came up in the Wahnfried household, not because it was taboo but because the children long assumed their dad had been on 'the right side' and therefore had no nasty secrets to conceal. When he mentioned the 'Third Reich' at all, Wieland did so either with evident disgust or bitter irony. Besides, didn't much of the press at home and abroad from 1951 hail him as the great innovator who by sweeping away traditional stage paraphernalia was creating a new and thought-provoking 'Wagner for our time'? Didn't he turn to left-wingers and Jews like Ernst Bloch and Adorno for inspiration, and encourage them to write for Bayreuth? To childish eyes, and even many adult ones, Wieland was thus a man of the present and future with no real past to atone for. Granny Winifred, on the other hand, had clearly been on 'the wrong side' – and still was. She talked to the Wieland brood about American 'propaganda' against Hitler, just as she had to Gottfried, and in her correspondence with old Nazi friends she would fondly refer to 'USA' – shorthand not for the United States of America but for '*Unser Seliger Adolf*' (Our Blessed Adolf). After moving back in 1957 from her Oberwarmensteinach 'exile' to the Siegfried-Wagner-Haus, thus becoming the closest possible neighbour to Wahnfried, she even took to giving tea parties for the likes of Emmy and Edda Göring (widow and daughter respectively of the former Reichsmarschall) and Ilse Hess (wife of Hitler's former deputy, languishing in Berlin's Spandau jail). Wieland warned his mother forthwith that he planned to build a high wall across the garden between her domain and his, and he was as good as his word. For the children it seemed plain who stood for the murky but evidently abominable past and who shunned it.

What, though, did Wieland really think and feel about his own role up to 1945? That remains largely a mystery. According to Wolfgang, neither he nor his brother needed to indulge in remorseful breast-beating over their personal records during the 'Third Reich'.[4] At any rate they did not do so. But every time Wieland went to and fro between Wahnfried and Festspielhaus he had to pass close to his former bolthole, the Lafferentz 'institute' linked to Flossenbürg concentration camp. Did he feel any shame or disgust as he sped by? If so, he bottled it up. Not only were few people aware that the new co-director on the Green Hill had worked at the 'institute'; the very fact that the place had existed at all was largely ignored or forgotten. It was not until the late 1980s that a happily inquisitive Bayreuth schoolgirl, Karin Osiander, jogged memories with details about the Flossenbürg offshoot that she unearthed for a history essay. Local journalists took up the topic and a thorough account by independent researchers was finally published in 2003.[5] Three years earlier the town of Bayreuth itself had got round to erecting a memorial plaque – inconspicuously sited on the fringe of a car park.

His own experience at the 'institute' apart, what passed through

Wieland's mind when he learned of the fate of those specially courageous souls who had dared to oppose Hitler: Pastor Dietrich Bonhoeffer, for instance, hanged in the Flossenbürg camp just before the war's end, or Hans and Sophie Scholl, Munich students guillotined in 1943? The Scholls were both younger than Wieland, but the leaflets they and other members of the *Weisse Rose* (White Rose) resistance movement covertly distributed were startlingly accurate about Nazi crimes, including the mass murder of Jews. Was the Bayreuth 'heir' less well informed despite (or perhaps because of) his special nearness to Hitler? Was Wolfgang? Or did they feel these were not matters of personal concern? After the war, or at least after 'denazification' had run its course, perhaps both brothers assumed that memories of the 'Third Reich' would steadily fade and embarrassing questions would become ever less likely. If so, that was an illusion they shared with many other Germans, especially in the 1950s – a comforting one, no doubt, but an illusion all the same.

Although Wieland spoke little of the all-too-recent past, his visible efforts to distance himself from it did not stop with his stage work. Venerable Wahnfried itself, still scarred and patched on the outside, had to yield within to the passion for clean lines and minimal clutter of the new Master and his hyperactive wife. Rooms were combined and made lighter, airier, the sofa given a bright new cover, family heirlooms banished to cupboards. The transformation may well not have been to Wolfgang's taste (let alone Winifred's) but the younger brother had no say in the matter, nor did he want one. He had set up house in the cramped quarters of the gardener's cottage well before Wieland returned to Bayreuth from his post-war 'exile' on the Bodensee, but he made no bid to take over the family seat or, later, even to share it. After a while he forbade Gottfried and Eva to play with his brother's children on the grounds that they were rowdy and foul-mouthed and in 1955, to general surprise, he bought a villa on the Green Hill just a few steps from the Festspielhaus. It was a typically shrewd move. Wolfgang seemed to be leaving his brother to 'rule the roost', but then Wahnfried still needed a lot of repair and was anyway expensive to run – in the long run probably *too* expensive. Leaving sentiment aside, and Wolfgang was anything but sentimental, the old place was frankly something of a millstone. With the new home that was to stay his base henceforth, Wolfgang placed himself strategically at the centre of the festival action and put several miles between his own family and his brother's across town; all Wagners, of course, but increasingly separated by parental enmity like Montagues and Capulets.

Did things have to go so wrong? On the surface, at least for the first few years, they seemed to be going very right. Under 'new management' the festival manifestly went from strength to strength – like the Federal Republic itself with its stable-looking government and burgeoning 'economic miracle'. By no means everyone approved of Wieland's productions or even of Wolfgang's less daring ones, but Wagnerians in Germany and far beyond had a fine time arguing fiercely about them and each year tickets became harder to come by. Already in 1953 average festival ticket sales reached eighty-six per cent of the house's capacity, and *Lohengrin*, Wolfgang's long-awaited first effort on the Green Hill, was wholly sold out. Funds from state sources as well as private sponsors were flowing in too, so that although more cash was still needed to renovate and modernise no one seriously suggested any longer that the show would not go on. For this success the brothers were initially given roughly equal credit. In fact, to most outsiders Bayreuth seemed to have the perfect team: Wieland the thoughtful, temperamental visionary, Wolfgang the good-humoured, level-headed business partner who, moreover, was no slouch on the artistic side. Lucky the enterprise, it was felt, that had such a tandem to run it!

For a host of reasons, professional and personal, that picture was too rosy by half. Even before 'New Bayreuth' was born, remember, Wolfgang had had cause to feel resentful of the big brother and 'heir' who had been dispensed from active service by Hitler, who had tried to flee abroad when the war was clearly lost and who for a time had seemed ready to make common cause with the 'treacherous' Friedelind. He, Wolfgang, had stuck to his post in Bayreuth in 1945, he had done most to head off the takeover bid by 'Cousin Franz' and he had stood down from artistic endeavour in 1951 to handle the business side. He dearly hoped to stage a production of his own the following year but Wieland had other plans and pushed them through with no real consultation. That set a pattern. The younger brother felt excluded from 'fireside chats' at Wahnfried on festival strategy and fumed that he was often left with the consequences when the plans went wrong.[6] By 1953 when Wolfgang was finally able to make his debut, Wieland had long since hit the headlines (and not only of the arts pages) with 'his' *Ring*, *Parsifal* and *Tristan*, the weightiest works in the Wagner canon. Wolfgang evidently hoped for advice on preparing 'his' *Lohengrin* but Wieland gave none, seemingly embarrassed that his brother was trying to make his mark on the Bayreuth stage at all. Aware of the tension between her sons, Winifred urged Wieland by letter to offer a helping hand because Wolfgang – 'the poor chap' – needed aid but could not bring himself to ask for it.[7] Her intervention achieved nothing. His mother was about the last person that Wieland felt disposed to heed.

If Wolfgang had clearly lacked all aptitude for theatre (as his foes inside and outside the family have often claimed), if he had limited himself to applying to the festival those managerial skills that would have taken him to the top in almost any business, the partnership with his brother would have been less fraught – albeit never easy. But since childhood, when he had pounded away in his workshop at home for a hobby, Wolfgang had been drawn to the nuts and bolts of stagecraft; he had learned a lot, mainly under Tietjen's tutelage, at the Berlin Staatsoper and in 1944 he had successfully produced one opera there himself (his father's *Bruder Lustig*). He might well have gone on to take charge of other pieces if the war had not forced the house to close a few months later. He was a tireless worker with an elephantine memory and for the most part he got on well with artists as well as stagehands. Naturally he wanted to show what he could do on his home ground, not just by balancing books but by facing up to the ultimate challenge of his grandfather's works.

Unfortunately for Wolfgang, he was up against a brother who from that very first *Parsifal* in 1951 was widely hailed as a theatrical genius – admittedly one capable of silliness and even perversity and not always quite as original as his greatest fans seemed to think. When Wieland trumpeted that the Master's music dramas had to be freed, above all through the imaginative use of lighting, from the 'sticky syrup' of traditional staging with its mediocre, naturalistic sets and slovenly routine, that sounded exciting, even shocking, to many Wagnerians descending on 'New Bayreuth'.[8] But it was very much what Adolphe Appia, so firmly shunned by Cosima, had been preaching well over half a century before and what innovative houses like the Kroll under Klemperer had practised – before the Nazis came to power. Even the Tietjen–Preetorius team had been more inventive in Berlin and Bayreuth than many post-war commentators, keen to put distance between themselves and the 'Third Reich', cared to acknowledge.

If Wieland, then, was not so much a revolutionary as a selective traditionalist with a restless mind, he was nonetheless one of the two most influential opera producers in Germany after 1945 (along with the Austrian-born Walter Felsenstein, who reigned for many years at the Komische Oper in East Berlin). At their best, his stark but symbol-laden stagings could haunt the memory as disturbingly and durably as the music they went far to match. Decades later many of the scenes he conceived were still the standard against which newer efforts tended to be measured and found wanting; the menacing outline of the wizard Klingsor in *Parsifal*, spotlighted in space like a white spider in a gigantic web; the phallic monolith towering above the doomed lovers in *Tristan*; the passionate 'outsider' Tannhäuser, dwarfed by the intimidating décor in the hall of Castle Wartburg and looking as vulnerable on the chequered floor as a lonely pawn on a chessboard. Wieland tended to shrug off Wagner's own, detailed stage directions as hints rather than instructions, but time and again people left the theatre feeling that what the grandson had shown them was what the Master must have *meant*. Nor was Wieland's success confined to Bayreuth. As his fame grew he became more and more busy in other houses, especially Stuttgart, and often in other repertoire – Gluck and Beethoven, Verdi and Richard Strauss, Berg and Orff. Wolfgang, for the most part, stayed at home minding the Bayreuth baby.

At times Wieland miscalculated. For one thing the lighting he favoured, especially in the early years, tended to be so subdued that key elements of the staging vanished in the gloom. Wags claimed the thrift-conscious festival was trying to save on electric power as well as scenery and in 1951, at least, there may have been something to that. More plausibly, in his single-minded drive to blot out all that was superfluous and force audiences to focus on the core of the dramas, Wieland indulged in overkill – led astray partly by the ultra-acute eyesight he had enjoyed from birth and honed as painter and photographer. He simply saw more than others did – more even than his close collaborator Paul Eberhardt, a veteran lighting technician with whom he worked exhaustively in the Festspielhaus, often right through the night. If old bulbs were exchanged between rehearsals for new ones of the same power, as like as not no one later would notice any change in the intensity of the lighting – bar Wieland who would start to fume and fiddle again with a scene that had seemed just right before.

That technical issue apart, Wieland's approach to staging Wagner was influenced by more complex factors to which he did not always admit. Clearly there was much in his grandfather's work he found not just superfluous but melodramatic and distasteful. When the critic Willy Haas asked him why he failed to show the end of the dramas as the Master had wished – no Senta leaping from a rock in *Holländer*, for instance, no swan arriving with a boat to bear off the hero in *Lohengrin* – Wieland responded that his interlocutor must have had a bad seat. 'I would have much preferred him to tell me frankly', Haas wrote, 'that the final scenes of many Wagner operas got on his nerves . . . and that he concealed as far as possible the culminating point.'[9] In *Meistersinger*, it was not just the final scene that got on Wieland's nerves but most of the preceding ones too. In his debut production of the piece in 1956 he removed so many signs of old Nuremberg that it would have been next to impossible for anyone to follow the plot who was coming to the work for the first time (and even in Bayreuth such people do exist). In his second attempt in 1963 Wieland put in more visual clues but, stretching the evidence of the score to breaking point and sometimes beyond, he drew the characters mainly as fools, boors or hooligans. He found several elegant explanations for these bizarre (non)realisations of what is usually seen as Wagner's most humane and naturalistic drama, but the most revealing one was that he wanted to avoid presenting *Meistersinger* as 'a dangerous mixture of Lortzing and the *Reichsparteitag*'.[10] In other words, here above all, he was trying to erase memories of the 'Third Reich' and almost certainly, although he naturally did not say so, to exorcise the ghost of his late benefactor 'Uncle Wolf'.

Finding the 'right' conductor proved almost as tough a task as achieving an 'ideal' staging. Ironically it was the veteran Knappertsbusch with his bias towards slow tempos and massive pathos, just the kind of thing Wieland eschewed, who appeared most often in the pit during the first years of post-war Bayreuth (ninety-five times until his death in 1965). This was a double irony, even, since Kna despised Wieland's productions – 'unprecedented nonsense' was one of the trenchant maestro's kinder descriptions – and boycotted the festival in 1953 because of them. He returned a year later, drawn by the 'spirit of Richard Wagner', as he put it, and thanks to coaxing by Wolfgang who thought more of Kna's approach than his brother did. On the face of it odder still, one of the conductors of Wieland's 1959 *Lohengrin* – for just three of a total of seven performances – was none other than Heinz Tietjen, making his first (and last) appearances in the Bayreuth pit since the *Kriegsfestpiele* of 1941. Had the 'heir' suddenly concluded that his former bitter foe, now Intendant (director) of the Hamburg Opera, was specially gifted with the baton after all? He had not. Two years earlier the canny old man had offered Wieland a production in Hamburg, one of the country's top houses, and in turn had extracted the pledge of a guest appearance as conductor in Bayreuth. Winifred, at least, was overjoyed.

Broadly speaking, Wieland favoured the lighter, lither sound – 'Wagner via Mozart', some called it – achieved by conductors like the seasoned Karl Böhm, the young Wolfgang Sawallisch and the (Belgian-born) Frenchman André Cluytens. The latter – significantly, as a non-German – was given charge of that first '*Meistersinger* without Nuremberg' and his passionate, propulsive *Tannhäuser* was judged by the Bayreuth boss to be without peer. Most of all, though, Wieland came to admire the avant-garde French composer and conductor Pierre Boulez, who surveyed the most complex of scores with a coolly analytical eye and who (although he had teething troubles in Bayreuth) could guide players through them with the skill of a traffic cop at a busy crossroads. The admiration was mutual. Perhaps if Wieland had lived longer his fledgling collaboration with Boulez, largely confined to a production of Berg's *Wozzeck* in Frankfurt in early 1966, would have flowered into a durable partnership.

Perhaps. Work with Wieland was never straightforward and it could end abruptly, with no thanks or even explanation given. Kurt Overhoff, once so close to 'the heir' and hopeful of a key *Festspiel* role, was coldly spurned early on – like Shakespeare's Falstaff when his erstwhile chum Prince Hal became king. Dietrich Fischer-Dieskau, post-war Germany's most renowned baritone, was not invited back after the 1961 season – apparently, he indirectly learned later, because he had argued with Wieland about his impractical headgear as Wolfram in *Tannhäuser*.[11] The conductor Joseph Keilberth, a festival stalwart in the early years, was dropped so summarily that he later looked pained at the very mention of Bayreuth.[12] It is true that to intelligent outsiders like Haas or the British publisher Victor Gollancz, who came to chat with him in his office between acts, Wieland seemed courteous and serene even if his work had just been hissed. Once in a while he would show real delight – when, for instance, he saw an artist had at last grasped what he wanted or that a scene he had long prepared seemed (at least for the moment) to be ideal. But to those who crossed or merely disappointed him he could be bitterly ironic and vindictive, his icy calm suddenly erupting in crude invective. Wolfgang was only one of many to suffer from Wieland's cynicism and scorn – but suffer he surely did. Even Nike, who adored her father and deeply admired his work, admits that she would not have liked to have had him for a brother.

Fame did not bring Wieland more equanimity; on the contrary, his exasperation seemed to grow with age and experience. Perhaps the more he grappled with his grandfather's works the more he felt persuaded (like Furtwängler at the end of his life) that the music had an emotional range no staging could adequately reproduce. Besides, with his new *Holländer* in the 1959 season he had served up once over all the staple dishes regarded as permissible in the Bayreuth diet (the *Ring* plus six others) and was about to embark on a second round. And then? Was the struggle to produce novel – let alone 'perfect' – cuisine with the same ingredients at the same table doomed to go on indefinitely, in harness moreover with a co-chef whose recipes he scorned? In a bid to pep up the menu he pondered bringing the Master's early *Rienzi* to the Green Hill for the first time, but after giving the piece, heavily cut, a trial production in Stuttgart he regretfully dropped the idea.

Growing artistic frustration with the Bayreuth straitjacket aside, Wieland badly needed more cash. He had a wife and four teenaged children to support, he faced the heavy costs for personnel and upkeep at Wahnfried and, unlike his mother and brother (but disastrously like his grandfather), he had no sense of thrift. When it came to staying in hotels, buying gifts or choosing clothes, only the best would do. As like as not Wieland would pay bills with a wad of banknotes that he drew almost absent-mindedly from a trouser pocket, as though signalling that 'there is plenty more where that came from.' There was not. His income naturally rose with his growing workload as an itinerant producer, but it failed to keep pace with his spending. Finally, in 1960 he tried to break free by applying for the post, quite prestigious and anyway steadily paid, of director at the Städtische Oper in West Berlin. The bid failed. Officially it was argued that Wieland would be unable to give the Berlin house the attention it deserved because of his

Bayreuth commitments; unofficially, rumours abounded of intrigue against him. Whatever the truth, Wieland would probably not have made a go of the job. Wolfgang had what it took to run a business, artistic or otherwise. His brilliant but moody, introverted, impractical brother did not.

Through all these peaks and troughs, Gertrud – adolescent sweetheart turned wife and mother, dancer and choreographer – was Wieland's closest, most enduring partner. Perhaps in the end she was also his biggest victim, although that description does scant justice to her role during much of a long and admittedly fraught relationship. Outsiders, even regular visitors to Bayreuth, usually underestimated the part she played – not surprisingly since she worked mainly in the background and her name popped up in the programme books, if at all, as a choreographer and (more vaguely) 'production assistant'. As for Wolfgang, he later insisted that there 'is no truth in Gertrud Wagner's recurrent assertion that she made an indispensable contribution to Wieland's productions'.[13] One can argue about the word 'indispensable' but Gertrud's role was undoubtedly a vital one, as Wieland himself acknowledged (albeit rarely in public). When a detailed account of his work was published in 1964, he handed his wife one of the first copies with the dedication, 'This should really be a book about *you* – without you there would be *no* picture and *no* concept.'[14] Nearly two decades before, early in the 'Nussdorf era', he had written that letter to her acknowledging that 'Without you I would never have found my way to the theatre.'[15] These were surely more than empty phrases. Wieland was never one to dole out undeserved praise, not even to Gertrud – perhaps especially not to her.

Of the two partners Gertrud was the more forceful and decisive – possibly the more independent-minded. It was she, drawn by her longing to make dancing her life, who had left Wieland and Bayreuth for Munich back in the 1930s; she who at the start of the war was already well on the way to a career of her own when Wieland was still dithering between painting and music; she who – from those very first productions in Altenburg and Nuremberg in the early 1940s – would time and again sweep aside Wieland's doubts with a brisk '*Das schaffen wir schon*' (We'll manage it all right). As in the cold, cramped quarters of the post-war Nussdorf chalet, so later in Wahnfried's spacious living room; the two would study scores together, swap insights, argue (often fiercely) – he usually sprawled in a chair, she prancing about showing how life could be breathed into a concept or an image.

Truth to tell, at the start of 'New Bayreuth' Wieland was still something of a novice, despite his stage experience in the war years. Astrid Varnay, his first Brünnhilde and Isolde, recalled that although 'he well knew what he wanted (seen pictorially) he was unable to show it to us physically. Each and every emotion was carried out with clenched fists, outstretched arms, straddle-legged . . . I, for one, couldn't imitate or make use of these gestures.'[16] Later, of course, he became far more adept, learning from the artists he chose and helped mould but also, in the first place, from his wife. It goes almost without saying that Gertrud in turn learned mightily from him; not just in Bayreuth but 'on the road' in productions at home and abroad. Even their holidays were 'working' ones, notably those they often took on the North Sea island of Sylt where the fierce gusts and the boom of breakers blew away cobwebs and fostered fresh ideas. The children on the whole were left to their own (de)vices.

No wonder Wolfgang, for one, looked balefully on this potent pair. Back in the 1930s and into the early war years he had got on well with Gertrud, sometimes – thanks to his sense of fun – better than the often sullen Wieland did. That had changed by the time the couple married, at the latest. Wolfgang began to feel, not without reason, that the ex-girlfriend was starting to 'take charge' of her new husband and to treat him, 'Wolfi', as the 'little' brother-in-law. '*Die Weiber lassen wir draussen*' (Let's keep the women-folk out), he tried to insist to Wieland, above all with a wary eye on Friedelind, when the two of them discussed restarting the festival after the war. In the history of Bayreuth, though, *Weiber* had never proved excludable for long. In the event it turned out to be Gertrud, far more than the long-absent Mausi, who took Wolfgang's place in an artistic partnership he felt by rights belonged to him; at least, she did until yet another woman burst on the scene and began to replace *her*, offstage as well as on.

Wieland's extra-marital affairs were long an open secret in Bayreuth. Gertrud got to know of them at the latest in 1954 when she returned early to Wahnfried from work on the Green Hill (rehearsing, as it happens, the erotic writhings of the *Tannhäuser* bacchanalia) and discovered her husband *in flagrante*.[17] She was surely hurt but she can hardly have been dumbfounded. Wieland had proved especially enticing to the opposite sex since his schooldays, he had often scorned the 'bourgeois' institution of marriage, he had continued to 'dilly-dally' during what amounted to his engagement and he had torn the ring off his finger immediately after the wedding. When finally caught out by Gertrud, he argued that as an artist he needed an 'open relationship' and encouraged her to seek the frisson of an occasional affair too. According to members of the family and close friends, Gertrud sought to follow this advice once in a while but the results evidently brought her little joy. For years she suffered from strange allergies and regularly consulted a psychiatrist. Throughout, though, she continued to work with her husband, if anything more intensively than ever, and seems to have assumed that his 'flings' would not threaten the special bond between them.

Nor did they do so, at least not until 1960 when the soprano Anja Silja – a former child prodigy from Berlin with boundless self-confidence, a strident voice and a cheeky tongue – breezed in to audition for the part of Senta in *Holländer.* Bayreuth was in a fix because Leonie Rysanek, the previous year's Senta, had pulled out and with only a few months left to the start of the new festival season no adequate substitute had been found. According to one version, fiercely rejected by Anja, it was Gertrud herself who persuaded a reluctant Wieland that the unlikely candidate, just turned twenty and with no Wagnerian stage experience behind her, would be simply ideal for the role.[18] Anyway the girl was hired. She sang Senta that summer, making one of the most triumphant debuts in Bayreuth's history, and later she and Wieland became lovers. Thus began a long liaison that with its mix of high passion and near farce – as well as phenomenal artistic achievement – gave as much fodder over the years to gossip columnists as to opera buffs.

Those who never saw *die Silja* perform on stage (she amazingly continued to do so into the new millennium) may well wonder what all the fuss was about. Her complete recordings of major roles are relatively few, but they are enough to reveal a voice that for lack of loveliness takes some beating. Wieland, for one, compared its metallic timbre to that of a child's trumpet. That, though, did not bother him – let alone the precocious Anja – and it would very likely not have bothered his grandfather, who set at least as much store by dramatic veracity as beauty of tone. For his very first Senta in 1843 (and his first Venus in *Tannhäuser* in 1845) the Master had chosen Wilhelmine Schröder-Devrient, a soprano whose acting he found so riveting that it more than made up for the fact that, as he once flatly put it, she had 'no voice'. Wieland clearly had this historical precedent much in mind. According to Anja, he signed and gave her a copy of what purported to be Schröder-Devrient's memoirs (only later discovering to his shock, she says, that the book was a pornographic novel issued under the great diva's name).[19]

Wieland was not the first seasoned professional to be enthralled by Anja'a talent and he was far from the last. Already in the late 1950s the young soprano had appeared before Georg Solti, then music director at the Frankfurt Opera and heading for world fame, to give what the maestro recalled decades afterwards as 'the most astonishing audition I have ever held'.[20] He engaged her on the spot. In the 1960s the veteran Klemperer insisted that she be the Senta in his recording of *Holländer* in London because 'musically and dramatically she is extraordinary'.[21] But it was Wieland above all who made Anja a star, drawing out of her in a phenomenal range of parts far more than even she thought she had to give. Within less than six years she took nearly twenty roles in close to forty of his productions – from Wagner's Brünnhilde and Isolde, Senta and Eva, Elsa and Elisabeth to Richard Strauss's Salome and Elektra; from Beethoven's Leonore (in *Fidelio*) and Verdi's Desdemona (in *Otello*) to Berg's Marie (in *Wozzeck*) and Lulu. She sang neither with the warmth of predecessors like Kirsten Flagstad and Frida Leider, nor with the heroically ringing tone of her contemporary Birgit Nilsson; but she habitually performed with such intensity and pathos that even her vocal idiosyncrasies seemed to be part and parcel of the roles she took – or rather, of the characters she became. In her prodigious ability to turn an apparent weakness into a strength probably her nearest rival was Maria Callas, except that Callas stuck mainly to the Italian repertoire, her stage career was ending as Anja's began – and she had no one constantly at her side with skill like Wieland's.

There was naturally a high price to be paid – professionally and personally – for this near symbiosis between Wieland and his *Wunderkind*. From the start, critics warned that by taking on such heavy and varied work so early in her career Anja would prematurely lose her voice for good. They were wrong but inevitably the pressure, intensified by the emotional stress of her affair with Wieland, *did* tell and she had to drop out of performances with embarrassing frequency – much to the delight, admittedly, of other aspiring sopranos for whom standing in for *die Silja* became something of a cottage industry. Such strains apart, even many well-wishers happy to acknowledge Anja's rare talent pointed out that she was neither faultless nor ideal for every role she took. Wieland, though, would not hear a word against her. Colleagues who failed to share his fixation tended to be ignored or dumped. When the Brussels Opera proposed taking someone other than Anja for a forthcoming *Tristan und Isolde*, he retorted that the house would have to do without him as producer. Brussels backed down. When Sawallisch, a Bayreuth mainstay for years, threatened not to conduct the planned new *Meistersinger* in 1963 if 'Fräulein Silja', were booked as Eva, Wieland simply shrugged. Sawallisch made good his threat and, indeed, never worked again on the Green Hill.

Anja claimed that the Bayreuth boss saw in her the Wagner type he had always sought – that of the self-sacrificing damsel ready to give up everything and endure everything thanks to her boundless love. Wieland himself was rather more explicit about what (artistic esteem apart) inexorably drew him to the vivacious nymph less than half his age. She was, he once wrote to her, just like the idealised girls of his early drawings – 'very long legs, blonde, red-blonde, somewhat ephebic (albeit with bosoms!!!!) – don't be angry, I'm long since over that stage.'[22] His feelings for her, he said, were in part like those of a father with a lot of Pygmalion thrown in. He might have added that, at the start anyway, she seemed so refreshingly uncomplicated: answering back at rehearsals when others treated him with a deference close to servility, shrieking with glee during games of mini-golf behind the Festspielhaus, joining in the raucous fun at a local beer festival. That he was widely seen as the victim of a classic mid-life crisis and was the object of countless nudges and winks, Wieland well knew. He was even able to look on his plight with a wry smile, comparing himself to a roaming Franconian bear of little brain that was rather fat, unstable and inclined to lose its hair with age. The beast could, however, be coaxed from its lair with honeyed words or perfume and it became amenable when stroked.[23]

If Wieland really did see Anja as wholly self-sacrificing then he deceived himself. Although she poured all her talent and many tears into the roles he fed her, that was not so much a sacrifice as the voracious embrace of a near-unique chance. Most young singers could only dream of such crucial backing and lightning fame at the start of their careers. It was not, though, stage success that Anja most yearned for, it was Wieland himself (though admittedly it was hard to disentangle the two). Convinced he was locked into a marriage that had long since broken down, she fought to detach him altogether from his wife with desperate energy but no lasting success. Gertrud continued her work with Wieland and was therefore constantly on hand, even for those productions 'on the road' in which, almost inevitably, Anja starred. Twice over on the sidelines of a fraught *Ring* in Cologne, the two women confronted one another and fruitlessly tried to 'clear the air'. Gertrud told her challenger to surrender and look instead for a nice doctor who was fond of music, advice that might be thought to show she had either lost contact with reality or somehow kept a sense of humour. In fact by this time she was plunging from bouts of furious activity to ones of deep depression, well aware that she was fighting not just for her husband but for her work – her life. Anja, needless to say, retorted that for her only Wieland would do.[24] For all her adaptability, the role of 'the other woman' was not one to which she was remotely suited – not even when it could be played out against more or less idyllic settings across Europe from Paris to Sorrento. Hotel rooms were no substitute for a shared base, let alone for a home.

Just once Anja spent the night with Wieland in his spartan bedroom at Wahnfried, an event she says both of them in retrospect judged 'uncomfortable and wrong'. She also stayed with him in the charming but impractical farmhouse on Sylt that he had rashly bought in 1963, in theory for Gertrud. The lady of the house was not present but her rival had the uneasy feeling that, somehow, she was. Nor did a bungalow near Bayreuth that Anja used for long spells before and during the festival turn out to be an ideal 'love nest'. Wieland visited her there often but rarely for long and never overnight. Furious at his premature departure she once pursued him back to Wahnfried in the darkness, constantly banging the front of her car against the back of his. Wieland sped on steadily as though unaware or uncaring, a typical reaction to her frequent tantrums and one that made her angrier still. Rarely, but then frighteningly, he too would explode – for instance on a nocturnal country drive during which Anja repeatedly refused money he offered her to buy a dress she coveted but thought too dear. Incensed, Wieland finally hurled the banknotes out into the gloom, stamped on the accelerator and bundled his dumbfounded mistress out at her door. That night she hardly slept a wink. Early the next morning, though, she drove back alone to the spot, found all the notes sticking to a field wet with rain and dumped the lot on Wieland's desk. He promptly bought her the dress and she kept it, like an heirloom or a trophy, ever afterwards.[25]

Maybe Wieland needed such *Sturm und Drang*, or thought he did, to stay creative; maybe it was in part what killed him. If it is really true that too much stress can prove fatal, then by the mid-1960s at the latest Wieland was a marked man. For all his work and fame beyond Bayreuth, he seemed chained indefinitely to sharing festival productions with a brother he regarded as inept. It may also be that, despite or because of his silence on the topic, he suffered inner torment over the specially privileged role he had enjoyed during the 'Third Reich'. That is quite feasible but, as matters stand, unprovable. He was surely plagued by the still heavier debts he had run up buying the house on Sylt, and in his emotional life, above all, he felt trapped. According to Anja, he latterly promised 'to think' about marrying her – she his Isolde, his Lulu, his *femme fatale* – but evidently thinking was as far as he got. Even when his four children, now young adults, begged him in a joint letter to end the anguish – with a divorce if need be – Wieland still could not make up his mind. He replied that he had as much 'love and esteem' as ever for Gertrud, that he also felt 'sincere' love for Anja and that he loved them, the children, above all. His inability to choose, he claimed, was born of sheer 'perplexity, not cowardice'.[26] Earlier he seems to have been just as 'perplexed' but in a letter to Anja he had put his position rather differently. While he could no longer live *with* Gertrud, he wrote, he could not live *without* her either.[27] In other words he felt there was no way out – or rather, only one.

In June 1966 an attack of nausea forced Wieland to break off a Bayreuth rehearsal and return to Wahnfried to rest. At the time no one panicked, least of all Wieland. He had suffered feverish colds earlier that year and, as usual, he had been working and travelling almost endlessly. He and others assumed the bout of weakness would pass and that he would soon be back preparing the season's offerings, especially *Parsifal*, in which Boulez was making his tensely awaited Bayreuth debut. They were wrong. After tests in a local hospital he was moved in early July to the Universitätsklinik in Munich for specialist treatment. For more than three months hopes were raised and dashed, plans laid and scrapped. It is unclear just when doctors realised there was no hope – that Wieland had a malignant tumour they considered inoperable and that invaded both lungs. At any rate the family was not told until the very end. Wieland, it seems, was *never* told but it is hard to believe he never guessed. Although he long used his hospital room like an office and was even able to take breaks – on Sylt, for instance, and in Anja's (usually empty) Munich flat – towards the end he coughed much blood and was confined to bed. He died just after four o'clock in the morning of 17 October, not quite three months before his fiftieth birthday. Gertrud and the children were with him.

As for Anja, she arrived at the clinic about an hour later by taxi from Vienna where she had been singing the night before in the premiere of a new production of Jacques Offenbach's *Hoffmanns Erzählungen* (Tales of Hoffmann).[28] Wieland had encouraged her to keep working, no matter what, and she had been busier than ever that year – taking half a dozen roles, large and small, in Bayreuth alone. She had snatched what time she could with him and had kept in constant touch by phone, but she too had not realised how serious his condition really was. Had she done so, no doubt she would have cancelled at least that Vienna engagement – in which case her life might well have taken a different turn. According to Anja, ten days before Wieland died the conductor preparing *Hoffmann*, André Cluytens, told her during a break in rehearsals that he was deeply in love with her. She confessed to feeling bowled over by this revelation. The elegant and charming maestro, whose skill on the podium Wieland himself so much admired, was a married man thirty-five years her senior. Did any of this percolate through to the patient in Munich? Indeed it did, because Anja phoned Wieland right away and told him. He heard the news with, she says, 'astonishment but understanding. Whether or to what extent he saw a danger in André's feelings I do not know. He did not need to because at this time there was no "advance" on my part.'[29] She admits that later her new suitor 'taught me what passion is', but their intense affair did not last long: André died just eight months after Wieland – of liver cancer.

Wieland's body was taken back to Bayreuth, first 'home' to Wahnfried for a day or two, then up to the Festspielhaus for what had all the trappings of a state funeral. Flags were flown at half-mast, the coffin at the front of the stage was almost smothered in wreaths, political and other dignitaries made speeches, the festival orchestra played Wagner and the chorus sang Bach. Brilliant organiser that he was,

Wolfgang got all that together, at Gertrud's behest, in barely four days. A suitable ceremony, most people thought, for so famous, so talented, so tragic a figure. It is doubtful whether Wieland would have agreed – he who had learned the hard way deeply to distrust pomp and circumstance, who had sought in his work to strip away all that was conventional and inessential. Later the same day, 21 October, he was buried in Bayreuth's municipal cemetery next to Siegfried – the father to whom in life he had never felt really close.

Shocked as they were, Gertrud and the children did not fully realise how vulnerable their position had suddenly become. They were soon to learn. Under a contract signed on 30 April 1962, the two brothers had pledged that when either of them died the other would take exclusive charge of the festival and pay the widow of the deceased a pension. This accord now took effect and left Gertrud with hardly a leg to stand on. Although she felt better placed than anyone to develop Wieland's artistic legacy in Bayreuth and elsewhere, she had precious little independent leverage, few effective allies and next to no money. Like his grandfather, Wieland had left no will, heavy debts and youngish offspring still needing financial support. In other words Gertrud found herself largely dependent on Wolfgang, the 'little brother' who had long deplored her 'interference' on the Green Hill and who had leverage in artistic circles far beyond Bayreuth. He stuck by his financial commitment to her but – unsurprisingly – massively opposed her efforts to step even partly into Wieland's shoes. Nor did she receive any backing from her mother-in-law. Winifred held that the festival now had to be run by a single, firm hand and threw her weight behind Wolfgang. Besides, she saw next to nothing in Wieland's (to her, mysterious and often repellent) productions that was worth preserving, let alone developing.

At first Gertrud and her brood still had the use of Wahnfried, but after a while they lost even that. Apart from the interim break after 1945, the old place had functioned as a director's residence and family home for nearly a century – from the days of the Master, through the Cosima, Siegfried and Winifred eras right up to Wieland's death. The new festival boss now put an end to this tradition. Although he had long since settled into his villa on the Green Hill and did not dream of moving down to Wahnfried, he did not want his late brother's family to be based there either. Arguing that the dilapidated pile had to be rebuilt as soon as funds could be raised, he put pressure on the occupants to quit. Winifred, firmly dug into her annexe behind the garden wall that Wieland built, fully agreed with Wolfgang. When the forester died, she shrugged, the forester's children just had to move out. In fact Gertrud and her offspring were usually absent anyway, she in the house on Sylt, they studying, odd-jobbing or starting careers far from Bayreuth. But for all of them Wahnfried had remained the common focus point, the tangible link to the past and especially to Wieland. Losing it was a blow that still smarted decades later. For the children, as Nike put it, it was as though a trap door had suddenly sprung open beneath their feet, pitching them into the unknown.

# 17

# End of Empire?

When Wolfgang took up the Bayreuth crown in 1966 at the age of forty-seven, next to no one dreamed he would rule for more than four decades – much longer than any of his predecessors from the Master and Cosima through Siegfried to Winifred. The new monarch himself, unexpectedly alone on the throne he had so far had to share, would no doubt have scoffed at the very idea. It was not even clear at the start that his kingdom would survive intact, let alone thrive. Wieland was gone and, like it or not, it was *his* work rather than his brother's that had proved the special draw for most of those who had flocked to 'New Bayreuth' since 1951. Would the crowds still come, even when those thrilling, shocking, ever-evolving productions had been phased out for good? For Wolfgang, Wieland dead and already a legend looked likely to prove still more of a challenge than Wieland living.

For the time being, it was true, the supremo on the Green Hill needed fear no serious challenge from the surviving members of the clan. Armed with the 1962 accord assigning him the succession should his brother die before him, Wolfgang was in a near-impregnable position; all the more so since he was backed privately and publicly by Winifred, still legal owner of the festival assets despite her (enforced) renunciation of the directorship seventeen years before. 'Little sister' Verena, mother of five and long resident by the Bodensee, had neither the ambition nor the experience to co-rule in Bayreuth. Wieland's gifted widow Gertrud had both, but she was vulnerable and could be held at bay. Franz Beidler in Switzerland – 'Cousin Franz' – was no longer even a distant threat. He continued to criticise the festival whose 'premature' post-war start under the two brothers he had so deplored; but he did not renew his bid for a say in running the show, and he would surely have foundered had he done so.

That left the pugnacious Friedelind, a regular presence especially after 1959 when she began running annual masterclasses on the sidelines of the festival. Winifred patronisingly welcomed these efforts on the grounds that they gave her 'problem' daughter something to do. Wolfgang glowered, fearing that his Atlantic-hopping 'big sister' aimed to muscle in on the festival proper via the back door. As it was, many outsiders assumed that thanks to her 'Bayreuth Festival Master Classes Inc.' (with offices in New York and the Festspielhaus) Friedelind had already become more or less a third force on the Green Hill. She had not, but for a time the success of her classes – probing every aspect of the art of opera from production and interpretation to history and architecture – suggested she might well forge a Bayreuth power base of her own at last. As even Wolfgang acknowledged,[1] she attracted outstanding speakers and coaches – from 'big names' like Pierre Boulez, Astrid Varnay, Walter Felsenstein and Gian Carlo Menotti, to experts on lighting, acoustics and psychoanalysis. Alongside the stream of lectures and workshops there were trips by minibus (often to the communist east) to judge rare fare like Prokofiev's *War and Peace*, Schoenberg's *Moses und Aron* – even Wagner's *Rienzi*, never staged on the Green Hill. Friedelind set a furious pace, selected the students herself and warned in advance that anyone interested in regular meals and sleep need not bother to apply.[2]

The Master himself, fierce advocate that he was of the *Gesamtkunstwerk* approach, would surely have favoured these efforts. A century before he had vainly urged King Ludwig to flank the building of a Festspielhaus with – just as important – the founding of a school, in the first place to train singers but later to foster all musical and theatrical skills. Cosima and Siegfried had each sought to follow up the idea but neither had got far: indeed the exaggerated 'speech-song' vocalism that the *Hohe Frau* had sought to impose through her Bayreuth 'style school' probably had her late husband turning in his grave. Friedelind with her interdisciplinary classes came closer to matching the original scheme, and she would no doubt have come closer still had she been able, as she dearly wished, to absorb the summer classes into an all-year-round training centre. As a permanent seat for the proposed institution the ambitious Mausi had her eye on nearby Schloss Fantaisie, that 'dream' castle with its superb park next to which Wagner and his family had first lived on their arrival from Tribschen in 1872.

Alas, as so often Friedelind's artistic aspirations outstripped her ability to raise cash. This was partly because she lacked a head for figures, partly because she favoured the American-style system of private sponsorship that was not readily transferable to the German – or European – context, in which public funding plays a far bigger role. Wolfgang scorned his sister's business naivety and in part he was right (although there would have been no Bayreuth festival, perhaps no Wagnerian music dramas at all, had the Master matched his own ambitions to his chronically empty purse). As for Wieland, whatever qualms he had about letting Friedelind gain influence on the festival itself, he had far more regard than his brother did for her talent and pluck. Besides, by the time her masterclasses began he was already looking for ways to reduce if not sever his own links with Bayreuth. When he died, Mausi lost not so much a real ally – the past had divided them too much for that – as an intellectual sparring partner whose questing spirit matched her own. Plagued by money troubles, her classes folded a year later – in summer 1967 – and she lost her only potential springboard, if not to the Bayreuth crown itself at least to greater influence at court.

Although he thus ruled the roost largely unopposed, Wolfgang faced a nagging question that could become urgent at any time: what would happen when his mother died? True, the 'old warhorse' seemed as sturdy as ever when she cantered through her seventieth birthday in 1967; but even barring bad illness or an accident it was hardly to be hoped, or feared, that she would survive into her nineties as Cosima had done. When she was gone the inheritance would be shared out not just between her three surviving children but with Wieland's brood too. Even if the trio of elders could reach accord on future strategy and finance for the festival, which was far from sure, there was no guarantee that the junior quartet, at odds with Wolfgang and chased from Wahnfried, would simply play along in harmony. Besides, as time passed the festival director became ever less hopeful that his own rebellious son Gottfried would 'see reason' and equip himself to take over one day on the Green Hill. In sum, with Winifred's passing the festival would probably face its end as a family enterprise – and might even sink altogether under waves of enmity. Happily for Wolfgang, his mother was at least as aware of the danger as he was.

*

Scraps between siblings, confrontation between young and old, unease about the future – none of that is uncommon, particularly not in a clan that has owned and run its own business for almost a century. But when Wieland died the Federal Republic itself was on the brink of a painful upheaval and, as so often before, the state of the Wagner family faithfully reflected the plight of the country at large. The reasons for the ominous and mounting tremors at national level were many, but an underlying one was economic. In 1966–7, after a decade and a half of mainly rapid growth, the country slid into a mini-recession with a small contraction of Gross National Product in real terms (after inflation) and the number of people out of work tripling to half a million. By the grim standards of later decades those woes look pretty mild, but for the land of the *Wirtschaftswunder* that had virtually defined itself throughout the 1950s in terms of surging production, exports and living standards the upset seemed dire. Chilling memories were revived of pre-Hitler Weimar, with its closely related economic and political chaos – all the more so since the Federal Republic's own democratic system had begun to look shaky.

The Adenauer era was over. The old chancellor had reluctantly stepped down in 1963 after fourteen years of office, sadly sure like so many aged autocrats that he had no fit successor – although, truth to tell, his own touch as government leader had become far from sure. The top job then went to Ludwig Erhard, a Christian Democrat who lacked Adenauer's iron but whose near-legendary economic skills seemed a guarantee that the boom of the 1950s would not go bust in the 1960s. Ironically, though, it was mainly thanks to a battle just three years later over how best to deal with a mounting budget deficit – itself linked to economic downturn – that the chubby, cigar-puffing chancellor lost power. At the height of the dispute the liberal Free Democrats stomped out of the government coalition in which they had been the junior partner, and Erhard lost his parliamentary majority. Wary of entrusting his own fate to the liberals, Erhard's successor, Kurt Georg Kiesinger, instead formed a 'grand coalition' with the Social Democrats – hitherto the Christian Democrats' biggest rival. That put the 'Sozis' into government power at national level for the first time in post-war Germany, but it also left the country with no parliamentary opposition to speak of. Conservatives hostile to making any deals with the political left moved off to swell the ranks of the far-right National Democratic Party, which was winning more support anyway as the jobless total grew. Left-wingers shocked by the 'sell-out' to the right began to desert the ranks of the Social Democrats and many, especially the young, took to the streets.

Two factors contributed mightily to this polarisation. The immediate one was the ('Ho-Ho-Ho Chi Minh') student revolt that swept much of the democratic world in the late 1960s, sparked mainly by the US intervention in Vietnam and fuelled by disgust over capitalism and 'bourgeois values' generally. In the Federal Republic this imported stimulus to youthful rebellion fatefully fused with a home-grown one – the intimidating 'grand coalition' and, in particular, its approval in 1968 of legislation giving the government special powers in a national emergency. Although the measure was circumscribed with parliamentary safeguards, many of its foes compared it to the Enabling Act that Hitler had used to win control of the Reich in 1933. It came, moreover, in an atmosphere made still more explosive by the death of a student, Benno Ohnesorg, shot by police during a demonstration in Berlin a year before. Not that the Berlin violence itself came as a bolt from the blue. It marked the (interim) climax of a long-growing confrontation between German youth and its elders – over many things but over the Nazi past in particular.

During much of the 1950s the question of responsibility for Nazi crimes had become ever less a subject of public debate or, seemingly, private concern. 'Denazification' as enforced by the victorious powers had come – and gone. The Federal Republic had joined the ranks of democratic nations and was needed as an ally; it had paid pretty heavy reparations, not least to Israel, and it felt rather proud to have risen from the ruins so soon. (Perhaps it felt prouder still to have won the 1954 football World Cup in Switzerland against all odds, an event recalled for decades afterwards as 'the miracle of Berne'.) Most Germans preferred to enjoy the goodies of the *Wirtschaftswunder* and draw a double line under what had happened before 1945, that time-barrier comfortingly defined as 'year zero'. If nonetheless forced to look back further, they could marshall plenty of reasons close to excuses for the birth and vileness of the 'Third Reich', from the fateful iniquity of the Versailles treaty to the bewildering speed with which the Nazis had moved to crush opposition once they were in power. Besides, it could be asked (but usually wasn't): hadn't the western wartime victors themselves appeased the Führer in the 1930s, welcomed his role as a 'bulwark against communism', even half-envied his ability to bring order out of chaos? Hadn't they and others failed to intervene decisively on behalf of the Jews even when the Nuremberg racial laws showed the way the wind was blowing? Such questions about guilt and responsibility were far from superfluous, but most Germans rightly realised they were not the ideal people to pose them – even in retrospect. Better, it was felt, to skirt the whole minefield in the hope that with time it would rust away to oblivion. Naturally there were those, among them a strong minority of trenchant authors and journalists, who deplored this attitude and fought against it, but the *Zeitgeist* was massively against them.

By the early 1960s, though, the mood was changing – in part because the outside world forced it to do so. For months on end in 1961, the painful past was literally brought home to millions of Germans via the high-profile trial in Israel of Adolf Eichmann, the SS officer who had organised the mass deportation of Jews to the death camps. Meanwhile communist East Germany was intensifying its written and verbal barrage against former Nazis holding key jobs in the Federal Republic. Although couched in puerile jargon and clearly meant to destabilise the 'ideological foe' in the west, many of the charges had too strong a basis in fact to be dismissed as 'mere propaganda'. They had, indeed, played a part in the enforced resignation in 1960 of Theodor Oberländer, the Bonn minister for refugees who was said to have colluded in war crimes in Poland. A few years before Adenauer could probably have shrugged off such a challenge to a member of his cabinet, but his power was on the wane.

Such outside pressure aside, the flagging domestic drive to unmask Nazi criminals had been given an unexpected boost in 1958 when the federal *Länder* agreed to set up a central office to coordinate their hitherto disparate investigations. The action was taken in response to a single particularly obnoxious case uncovered almost by chance; but as a result of it, and despite a subsequent decision by the Bundestag that broadly speaking blocked prosecution for Nazi crimes other than murder, the ugly face of the 'Third Reich' began to loom larger again in the public consciousness. It became virtually unignorable with the launching in 1963 of the first of the 'Auschwitz trials', in which more than two hundred of the camp's survivors testified in Frankfurt against those of their former persecutors who could be rounded up. In contrast to the Nazi ringleaders hauled before the Nuremberg tribunals nearly two decades before, most of the Frankfurt accused had been underlings in the chain of command. That, though, did not make their 'I was only obeying orders' defence and evident lack of remorse any the less shocking. If anything the very absence of a 'top person' as scapegoat helped underline how broad the connivance in brutality and slaughter had been.

All of this helped give a special, ultimately lethal, cutting edge to the youthful revolt in the Federal Republic in the late 1960s. In older democracies like Britain and France – even in an America agonisingly torn over Vietnam – an underlying attachment to the nation and its history survived all the demos and clarion calls to 'Marxist internationalism'. What, though, could young Germans find to be proud of about their *Vaterland* – a word likely to arouse embarrassment or contempt on the rare occasions it was used at all? In many youthful minds the Adenauer era was identified with stuffy conservatism and the – now-fading – *Wirtschaftswunder*. And before that? Defeat on the battlefield, and, so it seemed, responsibility for unprecedented mass murder. What honour could one have for fathers who shifted uncomfortably when asked what they did in the war; what respect for professors who prevaricated about their stance during the 'Reich'; what confidence in a political system that led to a 'grand coalition' – one, moreover, headed by a chancellor (Kiesinger) who had been a member of the Nazi party?

No wonder the rebellion in Germany turned so bitter nor that, in the Baader-Meinhof gang (later the Red Army Faction), it spawned a sect of youthful terrorists that left a trail of blood for years. The polarisation and violence might have become still more extreme had not a centre-left alliance between Social Democrats and liberals narrowly managed to oust the 'grand coalition' after a general election in 1969. Affirming that 'now Hitler has really lost the war', the Social Democratic leader and former wartime exile, Willy Brandt, became chancellor, the Bundestag enjoyed a real opposition again (this time made up of conservatives dumbfounded at losing government power after two decades) and, at least in part as a result, protest faded from the streets.

True to form, Winifred abhorred the rise of the 'Sozis' and pinned what political hopes she still had on the radical, nationalist right, especially the newly founded National Democratic Party that by the late 1960s had won seats in seven *Land* parliaments – though none in the Bundestag. She was delighted when the National Democratic boss,

Adolf von Thadden, attended the festival in 1968, and at least as happy a year later when Oswald Mosley, the former leader of the British fascists, turned up with his still-dazzling wife Diana (ex-Guinness, née Mitford). Not so Wolfgang. Keen to ensure memories were not jogged about 'New Bayreuth's' brown past, he implored his mother to keep her politics to herself, or at least within her own circle of *USA* ('blessed Adolf') fans. According to Winifred, her anxious son even offered her money to decamp for a time so that she would not become the focus of the National Democratic rally that was planned in the town, but eventually not held.[3]

That did not mean the festival director sympathised with the swing to the left in Bonn, let alone with young rebels whose noisy marches on occasion took them even to the hallowed ground of the Green Hill. To his annoyance – if hardly, by this time, surprise – his obdurate son Gottfried, still more critical of 'fusty' Bayreuth after swings through the 'cleansing air' of London and Paris, defended the demonstrators and buried himself in leftist literature. Still, whatever Wolfgang felt personally about the changes under way in politics and society, he realised the festival needed to take account of them in its approach to the works of the Master. He was also at least as well aware as anyone that with Wieland gone, his own relatively conservative productions would have to be supplemented with the work of outsiders. It nonetheless came as a shock to many of the Bayreuth faithful (and especially to Winifred) when the new *Tannhäuser* in 1972 was placed in the able but unloving care of Götz Friedrich, a sharp-eyed disciple of Felsenstein in communist East Berlin. What emerged gave a slant of 'socialist realism' to the piece that outraged the diehards but helped ensure, as Wolfgang surely hoped, that the festival stayed 'up to date' and in the news.

Unlike Gottfried, the Wieland children had never been in a clinch with their father – at least not over politics and history – and after 1966 they saw no cause to besmirch his memory. Why attack a revolutionary who, so it seemed, had fought on the right side from the start? Their critical fire was directed in the first place at their granny Winifred ('hailed' as a dragon in a birthday message they unkindly sent her), then at their 'ogre' Uncle Wolfgang – then, from various student bastions scattered across the country, at the conservative 'establishment' generally. Not that all members of the Wieland quartet campaigned with equal vigour. Curiously, it was the pensive, seemingly delicate, ballet-loving Nike – the second youngest child – who metamorphosed into the most 'way out' of the four. For a few years she shouted 'Ho Chi Minh' with the best (or worst) of her contemporaries, hopped from one student commune to another, sampled LSD and 'free love', and longed to get married in the 'socialist paradise' of Cuba – a yearning unfulfilled.

Fortunately for her intellectual and emotional education, Nike fell in love when she was just out of her teens with a Dresden-born composer, writer and broadcaster of Jewish origin called Wolf Rosenberg, who had fled to Palestine in the 1930s and returned to Germany after the war. Old enough to have been her father, vastly learned and blessed with a wry humour, Rosenberg quickly persuaded the starry-eyed young lady to drop her 'useless' course at the Munich conservatory and to place her studies in his hands. His abhorrence of the conventional in music, literature and lifestyle intensified her own, his favourite composers tended to become hers – from Berlioz through Mahler and Berg to Ligeti (with, along the way, deep bows of admiration before the 'modernity' of Richard Wagner and the insight of Wieland's productions). Later their ways parted. After a spell in the US fancying herself as a composer of electronic music, Nike settled in Vienna and became a pungent – sometimes feared – writer and critic. The Wagner name naturally helped her make her way, but for her breadth of knowledge and keenness of judgement she owed much to free-thinker Rosenberg.

Of the other two sisters Iris, the first-born child, immersed herself as a photographer and writer in the heady life of Berlin, putting Wahnfried, the festival and associated squabbles at an emotional as well as geographic distance. As for Daphne, the youngest and prettiest of the girls (named by her prescient parents after an irresistible nymph chased through a late opera by Richard Strauss), she became a busy Munich-based actress as much at home in Sartre as in Aeschylus. She also lent lustre to a marathon film epic about her great-grandfather Richard, and – hardly less appropriately – to a TV series showing how a German (industrial) dynasty came to throw in its lot with Hitler. At least in the early years, though, her life was as dramatic offstage as on – perhaps more so since she was wooed and won by Udo Proksch, an *enfant terrible* of Viennese society who pursued beautiful women and often-shady business schemes with equal vigour. Luckily for Daphne, her marriage to Proksch did not last long – albeit long enough for her ambitious spouse to head for Bayreuth in a bid to extract financial benefit from his famous new in-laws. He did not succeed. Shunned with rare unanimity by the whole clan, he was later jailed for murder in connection with a huge Austrian insurance fraud and died behind bars. Daphne meanwhile found a steadier partner in Tilman Spengler, a learned author of leftish views whose barbs of irony pierced many targets, Bayreuth and its public included.

Winifred thought little of these bids by the Wieland girls for professional and personal fulfillment – so different from the practical training that she had undergone before taking on a husband and family. Her granddaughters, she sniffed, refused even to *learn* housekeeping let alone do any. She thought still less of the flamboyant lifestyle of her grandson Wolf Siegfried, who had incurred her displeasure with a notable *bêtise* a year before his father died. While poking about in a junk room at Wahnfried, 'Wummi' had come across an old picture of his great-great-grandfather Liszt – one of those heirlooms that Wieland had cast into near oblivion when he and Gertrud modernised the family seat in the early 1950s. Impecunious as ever and less than enthralled by such evidence of distant ancestry, the young man assumed he could transform the seemingly forgotten object into a bit of ready cash with no questions asked. It turned out, though, that he had dug up near-buried treasure – an original portrait by the French neoclassical artist Jean-Auguste-Dominique Ingres dedicated to the Countess d'Agoult, Cosima's mother. The work landed in a Munich auction room and the family, under pressure from a livid Winifred, had to scrape up the funds to buy it back.[4]

The 'Ingres affair' was just one warning sign of how easily the Wagner heritage could be whittled away. Much of value had, of course, already been lost to the bombs that hit Wahnfried in 1945, and subsequently to souvenir-hungry occupation troops. As for that cache of the Master's manuscripts that had been bunkered away in Berlin, it had almost certainly gone up in smoke along with its owner – the Führer. Such 'blows of fate' apart, though, various other Wagnerian items somehow vanished from view in Bayreuth to pop up again, if at all, in unexpected places. Usually the articles in question were fairly trivial, peddled by this or that family member whose 'humble means', to coin Shakespeare's phrase, 'matched not his [or her] haughty spirits'. In some cases, however, the objects were far from negligible.

The original score of *Tristan*, for instance – one of the treasures

Wieland and Bodo Lafferentz had spirited away to their Nussdorf retreat near the end of the war – mysteriously turned up much later in Barcelona. Just how and why it got there remains a matter of dissent. Some claim that Wieland placed it there to be sold 'on the quiet' – although the noiseless disposal of such an object, worth a fortune on the open market, would hardly have been possible. Another version by a Bayreuth insider has it that the score was transferred to the 'safe haven' of Franco's Spain at the height of the cold war, for fear an east–west conflict might erupt on German soil. Exactly what happened then is also in dispute. Who first insisted on the return of the much-travelled opus? Was it Winifred, backed on this occasion by Friedelind who had long opposed any disposal of the Master's manuscripts? Or was it, rather less likely, Friedelind's old flame Gottfried von Einem? He claims that, thanks to a tip he was given in Switzerland, he managed to head off the score's impending sale in Barcelona and warned German authorities what was in the wind. (He also holds, incidentally, that he and his baroness mother were themselves offered – but refused – the original manuscript of the *Siegfried Idyll*.[5]) Anyway, there is no doubt that the *Tristan* score was finally lugged back somewhat furtively in a bag to Bayreuth, where it has rested in safety to this day.

Whatever her role in the *Tristan* case, it is clear that by the mid-1960s at the latest Winifred had become deeply worried about the gradual disappearance of heirlooms large and small. Naturally she was angry when objects simply vanished that had already been in place at Wahnfried when she had married Siegfried half a century before. Her reaction, though, had next to nothing to do with nostalgia or sentimentality. She knew as well as Wolfgang where the real wealth lay – not in the family home that badly needed rebuilding, nor in the Festspielhaus that drained funds year after year for upkeep and modernisation, but in the archive with its depleted but still precious (to true Wagnerians priceless) stock of scores, manuscripts, first editions, pictures and other mementos 'on which the Master's eye had rested'. In her view it was vital to keep this hoard intact – but could its cash value somehow be realised all the same, so that a tidy sum would flow into near-empty family pockets? Similarly, while it seemed unthinkable simply to sell off Wahnfried to the highest bidder, might not a way be found to have the place restored and preserved as a Wagnerian shrine at someone else's expense? Last but not least (especially not to

Wolfgang), how could the festival's long-term viability and artistic independence be secured while relieving the family of the financial risk?

The time had come for the rebirth of an old idea. Nearly a hundred years earlier, the debt-plagued Master had vainly proposed the creation of a publicly funded foundation to take over the festival and guarantee its survival. In 1914, Siegfried had claimed (honestly or not) that he and his mother were working on a similar scheme under which the Wagner legacy would be given in its entirety 'to the German people'. In 1946 Franz Beidler had drawn up his abortive plan under which the Nazi-tainted Wagners would have been dispossessed and the festival turned over to a foundation not exclusively German. Twenty years later, backed in principle if not always in detail by Wolfgang, Winifred began to compose her own variation on the same theme. At first she had in mind a solely Bavarian foundation run by a council on which the Wagners would always have a majority vote – and hence the power to appoint one of their number as festival director. That cosy concept came to nothing. Indeed, given the family friction and the number of public bodies that gradually became involved, it is a wonder that accord was reached on any scheme at all.

The search got off to a dreadful start in early 1968 when a family meeting called by Winifred to discuss her plan broke up amid mutual threats and insults. The press subsequently pounced with gusto on juicy details of the scrap, fed at least partly by Friedelind who had had a particularly bitter exchange with Wolfgang. As a result of this and other disclosures Mausi was forbidden by her livid brother to set foot in the Festspielhaus, a ban she nonetheless dodged at festival time with the help of Isabella Wallich, her old friend from London days. Tickets were obtained in Isabella's name and Friedelind crept into her seat at the last moment when the lights were being dimmed and there was less danger of being spotted. Recalling this covert operation many years later, the resolute English visitor wrote that had a 'guard' (i.e. attendant) sought to evict the two of them she would have stood her ground and staged a furious row.[6] No doubt Mausi would have done the same. Happily for both, and for the rest of the festival public awaiting the opening bars of *Walküre* with bated breath and devout demeanour, the Master's gatecrashing granddaughter remained unidentified.

Personal enmity apart, the Wagners long stayed at odds over the knotty practical questions arising from Winifred's original proposal. Was a foundation really the best solution? If so, did outsiders *have* to be involved in it? If they did, how best could the family retain influence? Crucially, how much cash could be raised, from whom, through the sale of which assets? The negotiations dragged on for a good five years before answers just about acceptable to everyone could be hammered out, and in the dramatic final phase Winifred landed in hospital for a while with heart trouble.

Thus it was not until 2 May 1973 that the charter of the 'Richard Wagner Foundation Bayreuth' could at long last be signed and sealed, creating a public institution into which the century-old family empire was subsumed. Naturally it was a painful occasion as well as an historic one, but the Wagners could console themselves above all with the thought that the sale of the archive lock, stock and barrel was netting them a tidy DM12.4m. More could easily have been raised had the items been sold piecemeal but, with varying degrees of enthusiasm, all members of the family came to agree that the collection should be preserved intact. It was therefore sold jointly to the federal government and two public bodies in Bavaria, who agreed to make it available to the Foundation on permanent loan. In the first place the whole sum thus raised was due to Winifred, who had inherited the estate and had the right to dispose of it – subject to legal restrictions written into her will with Siegfried. But she had long since pledged that any funds would be shared out forthwith among her heirs; one quarter of the balance to each of her three surviving offspring (Wolfgang, Friedelind and Verena), and the final quarter to be divided among Wieland's children (Wummi, Iris, Nike and Daphne). In one fell swoop, therefore, most of the family's financial worries were swept away – incidentally, a hefty bill for death duties was also averted.

To any outsider prepared to wade through it, the Foundation's charter no doubt seemed an unrewarding document – either unnecessarily complicated or boringly obvious.[7] It stated, for instance, that the new body aimed to preserve Wagner's 'artistic heritage for the general public in perpetuity', to promote understanding for his work, especially among the young, and to encourage research. Who, Wagner-phobes apart, could possibly be against any of that? But the document also stressed that the Festspielhaus would be made available 'for the purpose for which it was intended by its builder, that is solely for the festive performance of Richard Wagner's works'. That may, perhaps, have been the Master's ultimate purpose but he did not specifically say so. As already noted, at one time he was keen to see the 'Wagner festival' he dreamed of used to propagate new works by other German composers. It was Siegfried who formally imposed the 'only Wagner' restriction on the basis of a tradition founded by his mother. By enshrining it in the charter with all the force of the Master's (alleged) word, it has been easy ever since to throttle discussion about widening Bayreuth's repertoire.

The Festspielhaus was, in fact, the only part of the Wagner empire to be transferred direct to the new Foundation. Since the sale of the venerable pile was forbidden under the terms of the Siegfried/Winifred will, the family simply had to hand it over free of charge, along with its land and ancillary buildings. The case of Wahnfried was trickier. With the Master and Cosima buried in the back garden, it seemed disagreeable if not unethical to sell the place – and besides any purchaser would have to spend a lot on restoration. Finally the town of Bayreuth came to the rescue as financier and go-between. It bought the Siegfried-Wagner-Haus for DM600,000 but was given Wahnfried itself for nothing – on condition that both buildings (like the archive) be placed on permanent loan with the Foundation, and that Winifred be allowed to stay in the annexe to the end of her days. In the event, the town had to fork out for Wahnfried too. Rebuilding the place and turning it into a museum cost DM3.2m, half of which came from the federal government and the state of Bavaria together – but Bayreuth put in DM450,000.

Thanks to these complex arrangements, a lot of people had their fingers in the pie; more precisely, the financial weight of the various backers was reflected in the make-up of the Foundation's twenty-four-member council of trustees. Five votes each went to the federal German government and the state of Bavaria; two each to the town of Bayreuth and three other Bavarian outfits; one to the Society of Friends of Bayreuth (which had renounced its claims on sums it put up to modernise the Festspielhaus when the family owned it). The remaining five votes went to the various branches of the Wagner family – with the proviso that the number would be cut to four (and the Friends' share raised to two) when Winifred died. Those latter, relatively puny, figures were, of course, a far cry from the permanent majority for the family that Winifred had originally expected. Didn't they mean that the Wagners would be shunted onto the sidelines for good?

They did not. Wolfgang was – naturally – confirmed in office as director, the Festspielhaus was leased to him by the Foundation and his artistic independence was guaranteed. He thus remained responsible for running the festival and continued to bear the risks that went with the job; but he had powerful, committed backers and (along with the rest of the family) he was relieved of the worries of ownership. It was the kind of result the Master had dreamed of but had never been able to achieve. Moreover, the Foundation's charter specified that when it came to deciding on a future director the job would 'as a rule' be given to 'one or several members' of the Wagner family. This would only *not* be the case if 'other, more suitable' outside candidates applied. Should the council have doubts about how suitable a Wagner really was for the job, it would seek an expert report from the directors of leading German opera houses. In other words, the family was not wholly assured of victory in any future race for rule on the Green Hill – but it was given a head start. Bolstered by that comforting thought, and millions of Deutschmarks richer, the Wagners seemed well set for a calm and confident run-up to the festival's 1976 centenary. As usual, though, things did not stay peaceful for long.

# 18

# Time Present and Time Past

'If Hitler were to walk in through the door here today, for instance,' Winifred exclaimed in 1975, starting to stammer with joy at the very thought, 'I would be just as . . . as . . . as glad and as . . . as . . . happy as ever to see him and have him here.'[1] Seated in the Siegfried-Wagner-Haus that was now her home, the former Mistress of Bayreuth fondly recalled how the Führer ('he called me Winnie, I called him Wolf') had spent one festival summer after another in the selfsame building adjoining Wahnfried. The grateful guest had even told her longingly in 1936 how 'splendid' it would be if he could settle down there for good one day (presumably, bizarre though the notion seems, when he 'retired'). It is not clear how seriously Winifred took that statement at the time, but nearly four decades later she clearly relished the memory of it.

It was true, the old woman conceded in her marathon interview with Hans Jürgen Syberberg, one of the most controversial of German 'new wave' film directors, that Hitler had had a 'dark side' – but that did not count for her because she had never personally witnessed it. Besides, the 'negative' aspects of the 'Third Reich' had been 'basically' the work of other people like Julius Streicher (Gauleiter of Franconia and founder of the violently antisemitic weekly *Der Stürmer*) who had been 'simply impossible' and whom 'we all despised'. The 'Wolf' she knew had been full of Austrian tact and warmth – not to mention love of (Richard) Wagner – and he had, so she claimed, never disappointed her in all the twenty-two years (i.e. between 1923 and 1945) of their relationship. As a 'madly loyal' person, she was able wholly to separate her personal feelings for such a constant friend from everything that had gone on in the outside world. Admitting that this attitude might seem hard to understand, Winifred added with her habitual deep laugh dissolving into a bronchial cough (she was, to the end, a heavy smoker), that it would probably take a 'depth psychologist' to clarify her relationship with Hitler.

On any shortlist of unlikely screen classics, the film from which the above remarks are drawn would have to be placed high. Shot almost wholly in the Siegfried-Wagner-Haus over five days in April 1975, the black-and-white documentary lasts a good five hours – at least as long as *Parsifal* – and features a cast of just one. But since that one is Winifred, at seventy-seven still clear in mind if not in judgement and ever more garrulous in the face of Syberberg's seemingly innocent enquiries, the result makes for revealing and often riveting viewing. Of all the records available about the history of the clan in the twentieth century, this one – for all its distortion and occasional repetition – is probably the least dispensable. Trenchant, often humorous, seemingly devoid of self-pity (indeed, of any pity), the solitary star of the Syberberg epic brings her six decades in Bayreuth vividly to life – from her first meeting with Siegfried in 1914 and her early years of marriage under Cosima's eagle eye, right through to the bombing of Wahnfried and the festival's post-war rebirth. When the talk turns to Hitler, though, as it several times does, her words become fonder, her eyes brighter, her gestures more animated. It does not take a 'depth psychologist' to deduce that this is a woman in love – one whose infatuation might very well, decades before, have made her blind to the monstrous deeds of her idol in the 'outside world'.

Winifred later complained that Syberberg had tricked her into indiscretion, first by leaving her in the dark about how much he aimed to focus on the Nazi era, then by using comments she had not meant to reach the public. Perhaps so, although it is not wholly clear who may have been tricking whom. Winifred made her notorious 'if Hitler were to walk in' remark during a change of film reel but, apparently unbeknown to her, with the tape recorder still running. Her words were then inserted into the final film footage against a scene in which she, with her back to the camera, sits eating alone at the head of a long table – playing hostess, as it were, to old ghosts in a macabre version of that evergreen sketch 'Dinner for One'. That approach hardly seems to be playing fair (though Syberberg maintains that the film with this scene included was later seen and accepted by Wolfgang before its release).[2] On the other hand, Winifred does give every sign on screen of entering into the project with zest, plainly glad of the chance to get her version of her life and times – 'Wolf' included – off her chest at last. That impression is bolstered by Wolfgang's son Gottfried, who first made the contact between Winifred and Syberberg and who was present throughout the filming. In his view, the artful old lady knew very well what she was doing and took command of the proceedings right away. Before shooting began she had even phoned her friend Leni Riefenstahl, Hitler's favourite film-maker (of *Triumph des Willens* infamy), for tips on how best to present herself 'on set'.

Whether Winifred was used by Syberberg, or he by her, or each by the other, what she said on screen and off is plainly what she really thought. Much of it can have come as no surprise to her *USA* circle, nor to appalled Bayreuth artists like Fischer-Dieskau and the tenor James King, to whom the ex-director had happened to chat about her friend Hitler and the 'good old days'. But in this case she was courting, or at least risking, worldwide publicity and was doing so just one year before the festival was due to celebrate its centenary. In fact, not all reaction to her screen solo was downright hostile. At the world premiere in Paris in July, given as part of a festival of Syberberg's work, many of those present walked out before the end – evidently in boredom or incomprehension. When the film was shown in Germany towards the end of the year, Winifred received friendly letters not just from Nazi sympathisers but from people who simply felt she had been forthright on a topic her generation usually ducked. In general, though, the press reaction was ferocious, sparked above all by an ironic article headed '*Der gute Onkel von Bayreuth*' (The Good Uncle of Bayreuth) that appeared in the liberal Hamburg weekly *Die Zeit* soon after the Paris showing.[3]

At the start of the 1975 festival season and with centenary preparations well under way, Wolfgang suddenly found himself on the spot. Although he had known about the project from the first and had seen Syberberg's material in the wake of filming, he had evidently not expected the finished product to raise such a storm. Now he faced a public-relations debacle and the danger that, unless the damage could be quickly limited, demands to chop public funding for 'neo-Nazi Bayreuth' might become unstoppable. Accordingly, he stressed at a press conference that Winifred had long since had nothing whatever to do with the festival and that he was banning her from the Festspielhaus (or rather, as he more delicately put it, that he had asked her not to appear on the Green Hill until further notice).[4] Thus the weapon that he had already wielded against his elder sister and later turned on his son was used against his mother – for what transpired to be a full two years. Winifred was not even allowed to take part in the ceremony held in front of Wahnfried in July 1976, to mark the opening of the former family home as a museum – that scheme for which she herself had cleared the way with her drive for a Foundation. Sharp-eyed bystanders, though, caught an occasional glimpse of the fabled *persona non grata* peering out at the throng from a window of the Siegfried-Wagner-Haus, and cocking an ear as the festival choir launched the proceedings with (almost inevitably) the rousing '*Wach' auf!*' chorus from *Die Meistersinger*.

Oddly enough, when the Syberberg film was first released few people seemed struck that Winifred's comments tended to compromise her sons, the builders of 'New Bayreuth', as well as herself. Admittedly Wolfgang, as the 'little' brother, came off pretty lightly – although he can hardly have thanked his mother for telling viewers how, after being wounded in Poland, he had been brought flowers in hospital by a sympathetic 'Uncle Wolf'. But it was Wieland, the old woman

Banned! Winifred with Hitler as lapdog banned by Wolfgang from the 'Green Hill'. (E. M. Lang. *Süddeutsche Zeitung*)

stressed, on whom Hitler had specially bestowed so much of his own love of Wagner's music, who had been given every possible privilege and freed from war duty. Even if her eldest son had later felt unable to speak out in favour of his benefactor, Winifred added with ire, feelings of gratitude should at least have induced him to stay silent. Instead, she claimed, he had declared 'as far I am concerned, Adolf Hitler is finished' and with that 'the matter for him was over and done with'.

It is no surprise that, at the time, Wieland's offspring spurned this account of their father's early history, instead of pondering how much of it might be true and what more there might still be to learn. The children were naturally aware that in the grim and distant past Hitler had regrettably doted on the whole family – but whose fault had that been? They had long since dismissed their granny's rhapsodies about the Reich and were now simply angry that Wieland's hard, post-war work to free 'the real Wagner' from the shadow of Nazism was being, as they felt, gratuitously besmirched. Still, family reaction apart, it seems strange that Winifred's revelations did not prompt wider critical scrutiny of the role her offspring had played up to 1945. All the more so since the political climate in the Federal Republic was now far from conservative and other historical material, besides Syberberg's film, was starting to emerge of which the Wagners could hardly be proud.

When Bayreuth celebrated its centenary in 1976, the Social Democratic–Free Democratic government that replaced the 'grand coalition' in Bonn had been in power for almost seven years. In that time much had changed. Abroad, the left–liberal alliance had forged an *Ostpolitik* of reconciliation with the Federal Republic's eastern neighbours – a policy dramatically underscored in 1970 when Chancellor Brandt fell on his knees in Warsaw before the memorial to victims of the wartime ghetto uprising against the Nazis. At home, the partners had – as Brandt put it – 'dared more democracy', launching social and economic reforms that were in part ill-considered and too costly but that in the main swept the country with an exhilarating, much needed, wind of change. By mid-1974 Brandt had gone, brought down as government leader ostensibly over a spy scandal; but under his skilled and eloquent, albeit abrasive, successor Helmut Schmidt the coalition itself held together – and was to do so right through into the 1980s. Meanwhile Walter Scheel, formerly Brandt's closest ally as foreign minister and leader of the Free Democrats, had become federal president – and it was in this role that he turned up in Bayreuth as guest of honour for the main centenary ceremony.

Beneath the natural bonhomie that had made him a popular but sometimes underestimated leader, Scheel had a tough streak and if he felt the occasion demanded he could startle with his readiness to mince no words. So it was when he gave the keynote address to the serried ranks of Wagnerian and other dignitaries in the Festspielhaus on 23 July 1976.[5] At the very start, the president had the throng chuckling nervously with his ironic admission that he felt no urgent need to make a 'declaration of faith' in Bayreuth, let alone to journey there 'as a pilgrim'. The smiles, though, were soon to fade. Richard Wagner, Scheel noted, had viewed himself as the very embodiment of genius and had been so viewed by his acolytes in a late-romantic era shot through with pathos and *Weltschmerz* (world-weariness). Thus an 'irrational claim' had coincided with an 'irrational readiness' to accept it. But 'when seen by the light of day' did the music dramas really offer more elevated insights or a more profound experience than, say, Mozart's *Don Giovanni*, Goethe's *Faust*, Dante's *Divina Commedia* or Shakespeare's tragedies? Unquestionably, the president declared, Wagner had been 'one of the most important German composers', but that did not make Bayreuth 'the spiritual centre of the world'.

Bad enough, for many devotees present, that the Master should be classed simply as one fine composer among others – but there was worse to come. Scheel conceded that Bayreuth had enjoyed artistic triumph in the course of the past hundred years but – as a festival beloved and protected by Hitler – it had also been guilty of involvement in great wrong. Blame for that was due not only to 'those responsible for Bayreuth' who had thought they were fostering culture without noticing they were being instrumentalised for an evil policy, but also to all those democrats who had earlier abandoned the festival to the forces of reaction. Scheel stressed that he did not believe that Wagner's undoubted antisemitism had been responsible for Hitler's, as sometimes claimed; but Bayreuth was an institution in which Germans were able to recognise themselves and its errors had been those of the whole nation. He went on to declare:

We cannot just wipe away the dark chapter of German history and Bayreuth's history. Indeed, I believe the lessons that we have to draw from it are even more important than what Wagner has to tell us in his work. We have learned to distrust absolutist doctrines of salvation whether they come from the right, or from the left or out of Bayreuth. We have learned that subjecting oneself unconditionally to a man, a work or a nation leads into the abyss.

At least some of those present felt the president had struck the right note in the right place at the right time (although one could well argue over just what it was that Wagner *did* have, as Scheel put it, 'to tell us in his work'). But for old-guard Wagnerians the address was a shock and a scandal. Instead of being treated to a paean to the Master, or at least to such cosy platitudes as tend to be offered on 'official' birthdays, they had been forced to hear about Hitler, guilt and antisemitism on the hallowed ground where, as the brothers had put it in 1951, political discourse was taboo and art alone counted. Nor was the Festspielhaus ceremony the only centenary event to cause Wagner fans dismay, if not near-apoplexy. Far from it. Traditionalists had long feared the worst on learning that the centennial *Ring* was being put in the hands of two Frenchmen – the producer Patrice Chéreau, who had next to no operatic experience, and the conductor Pierre Boulez, that former Wieland protégé whose *Parsifal* performances in Bayreuth (from 1966–70) had been widely felt to lack weight and grandeur. These fears seemed massively confirmed when the Chéreau–Boulez anti-capitalist version of the tetralogy finally had its premiere, with prostitute Rhinemaidens peddling themselves around a hydroelectric dam and Hagen's vassals brandishing sub-machine guns. In later years, be it remembered, this production was hailed for its imaginative insight as well as its thrills. But at its first showing in July 1976, the howls and fistfights that broke out dwarfed by far even the booing and stamping that had greeted Götz Friedrich's 'socialist' *Tannhäuser* six years before.

The ghosts of the past brought Wagnerians no more comfort than the affronts of the present. Just four days after the Scheel speech, Cosima's long-inaccessible diaries – that million-word record of life with the Master between 1869 and 1883 – were unveiled (at least in part) at a Bayreuth press conference packed with German and foreign journalists. Interest was immense, not just because of the anticipated revelations but also thanks to the tortured history of the original books themselves (something hardly untypical in the Wagner family saga). Placed by Cosima in the care of her daughter Eva (Chamberlain) nearly seven decades before, the twenty-one elegantly handwritten volumes had been released for perusal to almost no one and – after a bitter scrap with the Wahnfried archivist Otto Strobel in the 1930s – Eva had passed the whole lot on to the town of Bayreuth for safety. She had even managed to exercise control beyond the grave, stipulating in her will that the diaries should be kept under wraps until thirty years after her death. Accordingly, the tomes thudded into the vault of a Munich bank and, despite flurries of litigation that finally delayed release even longer than Eva had intended, they were carted back to Bayreuth only in 1974. Thus Wieland, for one, never saw his grandmother's *magnum opus* except, perhaps, in a few bowdlerised extracts that found their way into the *Bayreuther Blätter* when he was young.

With the diaries 'home' again, a race began to edit and publish them in time for the centenary, then only two years away. In the event only half the contents, gathered together in a first 1,400-page volume, was ready for presentation 'on the day'. The world had to wait another year for the rest. Even so, there was quite enough to applaud and appal in that initial chunk, covering as it did the eight years to 1877 – from the Tribschen era through to the first Bayreuth festival against the background of the Franco-Prussian war and the founding of a united Germany. Although much had already been known in general, and more suspected, about the Wagners' trials and triumphs, Cosima's 'warts and all' inside story caused many jaws to drop. Alongside the Master's wild courage and sheer vitality, that even his fiercest critics could hardly fail to acknowledge, his rages and pettiness, his thanklessness and vindictiveness now emerged in excruciating detail. That Cosima had been a dedicated mistress, wife and muse was hardly news; but thanks to the ever more submissive tone of her entries, the history of her transition from a state of devotion to one of idolatry was chronicled as never before. Above all, it became clear for the first time how much antisemitism had been part and parcel of the Wagners' life – in bursts and with contradictions in the Master's case, implacably in that of the *Hohe Frau*.

Scheel had touched only briefly on antisemitism when he spoke of Bayreuth's role during the Nazi era, and Cosima's diaries had been completed long before Hitler first visited Wahnfried – indeed, six years before he had even been born. Nonetheless, both events – the speech and the publication (not to mention Winifred's film) – helped thrust into the foreground what was for Bayreuth the most tricky and painful of questions: how firm a connection might there have been between Wagner, Hitler and the Holocaust? In principle, of course, the issue was far from new. Thomas Mann, no less, had several times linked the Master's work to the spirit of Nazism, most famously in 1949 with his statement that 'There is much Hitler in Wagner.' Theodor Adorno, too, had claimed to find specific evidence of the composer's antisemitism in the music dramas[6] – a topic taken up sporadically by other writers. In Israel Wagner's music had in any case long since been boycotted because of the association it was felt to have with the mass murder of the Jews.

With the centenary, though, a fierce debate was sparked on the whole complex issue of Wagner, antisemitism and what Scheel called being 'instrumentalised' for an evil policy – all the more so since, alongside Cosima's diaries, several other books were issued that gave embarrassing insights into Bayreuth's past. In one, entitled *Richard Wagner – ein deutsches Thema* (Richard Wagner – a German theme), Hartmut Zelinsky, a Munich researcher, drew together a mass of hard-to-find historical material – much of it racist and nationalist – to document the Master's pervasive influence during the previous hundred years. Even for those who rejected Zelinsky's core thesis that the music dramas themselves were full of antisemitism, the evidence of a pernicious thread running from Wagner and Cosima through Chamberlain and his disciples to the 'Third Reich' looked hard to gainsay. Whether this was *the* crucial thread leading to Hitler and the Holocaust, or one among many, remains hotly in dispute.

Another publication by a young historian, Michael Karbaum, was if anything even more explosive, although at first glance it did not seem so. Unexcitingly called *Studien zur Geschichte der Bayreuther Festpiele* (Studies in the History of the Bayreuth Festival), Karbaum's book was one of a scholarly series commissioned several years earlier for the centenary and financed by the Fritz Thyssen Stiftung, a private foundation wholly independent of Bayreuth. From the first the planned volumes, covering such topics as Wagner's concept of music drama and the changing style of festival productions, looked bound to be thorough and balanced but mainly of specialist interest. Karbaum, however, not only combined a scrupulous historian's care for sources with a far from starry-eyed view of Bayreuth; he also managed to win the trust of Gertrud Strobel, daunting keeper of the Wahnfried archive (and widow of Otto Strobel who, in the same job, had run foul of Eva Chamberlain many years before). As a result he gained access to documents hitherto kept under lock and key – especially letters and memos from the Nazi era – and used pungent direct quotes from them to support a text of rare critical acumen.

Wolfgang only got to learn just what was up when Karbaum's completed manuscript, four years in preparation, was sent to him for perusal by the publisher in 1974. He was livid, to say the least – above all with the hapless Frau Strobel whom he accused of 'presumptuously and arbitrarily' handing over private material and of 'violating every basic principle governing the relationship between employer and employee'.[7] In his memoirs, Wolfgang stressed that 'it has always been difficult if not utterly impossible to divorce the Wagner family from the Bayreuth festival and regard them as two entirely separate things.' He can never have written truer words. But he went on to comment that the documents Karbaum had uncovered 'would at best have been a nine days' wonder and thus of no further importance had not Adolf Hitler's name kept cropping up in them'.[8] That point is also true, although many will feel it belongs more to the prosecution than the defence.

The irate festival director brooded over the manuscript until well into 1975, then returned it to the publisher without demanding changes. But astonishingly (and for Karbaum outrageously[9]) he passed on the documentation that went with it to Gottfried, who was feeding the eminent critic Hans Mayer with raw material for yet another centenary volume. It is hard to be sure why Wolfgang acted as he did, since he and his son were perennially at loggerheads. Did he conclude that, since the documents could hardly be prevented from reaching the public anyway, it would be better to go on the attack with them and show how 'open' the Wagners now were about their chequered past? Gottfried himself later maintained that, by poking about at Wahnfried and his granny's home, he had already seen much of the stuff that his father slipped to him. Be that as it may, all three volumes – Zelinsky's, Karbaum's and Mayer's – came to market in 1976, shedding much light into dark corners but leaving questions unanswered. In the meantime, Winifred had decided to put what 'evidence' she still possessed beyond the reach of any snooper. She gathered together her most sensitive private papers – believed to include letters from Hitler and a mass of material penned by Siegfried – and spirited them off to her favourite grandchild Amélie (an archivist daughter of Bodo and Verena Lafferentz) in Munich. There they have stayed ever since, at least as firmly guarded as Fafner's hoard. Even Wolfgang is said to have had no access to them.

Winifred evidently acted as she did, not just because of the fuss over 'her' film – resulting in her 'banishment' by Wolfgang – but because she was ever more suspicious of Gottfried's motives. At first she had welcomed her grandson's regular visits to the Siegfried-Wagner-Haus and his fascination with family history (of which his role in introducing her to Syberberg was one example). Gradually, though, she concluded that it was not just genealogical interest, let alone pride in tradition, that explained his constant presence on her doorstep. In that she was quite right. The inquisitive youngster who had stumbled so long before on first hints of the fateful family liaison with 'Uncle Wolf' had become an adult increasingly appalled as he dug more deeply into the past. Although Friedelind, the other great family rebel, had turned her back on Hitler she had never ceased to revere her father and grandfather. Gottfried, on the other hand, came to believe that there really had been a strong connection between Wagner's antisemitism and the Holocaust – and that Siegfried too had been a link in the chain. In his view, the family had loaded terrible guilt on itself but had failed adequately to acknowledge it, let alone pay the price.

Although Gottfried's doubts began early on, his 'conversion' came only slowly. His work on Kurt Weill in New York and Vienna for his doctorate surely played a role. So did the friendship he struck up in France with open-minded relatives of his great-great-grandfather Liszt (always regarded at Wahnfried as greatly inferior to the Master). Meanwhile, almost everywhere on his travels but especially – of course – in Israel, he came into painful contact with Jewish victims of the Nazis. By the end of the 1970s he had retreated from Bayreuth altogether, taking with him only two remnants of the past: puppets he had made as a child, and (symbolically?) the chair that had been used in his uncle Wieland's *Parsifal* to bear the guilt-plagued, salvation-seeking Amfortas into the hall of the Holy Grail.[10]

Ashamed of being German, and a Wagner to boot, Gottfried at one point thought of changing his name and becoming a US citizen; but he finally dropped the idea, repelled by what he called 'the obscene gulf' in America between rich and poor. After years of roaming when it seemed he would find neither a home nor a role, he at last settled down near Milan with Teresina, his Italian wife, and Eugenio, their adopted son – formerly a victim of mistreatment and poverty in Romania. From that base Gottfried sought to foster dialogue between a new – post-Holocaust – generation of Germans and Jews and fired one verbal and written salvo after another at Bayreuth and its history. His fiercely accusatory autobiography of 1997, *Wer nicht mit dem Wolf heult* (He Who Does Not Cry with the Wolf) can be seen as a response to what he felt were the holes and distortions of his father's memoirs, *Lebens-Akte*, issued three years before.

Perhaps it was young Gottfried's passion for prying and posing awkward questions that bit by bit stymied his relations with Wolfgang; or maybe it was because he was an unhappy child from the first that he began to seek out and rattle skeletons in the family cupboard. Whatever the truth of the matter early on, it was a much later shock that did most to seal Gottfried's break with his father and Bayreuth. Amid the centenary celebrations of 1976, Wolfgang separated from Ellen, his wife of thirty-three years' standing, and married his aide Gudrun Mack.

The two women in Wolfgang's life could hardly have been more different. Ellen (née Drexel), born in 1919, was a delicate former ballet dancer who had loved her career – at whose height in wartime Berlin she had met Wolfgang – but was privately shy and retiring. The Bayreuth festival public was aware of her, if at all, as a dainty, smiling presence, hovering near her husband on the Green Hill and – in the early years – clucking over her restless little son and daughter. She did not even try to involve herself in the family business and privately felt vulnerable before her formidable relatives, especially the domineering Winifred and (until she was driven away) the hyperactive Gertrud. Wolfgang's new wife, twenty-five years his junior, fitted the pattern of strong Wagnerian women far better. Born Gudrun Armann in East Prussia in 1944, she was a tireless organiser with a forceful manner and a manifest will to climb the Bayreuth ladder. She had managed to win the grudging respect of the hypercritical Wieland during her early days in the festival press office, and later further improved her Wagnerian credentials when she married Dietrich Mack, a scholar who co-edited the Cosima diaries. In 1976 she became the boss's secretary, his personal assistant – and his spouse.

Ellen never really recovered from the blow of divorce. Unable at the age of fifty-seven to find a new career, let alone go back to the world of dance, she first moved in with Winifred – who was at odds with Wolfgang over her own 'banishment' – then retired on a modest income to her birthplace of Wiesbaden. There she pondered the past, rereading and adding commentaries to voluminous diaries (another as yet unpublished source of family history) that she had kept ever since her engagement in 1942. In some ways, Gottfried felt closer to his mother as an adult than he had done in childhood, and her fate brought him lasting pain. When she died in a nursing home near Wiesbaden in 2002, he had her body taken to his new home town in Italy for burial. A photo of her, as a four-year-old sprite cavorting to a theme of Puccini, never leaves his desk.

Gottfried's elder sister Eva was naturally also shocked by her parents' split, in principle with still more cause. Since Wieland's death a decade before she had acted as a close aide to her father and had emerged as a far more likely choice than her brother to take over one day on the Green Hill. With the divorce, though, she was out – her place taken by her new stepmother who was just one year older than herself and who knew the festival 'ropes' from the inside as well as anyone bar the boss. The professional and emotional double blow might well have felled a fragile soul, but Eva was anything but that; on the contrary, in her pragmatism and toughness (a 'lady with sharp elbows' as one of her former associates puts it) she was her father's child. Wasting few words of sorrow or blame, she marched off and carved out a career as a music agent and consultant on singers to houses as renowned as Covent Garden and the Met. More than two decades were to pass before she really crossed swords with her father over the Bayreuth succession.

With his remarriage shortly before his fifty-seventh birthday, Wolfgang began a new life and went a long way towards drawing a double line under the old one. In the years to come virtually all his paternal affection was to be lavished on his and Gudrun's only child, a daughter born in 1978 and named Katharina Friderike. Did the fond father expect that the blonde little girl, who displayed much of his energy and next to none of his temper, would one day become Mistress on the Green Hill? Perhaps not at first, because it was plain that even if Katharina were to show enough talent for, and interest in, the Bayreuth directorship, she would not be ready for it until well into the next millennium. By that time, her father might be dead, her mother shunted aside and the succession settled some other way. But what other way? Whenever the touchy question came up, Wolfgang snapped that he saw no young (pre-Katharina) Wagner able to take on the top job or even willing to work hard to get it – as he had had to do.

This charge was plainly absurd. It was true that none of the younger set had been through the kind of intensive training that Wolfgang and Wieland, albeit in different ways, had enjoyed during the Nazi era under the benevolent eye of 'Uncle Wolf'. It was also true that Gottfried's efforts to forge a career in the theatre had proved sporadic, and had hardly been helped by the running feud with his influential father. But after an erratic start and a brief marriage that ended in divorce, the once-unruly Wummi – he of the 'Ingres portrait' scandal – had thrown himself with unexpected resolve into the theatre business, working as director and stage designer on literally dozens of productions at home and abroad. Although not blessed with his father's exceptional talent, he gained far more varied experience over the years than either Wieland or Wolfgang had had when they founded 'New Bayreuth'. Rashly, though, he failed to keep his own counsel or at least to content himself with seeking allies behind the scenes. In 1984, when the festival director reached what many regarded as the 'natural' retirement age of sixty-five, Wummi told an interviewer that he firmly aimed to take up the Bayreuth sceptre and that Wolfgang could not stop him. The 'real tragedy' of the situation, he claimed, was not so much that his uncle felt nothing for his late brother's children as that he felt nothing for his own – Eva and Gottfried.[11]

If the obdurate Wolfgang had needed encouragement to dig in his heels more firmly, which is admittedly unlikely, then his nephew's stinging public remarks supplied it. Pragmatically concluding that he was, after all, no irresistible force in the struggle for supremacy on the Green Hill, Wummi dropped theatricals and retreated to Mallorca with Marie Eleonore (Nona), his love of many years standing. There the two of them settled down on a spacious hillside *finca* and set up a thriving business building, restoring and fitting out choice properties for well-heeled clients. If Wummi pined for Bayreuth glory lost then he gave no sign of it, and in Eleonore he seemed to have found the ideal partner – a lively blonde, skilled as an interior designer and with a perfect pedigree. Born into a family of East Prussian aristocrats, she was not quite six years old when the Nazis slew her father – Count Heinrich von Lehndorff – for his part in the abortive 1944 plot to assassinate Hitler. Unlike Gottfried, Wummi was no crusader against Bayreuth's past, but he surely relished being linked to a family that – in marked contrast to his own – had tried to rid the world of the abominable Führer.

Practical stage experience such as Wummi had gained was obviously useful to any potential ruler on the Green Hill, but it was by no means a 'must'. If it had been, then neither Cosima nor Winifred would have qualified. Nor would Wolfgang, had outstanding originality as a producer been regarded as a prerequisite. Of the young aspirants who did not follow Wummi's career choice, both Eva with her international opera contacts and Nike with her sharp intellect and literary skill were clearly eligible for the shortlist of any unbiased judge. Had the assertive Wolfgang and Wieland daughters joined forces and (a tough but not impossible condition) quelled mutual friction in their common cause, they might even have turned out to be Bayreuth's 'dream team'. They would surely have been a daunting one. As a family rival ruefully put it, 'No man alive would stand a chance against those two if they got together.'

Wolfgang, though, was not to be budged – least of all by charges from interested parties that he was getting too old for the job. On the contrary, the longer he stayed in charge the more he came to seem as immutable a part of the Bayreuth landscape as the Festspielhaus in which he spent most of his waking life. Not that it was mere stubborness that kept him in place. The Wolfgang who had had a head for business even as a child and who had later kept the festival solvent while his brother earned most of the plaudits, now used all his canniness to bolster his position at the top. In one key move, he founded Bayreuther Festspiele GmbH (Bayreuth Festival Ltd.), of which he became the sole director and single shareholder and into which the assets of the festival were drawn. Under the 1973 charter of the Richard Wagner Foundation, the festival boss enjoyed artistic autonomy but also bore full responsibility for ensuring that the festival stayed viable as a business enterprise. By setting up the new limited-liability company in 1986, Wolfgang helped shield himself (and indirectly his family) from such risk as he had so far run as a private entrepreneur.

This unspectacular but effective coup was followed four years later by another. In June 1990, a contract was signed under which the Foundation leased the Festspielhaus to the Bayreuther Festspiele GmbH; not, in itself, a striking event – except that Wolfgang saw to it that the lease, like his employment contract with the GmbH, was open-ended. In practice this meant that he could not be replaced against his will, even if the Foundation board were one day to insist that it was time for a change. Theoretically his position could be made almost untenable and reasons found for naming a successor over his head; but under the terms of the lease he could not actually be ejected from the Festspielhaus unless he misused or damaged the place. If this confrontation scenario had been thought through, board members might have realised that the festival could eventually be doomed to have a hamstrung director *with* a theatre and a designated director *without* one.

In 1990, though, next to no one pondered over what (wrongly) seemed so theoretical a nightmare. When the lease was signed Wolfgang was just two months short of his seventy-first birthday and, it was thought, would probably bow out of his own free will before very long. Some board members did begin to have qualms a year later when the elderly boss, asked how long he planned to stay on, noted that Adenauer had become chancellor at the age of seventy-five – and had kept his job for fourteen years. On the whole, though, there seemed no compelling need to worry about the current director, let alone to start looking for a new one. Wolfgang might be overbearing and cantankerous but he knew the business from top to bottom – every stone and every creaking board in the Festspielhaus, every clause in every contract. Besides, the festival was manifestly doing well. Demand for the fifty thousand tickets available each year exceeded supply by up to a factor of ten. Wouldn't the Master himself have been thrilled?

Winifred did not live to see Wolfgang achieve so impregnable a position, but she did make her peace with him before she died. From 1977 she was allowed to re-enter the Festspielhaus and the following year she took a trip to Milan to see her son's production of *Tristan* at La Scala. On the whole she liked it, but then she had always preferred Wolfgang's work to Wieland's – let alone to the newfangled efforts by 'communists' that in her view now desecrated the Bayreuth stage. ('There are still places free in the asylum,' she is said to have snorted after suffering through part of the Chéreau *Ring*.) Although she continued to see her old *USA* friends and receive some young neo-Nazis too, the publicity she now aroused was minimal and gave the festival director no new headaches. Nor did her conduct bring a split in her perennially fraught relations with Friedelind, not even during the Syberberg affair itself. While the storm over the film was still blowing, mother and daughter went on a tour of Britain together looking for details of their ancestry. Naturally Mausi deplored Winifred's inability to change (the feeling was mutual), but the links that bound her to her mother, so often tested to the utmost, proved too strong to break – ever.

When the end came, Winifred was some way from home. While on a Christmas visit to Verena and her family at Nussdorf (by the Bodensee), the old woman was taken seriously ill and moved to hospital in nearby Überlingen. There she died on 5 March 1980 at the age of eighty-two – clear of mind and unsentimental to her last breath. Before the burial on 10 March in Bayreuth's municipal cemetery, her body was taken first to Wahnfried to 'lie in state', thence to the Green Hill for a ceremony with fulsome speeches and music performed by members of the festival orchestra and chorus. Outwardly, then, the procedure matched the one followed after Wieland's death in Munich fourteen years before. This time, though, feelings were far more mixed. For many of the clan, the loss of the matriach brought at least as much relief as grief. Besides, hadn't the deceased been pilloried only a few years before for her pro-Hitler remarks, and banned from the very place where she was now being honoured? The long-serving president of the Bayreuth 'Friends', Ewald Hilger, delicately hinted at this inconvenient history when he remarked that Winifred had never been 'guilty of the sin of cowardice in expressing her opinion'.[12] That was surely true. As for Bayreuth's lord mayor, Hans Walter Wild, he stressed that Winifred's name would be 'for ever' closely linked with the festival she had led with energy up to 1945, and with the town of which she had been an honorary citizen. Sadly, that may prove true too.

Friedelind survived her mother by just eleven years. To the end she remained as generous, impetuous and headstrong as ever, if anything more so thanks to the big family payout in 1973 that had made her a woman of means. Her former landlord and landlady in New York were given the trip of their dreams – to Israel, first-class and all expenses paid. Her old friend Isabella Wallich, desperate for cash to keep her recording company afloat, was saved in the nick of time when Mausi – apparently on impulse – phoned from a petrol station somewhere in Germany to offer funds.[13] The masterclasses that had foundered in Bayreuth were restarted with a still more ambitious programme, this time in Yorkshire. Alas, they too did not last, scuppered when local-authority backing for the project fell through. Instead, Friedelind redoubled efforts to promote her father's little-known music – heading an international Siegfried Wagner Society, financing recordings and organising public performances. Of the latter, probably the finest was the concert rendering of the opera *Der Friedensengel* (The Angel of Peace) given at London's Queen Elizabeth Hall in 1975. Stars including the sopranos Martha Mödl and Hanne-Lore Kuhse were in the cast, and more than thirty descendants of Wagner and Liszt (many meeting for the first time) were in the audience.

When seized with enthusiasm, as she usually was, Mausi could overrun the strongest doubter. She even managed to persuade a deeply reluctant Leonard Bernstein (who famously claimed to 'hate Wagner but on bended knee') to join her on a visit to the Master's grave at Wahnfried. What she really needed was a loyal business adviser with the canniness of her younger brother and the firmness to rein her in when she was in full flight. Not surprisingly, such a paragon did not come her way. She never married, but in Neill Thornborrow – an English pianist who as a teenager had attended her masterclasses in Yorkshire – she won a disciple who became like an adopted son to her. Indeed, he was often assumed to be her real son by those who saw the two of them together and thought they saw something Wagnerian in his features. 'Who's the father?' a Bayreuth diva was once nosy enough to demand of Friedelind. 'Parsifal,' she shot back, adding with a nod at Neill, 'and he's Lohengrin' – a joke maybe only Wagner cognoscenti can fully savour. It was this young Englishman whom Mausi, unorthodox to the last, eventually made her sole heir. All her belongings – books, letters, manuscripts, scores, pictures and her piano – went directly to him and were henceforth carefully preserved at his home in Düsseldorf, where he heads a theatrical agency. Much of her capital, as she stipulated, was used to set up a trust fund to finance cheap loans for promising young singers. Some of those to benefit have since made it to the Bayreuth stage.

Friedelind died of cancer at a clinic in Herdecke, a town in the Ruhr area of North Rhine-Westphalia, on 8 May 1991. She was seventy-three. Her body was not brought to Bayreuth, nor did an official ceremony in her birthplace mark her passing. She was cremated and, as she had wished, Neill Thornborrow took her ashes to Lucerne and scattered them there at a spot that she had asked not to be disclosed. Mausi had settled down in the Swiss city, close to the lake, some years before. She had no longer been keen on shuttling to America and had felt far from at ease in Germany. Besides, from her terrace she had an uninterrupted view across the bay to Tribschen – that idyllic villa where her grandfather had spent probably his happiest times, where her father had been born and where she herself had found refuge decades before from 'Uncle Wolf' and his pack. For the Wagner rebel and rover, Lucerne with its beauty and its memories was an appropriate place to rest at last.

# 19

# Time Future?

By the turn of the century – and of the millennium – the Wagner clan had become a widely scattered one. Eva lived in some state in Paris with her French husband Yves Pasquier, a film producer, and their son Antoine Amadeus, born in 1982. A year earlier Nike too had had a child – a daughter named Louise – by a Frenchman and later married a Swiss musicologist, Jürg Stenzl. From her spacious apartment hired by the Vienna State Opera, the 'bluestocking' of the family fired off one learned article and biting commentary after another, aimed mainly at displacing the solidly entrenched ruling caste in Bayreuth. Wits noted that the name 'Nike' was not only that of the Greek goddess of victory (and of much-fancied running shoes) but also of a largely outdated American missile system. It remained to be seen in the case of the Wieland daughter which of those associations proved the more apt.

From his base in Italy, Gottfried kept up his remorseless campaign to reveal the dark side of family history while in Mallorca his cousin Wummi enjoyed sun, sea and business success – Wagnerian strife, real or staged, far from his mind. Even those members of the clan who remained in Germany were, to a lesser extent, part of this diaspora. Of the brood that had grown up in Bayreuth in the 1950s, Daphne pursued her career as an actress in Munich, Iris hers as a writer and photographer in Berlin. Of the older generation, Verena still dwelt at her chalet home by the Bodensee as she had done since the war. With her husband Bodo long dead and her five children married, she was a solitary figure – but a spry and far from self-pitying one. As for Wolfgang, it almost goes without saying that he continued to live and move and have his being on the Green Hill, flanked by his strong-willed wife

Gudrun and their increasingly self-confident daughter Katharina. On occasion he *did* travel far afield, but virtually always in the service of the Master – even on a trip to Hawaii, the rather unlikely home of one of the world's most devoted Bayreuth fan clubs.

Bit by bit over the years, most Wagnerians had come to conclude that nothing less pressing than death would part the festival director from his post. In 1998 insiders had pricked up their ears when Wolfgang told them he would not stay on 'as a mummy or a robot', but it was hard to tell whether that remark had been meant as a pledge or a joke. Hence the surprise when in March 1999, five months before his eightieth birthday and two months before Katharina's twenty-first, the old man announced it was time to start the formal search for a new director. Did that imply he was ready, after all, to accept whichever candidate the board of the Foundation in its wisdom decided was best? By no means. It meant that he aimed to see Gudrun, then aged fifty-four, take command at some as yet unspecified point and hold the fort until, with luck, Katharina was ready and able to move in. Naturally he also planned to hold himself available, in the background as it were, to give his wife and – if he lived long enough – his daughter the benefit of his unmatched experience. To critics who later accused him of striving to keep his own branch of the clan in power no matter what, Wolfgang snapped that he had never seen the Gudrun-based solution as the only possible one.[1] But since he failed to specify another, at least in public, few people took this claim seriously.

Thus began what one of those most closely involved bitterly called 'a farce without humour'. The show did, in fact, have comic moments – for instance when a top representative of the Foundation compared the choleric Wolfgang to Rumpelstiltskin, that unsavoury Grimm wizard who created gold from straw but then, in a rage, destroyed himself. To anyone with a fairly long memory, the newly joined Battle of the Bayreuth Succession also had its ironic side. Half a century before, Wolfgang had urged his brother to help keep the family's *Weiber* (womenfolk) at bay in the running of 'New Bayreuth'. Now *Weiber* were ineluctably advancing to dominate the field, latching on to the tradition begun by Cosima and continued by Winifred. With Gottfried and Wummi standing aside, each for his own reasons, the struggle for the top job turned out in the first place to be one between Gudrun, Eva and Nike.

Admittedly each of these Valkyries had powerful male support – in

Gudrun's case from Wolfgang, in Nike's from Elmar Weingarten, seasoned manager of the Berlin Philharmonic Orchestra. Eva's choice of running-mate – Verena's youngest son Wieland Lafferentz – was almost too clever, since his qualifications were arguably even better than hers. Born in 1949, he had trained as a conductor, worked in orchestral administration in Dresden and now ran the prestigious Mozarteum in Salzburg. By teaming up with Eva, with his mother's blessing, Wieland gave notice that the Lafferentzes were by no means in Wolfgang's pocket as some commentators unkindly claimed. It eventually became clear, though, that he was not in Eva's pocket either. Urgently wanting more detail about future plans than his partner felt willing or able to give, the punctilious Mozart man broke with her and made his own bid for the Bayreuth crown.

Not surprisingly the Foundation saw no need to look beyond the family for someone who might be, as the statutes put it, 'more suitable' for the directorship. So many members of the clan were already chasing the prize – all but one of them, moreover, with impressively familiar physiognomy. Eva's strong features recalled those of the Master, Nike looked like Cosima reborn and Wieland closely resembled the youngish Franz Liszt. Only Gudrun, of course, lacked this superficial but not negligible advantage. On the other hand she had had vast practical experience on the Green Hill and seemed to guarantee relatively risk-free continuity. Of all the aspirants, it was Nike (with Weingarten) who produced easily the most far-reaching strategy for change and this was, in part, her undoing.[2] Far from everyone on the board could be called outstandingly imaginative or even well-versed in Wagner theatre, and when the Wieland daughter presented her vision of the festival's future at a meeting with her judges, numerous eyes around the table were seen to glaze. Her scornful public statements – describing Wolfgang's Bayreuth as a Wagnerian 'mishmash' and Gudrun as 'the laughing stock of the nation' – did not help her cause either.

To cut a long and painfully complex story short, on 29 March 2001 the board all but unanimously chose Eva as the next director and called on Wolfgang to step down after the 2002 season. It could have saved its breath. Already aware several months before that Gudrun looked unlikely to get the post, Wolfgang made plain that he regarded as unsuitable all the other candidates (or combination of candidates since, at one time, a 'troika' between Eva, Nike and Weingarten was mooted). Furious, the board members – especially the pace-setting Bavarian culture minister Hans Zehetmair – sought ways of prising the obdurate director out of his job, notably by threatening to cancel his Festspielhaus lease. But armed with the open-ended contracts that the Foundation itself had given him years before, Wolfgang was in no real danger, and after a few months Eva announced she was no longer available. Busy as a vocal talent-spotter for the Aix-en-Provence festival, she had no time to campaign fruitlessly against a father who, as she put it, still treated Bayreuth as his private fiefdom although the family had signed away ownership three decades before.

Naturally this debacle was covered at length and with glee by the press, even by those parts of it that were normally culture-shy. Growl though it might, the Foundation had been embarrassingly exposed as a paper tiger. Wolfgang could not be removed but he had achieved nothing – on the contrary, he had suffered a defeat at least as painful for his ambitious wife as it was for him. Suppose he were to die in the near future, or for some other reason be unable to carry on. Was it likely that the initially rejected Gudrun or the still unproven Katharina would be enthroned by the very body he had so thoroughly humiliated? Would Eva after all take up the crown she had stopped chasing? Would the whole selection rigmarole start again, perhaps with other or extra candidates? If so, who would have the authority to run the festival in the meantime? What Bayreuth now needed, it seemed, was some selfless figure from outside who was acceptable to all parties (family and Foundation), who knew the whole Wagner canon backwards, who would be ready to work at Wolfgang's side and who would take over on an interim basis if the director himself dropped out. It was hardly to be expected that such a paragon could be found – but found he was in the person of Klaus Schultz.

The new arrival – former viola player, dramaturg and manager all in one – had been a Bayreuth devotee, not to say fanatic, for much of his life. Born in 1947, he had managed as a teenager to smuggle himself into the orchestra pit of the Festspielhaus to watch the legendary Knappertsbusch at work, an intrusion old Kna spied from the corner of his eye but decided to ignore. After spells heading opera houses in Aachen and Mannheim, Schultz took over the Gärtnerplatz theatre in Munich, staging among other things *Das Liebesverbot* – one of those early works by the Master never given on the Green Hill. Professionally he admired Wolfgang's managerial skill but he had known

Wieland's wife Gertrud well too, and had made a touching speech to her children and other mourners when she died in 1998. In late 2001 he emerged as an intermediary between the fuming foes Wolfgang and Zehetmair, and after a three-way meeting in Munich he found himself with an extra job – modestly defined as that of 'freelance associate to the Bayreuth festival management'. In practice, that meant he was Wolfgang's right-hand man and would, if fate so decided, step into his shoes for a temporary, albeit unspecified, period.

With Schultz's appointment most of the heat went out of the succession dispute. Wolfgang stayed at the Bayreuth helm; Eva flitted between Paris and Aix; Nike – although never dropping her claim to the Green Hill – took charge of the summer festival in Weimar, an underfunded but imaginative offering of music, art and drama centred on the music of her great-great-grandfather, Liszt. Deprived of new thrills from the older members of the family, the press turned its attention to Katharina, now a rewardingly photogenic young lady far more relaxed with reporters than her father had ever been. With a ready smile and a toss of her blonde hair, she easily parried every question about whether she aimed to become the new (antiquated term!) *Hohe Frau*. But since she had long worked as an assistant in the Festspielhaus, had joined her parents in greeting the VIPs at the start of every season and had studied theatre in Berlin, it did not seem rash to conclude that she had her eye on the Bayreuth crown. Besides, from 2002 she became a producer in her own right – of Wagner in Würzburg and Budapest, Lortzing in Munich, Puccini in Berlin. Finally in 2007 she admitted she would like the Bayreuth directorship 'if the conditions are right' and sought to back her claim by tackling a new *Meistersinger* on the Green Hill in 2007 that same summer. Her maverick production drew jeers as well as cheers, but at least it kept her more than ever in the news.

Concentration on Katharina in the succession saga was natural enough but it had its drawbacks – not least for her. Inevitably her every new production was burdened by excessive expectations, positive and negative. A halfway imaginative bit of staging was promptly interpreted by well-wishers as Wagnerian genius showing through, modest flaws were damned by critics as evidence that the girl got work only through daddy's string-pulling. The truth was that Katharina had learned her theatrical handiwork well, that she could handle a team smoothly but firmly and that she had plenty of ideas, only some of them silly. If the invitations she received from one opera house after another were in part extended thanks to her father (and it would be naive to assume they were not), her productions themselves could hardly have differed more from his. One might almost conclude from her *Holländer* and *Lohengrin* that she was deliberately striving *not* to follow in her father's creative footsteps. If so, that was not unwise. When Wolfgang stepped down as a producer in 2002 (with *Meistersinger*!), his stagings in Bayreuth had been shown more than 460 times. Few if any of them made an indelible impact.

As a producer, then, Wolfgang was far from irreplaceable. Happily he either realised that himself or was too busy to do still more stage work, instead pulling in a string of notable outsiders – from Götz Friedrich to Patrice Chéreau, from Harry Kupfer to Jean-Pierre Ponnelle, from Peter Hall to Werner Herzog, from Alfred Kirchner to Heiner Müller. As a director, though, Wolfgang's like will never again be seen in Bayreuth, let alone elsewhere. Whoever takes over will certainly not get a contract for life from the now chastened and wary board, nor be able to run the business side more or less single-handedly. The days of 'management by walking around' on the Green Hill will be gone for good. Katharina's stage experience is obviously useful preparation for Bayreuth, but that alone does not qualify her to run the show. Like any future boss there she will need a partner to handle the ever more complex economic and budgetary side, ideally someone who knows the music business inside out but who will not get in her hair over artistic policy.

That, though, is the relatively straightforward part of the task. The tougher one is to decide where the festival should go from here. Many Wagnerians, of course, claim it should not go anywhere. With demand for tickets still vastly exceeding supply, it is argued that change is unnecessary and might well do harm. That view is misguided. It is true that Bayreuth has an all-but unique atmosphere it is well worth trying to preserve. Where else can one hear the works of a great composer given in the theatre he built in the town where he lived and is buried? And if in principle a member of the family is able as well as willing to run the show, so much the better. Suppose the Salzburg festival (admittedly less monomaniacal – as well as far dearer – than Bayreuth) found a Mozart descendant to manage things, wouldn't it snap him or her up? That said, Bayreuth badly needs to look to its laurels. Although the festival chorus remains unsurpassed, casts and orchestral playing at least as fine and often better can regularly be heard elsewhere – from Munich to Vienna, from Berlin to New York. As for the production side, naturally Bayreuth cannot often generate an outstanding homegrown talent like Wieland; but Wolfgang's policy of drawing in one outsider after another, originally sensible and necessary, has run up against its limits. The festival has long since ceased to set trends: it follows them and seems not to know which if any it prefers. Too often, moreover, there is a manifest disparity between the approach of the producer and that of the conductor to the work in hand – a flaw that in Bayreuth, of all houses, could and ought to be avoided. For most people who gain entrance to the sanctum after waiting perhaps a decade for a ticket, these ills are hard to admit. But in Nike's harsh description of the festival as a 'mishmash' there is sadly much truth.

Katharina believes a big part of the answer to the festival's future lies in an artistic partnership between herself and the talented maestro Christian Thielemann, long a Bayreuth regular. That might seem to make sense. But although the two have known each other for years and generally get on well, giving any one conductor – however fine – a preponderant say on the Green Hill could court disaster. The case of Karl Muck, who thought he was indispensable and who intrigued against gifted colleagues like Fritz Busch, is warning enough. That apart, Nike's proposals – largely pilloried or ignored since she put them to the board – make a good starting point for a new 'New Bayreuth' strategy. For one thing, she favours drawing the Master's early music dramas into the Bayreuth canon and building each season around a particular theme – underlining, say, the huge leap in technique and outlook that Wagner took between *Die Feen*, his first stage work, and *Parsifal*, his last. Seminars and performances of related compositions would be organised on the sidelines, new works commissioned, open-air concerts held and – perhaps – a less lavish Whitsun season added, mainly for young people. In the context of a broadly based summer academy, Friedelind's masterclasses would be reborn and would bear her name.[3]

Impractical, extravagant, rule-bending if not rule-breaking: those are some of the (politer) objections made to Nike's scheme. Her great-grandfather would have recognised them all only too well. It is, of course, impossible to say which ideas the Master would embrace or deplore if he lived now, but it is worth stressing yet again that it was not *he* who laid down the repertoire on which Bayreuth perennially insists. Perhaps he would emigrate to America, as he pondered in his last years, and make his works available for IMAX film theatres in multi-channel sound – a visual and acoustic miracle the Festspielhaus hardly begins to approach. This was, after all, the man who exhorted: '*Kinder! macht* Neues! Neues! *und abermals* Neues!' (Children! Do something *New! New!* and yet again *New!*).[4] His work thrives more than most people's on risk and dies easiest through routine. Even in Nike's long list of novel proposals, though, one vital element is missing. As it happens, the authoress herself indirectly drew attention to it in quite another context.

On 5 November 2005, the Vienna State Opera celebrated the fiftieth anniversary of its reopening after the war. The occasion was not quite as historic and thought-provoking as the Bayreuth centenary of 1976, although for the Austrians the house on the Opernring is a national symbol equalled, perhaps, only by the Vienna Philharmonic Orchestra (whose members are drawn from the ranks of the opera orchestra itself). Nonetheless, the anniversary was marked by a speech almost as controversial as the one that President Scheel had delivered on the Green Hill nearly three decades before. In one way the Vienna address was more striking than the Bayreuth one since it came not from a distinguished outsider but from an absolute insider – namely Ioan Holender, director of the venerable house since 1992.

As many of his listeners shifted uncomfortably, Holender recalled that the man appointed to head the opera at its rebirth in 1955 had been the very same one who had held the job in the last years of the 'Third Reich'. Moreover, the person chosen to produce the work that was given at the reopening premiere (Beethoven's *Fidelio*) had been in charge of all Prussian theatres under the Nazis. No one in Holender's audience needed reminding who was meant. The individuals in question were not exactly unknown in Bayreuth either. The *Fidelio* producer had been the ubiquitous Heinz Tietjen and the bounce-back director Karl Böhm (who had also, incidentally, taken over at the Dresden Opera after Fritz Busch went into exile from the Nazis in 1933). It was with Böhm that Wieland Wagner had aimed to produce a wartime *Ring* cycle in Vienna, but the plan could not be implemented and the house itself was bombed almost to bits in 1945. A Wieland/Böhm *Ring did* finally emerge, however – two decades later in Bayreuth.

Holender claimed simply to be taking a historic excursion, not sitting in judgement; but he went on to stress that after the war influential posts had been returned to those enjoying them *under* the Nazis and had not been offered to refugees *from* the Nazis. Most people saw that observation as anything but non-judgemental and reacted accordingly. One of the messages that flooded in to the opera as a result of the speech described the director as a 'characterless pig who really ought to be put down'. Many others, happily, took a different tack. One in particular praised Holender for referring unmistakably to the 'dark side' of what in 1955 had been so 'heavily symbolic' an event, and for urging more readiness to face up to painful history. This response was signed by none other than Nike Wagner and her husband. It could hardly be more applicable to Bayreuth itself – a place of symbols if ever there was one and anything but open about its past.[5]

There are many things to deplore in the Wagner family saga; among them Richard and Cosima's antisemitism (his sporadically vicious, hers implacable), the racist evangelism of Chamberlain – and the *Bayreuther Blätter*, Winifred's adoration of Hitler. They make for a peculiarly nasty tale. But in sum they do not show, for all the reasons set out earlier and despite strongly framed claims to the contrary, that the Master was particularly to blame for the Holocaust (the 'Wagner's Hitler' thesis). The evidence does not even support the related fable that is still more widely believed – that Wagner's music was specially palatable to the Nazis. Many twisting roads led to the 'Third Reich' and one of them, well trodden but – nonetheless – only one, passed through Bayreuth.

If the clan were to be sent to trial on its long, unlovely record, a defence counsel would no doubt plead extenuating circumstances. That is, it is true, a problematic line of argument. An extenuating circumstance for evil can almost always be claimed, be it late nationhood or a lost job, be it the Versailles treaty or childhood mistreatment, be it hyperinflation or a hopeless love affair. If everyone is somehow a victim then, ergo, there is no culprit – or at most, perhaps, one. *Ich bin's nicht, Adolf Hitler ist es gewesen* (I'm Not Responsible – It Was Adolf Hitler), as the title of a long-running Berlin play has it. Still, in the case of the Wagners a fair jury might well consider the defence reasoning persuasive. In their antisemitism Richard and Cosima were (admittedly influential) children of their time, and would, alas, have been so in most places in most times. Chamberlain and Winifred were two displaced Britons who sought to compensate for their early, desperate unhappiness with a specially fervent love of *Vaterland* – and Führer. As for Winifred's offspring, they had been little more than toddlers when the thrilling 'Uncle Wolf' burst on the scene. Is it any wonder that, with one exception somewhat later, they adored it when he became *the* top person and helped them on their way? Besides – a question that ought to be humbling – how would one have behaved oneself in similar circumstances?

What, though, when the war is over, when the dictatorship has been crushed and a working democracy born? Are circumstances still extenuating? When Winifred made her film with Syberberg, she had had thirty years to ponder the evidence that her friend Wolf had fostered murder and banditry on a colossal scale; that among countless other crimes he had decimated – with massive active and passive help – much of the Germany he and she professed to love. When Wieland died, he had had more than twenty years to come clean on his real record during the war years – as one who had been treated by the Führer like a son and who, straining after what he regarded as his full Bayreuth birthright, had used his privileged status to the very end. Wolfgang had had almost half a century to think over the past before, in his ill-structured and evasive memoirs, he concluded that he and his brother had had 'no reason to put on sackcloth or beat our breasts with remorse'. If ever a vital chance were missed for courageous reflection, this was it. It is not good enough simply to shrug off Winifred's execrable stance (let alone to find merit in her *Nibelungentreue*), nor to claim that Wieland's and Wolfgang's post-war work in Bayreuth justified their silence about what had gone before. The erstwhile Mistress of Bayreuth pressed on as incorrigible as ever and the brothers ducked responsibility behind the formula, 'Here it's art that counts.'

Doesn't that judgement amount to victimisation? Plenty of foreign Wagnerians were only too happy to flock to 'New Bayreuth' in 1951. Rival foreign recording companies vied with one another in the Festspielhaus in that opening year to capture the music dramas in all their tonal splendour. Evidently none of these enthusiasts agreed with Franz Beidler that, so soon after the Nazi era, the rebirth of a festival closely associated with Hitler was morally indefensible. Why pick on Wieland and Wolfgang, then, for failing to say 'Sorry, but now we consider our recent past we realise we should not be doing this'? Why even pick on Winifred when uncomfortable questions about responsibility and guilt deserve to be put in a far wider context? Weren't the British among the appeasers who let Hitler's Germany become strong in the first place? Didn't occupied France not so much acquiesce as vigorously collaborate in the deportation of Jews to the death camps? Didn't Swiss banks profit handsomely from looted Jewish wealth? Didn't the Americans as well as the Russians snap up Nazi experts after the war for their rival military purposes? The list can easily be extended. Besides, when 'New Bayreuth' was born the Germans were already becoming much-needed allies. 'Denazification' was, if not exactly a dirty word, at least a highly inconvenient one.

It is, then, far from the Wagners alone who have a shameful past to face up to – but that painful truth does not let them off the hook. Bayreuth is no provincial puppet show. Its artistic standards rise and fall but for much of its 130-year existence it has been the flagship, some would say the battleship, of German culture. As President Scheel observed, it is an institution in which Germans can see themselves reflected and its errors have been those of the whole nation. For once speaking rather too diplomatically, Scheel claimed that 'those responsible' for Bayreuth had not noticed that 'they were being instrumentalised for an evil policy'. He might rather have said that the Wagners were closer to Adolf Hitler than any other family in the 'Third Reich', that they and their festival joyfully accepted his patronage, that they did not consider carefully whether the policy for which they were being 'instrumentalised' was evil or not, and that they later showed next to no remorse – in Winifred's case just the opposite. What never came was the frank admission that 'We made a terrible mistake. We deeply regret it. We will explain as best we can how it happened, above all as a warning to those who come after us.'

Because the older generation (despite Friedelind's plucky example) failed to clear the air early on, the air has barely been cleared at all. For Wieland's children, it is surely hard belatedly to point a finger at a father one so deeply admired with one's head and loved with one's heart. Gottfried has fought for more openness but, in an eternal clinch with his father, he has also tended to disown the precious part of the Wagner heritage as well as the repugnant one. The town of Bayreuth, for which the festival is so welcome a source of revenue, has found it almost as tough to come to grips with the past (although individual citizens have made better stabs at doing so than their official representatives). In an embarrassing display of schizophrenia, near-veneration continues to be shown for Winifred the 'honorary citizen' while Winifred the Hitler-lover is passed over in near-silence. As for the modest memorial plaque belatedly erected to the inmates of the Bayreuth offshoot of Flossenbürg concentration camp, those keen to find it need to be unusually patient and sharp-eyed. By contrast, no one can miss the huge bust of the Master set on a pillar in the park before the Festspielhaus. A gift from the Bayreuth 'Friends', it is the work of Arno Breker, a sculptor much admired by Hitler – and by Winifred, who sat for him a few years before her death.

It is not too late to make amends. The family, in collaboration with the Foundation and the Wagner archive in Bayreuth, could and should back the preparation and publication of a scholarly history, in which independent judgement is backed by full documentation. The *Studien zur Geschichte der Bayreuther Festpiele* issued by Michael Karbaum in 1976 was excellent for its time and can serve as a model, but a lot of extra material has emerged in the past thirty years (some of it in this book). Much also remains under wraps and should be made available at last. One key, untapped source is the cache in Munich – very likely throwing more light on Siegfried and on the Hitler–Wahnfried connection – that Winifred put in the care of her granddaughter three decades ago. Another is the diaries that Wolfgang's first wife Ellen kept from 1942 and later collated with extensive commentary. Now in Gottfried's possession, these volumes could give more insight not least into the family's wartime doings and the birth of 'New Bayreuth'. Fuller use should also be made of the vast collection of documents that Friedelind left to Neill Thornborrow, part of which he has already generously made available. The resulting volume should have an introduction in which representatives of the clan's various branches present as honest a view as they can of their heritage in *all* its facets.

Isn't that crying for the moon? Not necessarily. Over more than half a century, the approach of Germans to the Nazi era – the effort to 'overcome the past' as it is over-ambitiously described – has been through several phases. The topic was largely buried in the 1950s, only to rise more shockingly and violently from the grave amid the student rebellion in the 1960s. The early 1970s brought something of a lull, followed – thanks not least to the showing in Germany of the American TV series *Holocaust* – by a broader public readiness to come to grips with the worst, the most unapproachable of all topics, the mass murder of the Jews. In recent years, from around the turn of the millennium, a new phase has emerged. To call it 'relaxed' would hardly be appropriate, but it is characterised neither by efforts to bury unsavoury facts nor by violent demands to reveal them. Many former Nazis and their victims have either died or are close to doing so. The post-war children who turned on their parents and fought against a 'cover-up' are now middle-aged (or even a bit older). Many of *their* children simply seem keen to learn as much as they can about that distant, repulsive but somehow also fascinating era – a desire to which a flood of books, films and television documentaries is responding.

At the same time, a lot of German firms that hitherto passed over their activities during the 'Third Reich' almost in silence have begun to issue histories that omit next to nothing. It is true that, in part, this new honesty has been stimulated by the court action of former victims, especially in the US. But broadly speaking, it is born of the realisation that in this case frankness is no longer hazardous; on the contrary, it tends to pay off handsomely. That is a lesson the Wagners, in their deeds and misdeeds ever a mirror of their times, should take to heart.

# Postscript

Since this book was first published in September 2007, much has changed on and around the Green Hill. In November that year, Gudrun Wagner died wholly unexpectedly after a minor operation in a Bayreuth clinic. She was only sixty-three. Several press commentaries referred to her as the 'secret ruler' of the festival. That was an exaggeration – but it was true that in recent years Wolfgang, now aged eighty-eight, had become ever more dependent on her.

Five months later, in April 2008, Wolfgang told the Foundation board that he would step down as director at the end of that year's festival, i.e. in August. The hunt promptly began for a successor. Wolfgang continued to favour Katharina but he knew that many on the board preferred Eva – just as they had done seven years before. So it was that, with Wolfgang's reluctant blessing, Katharina and Eva got together and produced a joint concept. Eva had originally been planning a bid with her cousin Nike for the directorship but she switched sides.

Finally in September 2008 the board voted in favour of Katharina and Eva as new joint directors. Time will tell whether the two half-sisters can work smoothly together to revitalise the festival and safeguard its future. Meanwhile, the need for the clan to come clean on its past remains as pressing as ever.

# Notes

Most references are to the original – usually German – texts. By no means all the works consulted have been published in English translation, and where translations *do* exist they are not invariably fluent or even accurate. For English versions of much of Richard Wagner's (admittedly often opaque) prose, for example, readers still have to rely on the archaic and sometimes misleading renderings of William Ashton Ellis. On the other hand, the invaluable *Selected Letters of Richard Wagner*, translated and edited by Stewart Spencer and Barry Millington, is a model of its kind. So is Geoffrey Skelton's prodigious translation of Cosima's diaries. These and a few other key English versions – for instance of books by Gottfried, Nike and Wolfgang Wagner – are noted below.

Even for German speakers, amassing a Wagner library is a complex and often costly business. For reference purposes, though, the CD-ROM *Richard Wagner: Werke, Schriften und Briefe*, issued in 2004 in the Digitale Bibliothek series by Directmedia Publishing GmbH, Berlin, is an inexpensive (€49.90) and invaluable tool. Besides including Wagner's *Mein Leben*, his letters and his other prose, this astonishing little disc contains the full text of Cosima's diaries and of noted works such as Carl Friedrich Glasenapp's six-volume biography of The Master. It is strongly recommended, and not only to the impecunious.

## ABBREVIATIONS OF FREQUENTLY CITED SOURCES

CWTB – Cosima Wagner, *Die Tagebücher*, 2 vols., Munich, 1976–7; English translation, *Cosima Wagner's Diaries*, London, 1978–80
KARBAUM – Michael Karbaum, *Studien zur Geschichte der Bayreuther Festspiele*, Regensburg, 1976
RWA – Richard-Wagner-Nationalarchiv, Bayreuth
RWML – Richard Wagner, *Mein Leben*, Munich, 1976; English translation, *My Life*, Cambridge UK, 1983
THORN – Neill Thornborrow archive, Düsseldorf
ZELINSKY – Hartmut Zelinsky, *Richard Wagner: Ein deutsches Thema*, Berlin/Vienna, 1976

## Preface

1. Wolf Siegfried Wagner, *Die Geschichte unserer Familie in Bildern*, Berlin, 1976, p. 9

## 1 A Sublime but Glaucous Sea

1. CWTB, vol. I, 1869–77, entry 6 June 1869
2. Ibid., entry 25 December 1870
3. Judith Gautier, *Auprès de Richard Wagner. Souvenirs (1861–1882)*, Paris, 1943, p. 75
4. Friedrich Nietzsche, *Ecce Homo*, 'Warum ich so klug bin', part 5
5. CWTB, vol. I, entry 3 August 1871
6. Ibid., entry 2 January 1869
7. Ibid., entry 3 September 1870
8. Ibid., entry 28 November 1869
9. CWTB, vol. II, 1878–83, entry 12 February 1883
10. CWTB, vol. I, entry 3 June 1869
11. Ibid., entry 4 June 1869
12. Ibid., entry 21 November 1874
13. Charles de Gaulle, *Vers l'armée de métier*, Paris, 1973, pp. 19, 20

## 2 Revolution and Reverse

1. Richard Wagner, *Sämtliche Briefe*, vol. I, 3rd edn, Leipzig, 2000, letter 3 May 1840
2. Eduard Hanslick, *Aus meinem Leben*, vol. I, Berlin, 1894
3. Heinrich Heine, *Zur Geschichte der Religion und Philosophie in Deutschland*, *Werke* vol. V, Berlin/Weimar, 1986, p. 144

4. RWML, p. 443
5. Alfred von Meissner, *Geschichte meines Lebens*, vol. I, Vienna/Teschen, 1884, p. 170
6. Richard Wagner, *Wie verhalten sich republikanische Bestrebungen dem Königthume gegenüber?*, *Sämtliche Schriften und Dichtungen*, vol. XII, Leipzig, 1911
7. Mikhail Bakunin, *The Reaction in Germany* (1842); English translation in *Bakunin on Anarchy*, New York, 1971
8. RWML, p. 356
9. Eliza Wille, *Funfzehn Briefe des Meisters nebst Erinnerungen und Erläuterungen von Eliza Wille*, Berlin/Leipzig, 1908, p. 64
10. Richard Wagner, *Sämtliche Briefe*, vol. VII, 1st edn, Leipzig, 1988, letter 12 June 1855
11. CWTB, vol. II, entry 22 April 1879

## 3 Ugly Duckling and Swan King

1. Thomas à Kempis, *The Imitation of Christ*, Book 2, chapter 3
2. Cosima Wagner, letter to Alfred Meissner, cited in Richard Graf Du Moulin Eckart, *Cosima Wagner: ein Lebens-und Charakterbild*, 2 vols., Munich/Berlin, 1929–31, vol. I, pp. 213–14
3. Marie Fürstin zu Hohenlohe, *Erinnerungen an Richard Wagner*, Weimar, 1938, p. 14
4. *Richard Wagner an Eliza Wille, Funfzehn Briefe*, Leipzig, 1908; this letter of 9 September 1864 first published in full in *Selected Letters of Richard Wagner*, trans. and ed. Stewart Spencer and Barry Millington, London, 1987
5. Letter from von Bülow to Liszt, 20 April 1856, cited in Max Millenkovich-Morold, *Cosima Wagner; Ein Lebensbild*, Leipzig, 1937, p. 82
6. Ibid., p. 81
7. RWML, pp. 745–6
8. CWTB, vol. I, entry 28 November 1869
9. *König Ludwig II und Richard Wagner, Briefwechsel*, 5 vols., Karlsruhe, 1936, letter 20 August 1865
10. Ibid., letter 11 October 1881
11. Ibid., letter 22 November 1881
12. Ibid., letter 7 October 1864
13. *Richard Wagner an Eliza Wille*, Leipzig, 1908, letter 26 September 1864
14. Richard Wagner, *Das Braune Buch, Tagebuchaufzeichnuungen 1865–1882*, Zurich, 1975, entry 8 September 1865
15. *König Ludwig II und Richard Wagner, Briefwechsel*, letter 30 August 1869 from King Ludwig to Hofrat von Düfflipp
16. Richard Wagner, *Die Kunst und die Revolution*, *Sämtliche Schriften und*

*Dichtungen*, vol. III, Leipzig, 1911
17. Friedrich Nietzsche, *Ecce Homo, Menschliches. Allzumenschliches* , part 2
18. CWTB, vol. II, entry 18 March 1880

## 4 The Fortress on the Hill

1. See notably Stewart Spencer, '"Er starb, – ein Mensch wie alle": Wagner and Carrie Pringle', *Das Festspielbuch* 2004, Bayreuth, and David Cormack, '"Wir welken und sterben dahinnen"; Carrie Pringle and the Flowermaidens of 1882', *Musical Times*, Spring 2005
2. CWTB, vol. II, entry 27 September 1881
3. CWTB, vol. I, entry 16 June 1869
4. Ibid., entry 16 May 1870
5. Ibid., entry 21 November 1876
6. *Ludwig II., Bemerkungen zur Nachricht von RW's Tod, Notizen des Hofsekretärs Ludwig von Bürkel,* quoted in KARBAUM, part 2, pp. 27–8
7. Quoted by Joseph Kerman in 'Wagner and Wagnerism', *New York Review of Books*, 22 December 1983
8. Martin Plüddemann, letter to Ludwig Schemann of 25 February 1896. quoted in *Cosima Wagner geb. Liszt*, Ausstellungskatalog, Bayreuth, 1987
9. See letters of 16 October 1881 and 29 September 1882 in Angelo Neumann, *Erinnerungen an Richard Wagner*, Leipzig, 1907
10. Richard Wagner, *Bayreuther Briefe (1871–1883)*, Leipzig, 1907, letter to Friedrich Schön 28 June 1880
11. Richard Wagner, *Vorwort zur Herausgabe der Dichtung des Bühnenfestspieles "Der Ring des Nibelungen"*, Leipzig, 1863
12. Felix Weingartner, *Lebenserinnerungen*, vol. I, Zurich, 1928, p. 269
13. Ibid., pp. 264–5

## 5 The Plastic Demon

1. Isidor Kaim, *Ein Jahrhundert der Judenemancipation und deren christliche Verteidiger*, Leipzig, 1869, p. 1
2. Joachim Köhler, *Wagners Hitler: Der Prophet und sein Vollstrecker*, Munich,1997; English translation, *Wagner's Hitler*, Cambridge UK, 2000
3. See in particular Jens Malte Fischer, *Richard Wagners "Das Judentum in der Musik"*, Frankfurt am Main/Leipzig, 2000, which usefully compares the texts of 1850 and 1869 and examines the public impact of each one
4. Ibid., p. 196
5. CWTB, vol. II, entry 2 July 1878
6. Ibid., entry 22 November 1878
7. Richard Wagner, *Ausführungen zu "Religion und Kunst"*, *"Erkenne dich*

*selbst"*, *Sämtliche Schriften und Dichtungen* , vol. X, Leipzig 1911. Article first appeared in *Bayreuther Blätter* 4, 1881, pp. 33–41

8. Ibid
9. CWTB, vol. II, entry 11 October 1879
10. See letter of 23 February 1881 in Angelo Neumann, *Erinnerungen an Richard Wagner*, Leipzig, 1907
11. Richard Wagner, *Religion und Kunst* (see note 7)
12. CWTB, vol. I, entry 19 September 1869
13. CWTB, vol. II, entry 16 December 1880
14. George Bernard Shaw, 'Bayreuth and Back', article of 13 August 1889, reprinted in *Shaw's Music*, vol. I, London, 1981, pp. 739–40
15. Gustav Mahler, *Briefe*, Vienna, 1996, letter of July 1883 to Friedrich Löhr
16. CWTB, vol. II, entry 23 April 1882
17. Herbert Killian, *Gustav Mahler in den Erinnerungen von Natalie Bauer-Lechner*, Hamburg, 1984, p. 122
18. Marc A. Weiner, *Richard Wagner and the Anti-Semitic Imagination*, University of Nebraska Press, 1997 – a thorough study recommended to all with open minds on this tricky topic
19. CWTB, vol. II, entry 26 December 1878
20. Hanjo Kesting (Hrsg.), *Franz Liszt – Richard Wagner Briefwechsel*, Frankfurt am Main, 1988, Wagner letter to Liszt 18 April 1851
21. Richard Wagner, *Briefe 1830–1883*, Berlin, 1986, undated letter to Carl Tausig, April 1869
22. Manfred Eger, *Wagner und die Juden, Fakten und Hintergründe*, Bayreuth, 1985, p. 51
23. Ibid. and, among many others, Robert Gutman, *Richard Wagner: the Man, his Mind and his Music*, Pelican Books, 1971, p. 303
24. For closely documented accounts of the Bethmann family history see: *Frankfurter Biographie. Personengeschichtliches Lexikon*, ed. Wolfgang Klötzer, Frankfurt am Main, 1994 (Veröffentlichung der Frankfurter Historischen Kommission XIX); Wolfgang Henningen, *Johann Jakob von Bethmann 1717–1892*, Bochum, 1993; Charles Dupechez, *Marie d'Agoult (1805–1876)*, Paris, 1989. I am grateful to members of the Bethmann family, the Bethmann Bank, the Institut für Stadtgeschichte and the Jüdisches Museum – all in Frankfurt am Main – for their advice and help

## 6 The Spin Doctor

1. For many details of Chamberlain's life, I am indebted to Geoffrey Field's indispensable *Evangelist of Race: The Germanic Vision of Houston Stewart Chamberlain*, New York, 1981. Additional biographical material

has been drawn from Chamberlain's *Lebenswege meines Denkens*, Munich, 1919, and Anna Chamberlain's *Meine Erinnerungen an Houston Stewart Chamberlain*, Munich, 1923

2. Paul Pretzsch (ed.), *Cosima Wagner und Houston S. Chamberlain im Briefwechsel 1888–1908*, Leipzig, 1934, p. 8
3. Dietrich Mack (ed.), *Cosima Wagner: Das zweite Leben, Briefe und Aufzeichnungen 1883–1930*, Munich/Zurich, 1980, p. 762
4. For a detailed account of the journal's history and influence see Annette Hein, *'Es ist viel "Hitler" in Wagner': Rassismus und antisemitische Deutschtumsideologie in den 'Bayreuther Blättern' (1878–1938)*, Tübingen, 1996
5. George Ainslie Hight, *Tristan and Isolde: an Essay on the Wagnerian Drama*, Montana, 2004 (reprint), chapter 2
6. Houston Stewart Chamberlain, *Richard Wagner*, Munich, 1895
7. Carl Friedrich Glasenapp, *Das Leben Richard Wagners in sechs Büchern dargestellt*, 6 vols., Leipzig, 1904–1911
8. Letter to Siegfried Wagner, 18 July 1896
9. Paul Pretzsch (ed.), *Cosima Wagner und HSC*, Cosima letter 23 August 1904
10. Paul Pretzsch (ed.) *Houston Stewart Chamberlain Briefe 1882–1924 und Briefwechsel mit Kaiser Wilhelm II*, Munich, 1928, Kaiser's letter of 31 December 1901
11. Ibid., Chamberlain letter of 20 February 1902
12. Chamberlain, *Die Grundlagen des 19. Jahrhunderts*, Munich, 1899, vol. I, p. 17
13. Ibid., p. 583
14. Theodore Roosevelt, *History as Literature*, New York, 1913, part 8
15. Pretzsch (ed.), *Briefwechsel mit Kaiser Wilhelm II*, Chamberlain letter 1 December 1908

## 7 Odd Man Out

1. Isadora Duncan, *My Life*, London, 1928, chapter 15
2. Siegfried Wagner, *Erinnerungen,* Stuttgart, 1923, last paragraph. For much supplementary biographical material, I am indebted to Peter Pachl's *Siegfried Wagner: Genie im Schatten*, Munich, 1988 and (in part) to Zdenko von Kraft's *Der Sohn*, Graz, 1969. For valuable insights into Siegfried Wagner's life and work, see also the *Siegfried Wagner-Kompendium I* (ed. Peter Pachl), Herbolzheim, 2003 – a volume that brings together the contributions made at the first international Siegfried Wagner symposium in Cologne in 2001
3. Pachl, photo of Siegfried's chalked-up remarks, opp. p. 436
4. Willi Schuh, *Richard Strauss*, Zurich/Freiburg 1976, p. 425

5. George Bernard Shaw, article of 15 November 1894, reprinted in *Shaw's Music*, vol. III, London, 1981, pp. 333–8
6. This recording and others of Siegfried conducting his father's works has been issued by Archipel on two CDs (ARPCD 0288-2)
7. Richard Graf Du Moulin Eckart, *Cosima Wagner: ein Lebens-und Charakterbild*, 2 vols, Munich/Berlin 1929–31, vol. II, p. 787
8. CWTB, vol. I, entry 5 November 1869
9. Edward Speyer, *My Life and Friends*, London, 1937, pp. 136–7
10. Claus Victor Bock, *Pente Pigadia und die Tagebücher des Clement Harris*, Amsterdam, 1962, p. 22. See also Ion Zottos, Clement Harris and the Wagner Family' in the *Siegfried Wagner-Kompendium I*, pp. 235–51
11. CWTB, vol. I, entry 17 December 1877
12. Siegfried Wagner, *Erinnerungen*, pp. 61–2
13. Siegfried Wagner, *Reisetagebuch 1892*, ed. Winifred Wagner, Bayreuth, 1935, p. 257
14. For perceptive comments on Siegfried and Wilde see Dorothea Renckhoff , 'Und die Seele ging weinend über die Sümpfe davon' in the *Siegfried Wagner-Kompendium I*, pp. 219–34
15. For a detailed account of the Beidler–Wagner family history see Dieter Borchmeyer, *Franz Wilhelm Beidler:Cosima Wagner-Liszt*, Bielefeld, 1997
16. Du Moulin Eckart (see note 7), vol. II, pp. 672–3
17. Dietrich Mack (ed.), *Cosima Wagner: Das zweite Leben, Briefe und Aufzeichnungen 1883–1930*, Munich/Zurich, 1980, pp. 685–6, letter 11 August 1906
18. For background on the proposed foundation, the controversy surround ing it and Cosima's will, see KARBAUM, part 1, pp. 57–9 and the related documents in vol. II

## 8 Wolf at the Door

1. Chamberlain, letter of 7 October 1923, reproduced in ZELINSKY, p. 169
2. Ibid., p. 170
3. For a full account of Winifred's life, see in particular Brigitte Hamann, *Winifred Wagner oder Hitlers Bayreuth*, Munich/Zurich 2002. A shorter and in part corrected edition was published in English in London in 2005 as *Winifred Wagner: A Life at the Heart of Hitler's Bayreuth*. Winifred herself gives many graphic details (in German) in *Winifred Wagner und die Geschichte des Hauses Wahnfried 1914–1975*, a five-hour film made by Hans Jürgen Syberberg in 1975 and since issued on video.

4. Siegfried, letter of autumn 1921, cited in Zdenko von Kraft, *Der Sohn*, Graz, 1969, p. 230
5. Von Gross, letter to Siegfried of 8 February 1924, cited in Karbaum, part II, pp. 41–2
6. Text carried in ZELINSKY, p. 169
7. Joachim Köhler, *Wagner's Hitler*, Munich, 1997, chapter 12
8. For a discussion of the disputed 'secret agenda' of *Glück*, see the *Siegfried Wagner-Kompendium I* (ed. Peter Pachl), Herbolzheim, 2003, pp. 144–7
9. Transcript of Siegfried letter to Rosa Eidam, Christmas 1923, RWA
10. See Kurt Ludecke, *I Knew Hitler*, London, 1938, chapter 12, for Ludecke's account of his meetings with the Wagners and Ford
11. Hitler, letter to Siegfried, 5 May 1924, RWA
12. Peter Pachl, *Siegfried Wagner: Genie im Schatten*, Munich, 1988, p. 418
13. Joseph Goebbels, *Tagebücher*, vol. I (1924–9), Munich, 1999, entry 8 May 1926
14. Joseph Goebbels, *Tagebücher, Sämtliche Fragmente*, vol. II, Munich, 1967, entry 30 May 1942
15. Henry Picker, *Hitlers Tischgespräche im* Führer*hauptquartier*, Berlin, 1997, entry night of 28 February–1 March 1942
16. ZELINSKY, p. 165
17. Text of the exchanges between Siegfried and Rabbi Salomon from June 1924 to July 1925, carried on the website of the *Siegfried Wagner Gesellschaft* – www.siegfried-wagner.org – under archive entries for 2001
18. ZELINSKY, p. 165
19. Picker, entry 28 February–1 March 1942
20. Siegfried, letter of 23 May 1930, quoted in Pachl, p. 438
21. Franz Stassen, *Erinnerungen an Siegfried Wagner*, RWA, p. 46
22. Siegfried Wagner, *Erinnerungen*, Stuttgart, 1923, p. 169

## 9 Three Funerals and a New Broom

1. Joseph Goebbels, *Tagebücher*, vol. I (1924–9), Munich, 1999, entry 8 May 1926
2. For Cosima's words as noted by Daniela and Eva between 1925 and 1930, see Dietrich Mack (ed.), *Cosima Wagner: Das zweite Leben, Briefe und Aufzeichnungen 1883–1930*, Munich/Zurich, 1980, pp. 752–66
3. Peter Pachl, *Siegfried Wagner: Genie im Schatten*, Munich, 1988, p. 428
4. Ibid.
5. Arnold Schoenberg, article in the *Rheinischen Musik-und Theaterzeitung*, 23 March 1912, cited in Pachl, p. 247

6. For text of the petition see KARBAUM, part 2, pp. 94–5
7. Ibid., pp. 82–4 for the relevant Winifred–Furtwängler correspondence between March and June 1932
8. Bruno Walter, *Thema und Variationen*, Frankfurt am Main, 1960, pp. 351–2; English version *Theme and Variations*, London and New York, 1947
9. Ibid., p. 353
10. Peter Heyworth, *Conversations with Otto Klemperer*, London, 1973, p. 70
11. Hannes Reinhardt (ed.), *Das bin ich*, Munich 1970 – a series of self-portraits of which Tietjen's is on pp. 169–205
12. Heyworth (see note 10), p. 67
13. Fritz Busch, *Aus dem Leben eines Musikers*, Berlin, 1971, pp. 195–6
14. Walter, p. 390
15. Walter Legge, article on the Bayreuth festival in the *Manchester Guardian*, August 1933, reprinted in Elisabeth Schwarzkopf, *On and Off the Record*, London, 1982, pp. 21–5

## 10 All the Reich's a Stage

1. Heinrich Heine, *Almansor – Eine Tragödie* (1821), first complete publication, Berlin, 1823
2. Joseph Goebbels, *Tagebücher*, vol. II (1930–4), Munich, 1999, entry 22 March 1933
3. Adolf Hitler, *Mein Kampf*, trans. Ralph Manheim, Boston, 1943, chapter 1. The state of Bavaria, which owns the copyright to all editions of *Mein Kampf* (apart from the English and Dutch), as well as the German federal government, oppose any copying or printing of the book in Germany. Old copies can, however, be legally bought and sold – subject to certain restrictions
4. August Kubizek, *Adolf Hitler mein Jugendfreund*, Graz, 1975, pp. 115–17
5. See Franz-Heinz Köhler, *Die Struktur der Spielpläne deutschsprachiger Opernbühnen von 1896 bis 1966*, Koblenz, 1968. For further analysis and interpretation of the statistics see Hubert Kolland, *Wagner-Rezeption im deutschen Faschismus* in *Bericht über den Internationalen Musikwissenschaftlichen Kongress Bayreuth 1981*, Kassel/Basle, pp. 494–503, and also Erik Levi, *Music in the Third Reich*, London, 1994, pp. 191–3
6. Köhler and Kolland, ibid.
7. Thomas Mann, *Wagner und unsere Zeit*, Frankfurt am Main, 1963. Article reproduced as *Auseinandersetzung mit Richard Wagner*, pp. 26–8

8. Hans Heinz Stuckenschmidt, 'Gestorbenes Bayreuth', in the *Neue Musikzeitung*, Jg. 49, 1928. Article reprinted in Susanna Grossmann-Vendrey, *Bayreuth in der deutschen Presse*, vol. III, 2, Regensburg, 1983, pp. 206–8
9. Bernhard Diebold, 'Der Fall Wagner', in the *Frankfurter Zeitung* , 30 September 1928. Article reprinted in Grossmann-Vendrey, pp. 208–11
10. Werner Jochmann (ed.), *Adolf Hitler, Monologe im Führerhauptquartier 1941–1944, Die Aufzeichnungen Heinrich Heims*, Hamburg, 1980. Remark on night of 24–25 January 1942, p. 224: 'Der *Tristan* ist doch sein grösstes Werk'
11. For background to and analysis of the Parsifal 'ban' see *inter alia*, Saul Friedländer, 'Hitler and Wagner', and Udo Bermbach, 'Liturgietransfer', in *Richard Wagner im Dritten Reich*, Munich, 2000 – a collection of texts of addresses given at a symposium in Schloss Elmau, Bavaria, July 1999
12. Alfred Rosenberg, 'Beethoven', article in the *Völkischer Beobachter*, 26 March 1927, marking the centenary of the composer's death
13. Alfred Rosenberg, *Der Mythos des 20. Jahrhunderts*, Munich, 1934, vol. II, part 4, 'Der aesthetische Wille'
14. Albert Speer, *Erinnerungen*, Frankfurt am Main/Berlin, 1969, p. 145; English translation, *Inside the Third Reich*, London /New York, 1970
15. Ibid., pp. 73–4
16. Traudl Junge, *Bis zur letzten Stunde*, Munich, 2002, p. 93
17. Ibid., pp. 66–93
18. Jochmann, *Adolf Hitler, Monologe* (see note 10), remark on night of 25–26 January 1942, p. 234: 'Wenn ich Wagner höre, ist mir, als seien das Rhythmen der Vorwelt'
19. Thomas Mann, *Wagner und unsere Zeit*, letter to Emil Preetorius of 6 December 1949, pp. 167–9
20. Ibid., letter to the editor of *Common Sense*, January 1940, pp. 153–60
21. Ibid., letter to Friedrich Schramm, 25 August 1951, pp. 181–2
22. Henry Picker, *Hitlers Tischgespräche im Führerhauptquartier*, Berlin, 1997, remarks on night of 28 February–1 March 1942, pp. 159–61
23. Adolf Hitler, *Mein Kampf*, chapter 15
24. Ibid., chapter 8
25. Jochmann, *Adolf Hitler, Monologe* (see note 10), remarks on night of 24–25 January, 1942, p. 225
26. Nike Wagner, *Wagner Theater*, Frankfurt am Main/Leipzig, 1998, pp. 299–300; English translation, *The Wagners: the Dramas of a Musical Dynasty*, London, 2000
27. Winifred Wagner, letter to Hitler 26 December 1934, Bundesarchiv Koblenz

28. For details of the festival's financing before and during the Nazi era, see KARBAUM, Anhang, pp. 150–3

## 11 Dissonant Quartet

1. Wolfgang Wagner, *Lebens-Akte*, Munich, 1994. p. 55; English translation, *Acts*, London, 1994
2. Friedelind Wagner, *Heritage of Fire*, the original manuscript written by Friedelind in English, New York, 1945, pp. 9–10; German translation issued in Bern, Switzerland, 1945; first published in Germany, Cologne, 1994
3. Frida Leider, *Das War Mein Teil*, Berlin, 1959; English translation (with some details corrected from the original), *Playing My Part*, London, 1966, pp. 99–100
4. J. B. Steane, *The Grand Tradition*, London, 1974, p. 240
5. See *inter alia* Nike Wagner, *Wagner Theater*, Frankfurt am Main/Leipzig, 1998, p. 299
6. Ibid., p. 302
7. See *inter alia* letter to Albert Knittel of 16 April 1932 in which Winifred writes of accommodation for 'Heinz . . . so long as we are not married'. Cited in Brigitte Hamann, *Winifred Wagner oder Hitlers Bayreuth*, Munich/Zurich, 2002, p. 222
8. David Lloyd George, article in the *Daily Express*, London, 17 September 1936
9. Letters of May and June 1933 from Lieselotte Schmidt to her parents, RWA. For copious excerpts from similar Schmidt correspondence up to 1937 see KARBAUM, part 2, pp. 77–80
10. Friedelind Wagner, *Heritage of Fire*, pp. 107–8
11. For a detailed account of the fate of Bayreuth's Jews during the Nazi era see Ekkehard Hubschmann, Helmut Paulus, Siegfried Pokorny, *Physische und behördliche Gewalt: Die 'Reichskritallnacht' und die Verfolgung der Juden in Bayreuth*, Bayreuth, 2000
12. Wolfgang Wagner, *Lebens-Akte*, p. 77
13. Renate Schostack, *Hinter Wahnfried's Mauern: Gertrud Wagner Ein Leben*, Hamburg, 1998, p. 163
14. Wolfgang Wagner, *Lebens-Akte*, p. 76
15. Ibid., p. 79
16. Ibid., p. 80
17. Ibid., p. 78
18. Friedelind Wagner, *Heritage of Fire*, p. 140

## 12 Mausi at Bay

1. Friedelind, letters to her aunts from June 1937, and from February and April 1938, RWA
2. Isabella Wallich, *Recording my Life*, London 2001, pp. 49–65
3. Berta Geissmar, *The Baton and the Jackboot*, London, 1944, pp. 205–6. The book appeared a year later in German as *Musik im Schatten der Politik*, Zurich, 1945
4. Friedelind Wagner, *Heritage of Fire*, p. 217
5. For background details of Friedelind's various stays in Britain before, during and after the war see the National Archives (NA), Kew, file ref. KV 2/1914. This material was first released in 2005
6. Friedelind Wagner, *Heritage of Fire*, pp. 186–7
7. Jonathan Guinness with Catherine Guinness, *The House of Mitford*, London, 1985, pp. 383–4
8. Ibid., p. 370
9. See Frida Leider, *Playing My Part*, pp. 170–2 and Friedelind Wagner, *Heritage of Fire*, pp. 206–8
10. Winifred in the film *Winifred Wagner und die Geschichte des Hauses Wahnfried 1914–1975*, dir. Hans Jürgen Syberberg, 1975
11. See *Heritage of Fire*, pp. 217–25. A fuller account of the Zurich meeting is given in the original manuscript, now in the possession of Friedelind's heir Neill Thornborrow. The original was shortened before publication, evidently by Friedelind with her American collaborator Page Cooper. Its extra detail does not, however, bring any basic new insights and the salient quotations are the same; THORN
12. Letter from Friedelind to Winifred, 29 February 1940, THORN
13. Friedelind Wagner, *Heritage of Fire*, pp. 209–10
14. Gottfried von Einem, *Ich hab' unendlich viel erlebt*, Vienna, 1995, p. 66
15. Ibid., pp. 67–8
16. Joseph Goebbels, *Tagebücher*, vol. IV (1940–1942), Munich, 1999
17. Syberberg film (see note 10)
18. Isabella Wallich, *Recording My Life*, pp. 68–9
19. For a balanced account of this period, including a brief reference to Friedelind's detention, see Ronald Stent, *A Bespattered Page: The Internment of His Majesty's most loyal Enemy Aliens*, London, 1980
20. All letters from which these extracts taken at NA, File ref. KV 2/1914 (see note 5)
21. Beverley Baxter, article in the *Daily Sketch*, London, 6 December 1940
22. Initial report of 'source 32a' after visiting Friedelind on 24 January 1941. NA KV2/1914 (see note 5)
23. Supplement to above dated 28 January 28th 1941, after 'source 32a' had been through Friedelind's suitcase. NA KV2/ 1914

24. Ibid.
25. Extracts from Friedelind's original speech carried by Süddeutscher Rundfunk in 1954 and re-broadcast by Südwestfunk on 21 May 2003

## 13 War – At Home and Abroad

1. Winifred in the film *Winifred Wagner und die Geschichte des Hauses Wahnfried 1914–1975*, dir. Hans Jürgen Syberberg, 1975
2. Wolfgang Wagner, *Lebens-Akte*, Munich, 1994. p. 112
3. Geoffrey Skelton, *Wieland Wagner: The Positive Sceptic*, London, 1971, p. 59 – quoting Kurt Overhoff in Austrian radio broadcast from Salzburg in 1969
4. Ibid., p. 69
5. Renate Schostack, *Hinter Wahnfried's Mauern: Gertrud Wagner Ein Leben*, Hamburg, 1998, p. 162
6. Ibid., p. 196
7. Winifred in Syberberg film (see note 1)
8. Ibid.
9. Gertrud Strobel, *Tagebuch*, entry 17 August 1941. See also Tietjen letter to 'Haus Wahnfried' of 21 August 1941, complaining of a 'basic change of attitude' towards him on the part of 'Wahnfried youth'; RWA
10. Henry Picker, *Hitlers Tischgespräche im Führerhauptquartier*, Berlin, 1997, entry 10 June 1942
11. Wolfgang, letter 3 April 1942 and Wieland letter – undated – of same month. Both reprinted in extract in KARBAUM, part 2, pp. 108–9; RWA
12. Extract in KARBAUM, part 2, pp. 107–8; RWA
13. Heinz Tietjen to Winifred Wagner. Extract in KARBAUM, part 2, pp. 109–10; RWA
14. Syberberg film (see note 1)
15. See Albrecht Bald, Jörg Skriebeleit, *Das Aussenlager Bayreuth des KZ Flossenbürg, Wieland Wagner und Bodo Lafferentz im 'Institut für physikalische Forschung'*, Bayreuth, 2003
16. Wulf Rüskamp (ed.), *Eine vollkomene Närrin durch meine ewigen Gefühle; Aus den Tagebüchern der Lotte Warburg 1925 bis 1947*, pp. 330–1
17. Skelton, *Wieland Wagner*, p. 79
18. Bald/Skriebeleit (see note 15), pp. 125–8
19. Wolfgang Wagner, *Lebens-Akte*, pp. 118–19
20. Schostack, *Hinter Wahnfried's Mauern*, p. 203
21. Wieland letter to Winifred, 5 January 1945, now in New York Public Library. Cited in Brigitte Hamann, *Winifred Wagner oder Hitlers Bayreuth*, Munich/Zurich, 2002, pp. 489–90

22. Cited in Skelton, *Wieland Wagner*, p. 77
23. Wolfgang Wagner , *Lebens-Akte*, p. 123
24. Schostack, *Hinter Wahnfrieds Mauern*, pp. 211–14
25. Wolfgang Wagner, *Lebens-Akte*, pp. 145–6
26. Winifred Wagner, letter 27 June 1946. Copy in the National Archives, Kew, File ref. FO 938/303

## 14 New Bayreuth?

1. *Das literarische Deutschland*, 2 Jg. Nr 16, Heidelberg, 20 August 1951. Article reprinted in ZELINSKY, p. 254
2. Ibid.
3. For details of Beidler's life and the (incomplete) text of his biography of Cosima see Dieter Borchmeyer, *Franz Wilhelm Beidler: Cosima Wagner-Liszt*, Bielefeld, 1997
4. Peter Heyworth, *Otto Klemperer: His Life and Times*, vol. II, Cambridge UK, 1996, p. 276
5. Hans Reissinger, 'Bayreuth, die schöne Stadt', in *Das Bayreuther Festspielbuch 1951*, pp. 44–7
6. Wolfgang Wagner, *Lebens-Akte*, Munich, 1994, p. 128
7. Ibid., p. 123
8. Wieland, letter to Winifred 11 July 1948. Cited in Renate Schostack, *Hinter Wahnfrieds Mauern*, Hamburg, 1998, pp. 241–2
9. Winifred in the film *Winifred Wagner und die Geschichte des Hauses Wahnfried 1914–1975*, dir. Hans Jürgen Syberberg, 1975
10. Wieland suggests the Monte Carlo solution in letter to Wilhelm Furtwängler 4 November 1947. Furtwängler opposes the idea. Cited in Schostack, *Hinter Wahnfrieds Mauern*, pp. 246–7. Also Wolfgang Wagner, *Lebens-Akte*, p. 152 on proposed sale of scores
11. Wolfgang letter to Wieland 5 April 1947. Cited in Wolfgang Wagner, *Lebens-Akte*, pp. 153–4
12. Wolfgang Wagner, *Lebens-Akte*, p. 129
13. Ibid., p. 154
14. Meyer letter to Beidler 28 August 1946. See KARBAUM, part 2, pp. 127–9
15. For Beidler's letter of 21 September 1946 to Meyer and his subsequent proposals for a Bayreuth Festival Foundation, see KARBAUM, part 2, pp. 129–34
16. See Borchmeyer, *Franz Wilhelm Beidler: Cosima Wagner-Liszt*, pp. 408–12 for details of Mann's – not unfavourable – reaction to Beidler's proposal
17. Franz Beidler, *Richtlinien für eine Neugestaltung der Bayreuther Festspiele. I Entwurf*, 31 December 1946. See KARBAUM, part 2, pp. 131–2

18. Heinz Tietjen, *Zum 'Wiederaufbau' der Bayreuther Festspiele*. Manuscript of 1 August 1947. See KARBAUM, part 2, pp. 134–5
19. Dieter Sattler letter to F. Meyer 29 January 1949, RWA. Cited in KARBAUM, part 2, pp. 137–8
20. See *inter alia* Winifred Wagner, *Aus der 'Denkschrift' für die Spruchkammer*, cited in KARBAUM, part 2, pp. 113–16
21. Richard Wilhelm Stock, *Richard Wagner und seine Meistersinger*, Nuremberg, 1943, p. 11
22. See *inter alia* Oswald Georg Bauer, 'Vierzig Jahre Neubayreuth (Teil II)', in *Programmheft IV, Bayreuther Festpiele 1991*, pp. 4–6
23. Ibid., p. 6
24. The National Archives, Kew, Winifred Wagner, file ref. FO 938/303
25. Die Berufungskammer Ansbach, Berufungssenat Bayreuth, 8 December 1948. Full text of judgement carried in Berndt Wessling, *Bayreuth im Dritten Reich*, Weinheim/Basle, 1983, pp. 284–303
26. See Albrecht Bald, Jörg Skriebeleit, *Das Aussenlager Bayreuth des KZ Flossenbürg, Wieland Wagner und Bodo Lafferentz im 'Institut für physikalische Forschung'*, Bayreuth, 2003, esp. pp. 66–73
27. Bauer 'Vierzig Jahre Neubayreuth (Teil III)', in *Programmheft V, Bayreuther Festspiele 1991*, p. 1
28. Ibid., p. 3
29. Sattler letter (see note 19)

## 15 The Road Not Taken

1. Letter to the *Musical Courier*, New York, 11 November 1949, THORN
2. Renate Schostack, *Hinter Wahnfrieds Mauern*, Hamburg, 1998, p. 251
3. Oswald Georg Bauer, Vierzig Jahre Neubayreuth (Teil III)', in *Programmheft V, Bayreuther Festpiele 1991*, p. 8. Wieland letter of 26 April 1949
4. Winifred letter to Friedelind, 7 April 1946, THORN
5. Letter of 20 June 1947, in which Winifred describes her 'unspeakable joy' on learning of Friedelind's aim to phone her, THORN.
6. Letter from Frida Leider to Friedelind, 2 December 1946, THORN
7. Letter from Friedelind of 5 December 1955 to Irving Kolodin, THORN
8. Friedelind Wagner, *Heritage of Fire*, New York, 1945, pp. 212–13
9. Winifred in the film *Winifred Wagner und die Geschichte des Hauses Wahnfried 1914–1975*, dir. Hans Jürgen Syberberg, 1975
10. Winifred letter to Friedelind 10 September 1939, quoting directly from a letter of Friedelind to her. This forms part of the correspondence uncovered by 'source 32a' in London in January 1941 (see chapter 12). The National Archives, Kew, NA KV2/1914
11. Friedelind Wagner, *Heritage of Fire*, pp. xiv–xv

12. *New York Times*, 5 April 1947
13. Friedelind's citizenship papers bear the number 6708462. Issued by William V. Connell, clerk of the District Court on 9 June 1947, THORN
14. Friedelind's talk carried by Süddeutscher Rundfunk in 1954 and re-broadcast by Südwestfunk on 21 May 2003
15. *New York Times*, 5 April 1947
16. 'Open letter' from Walter von Molo to Thomas Mann, printed in the *Münchner Zeitung* of 13 August 1945. This letter and subsequent correspondence on the same topic reprinted in full in J. F. G. Grosser (ed.), *Die Grosse Kontroverse: Ein Briefwechsel um Deutschland*, Hamburg, 1963. Von Molo letter, pp. 18–21
17. Thomas Mann, answer to von Molo printed in the *Augsburger Anzeiger*, 12 October 1945. Grosser (see note 16), pp. 27–36
18. Ibid., p. 31
19. Emil Preetorius letter to Thomas Mann of early 1946. Carried in Grosser, *Die Grosse Kontroverse*, pp. 57–61
20. Thomas Mann, radio broadcast of 8 May 1945 from California, later published in the *Bayerischen Landeszeitung*. Text printed in Grosser (see note 16), pp. 13–16
21. See 'Kummer in Bayreuth' in *Der Spiegel*, Hamburg, 24 March 1954
22. See London Metropolitan Police (special branch) report of 13 November 1954. In the National Archives, Kew, file ref. KV2/1914
23. See *Frankfurter Allgemeine Zeitung*, reports of 17 September 1954, 6 January 1955 and 15 March 1957
24. Wolfgang Wagner, *Lebens-Akte*, Munich, 1994, pp. 385–7
25. Friedelind Wagner, letter to Sabine Rapp, 15 February 1956, THORN

## 16 Sins of the Fathers

1. Gottfried Wagner, *Wer nicht mit dem Wolf heult*, Cologne, 1997, pp. 50–1. Published in England as *He who does not Howl with the Wolf*, London, 1998, and in the USA as *Twilight of the Wagners*, New York, 1999
2. Ibid., pp. 61–4
3. Gottfried Wagner, *Weill und Brecht, Das musikalische Zeittheater*, mit ein Vorwort von Lotte Lenya, Munich, 1977
4. Wolfgang Wagner, *Lebens-Akte*, Munich, 1994, pp. 145–6
5. See esp. Albrecht Bald, Jörg Skriebeleit, *Das Aussenlager Bayreuth des KZ Flossenbürg, Wieland Wagner und Bodo Lafferentz im 'Institut für physikalische Forschung'*, Bayreuth, 2003. Also Karin Osiander, *Dass Aussenlager des KZ Flossenbürg in Bayreuth*, Facharbeit am Gymnasium Christian-Ernstinum, Bayreuth, 1989; Peter Engelbrecht, 'V-2 Rakete in Bayreuth mitgebaut', in *Nordbayerische Kurier*, 7 October

1992, and Bernd Mayer, 'Das Geheimnis der "sehenden Bomb"', in *Fränkischer Heimatbote I*, 1995

6. Wolfgang Wagner, *Lebens-Akte*, pp. 178–9
7. Winifred letter to Wieland 14 March 1953. Cited in Renate Schostack, *Hinter Wahnfrieds Mauern*, Hamburg, 1998, p. 307
8. See Wieland Wagner, *Richard Wagner und das neue Bayreuth*, Munich, 1962, a useful compendium that includes Wieland's 'Denkmalschutz für Wagner?', pp. 231–5
9. Willy Haas, 'Wieland Wagner', in the programme book to *Götterdämmerung*, Bayreuther Festspiele, 1967, pp. 2–7
10. Wieland interview with the *Hessische Nachrichten*, 27 July 1956
11. Dietrich Fischer-Dieskau, *Echoes of a Lifetime*, London, 1989, pp. 209–10
12. Ibid., pp. 167–8
13. Wolfgang Wagner, *Lebens-Akte*, p. 181
14. Facsimile of Wieland's dedication in Schostack, *Hinter Wahnfrieds Mauern*, p. 367
15. Ibid., p. 196
16. Astrid Varnay, 'Wieland Wagner', programme book to *Das Rheingold*, Bayreuther Festspiele, 1967, pp. 20–4
17. Schostack, *Hinter Wahnfrieds Mauern*, p. 317
18. For the claim that Gertrud persuaded Wieland to employ Anja, see Schostack, *Hinter Wahnfrieds Mauern*, pp. 337–8. Anja Silja rejects this in her autobiography *Die Sehnsucht nach dem Unerreichbaren*, Berlin, 1999, p. 57
19. Silja, *Die Sehnsucht nach dem Unerreichbaren*, p. 60
20. Georg Solti, *Solti on Solti*, London, 1997, pp. 101–2
21. Klemperer letter to Peter Andry 2 August 1967. Cited in Peter Heyworth, *Otto Klemperer*, vol. II, London, 1996, p. 332
22. Silja, *Die Sehnsucht nach dem Unerreichbaren*, p. 50
23. Ibid. Wieland's *Der Eokalyptusbär* reproduced on pp. 132–3
24. Ibid., pp. 106–8
25. Ibid., pp. 83–4
26. Ibid. Wieland's reply of 29 July 1966 to his children cited on pp. 172–3
27. Ibid., p. 86. Undated letter from Wieland to Anja
28. Ibid., pp. 174–5
29. Ibid., pp. 197–201

## 17 End of Empire

1. Wolfgang Wagner, *Lebens-Akte*, Munich, 1994, pp. 287–90
2. For an eyewitness acount of one who took part in Friedelind's masterclasses, see John Mansfield Thomson, 'The Path to Bayreuth', in *Liber*

*Amicorum John Steele, A Musicological Tribute*, New York, 1987, THORN

3. Winifred Wagner letter to Gerdy Troost 16 January 1969. Cited in Brigitte Hamann, *Winifred Wagner oder Hitlers Bayreuth*, Munich/Zurich, 2002, pp. 605–6
4. See *inter alia* Nike Wagner, *Wagner Theater*, Frankfurt am Main/Leipzig, 1998, pp. 388–9
5. Gottfried von Einem, *Ich hab' unendlich viel erlebt*, Vienna,1995, pp. 69–71
6. Isabella Wallich, *Recording My Life*, London, 2001, pp. 211–13
7. For text of charter see *inter alia*Wolfgang Wagner, *Lebens-Akte*, pp. 446–63

## 18 Time Present and Time Past

1. Winifred in the film *Winifred Wagner und die Geschichte des Hauses Wahnfried 1914–1975*, dir. Hans Jürgen Syberberg, 1975
2. See Hans Jürgen Syberberg website, *www.syberberg.de*
3. *Die Zeit*, Hamburg, 18 July 1975
4. See *inter alia* article 'Politik ist im Festspielhaus weggewischt, Pressekonferenz mit Wolfgang Wagner', in *Nordbayerische Kurier*, 28 July 1975
5. Walter Scheel, 'Zum Mythos in der deutschen Geschichte, Rede zum 100jähriges Bestehen der Bayreuther Festspiele in Bayreuth 23. Juli, 1976', reprinted in Walter Scheel, *Reden und Interviews*, vol. III, S. 30–43, Herausgeber und Verlag: Presse und Informationsamt der Bundesregierung, Bonn, 1977
6. See Theodor Adorno, *Versuch über Wagner*, Berlin, 1952
7. Wolfgang Wagner, *Lebens-Akte*, Munich 1994, p. 102
8. Ibid., p. 103
9. See KARBAUM, p. 7, 'Vorwort' for expression of K's 'astonishment' at the use to which his material was put without his 'explicit permission'
10. Gottfried Wagner, *Wer nicht mit dem Wolf heult*, Cologne, 1997, pp. 195–6
11. *Harper's Bazaar*, German edition, April/May 1985. Wolf Siegfried Wagner interview with Karsten Peters
12. Walter Schertz-Parey, *Winifred Wagner: Ein Leben für Bayreuth*, Graz/Stuttgart, 1999, p. 304
13. Isabella Wallich, *Recording My Life*, London 2001, pp. 266–7

## 19 Time Future?

1. See Wolfgang Wagner statement of 8 February 2001, issued by the Bayreuth Festival press office. Also, from the same source, the statement

of 16 February 2001 in which Wolfgang calls for a '*Rückkehr zur Vernunft*' (return to reason) in the debate on the festival's future leadership, and notes that his employment contract was concluded 'for an indefinite period, that is for life'

2. See Nike Wagner and Elmar Weingarten, 'Kinder, schafft Neues! Tradition brechen – aus Treue zum Alten', article in the *Frankfurter Allgemeine Zeitung*, 30 May 2000
3. Ibid.
4. Hanjo Kesting (ed.), *Franz Liszt –Richard Wagner Briefwechsel*, Frankfurt am Main, 1988, Wagner letter to Liszt 8 September 1852
5. Details of the Holender speech and the reaction to it issued by the Vienna State Opera on its website, *www.wiener-staatsoper.at*

# Acknowledgements

The many instances of help I received in researching and writing this book far outnumbered the rare bids by this or that interested party to discourage or hinder. In the first place my heartfelt thanks goes to Daphne, Gottfried and Nike Wagner, as well as to Wieland Lafferentz, for talking to me about the Bayreuth festival and their family memories. Verena Lafferentz, Wieland's mother, replied at length to detailed questions submitted by letter. Neill Thornborrow, Friedelind Wagner's heir, gave unsparingly of his time on numerous occasions and kindly made available vital material from his archive.

Given its place in the family's history and its special atmosphere, the Siegfried Wagner House in Bayreuth – home of the National Archive of the Richard Wagner Foundation - made for an ideal spot in which to study and muse. Both Sven Friedrich and Günter Fischer at the Archive patiently dug out all they could in response to my sometimes tiresome requests, and talked with me at length about the family and festival, past and present.

Special thanks, too, to three Munich-based Wagner experts whose time I exploited insufferably over the years:; Jens Malte Fischer, who read the draft manuscript and made valuable suggestions; Klaus Schultz, who uniquely combines an insider's knowledge of the Bayreuth festival with an outsider's independence of view; and Michael Karbaum, whose carefully documented and boldly critical history of the festival in 1976 (sadly never translated into English) remains a model thirty years on.

For hints, tips and in some cases valuable counsel to 'think again', I am indebted more than I can say to: Albrecht Bald (Selb), Moritz Frhr. von Bethmann (Frankfurt am Main), John Deathridge (London),

Christoph von Dohnanyi (Zurich), Annelotte Elbrecht (Neu-Isenburg), the late Joachim Fest (Kronberg im Taunus), Geoffrey Field (New York), Sylvia Goldhammer (Institut für Stadtgeschichte, Frankfurt am Main), Ulrike Hessler (Bayerische Staatsoper, Munich), Gilbert Kaplan (New York), Hermann Kusterer (Bonn), Norman Lebrecht (London), Frans Lemaire (Zomergen, Belgium), Dietmar Müller-Elmau (Schloss Elmau, Upper Bavaria), Julian Nida-Rümelin (Göttingen), Peter Pachl (Berlin), Birgit Remmert (Oberlunkhofen, Switzerland), Dorothea Renckhoff (Cologne), Jörg Skriebeleit (KZ-Gedenkstätte Flossenbürg), Christian and Susanne Strauss (Garmisch), John Tomlinson (Lewes/Bayreuth), Marc A. Weiner (Bloomington, Indiana) and Heinrich Weltzien (Remagen). Naturally any errors remain my own responsibility.

Prizes for encouragement and extraordinary patience are richly deserved by Caroline Dawnay, my agent, and by the fine team at Faber & Faber, headed by Belinda Matthews and Julian Loose. The eagle-eyed Michael Downes in Cambridge was the very model of a collaborative copy-editor. As ever, Dorothea, my wife, makes it all worthwhile.

Jonathan Carr
7 May 2007

# Index

Figures in italics indicate captions. 'RW' indicates Richard Wagner.